City Dreams,
Country Schemes

THE URBAN WEST SERIES

City Dreams, Country Schemes

COMMUNITY AND IDENTITY
IN THE AMERICAN WEST

EDITED BY
Kathleen A. Brosnan
AND Amy L. Scott

UNIVERSITY OF NEVADA PRESS
RENO AND LAS VEGAS

THE URBAN WEST SERIES
Series Editors: Eugene P. Moehring and David M. Wrobel

University of Nevada Press, Reno, Nevada 89557 USA
Copyright © 2011 by University of Nevada Press
All rights reserved
Manufactured in the United States of America
Design by Kathleen Szawiola

Library of Congress Cataloging-in-Publication Data

City dreams, country schemes : community and identity in the American West / Kathleen A. Brosnan and Amy L. Scott, editors.
p. cm. — (The urban West series)
Includes bibliographical references and index.
ISBN 978-0-87417-851-7 (pbk. : alk. paper)
1. West (U.S.)—Social life and customs. 2. West (U.S.)—Social conditions. 3. City and town life—West (U.S.) 4. Community life—West (U.S.) 5. Group identity—West (U.S.) 6. City planning—West (U.S.)
7. Urbanization—West (U.S.) 8. Rural development—West (U.S.)
I. Brosnan, Kathleen A., 1960- II. Scott, Amy L. (Amy Louise)
F591.C54 2011
978—dc22   2011006985

The paper used in this book meets the requirements of American National Standard for Information Sciences—Permanence of Paper for Printed Library Materials,
ANSI/NISO Z39.48-1992 (R2002).
Binding materials were selected for strength and durability.

FIRST PRINTING
20 19 18 17 16 15 14 13 12 11
5 4 3 2 1

CONTENTS

Preface vii

Introduction 1
AMY L. SCOTT AND KATHLEEN A. BROSNAN

The Wishful West 10
JOHN M. FINDLAY

Part I

THE METROPOLITAN RETREAT TO THE ECO-URBAN 37

Crafting the Good Life in Irvine, California 39
STEPHANIE KOLBERG

Open-Space Politics in Boulder, Colorado 63
AMY L. SCOTT

Wilderburbs and Rocky Mountain Development 88
LINCOLN BRAMWELL

Middle-Class Migration and Rural Gentrification in Western Montana 109
RINA GHOSE

Part II

TOURISM, MEMORY, AND WESTERN URBAN IDENTITIES 131

Urbanity and Pastoralism in Napa Tourism 133
KATHLEEN A. BROSNAN

[v]

CONTENTS

Family Travel, National Parks, and the Cold War West   156
SUSAN S. RUGH

Public Art, Memory, and Mobility in 1920s New Mexico   178
JEFFREY C. SANDERS

Reclaiming Cannery Row's Industrial History   196
CONNIE Y. CHIANG

Seattle's Pike Place Market   218
JUDY MATTIVI MORLEY

Part III

FROM CULTURAL AND GEOGRAPHIC MARGINS
TO URBAN CENTERS   243

The Making of San Francisco's Queer Urban Scene   245
NAN ALAMILLA BOYD

San Francisco, Red Power, and the Emergence of an "Indian City"   261
KENT BLANSETT

Gay Male Rural-Urban Migration in the American West   284
PETER BOAG

Contributors   *307*
Index   *309*

[vi]

PREFACE

This collection of thirteen chapters by noted historians explores how new approaches to urban and rural development influenced the creation of community and identity in the twentieth-century American West. Each chapter considers how a specific western locale drew upon earlier utopian traditions to fashion new communities that purposely blurred the boundaries between urban and rural spaces. In so doing, the people of these locales sought the best of both worlds—the best landscapes, the best amenities, and the best people. Unlike earlier utopian projects, however, these westerners no longer believed that perfection was attainable, nor did they seek isolation from modern consumer culture. Instead, they shaped their metropolitan landscapes into spatial and cultural middle grounds that encompassed the cultural enrichment of cities, the security and social status of suburbia, and a natural aesthetic. In these communities, people forged new identities through restricted social space, common obligations, and shared experiences and interests, defining themselves by who was excluded as much as who was included.

The editors are grateful for the support they received in completing this project. This collection began as a conference called "Paradise Paved: Utopian Imaginations and the Southwestern City" at the University of New Mexico in April 2002. We are very grateful to Virginia Scharff, director of the Center for the Southwest at the University of New Mexico, who funded the "Paved Paradise" conference, and continued to provide ideas and encouragement as we moved forward with this collection. Judy Mattivi Morley did much of the organizing work for "Paved Paradise," contributed to the original proposal for this collection, and offered editorial comments on several of the chapters in this volume. John Findlay, Sylvia Rodriguez, Jeff Sanders, Amy Scott, Judy Mattivi Morley, Chris Wilson, Myla Vicente Carpio, and Pablo Mitchell presented conference papers. The University of New Mexico's Center for Regional Studies, directed by Tobias Duran, and the History Department also provided financial support for the conference. Evelyn Schlatter and Clark Whitehorn offered helpful editorial comments on the first draft of the manuscript.

PREFACE

The insights of Eugene Moehring, David Wrobel, and the anonymous readers elevated the central arguments of this volume. Matt Becker, Sara Vélez Mallea, and the staff at the University of Nevada Press brought this project into its final fruition.

Ultimately, we thank our families, friends, and colleagues at Bradley University and the University of Houston for their support and enthusiasm.

City Dreams, Country Schemes

Introduction

AMY L. SCOTT AND KATHLEEN A. BROSNAN

In *Looking Backward* (1888), Edward Bellamy tells the story of a man who falls asleep in 1887, awakens in 2000, and discovers a United States where goods are equitably distributed and capital is commonly owned. Steeped in socialist theory, his utopian vision critiqued industrial capitalism and argued that better alternatives existed.[1] *Looking Backward* was part of a larger literary tradition in which authors offered idealized visions of future communities as a means of satirizing religious, political, or economic conditions in their contemporary worlds.[2] Translated from the Greek, the term *utopia* means either "no place" or "good place." For Sir Thomas More, in 1516, it was the former; he believed perfection was unattainable.[3] In *The New Atlantis* (1626), Francis Bacon provided a counterpoint, the city of Bensalem, a fictional place where residents relied on scientific empiricism to build a peaceful and more prosperous society.[4] And throughout history people sought utopias where rational systems might overcome societal ills, communities where they might avoid religious persecution, or spaces where alternative ideologies might be tested and new identities formed.

Like Bellamy's protagonist, the contributors to this volume look backward from the twenty-first century, albeit from the perspective of history, to discover that idealized community visions, no matter how imperfectly implemented, shaped the landscapes of the American West and relations among its inhabitants. Bacon had located Bensalem on an island off North America's West Coast, and Americans frequently looked to the West and its mythic frontier for the fulfillment of their quixotic dreams. The region's presumed emptiness, its newness, and the opportunities it afforded led visionaries to believe they could forge stronger communities in the West.⁵ The social discourse of Bellamy and others inspired late-nineteenth- and early-twentieth-century planners to conceptualize urban environments that fostered social order, cultural cohesion, and a better quality of life through improved design, ordered development, and attention to the links between society and nature. They created an intellectual context in which western communities were planned and sometimes experienced.⁶

As John Findlay explains in our opening chapter, western cities became the focus of utopian community building in the nineteenth century, both in reality and on paper. Many migrants saw the region as a place where they might stand apart from the sweeping transformations of modernity. Other settlers and speculators laid out ambitious plats, envisioning prosperous cities that might dominate the region's resources and markets.⁷ In reality, contentious social relations forged in conquest, environmental limitations, and economic dependency thwarted the realization of the West as an ideal place for constructing independent communities from tabula rasa. Nonetheless, twentieth-century westerners continued to plan prototypical communities in the West. Perhaps they doubted that perfection could be realized, but ambitious planners still believed that societal improvements and stronger communities could be achieved, in part, by shading the lines between city and country.

This blurring of physical space became a central tenet of community building in the metropolitan West of the twentieth century, although it has earlier origins. Landscape architect Frederick Law Olmsted began experimenting with the integration of urban and ecological systems in his design of urban pleasure grounds in the 1860s. By the turn of the twentieth century, the influence of Olmsted and other landscape architects reached across the United States and across the oceans.⁸ Inspired by Olmsted, Bellamy, and others, Ebenezer Howard, a prominent British urban planner, published *To-Morrow: A Peaceful Path to Real Reform* in 1898 (reprinted three years later as *Garden Cities of To-Morrow*).⁹ Howard's influence crossed the Atlantic, and his ideas on community design and social improvement influenced the city builders of the American West, including Frederick Law Olmsted II. Like Bellamy, Howard accepted the notion that contemporary society was transitory and that hierarchical planning by experts would enable people to avoid the worst aspects of industrialization in the future. However, Howard rejected the centralization of authority inherent in Bellamy's socialist critique and instead devised a model community that balanced private initiative and collective enterprise.¹⁰

As Thomas Bender observes, "In both popular and academic discourse, the word *community* has quite positive connotations that are associated with visions of the good life. Yet there is, and always has been, an undercurrent of fear associated with the idea of community." Some Americans worried that urban industrialization had undermined the small-town values that once shaped their lives.[11] Howard proffered an alternative vision of a modern society free of slums and poverty where planned communities were surrounded by agriculture and successfully integrated town and country. Howard's "garden cities" sought the best that each offered (the city's culture and economic drive and the country's connection to nature's restorative powers), while avoiding their worst (urban industrial blight and rural isolation and stagnation). Howard's attempts to realize his vision in the multicentered British towns of Welwyn and Letchworth proved less than successful. Nonetheless, in his elevation of the planning profession, in his primacy of the town-country magnet, and in the exclusory nature of his model communities that by definition were designed for only a few thousand, he and other planners anticipated later efforts to obtain perfected communities in the modern American West. Echoing these earlier visions, westerners experimented with the proper balance of individual creativity and private initiative, expert planning, and governmental authority in the construction of physical space and community identity. By the early twentieth century, every major western city had hired an urban planner who, more than likely, was familiar with the planning language and social philosophies espoused by Olmsted, Howard, and Bellamy.

As John Findlay's introductory chapter makes clear, some community-building enterprises in the twentieth-century West were consistent with earlier social movements in that they often involved efforts to avoid the perceived evils of industrial America through communalism.[12] The region's first utopian colonies had consisted of groups of people who possessed visions of idealized life and attempted to establish communities that modeled new social patterns that outsiders might follow. The essential element, for the West's early communitarians, was withdrawal from a modernizing America. These nineteenth-century settlers did not seek to transform American society but instead retreated to a home place where they might separate themselves from the larger society and begin anew.[13]

The other chapters herein reveal that twentieth-century urban, suburban, and exurban visionaries in the American West shifted from hopes of perfection and no longer sought isolation from consumer culture. Individuals did not believe that they could fully escape the realities of modern life, and most did not wish to. Rather, as the chapters suggest, the planners, government officials, business owners, residents, and tourists who shaped the region's cities during the twentieth century increasingly championed less idealistic visions of community. Developers, builders, and activists continued to plan idealized communities in the American West, but they also compromised pragmatically, creating new kinds of living spaces that played a role in the development of more modern and diverse urban identities. Like Ebenezer Howard, westerners wanted the best of both worlds—modern urban amenities in the midst of a garden. As John Findlay argues in *Magic Lands*, "The urban West—with its central cities, suburbs, and nearby countryside—offered Americans a unique opportunity to live according to their preferences."[14] Consequently, they began to shape their metropolitan landscapes into spatial and cultural middle grounds that encompassed the cultural enrichment of cities, the familiarity of suburbia, and a western wilderness aesthetic. The communities that emerged from these mottled landscapes were defined by place but also by what a specific place offered. In these communities, people found cohesion through restricted social space, common obligations, and shared experiences and interests.[15]

The shift away from urban planning that aimed at achieving alternative communitarian social philosophies was tied partly to a growing American assumption that successful, enjoyable metropolitan living depended on individual material acquisition and consumption. The new affluence and increased mobility of a modernizing nation meant that twentieth-century Americans sought additional, often more material, elements in their idealized communities. Affluence and mobility, consequently, created the necessary conditions for the rise and expansion of middle-class suburbs. As the twentieth century progressed, the majority of Americans placed their aspirations for financial security and community life on a home in suburbia. For Robert Fishman, the suburbs represented an attempt to create community through a collective vision of individual private property. Fishman argues in *Bourgeois Utopias* that suburban design expressed "complex and compelling visions of the modern family freed from the corruption of the city, restored to harmony with nature, endowed with wealth and independence, yet protected by a close-knit, stable community."[16] Suburban living represented a solution to Americans' long-standing discomfort with the historical processes of urbanization and community building. In their suburban dreams, Americans articulated a new vision of the good life, incorporating a pursuit of material goods rather than a search for a spiritual haven.[17]

Twentieth-century westerners increasingly believed that certain physical forms determined the nature of their communities and worked to incorporate the best of the city and the best of the country in their living space. Urban history has often focused on the metropolis as the quintessential urban form in the study of modernization and its impact, but this volume considers places that blur distinctions and people who sought identity through the modern consumer lifestyle in these places.[18] At the same time, "the terms of production have infiltrated the language and conceptualization of urban history," according to Lizabeth Cohen. With the advantages of modern technology, westerners did not abandon urban life but instead muddied the distinctions between traditional spaces, developing lifestyles that combined the benefits of rural environs with urbane features. The history of consumption has demonstrated how people have constructed identities through acquisitions. Likewise, westerners found social status in styles of living grounded in privileged space and material comfort. As physical space shaped identity, consumer behavior reshaped regional landscapes. Suburban and county governments developed a wide range of techniques to protect the land uses, lifestyles, and identities that constituted the western metropolitan ideal.[19]

However, identity in reformed or newly formed western communities relied on more than acquisition. Suburbs and exurbs often became exclusory places because a certain level of material comfort was beyond the means of large segments of the population. Others were denied access on the basis of race or gender discrimination.[20] Community development involved the establishment of social and cultural boundaries. By reshaping physical space, through planning and other activities, those in authority tried to eliminate supposed sources of disorder.[21] While western suburbs remained comparatively more available to minorities than they had been in the Northeast or Midwest, exclusion remained important to the western suburban identity and offered a connection to the practices of earlier utopian efforts.[22] New communities and city forms often reflected members' efforts to distance themselves from people and activities perceived as less desirable. In the American West, as elsewhere in the nation, people attempted to create small sanctuaries such as master-planned communities, wilderburbs, or exclusive tourist getaways. Consequently, westerners' identities were increasingly shaped by exclusive urban forms that enforced physical and cultural distance between residents and the "other."

The westerners who are revealed in this book constructed diverse communities and metropolitan forms—cities, suburbs, university towns, mountain exurbs, amenity-rich tourist getaways, and politicized neighborhood enclaves—which they usually defined in opposition to other less desirable places. Convinced that western cities experienced fewer urban problems than their eastern and southern counterparts, westerners imagined their cities as dynamic, pliable places that were more easily transformed and improved.[23] Consequently, as they planned new towns or developed older ones within metropolitan regions, they often rejected the eastern models of cities and suburbs, constructing spaces and cultural identities that revealed alternative understandings of modern urbanity.

We have divided the thirteen chapters of this book into three parts. The first part, "The Metropolitan Retreat to the Eco-Urban," explores the movement of middle-class and wealthy urban residents to sanctuaries on the metropolitan fringe—university towns and foothill communities. The second part, "Tourism, Memory, and Western Urban Identities," contemplates the ways in which tourism shaped landscape and social status in the American West. The final part, "From Cultural and Geographic Margins to Urban Centers," suggests that westerners who found themselves marginalized for their ethnicity or sexual orientation sometimes discovered social cohesion and shared identities in the urban cores and central city neighborhoods that previous inhabitants had deserted.

Taken as a whole, the chapters in this collection examine some of the ways that westerners conceptualized, built, and inhabited urban space in the twentieth century. As these narratives collectively demonstrate, the creation of a western urban ethos and new city forms was a contested process. As westerners tried to create livable urban communities, diverse voices championed frequently changing visions of a western urban ideal. Although their visions of an ideal community—whether urban, suburban, or exurban—were often compromised, new discourse and practices, including some fanciful thinking, led to social transformations and new political identities, crafted distinct regional urban forms, and created urban spaces where touristic fantasies could be acted out. These westerners sought safe havens and were eager to avoid their own versions of dystopia, places characterized in literature and popular culture by poverty, pollution, oppression, violence, or anonymity. In fiction such as Ray Bradbury's *Fahrenheit 451* or Aldous Huxley's *Brave New World,* urban spaces and authoritarian governments separated people from nature and its restorative powers.[24] Thus, some westerners found in the cities connections to a sanitized past or the chance for restoration and self-realization and sometimes expressed identities that would have brought them scorn elsewhere. In the end, the interconnectedness that defines the modern world perhaps has made the realization of isolated communities—whether within the city or outside its perimeter—little more than a myth. At the end of the twentieth century, the idealized communities that twentieth-century westerners had hoped to create grew more culturally diverse and politically complicated. They remained contested spaces and works in progress.

INTRODUCTION

Notes

1. Edward Bellamy, *Looking Backward, 2000-1887* (Boston: Ticknor, 1888), discussed in Robert Fishman, *Urban Utopias in the Twentieth Century: Ebenezer Howard, Frank Lloyd Wright, and La Corbusier,* rev. ed. (Cambridge: MIT Press, 1994), 33.

2. This literary tradition includes classic works, such as Plato's *Republic* (ca. 360 BCE), St. Augustine's *City of God* (ca. 426), and Sir Thomas More's *Utopia* (1516), and modern fantasies such as James Hilton's *Lost Horizon* (1933). See Plato, *The Republic,* translated by Desmond Lee, 2nd ed. (New York: Penguin Classics, 2003); Augustine of Hippo, *The City of God,* translated by Henry Bettenson (New York: Penguin Classics, 2003); Sir Thomas More, *Utopia* (Leeds: Scholar Press, 1966); and James Hilton, *Lost Horizon* (New York: Grosset and Dunlap, [1933]). See also Joseph Levine, "Intellectual History as History," *Journal of the History of Ideas* 66 (April 2002): 189–200; and Barbara Goodwin, introduction to *The Philosophy of Utopia,* edited by Barbara Goodwin (London: Routledge, 2001), 1–9.

3. Robert V. Hine suggests that "the expression 'utopian' since the time of Thomas More has connoted unreality and impracticality.... But 'utopian' also denotes an ideal to which men aspire, concrete and real to its proponents, though visionary to its detractors" (*California's Utopian Colonies* [New Haven: Yale University Press, 1953], 4–5).

4. Francis Bacon, *The New Atlantis; and, The Great Instauration,* rev. ed. by Jerry Weinberger (Arlington Heights, Ill.: Davidson, 1989).

5. Richard White, "The Frontier in American Culture," in *The Frontier in American Culture,* edited by James R. Grossman (Berkeley and Los Angeles: University of California Press, 1994), 25; Hine, *California's Utopian Colonies,* 9; Walter Prescott Webb, *The Great Plains* (Waltham, Mass.: Ginn, 1931). Contemporary scholars appropriately retreated from the ethnocentric aspects of Turner's thesis over the past century, while urban historians challenged his conclusion that cities were the final stage in frontier development. Rather, Richard Wade, William Cronon, and others argue that cities were at the forefront of Euro-American settlement. See Richard Wade, *The Urban Frontier: The Rise of Western Cities, 1790-1830* (Cambridge: Harvard University Press, 1959); William Cronon, *Nature's Metropolis: Chicago and the Great West* (New York: W. W. Norton, 1991); and Kathleen A. Brosnan, *Uniting Mountain and Plain: Urbanization, Law, and Environmental Change Along the Front Range* (Albuquerque: University of New Mexico Press, 2002).

6. John Findlay, *Magic Lands: Western Cityscapes and American Culture After 1940* (Berkeley and Los Angeles: University of California Press, 1992), 2.

7. Perhaps the most famous utopian venture in the West involved the Mormons' efforts to escape religious persecution and develop their unique urban community along the Wasatch Mountains in Utah. Although it deviated in some details, Salt Lake City called forth the "square cities set in the middle of their agricultural lands and thus comprising the kind of rural-urban unit or city-state that (founder Joseph) Smith envisaged and Brigham Young

later provided" (John W. Reps, *The Making of Urban America: A History of City Planning in the United States* [Princeton: Princeton University Press, 1992], 472). In its origins, it offered community members an identity defined by faith and grounded in entrepreneurial skill.

8. Greg Hise and William Deverell, *Eden by Design: The 1930 Olmsted-Bartholomew Plan for the Los Angeles Region* (Berkeley and Los Angeles: University of California Press, 2000), 8.

9. Ebenezer Howard, *Garden Cities of To-Morrow*, edited by F. J. Osborn (Cambridge: MIT Press, 1965). Regarding the Bellamy movement in the United States, see Hine, *California's Utopian Colonies*, 85–90, 161–64.

10. Fishman, *Urban Utopias in the Twentieth Century*, 35–36.11. Thomas Bender, *Community and Social Change in America* (New Brunswick: Rutgers University Press, 1978), 3–4. See also Cronon, *Nature's Metropolis*; Matthew Klingle, *Emerald City: An Environmental History of Seattle* (New Haven: Yale University Press, 2007); Philip Dreyfus, *Our Better Nature: Environment and the Making of San Francisco* (Norman: University of Oklahoma Press, 2008); and Richard A. Walker, *The Country in the City: The Greening of San Francisco* (Seattle: University of Washington Press, 2008).

12. Frances Fitzgerald, *Cities on a Hill: A Brilliant Exploration of Visionary Communities Remaking the American Dream* (New York: Simon and Schuster, 1987); Timothy Miller, *The Quest for Utopia in Twentieth-Century America, 1900–1960* (Syracuse: Syracuse University Press, 1998), 4–9.

13. Hine, *California's Utopian Colonies*, 5.

14. Findlay, *Magic Lands*, 2.

15. Bender, *Communities and Social Change*, 6–11.

16. Robert Fishman, *Bourgeois Utopias: The Rise and Fall of Suburbia* (New York: Basic Books, 1987), x.

17. Lewis Mumford, *The Culture of Cities* (New York: Harcourt, Brace, 1938), 51.

18. James J. Connolly, "Decentering Urban History: Peripheral Cities in the Modern World," *Journal of Urban History* 35 (November 2008): 3–4.

19. Lizabeth Cohen, "Is There an Urban History of Consumption?" *Journal of Urban History* 29 (December 2003): 87; Carl Abbott, "The Suburban Sunbelt," *Journal of Urban History* 13 (May 1987): 286–87.

20. Margaret Garb emphasizes the importance of exclusion in the formation of urban neighborhoods in "Drawing the 'Color Line': Race and Real Estate in Early Twentieth-Century Chicago," *Journal of Urban History* 32 (July 2006): 773–87.

21. Patricia Burgess, "Discovering Hidden Histories: The Identity of Place and Time," *Journal of Urban History* 26 (July 2000): 647.

22. Louise Nelson Dyble, "Revolt Against Sprawl: Transportation and the Origins of the Marin County Growth-Control Regime," *Journal of Urban History* 34 (November 2007): 38–66; James S. Duncan and Nancy G. Duncan, *Landscapes of Privilege: The Politics of the*

INTRODUCTION

Aesthetic in an American Suburb (New York: Routledge, 2004), 4. Regarding minority suburban populations, see Abbott, "The Suburban Sunbelt," 283.

23. Findlay, *Magic Lands,* 2.

24. Ray Bradbury, *Fahrenheit 451* (New York: Ballantine, 1953); Aldous Huxley, *Brave New World* (Garden City, N.Y.: Doubleday, Doran, 1932).

The Wishful West

JOHN M. FINDLAY

"Thus in the beginning all the world was *America*." John Locke's statement from his *Second Treatise of Government* (1690) exemplifies the pervasive European and Anglo-American perception of the New World, and especially its western reaches, as a tabula rasa. Not knowing what the West in fact contained, Europeans and Anglo-Americans have often been disposed to imagine the best-possible scenarios for this blank slate. So first Estevánico and then Coronado, in the late 1530s and early 1540s, toured the Southwest in search of the seven cities of Cíbola—the first utopias in the Southwest to seduce the nonnative imagination. And so Thomas Jefferson, in advising André Michaux in 1793 what to look for during a proposed exploration of the northern Rockies in search of the Northwest Passage, instructed the French naturalist to head up the Missouri River because "it would seem by the latest maps as if a river called the Oregon [today's Columbia] interlocked with the Missouri for a considerable distance, and entered the Pacific Ocean not far southward of Nootka Sound."[1] What could have encouraged Jefferson to conceive that two river systems would miraculously "interlock"? How could Coronado have imagined seven golden cities on the desert and plains, each wealthier than the Aztec capital at Mexico City? Why did Locke construe the precontact Americas as a vacuum? Wishful thinking.

This chapter concerns one particular manifestation of wishful thinking. As blank slates, America in general and the West in particular have been especially attractive to those Europeans and Anglo-Americans bearing plans to create model communities. Puritans, proposing in the early seventeenth century to erect "a city upon a hill," helped to set a precedent of blending westward migration with attempts at radical improvement to forms of community. Later groups saw blank slates not just in the regional environs but also in large swaths of urban fabric; wishful thinking applied to new towns as well as to new worlds. Since the 1840s utopian practice and utopian rhetoric defined the West as the most promising region in the country for implementing plans to perfect Americans' ability to live in communities. Bringing scholarship on American utopianism into conversation with scholarship on the urban West helps account for why utopian practice and utopian discourse have been constants west of the Missouri River, while also exploring how western utopianism developed in stages after 1840.

Note the distinction between *utopian practice* and *utopian rhetoric*. On the one hand, the West has hosted more than its share of America's utopian colonies. That is, the region became home to a disproportionate number of experimental communities, many conceived as models by which the larger society would be transformed. In most instances, these utopian colonies were located at some distance from cities, so it would be mistaken to claim that their influence on the urban West was always direct and forceful.

Utopian discourse, on the other hand, permeated thinking about western towns of all sizes. This discourse grew out of a long European tradition of imagining perfected forms of community, often rendered in literature about the future. Cities in the American West, in both the nineteenth and the twentieth centuries, have been frequently conceived and reconceived—by boosters, planners, inhabitants, and others—in terms of such high expectation that the language about them has echoed that surrounding utopian colonies.

These two strains of western utopianism were not isolated from one another, although they are singled out here for analytical purposes. Utopian ideas and utopian colonies intersected in many ways, often in the same individuals, even though they represented divergent approaches to the project of perfecting society. It must be added that the decisive majority of utopian practice and discourse, in the United States as a whole and the West in particular, has been the product of white, mostly well-educated men. These utopians have advanced specific proposals for women, children, and people of color, but utopianism as described here (and primarily as found in the secondary literature) has largely been the product of relatively privileged people in American society. Even so, this particular form of wishful thinking has exerted a striking amount of influence on the West. And the West has had a significant influence on American utopianism.

Since the antebellum period western states and territories have played host to either a majority or a plurality of intentional communities in the United States. Robert V. Hine writes, "More than one hundred communitarian experiments were started in America in the first half of the nineteenth century, and at least seventy-five percent of them were on the frontier of their day." Virtually none of the utopian ideas or residents originated on the frontier, to be sure; rather, coming "from Europe and the East," they went to western soil to flourish.[2] Following the Civil War, "the frontier still offered both land and social space for launching new ventures." Of the more than 140 cooperative colonies inventoried by Robert S. Fogarty for the period 1860–1914, more than half were located in the trans-Mississippi West. Although there are no reliable lists of American intentional communities for the first half of the twentieth century, Hine reports that between 1850 and 1950 California customarily led the nation in the number of utopian colonies, while Washington State generally ranked second, so one may speculate that the West continued to have more than its share of utopian colonies.[3]

A resurgence of communitarian activity after 1960 produced additional intentional communities. Timothy Miller has tabulated almost fourteen hundred communes for 1960–75; 40 percent of them were located in the Pacific states, and another 11 percent were located in the Rocky Mountain and Great Plains states.[4] In other words, more than half of America's utopian colonies in the 1960s and early 1970s lay west of the Missouri River. (In 1970, for the sake of comparison, the same region contained just over 26 percent of the U.S. population.) Finally, to try to bring matters more up-to-date, the 1995 edition of *Communities Directory: A Guide to Cooperative Living* located 44 percent of all intentional communities in the Plains, Rocky Mountain, and Pacific states. California ranked first among the fifty states with ninety-four, Washington stood third with twenty-seven, Colorado sixth with twenty-two, Arizona ninth with nineteen, and Oregon and Texas tied for twelfth with seventeen each.[5] In sum, over the past two centuries successive Wests have had far more than their share of American utopian colonies.

What has accounted for the West's special relationship to intentional communities? In fact, certain frontier conditions—for example, the anti-intellectual climate, the remoteness from cosmopolitan centers—were not conducive to intentional communities. Yet most utopians went west anyway because they believed that they needed to withdraw from mainstream society in order to build a successful model for the future. More than any other region, the West has seemed to provide the isolation that utopians required. As a blank slate before wishful minds, writes Dolores Hayden, it has appeared to be "a spatial vacuum on which hopeful ideal-ists imposed an imaginary geography of fecundity, equality, and self-sufficiency." Moreover, socially the West has been assumed to be in its formative stages and therefore more susceptible than other regions to the reforming influence of a utopian colony. George Ripley, founder of Brook Farm in Massachusetts, explained in 1847: "There is so much more pliability of habits and customs in a new country, than in one long settled, that an impression could far more easily be produced and a new direction far more easily given in the one than in the other. An Association which would create but little sensation in the East, might produce an immense effect in the West." Finally, communitarians expected not only that a malleable West would more likely be influenced by utopian colonies but also that its rapid rate of growth would ensure speedy diffusion once model communities had been adopted. In 1854 the French Fourierist Victor Considérant, upon creating a utopian colony in Texas, speculated: "If the nucleus of the new society be implanted upon these soils, to-day a wilderness, and which to-morrow will be flooded with population, thousands of analogous organizations will rapidly arise without obstacle, and as if by enchantment around the first specimens."[6]

After the Civil War, even as the West grew more settled, utopians still subscribed to the belief that the region remained more receptive to model communities than other parts of the country. Communitarians (like most other Americans) have held on to the idea of a West of wide-open spaces and comparatively plastic, malleable institutions. In the late nineteenth and twentieth centuries, moreover, the appeal of the West's natural amenities heightened its reputation as a haven for intentional communities. Increasingly, utopian colonists recruited converts by advertising "the attractions of the climate, . . . the fruitfulness of the land, . . . the garden that the cooperators would settle and help bring to blossom."[7] As its population expanded, furthermore, the West produced more of its own utopian ideas and colonists, rather than relying so much on imports from the East and Europe, and those colonists spoke about their efforts in distinctly regional terms. The inhabitants of the experimental community of Llano del Rio, founded in Southern California in 1914, not only came primarily from west of the Rockies but also envisioned their influence in regional terms. They expected to see the colony "repeated, multiplied, the Llano idea carried irresistibly throughout the west, conquering prejudice, spreading hope, extending the cooperative idea."[8]

Colonies such as Llano del Rio resulted in some measure from an affinity between expansion and utopianism that accompanied Americans' spread across North America but was much less characteristic of the colonizing efforts of European rivals. Simply put, the system of colonization employed by the United States gave greater encouragement to utopians because it offered more incentives and greater autonomy to nonelite migrants and because it entailed less centralized control. Of course, most westering Americans (particularly those heading toward areas where extractive economies prevailed) proved uninterested in communitarian experiments. Indeed, the greater individualism inherent in the American system of colonization likely produced a more atomistic society, yet that system also offered much wider latitude for individuals to coalesce into experimental communities.

Whereas utopias in the nineteenth-century United States drew heavily on ideas from across the Atlantic, European schemes of colonization proved inhospitable to utopians, as shown by examples on the Pacific Coast, because of their more centralized approach to controlling territory and because they offered minimal opportunity for nonelite migrants to shape communities to their own tastes. Eighteenth-century Spain colonized Alta California through the hierarchical institutions of the army and the Catholic Church, which created presidios and missions along the coast. It founded civilian communities only as an afterthought, and because these pueblos were created primarily to provision the presidios, they were constantly subject to military discipline. Russian colonization in Alaska proceeded in a somewhat similar fashion, with a czar-chartered monopoly (the Russian-American Company), the Russian Navy, and the Russian Orthodox Church running the show.

British fur traders on the Northwest coast, during the first half of the nineteenth century, best articulated the Europeans' more centralized approach that vigorously discouraged nonelite migrants from creating communities of their own making. The Old World philosophy was spelled out at midcentury in correspondence between officials of the Hudson's Bay Company over how to bring settlement to Vancouver Island. In 1849 chief factor James Douglas, the fur-trading company's top official on the scene, proposed giving parcels of two to three hundred acres to families willing to settle in the vicinity. Douglas had seen the appeal of "free land" to Americans in the Oregon Country and thought that the British would benefit by offering a comparable incentive to migrants. But writing from London, the governor of the Hudson's Bay Company strongly disapproved of the idea. The home office insisted upon a method of colonization that, rather than permit the kind of latitude that wishful individuals enjoyed under the American system, was designed to prevent any innovation that might upset the social order as understood back in England. "The object of every sound system of colonization should be, not to re-organize Society on a new basis, which is simply absurd, but to transfer to the new country whatever is most valuable, and most approved in the institutions of the old, so that Society may, as far as possible consist of the same classes, united together by the same ties, and have the same relative duties to perform in the one country as in the other."[9]

British and American strategies for settling the North American West in some ways could not have been more different. The British wanted to avoid squatting on and speculating in land, while the American system encouraged it. The British wanted to transfer intact their system of social classes to the Pacific slope, while Americans outside the slave South mostly disapproved of such a system in the first place and expected that westward expansion would in any event weaken class lines. The British rejected as "simply absurd" the idea of reorganizing society on a new basis, while the more decentralized American system offered a seemingly endless supply of blank slates on which social reformers could draw up new societies. In the nineteenth century most westering Americans, like most Europeans, no doubt preferred to transplant to new countries the familiar institutions of the old society, but the U.S. colonizing system nonetheless proved much more tolerant of those who imagined that movement westward across the continent would entail experimentation with forms of community.

For many Americans, going west implied social progress. Writer Marilynne Robinson, in spite of her "governing assumption that history is a dialectic of bad and worse," affirms the connection between migration and social reform running through much of U.S. history: "There was a Utopian impulse, the hope to create a model of a good human order, that seems to have arrived on the *Mayflower*, and which flourished through the whole of the nineteenth century. . . . The American frontier was what it was because it expressed a considerable optimism about what people were and what they might become." And this optimism continued into the twentieth century, by which time a strong connection had been made in many minds between mobility and uplift. The psychology of population movement (from east to west, as well as from rural to urban places, from urban to suburban places, and from one metropolitan area to another) made the West particularly receptive to utopian ideas. George W. Pierson has noted the distinct connection in American culture between "movement" and "improvement." Whether moving away from something objectionable or moving toward something preferable (and utopians did both), westering people customarily anticipated a different and better life once they arrived at their destinations. This regional optimism in some ways grew even stronger after 1900, when the impulse to imitate the East diminished. Westerners increasingly found fault with eastern towns and more often viewed their own cities as places that could avoid the mistakes made elsewhere and produce communities more suited to the modern age as well as to the West's superior natural environs.[10]

What Robinson calls "optimism about what people were and what they might become" focused for the most part on the potential of adult white men (and, to a lesser extent, adult white women and white children) with some resources at their disposal. Yet other groups often came within the purview of Americans' utopian impulse. The architects of Indian reservations, when the institution was becoming the mainstay of U.S. policy during the mid-nineteenth century, drew upon the same thinking that inspired not only communitarians but also abolitionists, women's suffragists, and reformers of prisons and asylums during the antebellum era. Like Brook Farm or New Harmony, Indian reservations were imagined by some non-Indians as capable of solving a wide range of social problems. In 1853 a San Francisco newspaper, echoing the promises of federal agents, predicted that reservations would transform Indians within five years "from a state of semi-barbarism, indolence, mental imbecility, and moral debasement, to the condition of civilization, Christianity, industry, virtue, frugality, social and domestic happiness, and public usefulness."[11]

During the late 1870s the utopian movement merged with reservation policy in the person of Nathan Meeker. Meeker had explored and participated in utopian communities during the antebellum period. He also published a novel, *The Life and Adventures of Capt. Jacob D. Armstrong* (1852), in which a shipwrecked sailor persuades South Pacific natives "to give up barbarism and adopt a Utopian civilization of modern arts and industries, stripped of all vice." A close association with newspaper editor Horace Greeley led in 1869 to Meeker's becoming the leader of the communitarian Union Colony at Greeley, Colorado. Within a few years the Union Colony drifted away from its founding principles and left Nathan Meeker in debt. Seeking to recover financially and continue his reform efforts, Meeker sought an appointment from the Office of Indian Affairs and in May 1878 was assigned to the White River Agency in northwestern Colorado. After rereading the works of French utopian philosopher Charles Fourier, rededicating himself to the principles of cooperation, and recruiting employees from the moribund Greeley experiment, Meeker set out to make the Ute Indians his next utopian project. At the White River Agency, Meeker's ideals collided head-on with the intractable problems of reservation policy; his "curt, brusque, impatient manner" only made matters worse. Bemoaning the glacial pace of acculturation, and seeking to accelerate the conversion of the pastoral Natives to farming, Meeker created a demonstration field in

1879 by ordering that a Ute corral and pasture be plowed. Natives responded with hostility, and Meeker, increasingly fearing for the safety of his family and employees, summoned the military. In the ensuing skirmishes the Utes torched the Indian agency and shot, killed, and mutilated Meeker.[12] One person's utopia all too easily became another person's hell.

The high expectations for reservations and reservations' failure to live up to those expectations remind us of why the adjective *utopian* sometimes serves as a pejorative in our culture. Those who predicted that reservations would produce miracles clearly promised more than could be delivered, as did the typical founders of utopian colonies. The promotion of new forms of intentional communities—whether designed for the acculturation of Native Americans, the harmonization of families, or the salvation of souls—entailed a blizzard of extravagant claims about fantastic improvements, rapid transformation, and social reform. In short, advocates of utopian colonies sounded a great deal like the legions of promoters associated with cities and towns of the American West during the nineteenth and twentieth centuries. In fact, urban boosters and their allies ensured that although most westerners probably never came into direct contact with actual communitarian activity, they were exposed to a heavy dose of utopian discourse.

Conventional understandings of the utopian and the booster tend to put the two types at opposite ends of a spectrum. The former seems altruistic and idealistic, the latter untrustworthy and base. Yet historian David Hamer argues persuasively that many urban boosters took some of their extravagant claims quite seriously. "The negative, manipulative side of boosterism undoubtedly existed," Hamer explains. "But the other side was a strong vein of utopianism." Boosters' campaigns "were usually invoking . . . a broad utopian vision of what towns and cities should be and, in the case of their own town at least, certainly would be like. If one believed even a small part of their rhetoric, then one would be accepting that a type of community was in the process of realization in which most of the major social problems which confronted humankind would cease to exist and economic prosperity and social harmony would reign."[13]

The case of African American boosters in Los Angeles illustrates the congruence between promoters and utopians. Many black leaders portrayed Southern California as a promised land for African Americans by claiming that the region surpassed what other regions offered for blacks. Of course, these individuals also promoted Los Angeles for the same reasons that other boosters did—to stimulate the economy, increase their income, and heighten the city's and their own reputations. Yet they expressed a utopian impulse, too, focused on improving conditions for the race. Their rhetoric highlighted the relative improvements to community available to blacks in the near term, while envisioning absolute gains over the long term. They trumpeted the idea that African Americans would find in Los Angeles a place where they would receive better treatment. They genuinely believed that they described a community that improved on race relations elsewhere, but they also hoped that whites in Southern California, upon hearing their words of praise, would work harder to live up to them.[14] African American spokespeople promoted Los Angeles in both worldly and wishful ways.

Boosters and utopians were not altogether one and the same, yet their perceptions of and approach to the West bore striking similarities. To both groups the West, in comparison to the East, seemed more receptive to change, less set in the old ways. Like utopians, boosters imagined that they were working with a blank slate. The urban equivalent of John Locke's empty continent was often a gridiron plat waiting to be filled in. In the fashion of utopian colonists, boosters founding new towns approached their tabula rasa with a plan in their minds and a long list of superlatives at their disposal. Other boosters, set more on reforming existing towns than on founding new ones, shared utopians' belief that the West's dynamic rate of growth made it much more capable of embracing improvements to community. They expected that newcomers committed to a better plan would simply overwhelm the impure inhabitants and imperfect designs of older towns.[15]

Promoters' expectations for western towns thus soared quite high. In 1890 one claimed for Helena, Montana, "a society in which even the cynic can find no fault—a society in its moral structure as pure as in any community on the face of the earth." Farther west, Jeff W. Hayes, the businessman who introduced the telegraph to Portland, Oregon, not only boosted his adopted town in conventional ways but also penned utopian fiction about it. Two of his stories, modeled after Edward Bellamy's famous novel, adopted the themes of looking ahead to a perfected Portland by "looking backward" through the eyes of someone who had seen the city in 1999. Visions of a utopian Portland at the end of the twentieth century represented the culmination of changes advocated by promoters like Hayes at the start of the century.[16] Boosters' efforts on behalf of western towns were abetted by collaboration with the growing advertising industry and the rising corps of professional urban planners.

As time passed, eastern points of reference took on new meaning for wishful western cities. In the nineteenth century most westerners aspired to imitate more than they aspired to improve upon the East, but those who spoke in utopian terms often found that urban conditions along the Atlantic seaboard made a useful foil for their purposes. The alleged improvements that western towns generated implied eradication of the problems that seemed characteristic of cities in the East—congestion, poverty, crime, unassimilated foreigners, pollution. Thus, one promoter of Colorado Springs viewed the nearby environs as "the inner temple of Americanism . . . , where Republican institutions will be maintained in pristine purity," in contrast to the "eastern seaboard," which was conceived as "a sort of extensive Castle Garden to receive and filter the foreign swarms." By the early twentieth century industrialization, urbanization, and immigration were advanced enough in such cities as Seattle, San Francisco, and Los Angeles that some utopians believed that "the West was breeding the same circumstances against which eastern and European communitarians had earlier sought release."[17] On the other hand, the urban West now felt much less need to imitate the East. Despite the accelerating urbanization and industrialization of the region, many still thought that its urban forms and institutions, not to mention its increasingly appreciated natural settings, produced an urban way of life that improved significantly upon what existed elsewhere. The West continued to have more than its share of utopian practice and utopian discourse through the twentieth century.

Although utopian activity and utopian discourse have been constants in the trans-Missouri West since the 1840s, the forms they took and the meanings they expressed were not uniform across the decades or between groups. Utopianism in the West may be divided into four primary phases during which the number of experimental communities and the amount of idealistic discourse surged notably. These eras of particularly active utopianism—the antebellum period (1840–60), the industrial and progressive period (1885–1917), the period of federal communities (1933–50), and the period of corporate culture and counterculture (1960–75)—corresponded to key shifts in regional and national conditions, as others have noticed. For example, Brian J. L. Berry argues that increases in communitarian experimentation have neatly coincided with the periodic downturns, or "troughs," in the fifty-five-year Kondratiev waves that have characterized the U.S. economy. To explain such "exquisite contrapuntal dynamics," Berry suggests that "depressed prices and asset values" create a "downwave psychology" that in turn encourages people to seek relief and security in new forms of community.[18] Even if one does not endorse Berry's interpretation entirely, his chronology mirrors the pattern of four phases of western utopianism described here.

The first stage of utopian activity and rhetoric began with the extension of antebellum reform and religious fervor from the Northeast to the West in the mid-

1840s. Like some other religious communitarians of the period, members of the Church of Jesus Christ of Latter-day Saints endeavored to reorganize and perfect society in anticipation of the Second Coming of Christ, which they regarded as imminent. Their own mistakes as well as the hostility of Gentiles drove the Mormons in the 1840s from the Mississippi Valley to Utah, where they built the most utopian of all large towns in the region.

Salt Lake City is the western community where practice and discourse merged most fully and for the longest time. Its design grew out of both the Latter-day Saints' theology and their efforts to avert the disasters and tensions that had undermined Nauvoo, Illinois, and other Mormon settlements. Like other utopian colonies, the Mormon Zion stood isolated from mainstream society—partly to prevent governmental interference in Mormon theocracy and to keep hostile non-Mormons at a distance. Saints also organized the town so as to keep worldliness at bay: Planners blended rural and urban landscapes, religious leaders allocated city lots according to need, and the church forbade real estate speculation and subordinated property rights to a common spiritual purpose as well as to the economic ideals of self-sufficiency and cooperation. Over the course of the later nineteenth century, the Mormons' control over the city diminished (Gentiles outnumbered Mormons in the town by 1890), and the church had to make concessions to its members' individualist inclinations. But the extraordinary level of central planning and control set Salt Lake City off sharply from not only other western cities but also the typical American city of the day. Gunther Barth writes that Mormons' "successful application of a definite plan to urban development antedated, by half a century, the beginning of modern city planning that shaped the Chicago World's Fair of 1893."[19]

Salt Lake City was not the Mormons' only effort at utopia. The Saints planned numerous towns in and around Utah that embodied the church's communal ideals. Moreover, with Brigham Young urging anew in the 1860s that "people must overcome selfishness and prepare for the millennial reign of Christ," the church launched the United Order movement in order to maximize economic cooperation and self-sufficiency. The initiative produced a variety of cooperative communities, most of which did not last long. Over time Mormons' different utopian efforts, faced with the postponement of the Second Coming and other worldly realities, have had to make "creative adjustments."[20] Yet the effects of Mormon communitarianism have lingered. Salt Lake City in particular—a long distance in time and space from the Burned-Over District of upstate New York where Joseph Smith started the church—attests to the persistence of Jacksonian-era utopianism up to the present. It shows how activities and discourses from one century spill over—albeit in modified form—into another.

Salt Lake City stands apart because, among other things, it embodies preindustrial designs in our postindustrial world. This background also made it distinctive very quickly in the American Far West. Shortly after its founding, other towns and cities began to emerge, largely in the course of the development of mining, logging, stock raising, and other extractive activities. Cities like San Francisco and Denver reflected the industrialization of the region. With industrialism came a new phase of utopian activity and rhetoric, beginning in limited fashion in the 1850s, peaking between 1880 and 1917, and then tapering off. In these years, much utopian activity and discourse were shaped by the requirements of economic production, the polarization of social classes, and the upsurge of radicalism in the West. The period's characteristic communities were the company town and the socialist colony. Both were conceived in large part as responses to the wrenching economic changes of the time, although other motives also influenced them.

Company towns in the American West were first created in the 1850s and 1860s in order to recruit and retain workers in the isolated places where logging, mining, and milling occurred. In the absence of other communities, companies provided the infrastructure and services needed to house, feed, and care for employees. Through such institutions as the company store, the owners of these towns also exploited and manipulated workers. Particularly after 1880, company towns became embroiled in the sharp class tensions that increasingly characterized Far Western industry. Corporations saw them as tools for fighting working-class interests. Some companies excluded labor organizing and organizers from town and canceled the leases of workers whose actions and rhetoric they disapproved of. Other companies provided a measure of planning and amenities in towns as a way to establish a higher standard of living and, it was hoped, reduce inhabitants' interests in unionization.[21] The provision of planning and amenities was often depicted in utopian terms.

For example, when the Long-Bell Lumber Company saw that it was running out of trees in southeastern forests during the second decade of the twentieth century, it moved its operations to southwestern Washington State and built the community of Longview as its regional headquarters and mill town. It did so in part because it needed to house workers near the new plant and in part to profit from real estate development. But the company, accustomed to working in the nonunionized South, was also wary about the Pacific Northwest's reputation for workers' unrest, and it hoped to mute class tensions by providing decent living conditions in its new town. To these ends Long-Bell hired J. C. Nichols, planner of Kansas City's famous Country Club district, to help lay out the town, and in a nationwide advertising campaign it trumpeted planned and packaged Longview as "a wonder city in a wonderland" and "the city practical that vision built."[22] Promoters often touted company towns with wishful words. Little about them was ideal, but many endured into the mid-twentieth century.

By contrast, the West played home to a host of relatively short-lived utopian colonies between 1880 and 1920, many of which were conceived as socialist responses to industrialism. Perhaps the most famous socialist colony was Llano del Rio, located inland from Los Angeles. Llano differed from most others because a woman, architect Alice Constance Austin, exerted significant influence on it through her "socialist feminist design." Begun in 1914, Llano del Rio dissolved in 1917 "after its self-styled 'socialist' banker foreclosed the group's mortgages."[23] A concentration of socialist colonies appeared between 1885 and 1917 around Puget Sound, sporting earnest names like Equality, Freeland, Home, and Harmony. In these instances, founders followed the lead of earlier utopians who regarded the West as a place with malleable institutions and attitudes. Leftists viewed Washington as the most progressive state in the nation and assumed that utopian experiments had a better chance of success there. Its reputation as a haven for radicalism was not always well deserved. Yet hostility from conservative neighbors and capitalist interests was only one reason that socialist utopian colonies failed. Experimental communities on Puget Sound, for instance, collapsed more from internal problems than from external pressure.[24]

At roughly the same time that company towns and socialist colonies appeared, the rise of the profession of urban planners also came to influence western utopianism. In Europe and North America, this development was related in important ways to industrialization, but it stemmed as well from the intellectual, cultural, and political mixture that in the United States has been labeled the Progressive movement.

Urban planning has certainly produced more utopian discourse than utopian practice, yet its contributions to conceptions of western cities have loomed large. In some respects urban planners were like boosters with blank slates in their hands; indeed, in most instances civic elites *hired* these professionals as allies and experts and recruited them to the cause of promotion. But in contrast to boosters and other more ordinary developers of towns, planners made laying out cities into both an art and a science. Reflecting Progressive concerns for efficiency, rationality, and expertise, planners proposed to apply professional training and judgment to rationalize the city and create a more perfect urban form by developing comprehensive plans.

Critics have suggested that modernist urban planning is at bottom an inherently utopian exercise. *Utopian* has negative connotations in this context, implying either a quite unrealistic conception of the city or, worse, an authoritarian approach by which the powerful few serve their ends by imposing discipline upon the urban many.[25] Although this view deserves consideration, planners (like boosters) need to be contemplated in more complicated terms. Among other things, planners were reformers trying to address such real and mundane matters as sanitation and safety. Moreover, utopian planning made positive contributions to cities if for no other reason than by encouraging dialogue about the differences between what is and what could be, the present and the future, the worldly and the wishful. Those who use the city have a lot to learn from those who would design and redesign it—and vice versa.[26] And outside of Salt Lake City most western urbanites made it clear that they would never be too obedient to master plans.

In the years after 1900 virtually every major western city—generally prodded by business interests intending to help promote and expand their town—hired a prominent planner, engineer, or landscape architect to draw up a master plan. Mostly hailing from the East, these experts introduced scientific and artistic rigor to thinking about urban futures. Their plans clearly made another kind of utopian statement about the western city. Whereas getting plans drawn up was one thing, getting them approved, funded, and implemented was another. Western cities generally rejected the more comprehensive plans, or else failed to implement them fully after adopting them. Often the business elites who had urged large-scale planning in the first place lost interest when presented with actual proposals and cost figures. In other cases voters rejected ambitious designs, for diverse reasons.[27] Comprehensive plans for cities thus shared the same fate as the several sites for international expositions, which had been produced during the same era, by the same combination of hired experts and local elites, often for the same booterish reasons.[28] Both the master plans and the short-lived fairgrounds were forms of utopian discourse about the western city.

The impact of professional planners was felt far and wide, of course. Their efforts—wishful and otherwise—were not restricted to the American West. By the 1930s planners actually exerted influence in the New Deal administration of President Franklin D. Roosevelt and in that capacity helped to usher in the third phase of utopian activity and rhetoric—the period of federal communities. Heretofore, the planning of western towns had primarily been the responsibility of private interests, nonprofit organizations, or local governments. But in response to the Great Depression the national government began leading the way in urban planning. Among many other initiatives in urban policy and development during the decade, federal agencies created about one hundred remarkably varied planned communities—some for resettlement of the unemployed, some as model farming communities, some as greenbelt towns designed to demonstrate rational planning.[29] Most of these towns were not located in the West. Rather, New Dealers tended to provide the region with massive public works projects, which in turn were accompanied by such model federal towns as Boulder City, adjacent to the Hoover Dam, and the city of Coulee Dam, next to the Grand Coulee Dam. Uncle Sam's communities stood in contrast to the chaotic towns and construction camps located nearby.

New Deal towns did not exert much direct influence on the wishful West, but they did provide a model for a more striking set of federal communities that emerged after 1940. In mobilizing for global conflict, the federal government rebuilt the West on an immense scale, often treating the region as a blank slate as it set about meeting national security needs. Programs during World War II and the cold war to build and test atomic bombs gave to the region a disproportionate share of weapons work. The West attracted nukes just as successfully as it attracted utopians, and carefully planned, precisely managed, federally owned towns arrived as part of the package. The design of wartime Los Alamos, New Mexico, and Richland, Washington—two of the Manhattan Project's three major settlements—drew upon New Deal precedents as well as the army's utilitarian ethos for communities. With increased weapons production after the war, both towns underwent expansion that incorporated suburban motifs. Their distinctive design and privileged populations, and their association with the potentially liberating advances of nuclear science, earned for Richland and Los Alamos reputations as "Atomic Age" utopias.[30] That the public regarded these federal towns as exemplary reminds us of the tremendous trust most Americans had in their government in the 1940s and 1950s. Hard as it is for some to accept today, the perceived triumph of the Manhattan Project—at making bombs, ending the war, building towns, accelerating technological progress—was an important pillar of that trust, as well as a source of utopian discourse about the future.[31]

Of all the decades of western utopianism, the 1840s and the 1940s remain the only ones to produce substantial and enduring cities that continued to live up to some of their utopian billing. A primary reason seems obvious: The Mormon

Church and federal defense agencies have stood apart in their power to define a common purpose, command resources, and enforce discipline among townspeople. In contrast to the average western city, and in contrast to utopian colonies that typically came and went quickly, modern Salt Lake City, Richland, and Los Alamos still demonstrate some of their original ideals and designs.

Although Richland and Los Alamos seemed to live up to their utopian billing, the government consciously decided against building any more federal nuclear communities during the early 1950s. A nation devoted to opposing communism was no place to build more towns that, no matter how successful, were planned, owned, and operated by the government. This decision may be said to mark the end of the third phase and the beginning of the fourth phase of utopian practice and discourse. Since the mid-1950s there have been many new communities in the wishful West. They have ranged widely, from so-called hippie communes to retirement villages such as Leisure World, with each more likely to serve a narrower demographic or socioeconomic clientele than before. One orientation common to most of the newer efforts is that, in contrast to other eras of community building, this period has been much more concerned about the wants of consumers rather than the needs of producers. Another theme has been a greater concern about the environment—either as a set of amenities to be consumed or a set of resources to be protected.

One might ascribe recent western utopianism to two major sources—corporate culture, which was more likely to produce utopian rhetoric, and the counterculture, which was more likely to produce utopian practice.[32] Corporations produced a plethora of new model towns for different purposes and promoted them with an array of claims about their promise for improving the way Americans lived in community. Again, this pattern was national, not regional, in scope, but it reached its fullest expression in the postwar West, where it found encouragement from rapid population growth and cultural change. The master planning of large tracts of usually suburban land, often following a central theme, characterized many of these towns. Thus, Irvine became a new town planned around a campus of the University of California, while Sun City, Arizona, pioneered a new suburban way of life for retirees. At one point the promise of "new communities" seemed so substantial, particularly in terms of combating urban sprawl, that the federal government showed considerable interest in guiding and subsidizing them, but this interest proved short-lived.[33] As in previous periods, some boosters of such new towns could be quite sincere in their efforts to create models worthy of emulation by others. The developer of Valencia, California, for example, expected the planned community to become "an island of reason in the path of the metropolitan sprawl." But few home buyers shared his hope; they cared more for peace and quiet and higher property values.[34] Consumers often paid little attention to the utopian claims made by corporate culture on behalf of their communities.

In the realm of utopian practice, although counterculture communes proved to be tremendously varied, they generally lacked the kind of strong central authority that a real estate development company, let alone the U.S. Army or the Mormon Church, could provide. The inhabitants of experimental communities during the 1960s and 1970s proved more successful at criticizing mainstream culture than at developing a model community for others to replicate. Indeed, compared to earlier generations of utopians, fewer communitarians of this period intended to provide an example for others to follow. And most of the communities they created proved short-lived. In the antebellum era Joseph Smith had conceived the Mormon Church as a haven from "the excesses of individualism and pluralism."[35] Many modern utopias embraced individualism and pluralism—even though those traits functioned as solvents that weakened community ties.

For all their disintegrative tendencies, countercultural utopian colonies flourished in the 1960s and 1970s; some remnants survive today, albeit in diluted and diminished form. The environmentalist concerns of many utopians in this period shaped numerous communities, including nine lesbian land collectives in 1970s Oregon, and encouraged among them a romantic and often idealized reverence for Native Americans' relationship with nature. In keeping with the back-to-the-land ethos of many participants, at least half of the experimental communities were located at some distance from cities and suburbs. However, many of those who populated communes went there directly from much larger cities and towns. For example, Timothy Miller describes an exodus to rural communes from the Haight-Ashbury district of San Francisco, following 1967's Summer of Love. More important, the small groups that conceived and founded numerous communes—whether for secular or spiritual reasons—met and got organized in larger cities. Los Angeles and the San Francisco Bay Area were particularly fertile breeding grounds for utopian colonizers, and so were such college towns as Berkeley, Boulder, and Albuquerque. Relatively few communes appeared on the Great Plains, but a striking number grew up in and around the university towns of Lawrence and Manhattan, Kansas. Most participants in this era of experimental communities were youthful, white, and of middle-class background; males tended to dominate leadership positions. Finally, in contrast to previous phases, inhabitants displayed a sense of humor when naming communes after 1960. They treated the world to the Bad Manners and Psychedelic Sheep Ranch communes in Kansas; the Reality Construction Company, the Magic Tortoise, and the Last Resort near Taos; the Blue Fairyland, Floating Lotus Opera Company, and Good Times communes in Berkeley; the Candy Ass House and the Peace, Bread, and Land Band in Seattle; and in Oregon the CaveCampKids Commune, the Coagulators, the Sunny Ridge Occult Society and Candy Store, and Maggie's Farm.[36]

The transience and sense of humor that characterized 1960s communes move one to wonder just how seriously to take utopias in western American history. Was utopianism just a phase (or four phases) that society went through? The question deserves pondering, given that Americans are so frequently dismissive of utopianism. They deploy the adjective *utopian* to connote impractical, unrealistic, or naive—all traits regarded as undesirable in our pragmatic, get-ahead culture. Even students sympathetic to utopian ideals have grown cynical. Zeese Papanikolas surveys several nonnative efforts at utopia in the West and comes away discouraged: "One by one they all die. Mormonism becomes a respectable Protestant religion, the Wobblies get driven out of Goldfield by the operators and the U.S. Army. . . . Llano, Icaria, Kaweah . . . these would-be-utopias of the American West are gone for good, and some day, when on some wind-blown New Mexican mesa or among the dripping redwoods of the Mendocino coast, the last hippie crawls out of the last broken-down schoolbus and gives the final mystical sign of peace, even the idea of utopia may be gone."[37]

Papanikolas's judgments about utopia seem to be based on a very narrow measure of success and failure. Asking whether a utopian project survived to realize the original visions of its original founders sets an impossibly high standard. Of course, many utopians themselves have contributed to this impossibly high standard by portraying their destination as a fixed state of perfection. Yet utopias change and evolve, just like everything else.[38] Moreover, in doing so they still deserve our attention—indeed, their mutability probably makes them *more* deserving of our attention. Most utopian experiments have "failed" to achieve their exalted initial visions, but the same could be said about virtually any realm of human striving. In our society, for example, most urban master plans, many small businesses (including most restaurants), and over half of all marriages "fail," yet nobody requests the end of planning, entrepreneurship, or weddings. Such wishful ventures possess some redeeming value for the larger society; few would argue that their inability to attain some sort of ultimate goal meant that they did not contribute in a meaningful fashion to the broader good.

If utopian projects are held to a slightly less lofty standard, I think that we can see that this particular realm of human striving actually endures in significant and illuminating ways. Take just a few examples from the West. Utopia lives on in Utah and the Mormon West; saying that it "died" when Mormonism became "a respectable Protestant religion" is much too simplistic. Surely, Mormonism changed—made "creative adjustments"—in many ways; its wishfulness had to accommodate the worldliness with which Mormons needed to coexist. But change has by no means implied the abandonment of all idealism. Utopianism is one of the reasons Utah remains different.[39] And the adaptations that Mormon utopianism has undergone make it more—rather than less—interesting to study.

Not all westerners share Mormon ideals or regard Utah as a state in which they would wish to live. Fortunately for them, the West has proved large enough to host many utopian projects. Following impulses different from those of the Church of Jesus Christ of Latter-day Saints, other utopians have created different kinds of wishful places. Another contributor to this volume, for example, describes Boulder, Colorado, as a community shaped over the years by sets of high ideals. Like Utah, Boulder never became a fully realized expression of the utopian sentiments behind it, but it continued to embody, if only imperfectly, the wishful thinking of earlier generations.

Boulder and Salt Lake City are just a few examples of towns influenced by utopian practice and utopian discourse. The American West has shaped substantially, and been shaped substantially by, different kinds of utopianism—in such forms as social and reform movements, boosterism, urban planning, and federal towns. The sheer number of participants in different kinds of utopian ventures has been surprisingly high. Timothy Miller, for example, estimates that there were "probably tens of thousands" of communes founded in the United States between 1960 and 1975 and argues that their influence extended beyond their own limited life span and membership.[40] The simple numbers of participants also suggest that we ought to take utopianism seriously. The desire for a more perfect kind of community (coupled with a willingness to act upon that desire, if only for a brief period) has marked American society.

Papanikolas's remarks to the contrary, moreover, this desire remains powerful, particularly in the American West. Many people long to identify with a better future. Consider, for instance, the regional influence of recent utopian fiction. In 1975 a Berkeley writer named Ernest Callenbach published the novel *Ecotopia*. Set twenty-four years into the future, in 1999, the book portrayed how a part of the United States—northern California, Oregon, and Washington—had seceded from the rest of the country in 1980 and established the new country of Ecotopia, an ecological utopia. The fictional new nation outlawed the internal combustion engine, did away with most cars, replaced many city streets with streams, and planted flowers in potholes. It prided itself on a no-growth economy that recycled virtually all wastes, ran on solar power, and reduced the average workweek from forty to twenty hours. The standard of living declined, but most Ecotopians did not seem to mind. They lowered their material expectations, found ways to enjoy their newfound leisure time, and derived satisfaction from living harmoniously with nature. They became better-rounded people; men in particular got more in touch with their "feminine" sides. Indeed, women's influence was critical in redirecting and running the society.

Ecotopia is not great fiction. For one thing, it tends to read as a male fantasy about the benefits of feminism. For another, there is one glaring contradiction that defies readers' suspension of disbelief: In order to attain their independence, Ecotopians used nuclear blackmail by threatening to detonate atomic bombs in major American cities if they were not granted their autonomy. Many observers concurred that, as a work of fiction, *Ecotopia* left something to be desired. Twenty-five publishers rejected the manuscript before it was issued by a Berkeley collective, Banyan Tree Books. Yet the novel began to attract adherents, and it soon racked up so many sales that Bantam Books bought it up and sold thousands of paperback copies. The book succeeded because many buyers regarded the novel not as good fiction but as a kind of wishful nonfiction, a forecast of how the future could or should evolve. The publisher encouraged this perception by marketing the book not as a novel but as one in a series of "Bantam New Age Books: A Search for Meaning, Growth, and Change." Ralph Nader reinforced the notion that *Ecotopia* was something other than fiction when he endorsed the book in a blurb, claiming, "None of the happy conditions in Ecotopia are beyond the technical or resource reach of our society."[41]

Ecotopia proved especially popular among readers in the Pacific Northwest, where the plot apparently possessed a certain resonance. As late as 1979, when the novel was still selling at a rate of one thousand copies every month, Callenbach estimated that at least half of the sales took place in the Pacific Northwest. The idea that the American Northwest was becoming a kind of ecological utopia gained popularity outside the region as well. In 1979 the British magazine *New Scientist* labeled the Pacific Northwest "ecotopia." Then in 1981 journalist Joel Garreau published a trendy book called *The Nine Nations of North America*. Garreau asked readers to put aside old political boundaries and recognize the new geographic, economic, and cultural realities remaking North America into different zones. These included Mexamerica (Mexico and the American Southwest), Quebec (separated from the rest of Canada), the Foundry (the industrial Northeast), the Empty Quarter (most of western Canada and the American Great Basin and Rocky Mountains), and Ecotopia (the coastal strip running from Monterey, California, to Anchorage, Alaska, including the western half of the Pacific Northwest). Garreau argued that, in some measure, Callenbach's Ecotopia was coming into existence in northwestern California; coastal Oregon, Washington, and British Columbia; and southeastern Alaska. In ensuing years others made similar claims for an exceptional, environmentally aware region, while changing the emergent nation's name to Cascadia.[42] In short, Callenbach's utopia took on a life of its own.

Identifying strongly with the idea of an ecological utopia posed certain problems. One might be summarized as the paradox of extinction in Ecotopia. During the 1980s and 1990s the regional crises of the endangered spotted owl and the endangered species of salmon seemed to suggest that the Northwest's identification with Ecotopia entailed a certain amount of denial. For another, American proponents of Ecotopia or Cascadia as a transnational region have proved rather cavalier about international boundaries. By incorporating British Columbia, the imagined nations of Ecotopia and Cascadia seemed like just another U.S. challenge to the integrity of Canada. Yet readers' wishfulness in responding to the idea of an ecological utopia is less important than the warm reception they have given it. There remains in the West a strong inclination to identify oneself with a better future, to connect with a vision of an improved world and a more perfect community. The success of T. C. Boyle's 2003 novel *Drop City*, which imagines in rather upbeat fashion the migration of a 1970 commune from northern California to the Alaskan interior, hints that Americans remain at least partially optimistic about the notion of a utopian West.

Even if we wanted to drive utopianism to extinction, we could not. There will always be more "downwave psychology" prodding people to search for improved forms of community. There will always be another hippie—in Mendocino, New Mexico, or some other part of the wishful West—ready to climb back into the broken-down school bus.

Notes

1. Jefferson cited in Jeanette Mirsky, *The Westward Crossings: Balboa, Mackenzie, Lewis & Clark* (1946; reprint, Chicago: University of Chicago Press, 1970), 242–43. These instructions foreshadowed the ones Jefferson gave to Meriwether Lewis a decade later.

2. Robert V. Hine, *The American West: An Interpretive History* (Boston: Little, Brown, 1973), 264. In using the words "the frontier of their day," Hine raises the matter of just what is meant by *frontier* or *West*. Scholars of American utopianism have used *frontier* rather loosely, and only sometimes have they been careful to note different zones of advancing U.S. interests. *West* herein is defined as the region lying beyond the Missouri River, unless context or specific phrasing suggests otherwise. *Wests* refers to successive frontier regions.

3. Robert S. Fogarty, *All Things New: American Communes and Utopian Movements, 1860–1914* (Chicago: University of Chicago Press, 1990), 10, 227–33; Robert V. Hine, *California's Utopian Colonies* (1953; reprint, New Haven: Yale University Press, 1966), 6. Donald E. Pitzer, comp., "America's Communal Utopias Founded by 1965," in *America's Communal Utopias*, edited by Donald E. Pitzer (Chapel Hill: University of North Carolina Press, 1997), 449–91, is an extensive but unwieldy list. Among other things, it includes Catholic religious orders that other lists normally exclude.

4. Hine, *American West*, 267; Timothy Miller, *The 60s Communes: Hippies and Beyond* (Syracuse: Syracuse University Press, 1999), 249–85. Miller's listing, like any inventory of utopian colonies, is not comprehensive. He admits that it covers only a fraction of the thousands of communes that existed. My calculations refer to only those communes definitely situated inside or outside the trans-Missouri West.

5. Fellowship for Intentional Community, *Communities Directory: A Guide to Cooperative Living* (Langley, Wash.: Fellowship for Intentional Community, 1995). These data are even more unreliable than Miller's. Communities nominated themselves for inclusion; claims were not verified.

6. Arthur Bestor, "Patent-Office Models of the Good Society: Some Relationships Between Social Reform and Westward Expansion" (1953), reprinted in Arthur Bestor, *Backwoods Utopias: The Sectarian Origins and the Owenite Phase of Communitarian Socialism in America, 1663–1829*, 2nd ed. (Philadelphia: University of Pennsylvania Press, 1970), 233, 239–40; Dolores Hayden, *Seven American Utopias: The Architecture of Communitarian Socialism, 1790–1975* (Cambridge: MIT Press, 1976), 15; Bestor, "Patent Office Models," 248, 249.

7. Fogarty, *All Things New*, 10. As an example, the colonists at Icaria Esperanza, on the Russian River in California, during winters in the 1880s sent leaves and flowers along with their letters to acquaintances in Iowa, trying to lure them to California (Hine, *California's Utopian Colonies*, 68).

8. Hayden, *Seven American Utopias*, 290, 293.

9. Archibald Barclay to James Douglas, December 17, 1849, cited in Margaret A. Ormsby, *British Columbia: A History* ([Toronto]: Macmillans in Canada, 1958), 100–101. I am indebted

to Jeremey Mouat for this quotation and for directing me for additional background to Margaret A. Ormsby, introduction to *Fort Victoria Letters, 1846–1851*, edited by Hartwell Bowsfield (Winnipeg: Hudson's Bay Record Society, 1979), li–liv.

10. Marilynne Robinson, "My Western Roots," in *Old West—New West: Centennial Essays*, edited by Barbara Howard Meldrum (Moscow: University of Idaho Press, 1993), 169–70; George W. Pierson, *The Moving American* (New York: Alfred A. Knopf, 1973), 12. See also John M. Findlay, *Magic Lands: Western Cityscapes and American Culture After 1940* (Berkeley and Los Angeles: University of California Press, 1992).

11. See John M. Findlay, "An Elusive Institution: The Birth of Indian Reservations in Gold Rush California," in *State and Reservation: New Perspectives on Federal Indian Policy*, edited by George Pierre Castile and Robert L. Bee (Tucson: University of Arizona Press, 1992), 18–20, quote on 19.

12. On Union Colony, see Hayden, *Seven American Utopias*, chap. 9. The conflict at the White River Agency, especially the role of Meeker's utopianism in it, is treated in Marshall Sprague, *Massacre: The Tragedy at White River* (Boston: Little, Brown, 1957), first quote on 10–11; Robert Emmitt, *The Last War Trial: The Utes and the Settlement of Colorado* (Norman: University of Oklahoma Press, 1954), 50, 73–74, 122–25; Mark E. Miller, *Hollow Victory: The White River Expedition of 1879 and the Battle of Mill Creek* (Niwot: University Press of Colorado, 1997), 5, 13, 27; and David Boyd, *A History: Greeley and the Union Colony* (Greeley, Colo.: Greeley Tribune Press, 1890), 319–56, second quote on 343.

13. David Hamer, *New Towns in the New World: Images and Perceptions of the Nineteenth-Century Urban Frontier* (New York: Columbia University Press, 1990), 61–62.

14. William Deverell and Douglas Flamming, "Race, Rhetoric, and Regional Identity: Boosting Los Angeles, 1880–1930," in *Power and Place in the North American West*, edited by Richard White and John M. Findlay (Seattle: University of Washington Press, 1999), 117–43.

15. William Alexander McClung, *Landscapes of Desire: Anglo Mythologies of Los Angeles* (Berkeley and Los Angeles: University of California Press, 2000), argues that Anglo conceptions of Los Angeles revolved in large part around the idea that the city represented Utopia.

16. Hamer, *New Towns in the New World*, 61–62; Howard P. Segal, "Jeff W. Hayes: Reform Boosterism and Urban Utopianism," *Oregon Historical Quarterly* 79 (Winter 1978): 345–57.

17. Hamer, *New Towns in the New World*, 69; Hine, *American West*, 266.

18. Brian J. L. Berry, *America's Utopian Experiments: Communal Havens From Long-Wave Crises* (Hanover, N.H.: University Press of New England, 1992), chap. 2, esp. 25–26.

19. Information about Salt Lake City comes primarily from Gunther Barth, *Instant Cities: Urbanization and the Rise of San Francisco and Denver* (New York: Oxford University Press, 1975), chap. 2, quote on 59.

20. The term is from Leonard J. Arrington and Davis Bitton, *The Mormon Experience: A History of the Latter-day Saints* (New York: Alfred A. Knopf, 1979), 243, where it is noted that "the church abandoned its traditional promotion of cooperative and group economic

enterprises" while trying to preserve as many other "traditional goals as national sentiment would permit."

21. James B. Allen, *The Company Town in the American West* (Norman: University of Oklahoma Press, 1966), is one starting point on this topic. See also Linda Carlson, *Company Towns of the Pacific Northwest* (Seattle: University of Washington Press, 2003).

22. John W. McClelland Jr., *R. A. Long's Planned City: The Story of Longview* (Longview, Wash.: Westmedia, 1998), chaps. 4, 7.

23. Hine, *California's Utopian Colonies*, chap. 7; Hayden, *Seven American Utopias*, chap. 10, esp. 299, 300.

24. Charles P. LeWarne, *Utopias on Puget Sound, 1885–1915* (Seattle: University of Washington Press, 1975), 229–37. On Washington's progressive reputation, see also Carlos Schwantes, *Radical Heritage: Labor, Socialism, and Reform in Washington and British Columbia, 1885–1917* (Seattle: University of Washington Press, 1979).

25. The following works criticize planners for their "utopian" approach to cities, although each author adopts a different tack: Jane Jacobs, *The Death and Life of Great American Cities* (New York: Random House, 1961); M. Christine Boyer, *Dreaming the Rational City: The Myth of American City Planning* (Cambridge: MIT Press, 1983); and Leonie Sandercock, *Towards Cosmopolis: Planning for Multicultural Cities* (Chichester, England: John Wiley and Sons, 1998).

26. On the important distinction between designers and users, see Amos Rapoport, *The Meaning of the Built Environment: A Nonverbal Communication Approach* (Beverly Hills: Sage Publications, 1982), 76, 15–22; and Amos Rapoport, *Human Aspects of Urban Form: Towards a Man-Environment Approach to Urban Form and Design* (Oxford: Pergamon Press, 1977), 14–15, 24–25, 52.

27. Judd Kahn, *Imperial San Francisco: Politics and Planning in an American City, 1897–1906* (Lincoln: University of Nebraska Press, 1979); Mansel Blackford, *The Lost Dream: Businessmen and City Planning on the Pacific Coast, 1890–1920* (Columbus: Ohio State University Press, 1993); William H. Wilson, *The City Beautiful Movement* (Baltimore: Johns Hopkins University Press, 1989), chaps. 7, 10; Greg Hise and William Deverell, *Eden by Design: The 1930 Olmsted-Bartholomew Plan for the Los Angeles Region* (Berkeley and Los Angeles: University of California Press, 2000).

28. Robert Rydell, *All the World's a Fair: Visions of Empire at American International Expositions, 1876–1916* (Chicago: University of Chicago Press, 1984).

29. Berry, *America's Utopian Experiments*, chap. 16; John Hancock, "The New Deal and American Planning: The 1930s," in *Two Centuries of American Planning*, edited by Daniel Schaeffer (London: Mansell, 1988), 197–230.

30. Bruce Hevly and John M. Findlay, "The Atomic West: Region and Nation," in *The Atomic West*, edited by Bruce Hevly and John M. Findlay (Seattle: University of Washington Press, 1998), 3–9; Carl Abbott, "Building the Atomic Cities: Richland, Los Alamos, and

the American Planning Language," in *The Atomic West,* edited by Hevly and Findlay, 90–115; John Findlay, "Atomic Frontier Days: Richland, Washington, and the Modern American West," *Journal of the American West* 34 (July 1995): 32–41; Jon Hunner, *Inventing Los Alamos: The Growth of an Atomic Community* (Norman: University of Oklahoma Press, 2004).

31. Heather Fryer, *Perimeters of Democracy: Inverse Utopias and the Wartime Social Landscape in the American West* (Lincoln: University of Nebraska Press, 2010), assesses the surge of federal community building in the West during World War II. Grouping together as "inverse utopias" the atomic town of Los Alamos, New Mexico, the housing project of Vanport, Oregon, the Klamath Indian Reservation in Oregon, and the Topaz Relocation Center in Utah, where peoples of Japanese descent were incarcerated, Fryer highlights the repressive and coercive dimensions of communities built as part of the U.S. government's mobilization for war.

32. Some practicing youthful communes were organized by fairly mainstream religious groups and so confound the distinction between mainstream culture and counterculture.

33. See Raymond J. Burby III et al., *New Communities U.S.A.* (Lexington, Mass.: D. C. Heath, 1976). On Irvine, see William Benjamin Piggot, "The Irvine New Town, Orange County, and the Transformation of Suburban Political Culture" (Ph.D. diss., University of Washington, 2009).

34. Findlay, *Magic Lands,* 181–93, 291.

35. Hayden, *Seven American Utopias,* 321, notes that communes of the 1960s seldom expected the rest of society to follow their example. On Smith's motives, see Leonard J. Arrington, Feramorz Y. Fox, and Dean L. May, *Building the City of God: Community and Cooperation Among the Mormons,* 2nd ed. (Urbana: University of Illinois Press, 1992), 2, 13. Regarding the individualism of the 1960s and 1970s, Brian J. L. Berry titles his chapter on postwar utopian experiments "Pathways to Self-Realization" (*America's Utopian Experiments,* chap. 18).

36. This paragraph is largely based on Miller, *60s Communes.* On the exodus from San Francisco, see chapter 4. The names come from pp. 249–85. On demographic traits, see xxiv, 170, 212. Hayden, *Seven American Utopias,* 322, notes the environmentalism and the high regard for Native Americans, and Catherine Kleiner, "Nature's Lovers: The Erotics of Lesbian Land Communities in Oregon, 1974–1984," in *Seeing Nature Through Gender,* edited by Virginia Scharff (Lawrence: University Press of Kansas, 2003), 242–62, documents similar attitudes.

37. Zeese Papanikolas, *Trickster in the Land of Dreams* (Lincoln: University of Nebraska Press, 1995), 94.

38. Sandercock, *Towards Cosmopolis,* 163, suggests that the most reasonable type of utopia to offer is one that can never be fixed or attained, so she imagines "a postmodern Utopia to which I will not ascribe built form, and which I insist can never be realized, but must always be in the making."

39. On the persistence of communal ideas among Mormons, see Dean L. May, "One Heart and Mind: Communal Life and Values Among the Mormons," in *America's Communal Utopias*, edited by Pitzer, 153–55.

40. Miller, *60s Communes*, xiii, xiv, xx.

41. Ernest Callenbach, *Ecotopia: A Novel* (1975; reprint, New York: Bantam Books, 1990).

42. Joel Garreau, *The Nine Nations of North America* (Boston: Houghton Mifflin, 1981), 251–52. On Cascadia, see Alan Artibise, "Cascadian Adventures: Shared Visions, Strategic Alliances, and Institutional Barriers in a Transborder Region" (paper delivered at the "On Brotherly Terms" symposium, University of Washington, Seattle, September 13, 1996).

Part I

THE METROPOLITAN RETREAT TO THE ECO-URBAN

In the twentieth century community development in the West was often a synthetic response aimed at balancing residents' desires for culturally rich urban living, stable community life, and access to nature. In Irvine, California, as Stephanie Kolberg explains, planners rejected the chaotic sprawl that defined Greater Los Angeles. Inspired by Ebenezer Howard's garden-city model, Irvine's master planner, William Pereira, organized the city around multiple centers, or villages, which included residences, schools, and small shopping venues. Like many of the earlier utopian efforts described by Findlay, Irvine required a top-down plan that detailed land uses and architectural styles. Although the master-planned community afforded middle-class consumers access to the leisure-based lifestyle of Southern California, Kolberg concludes that the company's quest to provide residents with familiarity, order, and security resulted in racial and class exclusivity.

Boulder, Colorado, another university city, traces its origins to the nineteenth-century Colorado gold rush. Boulder's early planning history was marked by the mutual desire of boosters and environmental preservationists to protect and capitalize on the natural beauty of nearby forests and mountains. As Amy Scott describes, a grassroots movement emerged after World War II to control urban expansion through the preservation of open space. While activists simultaneously tried to protect an urban way of life that was defined by interactions with the natural environs, they developed an ecological planning tradition in Boulder. In both Irvine and Boulder, planners and residents acknowledged the connections among the urban economy, the environment, and postindustrial, leisure-centered consumer lifestyles. In these university towns, planning, both at the corporate level and through public activism, has played a significant role in shaping the cityscape and the communities that emerged.

Westerners increasingly exploded the traditional triumvirate of city, suburb, and country, hoping to create urban spaces that embodied the most desired characteristics of all three community models. In these efforts to create new urban forms suited to the region, nature became, as Matt Klingle observes, "an instrument to define and enforce the idea of community." After World War II developers built exurban community clusters on unincorporated land in the foothills and ridges near Park City, Utah, and Missoula, Montana, attracting middle- and upper-class migrants from the nation's larger cities. These migrants were not content with temporary scenic grandeur; rather, as essays by Lincoln Bramwell and Rina Ghose demonstrate, they expected permanent suburban amenities in the wilderness. Bramwell's essay discusses the emergence of "wilderburbs," privately financed clusters of homes in the rural valleys and along the mountain slopes of the Rocky Mountain West. Wilderburbs are neither wild nor suburban, but instead offer residents an opportunity to be closer to nature while enjoying the security and cultural amenities associated with cities. As Ghose demonstrates, the Rocky Mountain region has experienced significant urban and suburban population growth in the past decade, caused mainly by in-migration, which has changed the region's land use, housing, resource allocation, economy, and public policies. Focusing on recent migration to Missoula, Montana, Ghose analyzes the demographic characteristics and migration motivations of newcomers, arguing that the consumption patterns of middle-class amenity migrants have resulted in increasingly rural gentrification in western Montana. With rising housing prices and a new emphasis on social amenities, powerful new expressions of localism and self-interest reshaped community and landscape in the Rocky Mountains. Bramwell and Ghose reveal the economic and environmental limitations that occurred as the lines between country and city were blurred. "Place making," as Matt Klingle writes, "is neither disinterested nor innocent."[1]

Note

1. Matthew Klingle, *Emerald City: An Environmental History of Seattle* (New Haven: Yale University Press, 2007), xii, 4.

Crafting the Good Life in Irvine, California

STEPHANIE KOLBERG

Amid the seemingly undifferentiated post–World War II sprawl of Southern California, a private company put forth plans for a brave new city, plans that aimed to foster a heightened sense of community through "village life" and through the integrated presence of nature. The new city would provide a respite from the perceived monotony of the faceless Southern California suburb by blending architectural diversity, extensive greenery and open space, and differentiated neighborhood centers, culminating in a master-planned California Dream land for the contemporary consumer. Carefully landscaped pods of industry and commerce would dot the city, and the unique personalities of each neighborhood would inspire feelings of belonging and security not thought possible in the larger, more disconnected metropolis. The entire city was to be developed under the aegis of a single entity, the Irvine Company, which offered to impart a more centralized method of development than the piecemeal approaches found in other parts of the region. Through a model that offered a unified design of neighborhood differentiation, and by utilizing marketing imagery that promised cohesion and balance, Irvine's community builders wove their own version of the new twentieth-century city, a city banking on the allure of a tidily planned future in the face of mid-twentieth-century disaffection and alienation.[1] The American habit of "starting over" had, yet again, been simply too hard to resist.

Given the long tradition of antiurbanism in the United States, and coming on the heels of postwar suburban discontent, Irvine's plan appeared poised to provide (upper-middle-class) Americans with the kind of city they had been tacitly asking for for decades: a quiet, "tasteful" landscape designed to minimize conflict and maximize comfort, privately financed by a corporation in order to lower uncertainty.[2] This chapter will examine the transformation of Irvine as it evolved from frontier ranch lands to future-oriented new city and will explore those promotional images of Irvine that forged its initial mediated identity. The discussion will conclude with a current look at one of the key recreationally oriented Irvine villages—the Village of Woodbridge. From the selection of Irvine in 1959 as a site for a new University of California (UC) campus to the first few years following its incorporation in 1971, the narrative of the new city evokes the stubbornly persistent garden-city ideal that is forever reemerging from the wastelands of the steel and concrete metropolis—or, in this case, from the threat of the "faceless, shapeless everything-in-a-row suburbs." With the new city of Irvine, once slated to become "the largest planned city on the North American Continent," the suburban dream could emerge triumphant, this time stocked with many of the accoutrements of a full-scale city.[3]

Whereas some have viewed master-planned communities as attempts to retreat from modern life, Irvine's marketers frequently touted the advantages of modernity and the progressive nature of development, as the new city was to utilize the best-available tools of contemporary society in order to create a more nature-infused, rational order.[4] In this way, Irvine's marketed narrative embodies the apex of the modernist creed: an unwavering faith in large-scale order and rationality, with a premium placed on comfort and smooth efficiency. Although occasionally drawing from Irvine's ranching past to create a sense of continuity and intrigue, Irvine's image makers had to convince consumers that their "city of the future" would be a bourgeois paradise in which comfort, cultivated nature, and exaltation of "the plan" would culminate in an island of calm amid the Southern California population barrage. The story of Irvine's marketed image is the apotheosis of a California Dream that exalted consumer pleasures and a recreationally themed lifestyle, all wrapped up in a tidy city of familiars, the city as product, a story that, in a way, embodies antimodernist fears of an increasingly comfort-obsessed public.[5]

From Feedlots to Swimming Pools

The master-planned city of Irvine, California, gained its roots in agricultural beginnings when, in 1864, James Irvine and partners purchased the land that was to become the Irvine Ranch. The original 120,000-acre swath of land (now 93,000 acres) forty miles south of Los Angeles was composed of Spanish and Mexican land grants that included Rancho San Joaquin, Rancho Lomas de Santiago, and a portion of Rancho Santiago de Santa Ana.[6] In 1876 Irvine bought out his partners to become the sole owner of the ranch and ultimately shifted the land use from sheep grazing to cattle raising. Upon Irvine's death in 1886, his son, James Irvine II, inherited the ranch, and with the establishment of the new County of Orange in 1891, Irvine II formed the Irvine Company in 1894 as a cohesive body to manage ranch operations. The ranch then took an agricultural turn as it moved into the cultivation of corn, beans, and barley and eventually entered the citrus market in the 1910s and 1920s.[7]

James Irvine II formed the James Irvine Foundation in 1937 in order to keep the ranch lands together.[8] When Irvine II died in 1947, he left control of the Irvine Company to the foundation, and his son, Myford Irvine, became the president of the Irvine Company. Because of mounting pressures to urbanize, Myford developed several housing enclaves on the ranch lands, complete with community centers and other recreational facilities. The booming Orange County population, which grew from 220,000 in 1950 to 704,000 in 1960, put increasing pressure on the Irvine Company to develop its land. In addition to this massive population influx, the wheels of urbanization had further accelerated when the University of California regents selected Irvine as the site for a new UC campus in 1959.

The regents enlisted the help of renowned architect William Pereira in selecting the site for the future university. Not only was Pereira an accomplished architect, but he also had a keen interest in the workings and design of cities. Based on Pereira's recommendation, the UC regents selected Irvine for the new campus because its vast undeveloped space presented a chance to build an entirely new community around the university.[9] Once the site was confirmed, the Irvine Company gifted one thousand acres to the new university, and the school subsequently purchased an additional five hundred adjoining acres.

Commissioned to develop the master plan for the new university and its surroundings, Pereira, in 1960, revealed his plan for "a university-oriented community to be organized along the lines of the venerable garden-city model."[10] Englishman Ebenezer Howard first proposed the garden-city model in his 1898 book *To-Morrow: A Peaceful Path to Real Reform*. Howard's plan was to combine the best features of the town and the country by incorporating a series of small, dense villages separated by green space and grouped around a vibrant, urban center. As Lewis Mumford noted, "The Garden City, as Howard defined it, is not a suburb but the antithesis of a suburb; not a mere rural retreat, but a more integrated foundation for an effective urban life."[11] Similarly, Pereira's plan for Irvine was for a fully functioning new city—a city interconnected with the larger region, but definitely not a bedroom-community suburb.

Pereira was far from the first to adapt elements of Howard's garden-city plan, and that model is in fact seen as one of the strongest influencers of American suburban design. The greenbelt towns of the 1930s Resettlement Administration were among the first American developments influenced by Howard's model, and in the 1960s American developers—some funded by the government—again turned to the garden-city model in search of a palliative to the growing urban crisis and proliferating sense of suburban ennui, leading to the development of a string of "New Towns." Of the government-funded New Towns of the 1960s and 1970s, only the Woodlands, just outside of Houston, Texas, continues to thrive today. The most well known of the New Towns—Reston, Virginia, and Columbia, Maryland—were both privately financed.

In paralleling the New Town project of creating entirely new cities, Pereira originally conceived of Irvine as a ten thousand–acre university-centered town, with a proposed population of one hundred thousand. The resulting community was, in Pereira's words, to embody "a real link between town and gown, a place intimately connected with the center of learning." The new community would resemble classic American and European college towns and was to have an intimate pedestrian-oriented design with densely grouped offices, shops, residences, and restaurants situated near the campus. "These communities will not be dominated by the auto," explained Pereira. "They will be walking communities where women can stroll to the shops with their children just as their grandmothers did." Pereira's desire for a walking community can be seen as a revolt against the environmental degradation that had resulted from the proliferating car centrism of late-1950s Southern California.[12]

Pereira's Irvine plan was also informed by alternate models of urbanism, as Pereira had spent a great deal of time analyzing what worked best in the great cities of the world, though, referring back to an American model, he noted that his plan was intended to "revitalize the basic meaning of a community, somewhat on the pattern of a colonial New England town with political and civic interests taking the place of religious ties." The Irvine Company embraced Pereira's design and, believing the entirety of the Irvine Ranch would ultimately be developed in the future, commissioned him to draw up a plan for the rest of the Irvine Ranch. The Irvine Ranch plan allowed Pereira to integrate his many ideas of what the ideal city should look like, and it has been reported that the master plan for Irvine became Pereira's favorite project.[13]

With a comprehensive plan in place, the Irvine Ranch barreled forward along the road to urbanization, and in 1965 UC-Irvine (UCI) opened, as did its adjoining residential center, University Park Village. The village of Turtle Rock was completed in 1967, and in 1968 University Park Center became Irvine's first neighborhood retail hub.[14] Bolstered by California's burgeoning cold war defense industry, Irvine had, by the 1960s, attracted an array of aerospace and electronics research firms, creating a large high-tech income base for the amenity-rich new city. The area's rapid rise to prosperity and the recreationally themed lifestyle that followed led some to view the new city as an almost impossibly idyllic and successful example of new community design. As former Irvine official Charles E. Thomas said of the embryonic city in 1964: "[It] is the kind of place that people have only been able to dream about up until now. . . . Picture a community where children can walk to school without ever crossing a street, where a family can walk barefooted over lawns to their neighborhood swimming pool. Picture a community where a man with a low-medium income can live in an apartment building overlooking a golf course."[15] Such utopian language betrays an ambitious and distinct vision for the new city, a vision that placed a premium on a sense of security made possible by a carefully laid plan unfolding against a backdrop of meticulously manicured nature. This new dream city, which had been slated as a massive experiment in community design, would craft an image steeped in Edenic simplicity and, in this example at least, the promise of the California Dream for all.

Countless commentators expressed a vast sense of hope toward the new community, and in a 1967 article titled "The Making of a City," author Myron Roberts described Irvine as representing the dawn of a great Southern California cultural jackpot. "If this were the time of the Renaissance," ventured Roberts, "and California were Italy, one could predict—without much exaggeration—that very soon the Irvine Ranch will be a city as rich as Genoa, as well educated as Florence, as luxurious as Venice." The careful planning of Irvine would presumably prevent the haphazard growth embodied by other California cities: "Thus, hopefully, Irvine will not be merely another clean, comfortable California suburb where people can enjoy their swimming pools undisturbed by civilization, but a *community* made up of interesting and involved people, a place where minds and souls will be at least as healthy and attractive as the tanned young bodies that soon will occupy these rolling hills and bask under the hot white sky." Such comments betray a desire for a sense of substance and depth, yet a depth still bathed in the glow of a California promise. As historian Kirse Granat May writes in *Golden State, Golden Youth*, the popular California image of the mid-1950s–'60s, especially of California youth, embodied an exaggeration of larger trends within the United States that included a near obsession with "mobile, capitalistic, outdoorsy, consumer-oriented . . . harmless, well-meaning fun."[16] With a new university at its center, Irvine represented to some a more sustainable and serious plan for the future, a maturation into a grown-up version of the pleasure dream.

Although University Park Village was initially at its core, Irvine, or "University City" as it was once dubbed, did not long maintain its university-centered orientation, at least not solely. While a *Los Angeles Times* reporter had quipped in 1964 of Irvine that "probably never before in history has a city started off first with a university and then with a golf course," by 1970 Irvine had become more golf course and less university. Partly due to increased student activism on campuses and preferring to highlight the region's growing affluence, Irvine's promoters soon moved away from the original town-and-gown emphasis, with one Irvine official stating, "The university is as central to our plan as ever. It's just that with all this campus violence, it's not a very good time to be talking about a university community to the public or to our investors."[17]

This shift in emphasis was also connected to a reworking of the original plan, and in March 1970, based on the work of an entire team of planners, the Irvine Company unveiled its revised plan for Irvine, a plan that covered fifty-three thousand acres and included a projected population of 430,000 by the year 2000. This new version of Irvine was billed as "the largest planned city on the North American Continent."[18] The orderly development of the ranch lands was seen as a far better alternative to the piecemeal merchant-builder sprawl that had engulfed much of Southern California. Playing off the public's growing criticism of traditional postwar suburbs, the Irvine Company seized a golden opportunity to provide the public with a relatively recent product—an entirely master-planned, amenity-packed, fairly self-sufficient new community. Fearing annexation attempts by neighboring cities and eager to eke out a more independent existence, the residents of Irvine voted to incorporate in 1971, and the City of Irvine was officially born.

At the center of this plan—and a strong component of the original Pereira design as well—was the concept of the village. According to Irvine Company definitions, villages were to be visually distinct settlements with a unifying theme and were to be large enough in population density to support the everyday conveniences of the residents and coherent enough to be clearly distinct from other villages in the area.[19] Villages would be the major building blocks of the new city, and the coherent uniformity of each would help create a feeling of community and stave off fears of monotonous amorphousness. This sense of distinctiveness would be one of the key selling points of the new city.

Though Irvine's planners had clearly gone to great lengths in designing and marketing this idealized environment, some less ideal realities still surfaced. In the late 1960s the average price for a single-family home in Irvine was thirty-five thousand dollars, more than twice the Orange County average. The high volume of white-collar jobs in Irvine's office parks and the high standard of living typically afforded their employees led the Irvine Company to continue its focus on amenity-packed, high-end housing. Partly because of this, public scrutiny from critics and housing advocates over the lack of affordable housing within the area prompted the Irvine Company to propose the moderate-income Village of Valley View in 1973. In council meetings, however, Irvine residents expressed concerns about increased traffic, declining property values, and fears of hostility to racial and class integration. Residents spoke so vehemently against the plan that the development was scrapped entirely.[20] The Irvine Company was well aware of these tensions, as key Irvine planner and then Irvine Company vice president Ray Watson had commented: "When Columbia [Maryland] started, they ran full-page newspaper ads showing pictures of interracial couples. Back there, that went over great. But if I tried it here, I would scare off every white person I had even the slightest hope of getting."[21] Despite such discomfort over racial and class integration, officials did devise some measures to address the issue of affordable housing. Though the City of Irvine had declined to participate in federally assisted housing programs, in 1974 Irvine became the first city in Orange County to require that 10 percent of its housing be reserved for moderate-income use. Unfortunately, this allocation still fell far below the current and projected needs.

Irvine's plan, for the most part, thus ultimately served as a model of what the future of the American-built environment could be for those willing and able to pay. In perusing promotional literature for the City of Irvine, the picture that emerges is of a place in revolt against the perceived negative aspects of cities and suburbs alike. Although the liberal use of tight aesthetic controls within master-planned cities like Irvine has been the focus of much criticism, Irvine employed that image-crystallizing device to effectively appeal to those imbued with a longing for familiarity, order, and security—hallmarks of the original suburban dream. Whereas Southern California appeared engulfed by disorder and unpredictability, the master-planned Irvine would lift planning and stability to near-religious proportions, creating a retooled version of the suburban California Dream for a new generation of consumers.[22]

Building the Master-Planned Identity
Reimagining Ye Olde Frontier

The story of Irvine's beginnings is steeped in the romance of the Old West. The Irvine Company frequently portrayed James Irvine, the founder of the Irvine Ranch, as a frugal and rather prudish man who, nonetheless, had an amazingly pioneering business spirit. The company described him as "an honest farmer with a real feeling for the land," a man who "was too much of a man not to be himself."[23] Although Irvine was more of an entrepreneur than a cowboy, he was granted many of the rough-and-tumble traits of a classic Old West figure and was often pictured mustached, with a hard look on his face, and wearing a wide-brimmed hat and carrying a rifle, his dog at his side. In a series of sixty-second radio spots from 1966 and 1967, the Irvine Company used frontier and cowboy imagery to market the future site of the City of Irvine, drawing liberally from the region's romanticized past. The ads wove a past steeped in adventure and lurking danger and created a sense of history generally missing from new communities: "Woven into the tapestry of time is a daring tableau, Orange County and Irvine Ranch land has a bandit-ridden frontier, with gunfights and robberies, cattle rustling, highwaymen. . . . The forming of the Irvine Ranch brought stability and organization to the Santa Ana Valley. Arid lands gave way to cultivated fields. Beautiful homes now stand where coyotes once howled to the wind. And from the abyss of time past, emerges the finest place in America to live, work and play." Such ads represent an attempt to endow the region with a sense of continuity where a past rampant with stagecoaches and outlaws could give way to the ranch's future destiny: a new city filled with master-planned subdivisions and bougainvillea-lined jogging paths. The transition from an older romanticized American ideal of the invigorating, untamed frontier and the rough-hewn, land-based lifestyle that accompanied it gave way to another romanticized American ideal—the tranquil, cultivated garden community of the future. Kevin Starr has discussed the prominence of this California image at the turn of the century, the myth of a California history with "a pastoral past, progressive and colorful present, imperial future—a proud and optimistic fable, one that conferred a sense of importance and glamour upon a remote, underdeveloped region." Irvine's "pioneers," as some residents called themselves, moved to the city to become active participants in local government and in the modern evolution of Orange County, bringing it toward a more rational, cultivated order that banked on open-space concerns even, ironically, as the company decimated existing open spaces.[24]

The rapid postwar loss of undeveloped land, which was certainly viewed with despair by many Californians, could be sold placatingly as simply the next (master-planned and hence *reasonable*) step in the progress of Southern California civilization. Of course, the extent to which consumers accepted this idea is uncertain. Environmental historian Adam Rome details the connection between suburban development and the rise of American environmentalism in his book *The Bulldozer in the Countryside,* in which he notes that in the immediate postwar era, "every year, a territory roughly the size of Rhode Island was bulldozed for urban development." Rome discusses the impact of such environmental degradation on the psyches of consumers who had, despite the optimism of the previous generation, ceased to view home builders and developers as heroes. Instead, the loss of beloved play space for children had led to increased environmentalist concern, as parents worried that their kids' favorite fields and meadows would disappear forever with the rapid-fire spread of housing developments.[25] Because suburban dwellers had come face-to-face with the ravages of urbanization, developers had to take their concerns into serious consideration if they were to attract potential residents. Irvine's plan for the inclusion of significant open space and greenery provided a modicum of relief for those increasingly wearied and worried by the prolific blacktopping of the region.[26]

Environmental concerns, however, played a relatively small role in the marketed image of Irvine, while ideals of consumeristic splendor and pleasure fared prominently. Several ads attempted to bridge the gap between the past "good life" of hardworking *production* and the future good life of passive, recreationally themed *consumption* by highlighting the apparently timeless materialism of the past. For example, one ad told the story of a legendary but never-found treasure purported to be buried on Irvine land. Though that treasure proved to be a myth, the master plan for Irvine would bring "contemporary man closer to his dream, for the treasure of today is living comfort, pleasure. Westcliffe Plaza, in Bayside shopping center on the Irvine Ranch, offers consumer products . . . [t]reasures in consumer delight and satisfaction."[27] In this way, an allusion to California's Gold Rush past was made to blend seamlessly into the contemporary California Dream. In putting faith in a more "realistic" plan for the good life, the development of the Irvine Ranch could become the most modern stage of the endlessly unfolding tale of westward expansion and the search for wealth, where future residents could be implicated in the drama by purchasing goods, or perhaps a home, as connections to the land would ultimately give way to a consumer society of sparkling products.

CITY DREAMS, COUNTRY SCHEMES

Modern Plans for Modern Problems

The drama of westward expansion and modernization, however compelling a narrative, did threaten to verge on catastrophe. Between 1940 and 1960 the population of Orange County grew an amazing 385 percent, a growth rate that was "three times the state average and eleven times the national average." As historian Lisa McGirr observes, "This growth was, in a very real sense, a modern-day version of the California gold rush—making Orange County the new frontier West of the second half of the twentieth century."[28] Many Irvine Ranch ads of the time mixed frontier imagery with alarmist reactions to California's rapidly expanding population, an approach that added a palpable sense of urgency by drawing parallels between the contemporary situation and the mushrooming of nineteenth-century frontier towns. Such ads seemed bent on awakening Southern California residents from their Arcadian dream states and snapping them into the reality of a more complex future by relying on the language of both natural and technological disaster, blending lingering cold war fears of annihilation with pressing realities of strained natural resources. In this way the growing tension between the golden dream of sunshine, swimming pools, and fresh starts and the potential for its destruction based on its own popularity lent credence to the possibility that large-scale planning would allow residents to both indulge in and preserve this much-coveted ideal.

In a 1969 advertising supplement in the *Orange County Register*, the Irvine Ranch is said to have given way to "the human flood" that flowed "around the borders of the cattle domain clamoring for entrance to sites for homes, shops, factories, stores, parks, schools, universities, churches and playgrounds." Untamed, this "population bomb . . . mushrooms on three sides and over the center of Irvine Ranch with an impact not yet fully assessed."[29] The Irvine Ranch would deal with this "human hurricane" by devising a plan that would bring a "tasteful dispersion of the flood that, uncontrolled, could cover a fine land in a cloak of tawdriness." Unchecked, this surge of humanity could potentially destroy pristine Orange County and turn it into a clone of its chaotic northern cousin, Los Angeles. Just as so many modernist planning visions of the early 1900s were a result of attempts to accommodate and tame massive urbanization in a manageable way, so too the design for the Irvine Ranch offered a vision of calm rationality and foresight via a holistic and all-encompassing master plan. Even Irvine's dwindling ranch operations had tasted modernity, as the ranch's few remaining cattle were "now managed not by a foreman but a corporate team of fiscal-economic experts for the Irvine

Company." Such futuristic language is rife with calls to efficiency and "progress" and stands in stark contrast to the images of alarm and chaos used to describe the population explosion. Irvine's "utopian" plan could then more effectively be assumed as the reasonable choice in light of the clearly dystopic alternative of a less ordered future. A profound faith in the apparatuses of modernity is evidenced in the vision of the new Irvine as "a mecca for the good life softened and beautiful as never before in history by the machines of a fantastic technology."[30] Such imagery betrays an underlying nervousness over the defense of both class and aesthetic identity and suggests an optimism that technology would finally be able to create a perfect—and up-to-date—middle landscape.

This fantastic technology would also allow for a better way of life, a life of more rational order. "Tomorrow can't be left to chance," warned a 1973 Irvine Company brochure addressed to new residents. "It has to be planned for. Today. And yesterday. The Irvine Company has been planning . . . Planning every important detail of your new world." Whereas fears of paternalism partially led to the eventual downfall of government-funded New Towns, similar fears of *corporate* paternalism appear absent from Irvine's marketing materials, as the same 1973 ad gleefully embraced the kind of big-brother involvement that surely would have caused chills to run down the spines of the anti–big government crowd: "At first glance, the Plan seems to indicate only the *physical* layout of the proposed development. What goes where. And how the streets will be laid out. In reality, the Plan indicates the kind of *community* which can result—if the Plan is followed."[31]

A City of Edenic Villages

In promoting this well-reasoned city of the future, marketers presented a newfangled, nature-infused enclave—the city as haven, almost womblike in its sense of security. In this way Irvine would cast aside old notions of the city as industrial jumble, a land of frantic energy, confusion, and unpredictability. The Irvine Company promised instead a different kind of urbanism, an urbanism of tranquil peace and serenity, where the "balance between man and nature" would be lovingly restored. One 1970 advertisement entitled "Progress" best emblematizes this approach, as a full-color pictorial showcases scenes of pastoral urbanism from the vantage point of a little blonde girl as she recites a lengthy poem about her ideal city. As the girl window-shops with her mother, waves to her office-bound father, and frolics in various idyllic settings involving sailboats, grassy fields, and immaculate storefronts, she praises, essentially, the foresight of the Irvine Company. In lauding green grass and flowers, a lack of "smog and uglies," "neat and clean" park-like offices, and "food that God first found . . . not just a plastic package treat," the ad effectively weaves in environmentalist concerns using only mildly politicized language.[32] The message is that a pollution-free, pastoral-tinged, purified environment is essentially what all kids (at least pretty blonde kids) are dreaming about and is what they are certainly owed. Irvine's ad captures declining open-space fears perfectly, addressing such concerns through its promise to accommodate kids' desires for roaming room and parents' desires for smog-free, pleasant consumption and office parks nestled among greenery.

It is no surprise, then, that the chance to move to a city with a relative abundance of greenery was a major selling point for those who could afford it.[33] One 1960s marketing brochure for University Village explained that William Pereira's design was intended to bring a restful atmosphere to the community via trees, flowers, shrubs, and park benches, resulting in "an immeasurable sense of family well-being and the tranquility that all of us seek." The inaugural edition of the *Voice of the Turtle*, a newsletter for the residents of the Turtle Rock neighborhood, took a similar but more sanctified approach by including a verse from the Song of Solomon: "Rise up, my love, my fair one, and come away. For lo! The winter is past, the rain is over and gone; The flowers appear on the earth; the time of the singing of birds is come, and the voice of the turtle is heard in our land."[34] This biblical reference implies the degree of ambition of the Irvine project, bestowing a further sense of grandiosity and utopianism to the new community.

Representations of a modern-day Garden of Eden within a chaotic, denaturalized world may have seemed like a rejection of modern life and the modern world, but Irvine's encouragement of an opulent if nature-soaked lifestyle can hardly be seen as espousing Luddite sensibilities. Many ads *embraced* modernity and depicted a grassier environment as a *benefit* of modern technology rather than as a retreat from it, as did a 1970 advertising insert in the *Los Angeles Times Home Magazine* that hailed Irvine's "better environment for you" as a place that was "Uncrowded. Clean, airy, open. Everything conveniently close by. Designed for tomorrow. The place where urban sprawl ends. Where the future of man can start today."[35] Similarly, in a 1971 visitor's guide, grandiose and futuristic language heralded the Irvine Ranch as "a totally new living concept . . . in a complex of communities planned by some of the greatest environmental scientists and artists of our time." The brochure elaborates:

> Pastoral beauty is all about you in the vast reaches of the IRVINE RANCH. Quiet meadows for picnicking; mountain heights and wilderness valleys for hiking, riding, and exploring;

providing an island of greenery in the midst of a projected 30,000,000 population megalopolis stretching from Santa Barbara to San Diego. The IRVINE RANCH master plan thus recognizes the needs of civilized man for breathing space, natural country near at hand; the tranquility of fields under cultivation; trees, lakes, streams and parks. This is all a part of the better life being readied for you today on IRVINE RANCH.[36]

William Whyte, author of *The Organization Man* (1956), became—in light of the growing concern over the costs of postwar suburban growth—one of the biggest advocates of open-space preservation in the 1950s–1960s and championed the idea of cluster or planned-unit development in which smaller individual lot sizes would make way for larger communal open spaces.[37] Irvine's marketers and planners were well aware of these ideas, and thus explicit reference to parks and greenery in particular added to the appeal of the new city. In opposition to dystopian visions of the future in which concrete and pollution had left the world in a denaturalized, smoking heap of metal, the future as presented by the Irvine Company foretold a return to green, verdant fields and grassy meadows; they were tamers of the ugly postindustrial city, an ideal meant to instill a sense of calm and trust in jittery home buyers of population-boom Southern California.

In addition to open space, Irvine also promised to deliver a better downtown. Before the Irvine Spectrum Entertainment Center was completed in 1995, the Newport Center served Irvine residents in a downtown cleansed of aesthetic blight. This new-style downtown, image makers contended, would be devoid of the congestion, tawdry neon signs, and light-obstructing skyscrapers that defined many urban centers. The Newport Center—the "sparkling downtown-in-a-park"—was regaled as a downtown to truly *enjoy*, as it would have plenty of "grass to sit on . . . and fountains and goldfish ponds to look at." Similarly, UC-Irvine was described as a good place in which to bike and walk around—a "university-in-a-park." Even the Irvine Industrial Complex was noted as being an attractive neighbor, boasting "more grass than Griffith Park." In addition, "Trees, fountains and flowers decorate the buildings. Many of the parking lots and loading areas are hidden from view by grass and shrubbery." A 1974 ad seamlessly integrated Irvine's past, present, and future, in which large-scale development was meant to seem as organic as plants and animals: "One hundred years ago, it was called the Irvine Ranch. Then, where sheep once grazed, orchards bloomed. And the next harvest came up in skylines. The ranch was becoming the city of the future." In this way, Irvine's promoters highlighted both a dwindling agricultural past and a future of garden-infused urbanism, allowing Irvine to become the new twentieth-century city cleansed of all grit and tawdriness, a city where families had reclaimed the streets and the corner pub had morphed into an open-space nature reserve.[38]

While greenery was one of the biggest allures of the new city, home owners were also courted by the notion that they would be able to walk into a ready-made sense of belonging via Irvine's distinctive "villages." "In times past, throughout the world," noted a 1973 brochure, "people gathered in villages. For comfort. Security. Convenience. To share life's joys and responsibilities with neighbors." The cozy familiarity made possible by the planned villages of Irvine would provide an alternative to a seemingly oppressive landscape in which "people are scattered across shapeless suburbs. With few shared interests, little sense of community, nothing to bring them together." In this way the distinctive visual style of each separate Irvine village would inspire an easy sense of belonging and of knowing one's place, in contrast to the feelings of identityless instability assumed to be the case in less rationally ordered and less architecturally coherent regions: "What's so special about an Irvine Village? Well, the people who live in one can tell you exactly where it begins. And where it ends. And what's in it. And who's from it. (Do you know your community that well? Or do you live in one of those faceless, shapeless everything-in-a-row suburbs?)"[39]

The Irvine plan would supposedly provide the structure within which community ties could flourish, allowing stability, comfort, and familiarity to take over, assumedly prompting one Turtle Rock resident to note, in the early 1970s, that Irvine was "like an old-fashioned neighborhood. [A place where] you know your neighbors and your neighbor's children. And you do things together." One Eastbluff resident similarly proclaimed, "This is the first time I've lived someplace where the grocery clerks actually know my name."[40] As concerns of "otherness" were at least partly behind a distrust of urban life, Irvine would rise as a city composed of familiars, marking, in some ways, the death of the stranger. This new city would not be a place where one simply slipped into anonymity; rather, this would be a place where clerks actually knew your name and issues of "strangeness" would ideally be dissolved by a unified aesthetic. Whether residents of Irvine actually felt a strong sense of community connection was debatable, but the continuous touting of this ideal throughout the marketing literature reveals its appeal.[41]

Irvine's image as a cultural landscape is thus one awash in the symbols of perceived low density and "pleasantness." As environmental-behavior scholar Amos Rapoport has noted, in the United States, perceived low density is one of the largest factors in creating a positive place image. Elements of perceived low density include an abundance of parks and open space, greenery, a strong sense of control, and a low number of strangers.[42] All of these factors have weighed heavily in both the design of Irvine and its marketed image, and the professed friendliness and familiarity of the Irvine villages dovetail strikingly with Rapoport's connection between a lack of strangers and a positive place image. All of these symbols trigger the new city as classically suburban, which raises a question: To what degree can a city espousing garden-city ideals be accepted as being on the same playing field as sites of more traditional urbanity?

In order to get a better sense of how exactly the ideas and imagery behind the new City of Irvine have been realized today, it may be instructive to look at one of the key villages of Irvine, the Village of Woodbridge. How have ideals of tranquillity and nature been worked into the village landscape, and in what ways do the area's aesthetic markers embody a particularly "Irvine" way of life? Does Woodbridge, as a microcosm of the city, seem to embrace the idea of cozy villages that promoters of the new city seemed most excited about, and if so, what can such a setting contribute to the idea of urbanism in the twenty-first century?

The Woodbridge Way of Life

The Village of Woodbridge is one of the oldest villages in Irvine. Established in 1975, it is also one of the most lauded villages of Irvine, and thus serves as a key example of the idealized "Irvine way of life." Woodbridge is a "recreation-oriented" community built around two large artificial lakes that are intended not only as aesthetic enhancements to the neighborhood but as sites for water sports like fishing and boating. A 1982 *Christian Science Monitor* article may have had Woodbridge in mind when it called Irvine "a rival to anything Disneyland can offer . . . [and it] is like no other ranch in the world." On the Woodbridge Village Association Web site, an article commemorating the twenty-fifth anniversary of Woodbridge featured an interview with Ray Watson—former Irvine Company president, Disney chairman, planner, and "the man in charge of designing and creating Woodbridge Village Association"—in which Watson was pictured posing next to a large "Watson-land" poster. Watson's head had been superimposed onto various cartoon bodies of Disney icons such as Prince Charming, Aladdin, and Tinkerbell. In line with this fantasy feeling, Bob Figeira, the first executive director of Woodbridge, reminisced about "hiring students to come to the lagoon to swim and boat on weekends while the model homes were open in order to give visitors a more concrete image of the activity that was to be a part of Woodbridge." Woodbridge was noted as being so popular that the company received more than fifty thousand inquiries from potential buyers before it even opened.[43]

Potential residents were presumably at least partly attracted to Woodbridge for its outdoorsy aesthetic and feel, an aesthetic that many would seek to maintain. Although the legendarily extensive regulations of suburban home-owner associations have been easy targets for critics of master-planned communities like Irvine, the meticulous attention to the maintenance of a certain look does reveal much about issues of class and about the faith many place in a series of aesthetic policies. Like those of many home-owner associations, the *Woodbridge Village Association Membership Manual* contains countless rules governing the appearance of the neighborhood, rules that engage such particularities as correct shades of paint for houses and fences, the proper parking of large vehicles, the number of hours garage doors may legally be left open, and the correct (discrete) placement and size of satellite dishes and security decals. One rule from the 1984 manual governs the color of car covers, specifying that "color and design of covers are subject to approval by the Board. Standard grey and light green covers are considered acceptable. Any other color or design must first be approved by the Board or its designated committee."[44] This sense of control over the community aesthetic seems most focused on creating a streamlined, nonjarring environment, at all levels.

According to Kevin Chudy, community relations manager of Woodbridge Village, a neighborhood's covenants, conditions, and restrictions are put into place by the developer well before the first residents have moved in. These CC&Rs are recorded with the county and cannot be changed without a vote. The process is lengthy and extensive, and it only occurs—if ever—over major issues of contention. The CC&Rs laid out by the developer—in this case, the Irvine Company— define a neighborhood's common areas and common guidelines and grant power to the community's board members to write the more specific "rules and regulations" for that community. The rules and regulations are largely determined by the board members and are more easily altered than the CC&Rs, as residents may propose additions or changes at any time. New home owners must sign a contract agreeing to observe the neighborhood's CC&Rs and rules and regulations.[45]

Such extensive guidelines, especially those relating to the minutia of building appearances, could serve as evidence of what design critic Virginia Postrel has called "the rise of aesthetic value," which she claims is embodied by the public's increased interest in design, style, and beauty. But these meticulous rules also express a fear of chaos and of the unknown, a belief that without such stringently enforced aesthetic controls, the neighborhood may collapse into ugliness and disarray. In Irvine the ability to govern community aesthetics restores a more "pleasant" sense of order and security and ensures a sense of "niceness" saturated with class-based ideals.⁴⁶ Geographers Nancy Duncan and James Duncan discuss the highly political nature of the aestheticized landscape in their 2004 book, *Landscapes of Privilege*, in which they study the wealthy New York City–area suburb of Bedford. The authors maintain that in Bedford, adherence to a particular pastoral aesthetic was used as a defense to establish individual and community identity, often "against and in contrast to an outside world." They argue that "a high degree of attention on the part of suburban residents to the visual, material, and sensual aspects of place and place-based identity leads to an aestheticization of exclusion. A seemingly innocent appreciation of landscapes and desire to protect local history and nature can act as subtle but highly effective mechanisms of exclusion and reaffirmation of class identity."⁴⁷ In a new city like Irvine, the defense of a particular aesthetic may be the most logical shortcut to cultivating a sense of collective identity, but it seems an unfortunate by-product of California master-planned communities that the preservation of open space and greenery would come to be associated with a certain upper-middle-class aesthetic and conservatism instead of a more populist inclination toward the sharing of natural beauty.

The Woodbridge Village Association publishes a monthly newsletter called *Reflections* in which local village events are discussed, events such as arts-and-crafts fairs, swim clubs, board meetings, and Jazzercise classes; it is a potpourri of information and local color designed to enhance community connections. It is not unlike other neighborhood-association newsletters found across the nation. One of the more interesting aspects of *Reflections* is a regular feature called "Home of the Month," which "intends to recognize homeowners in the Village who have helped to protect the Woodbridge way of life by maintaining the exterior of their home in excellent condition." According to the November 2004 installment, people can protect this way of life by showing excellence in "the condition of their paint, landscaping, roofing material, fencing, walkways and driveway, garage door and mailbox and post, and [in] the home's general curb appeal." Winners of this award are presented with a Home of the Month plaque and are thanked for "their contribution to the Woodbridge way of life."⁴⁸

February 2005's winners, whose "attractive Creekside property has undergone a substantial renovation," were congratulated for their "new roofing, new fencing, hardscape including a stucco wall with a brick cap and brick ribbons on the driveway, a new garage door, a new exterior color scheme, a patio cover, built-in cooking area, patio heaters and lighting and retractable awnings."⁴⁹ The use of defensible-space imagery—defined as the maintenance of a certain look that can "protect" one's lifestyle—speaks of the intensely important role aesthetics plays in the master-planned community and in the creation and maintenance of group identity. To not defend the village aesthetic would be to introduce the potential for a destabilized sense of community and a lack of unity, the opposite of what Woodbridge—and Irvine—seems to be about.

When I first visit Woodbridge it is a Saturday afternoon, and there is a fairly large crowd at the Woodbridge Village Center. The shops, which include Barnes and Noble, FasTracKids, Jitterbugs Toys, Karma Centre, and Rainbow Kids Hairstyling, among others, are arranged around a central courtyard. The center's movie theater is called the Woodbridge Family 5. Two large fiberglass sculptures—one a frog, the other a toad—are set in a sandbox at the center of the courtyard. The frogs are a hit with the kids, which is a good thing, since the vast majority of village visitors seem to have them. It is a sunny afternoon, and everyone appears to be having a good time.

I walk around to the rear of the center, to a large drainage ditch flanked by grassy hills. Two teenagers skateboard across the curbs of the jogging paths. The ditch is empty except for a few small stagnant pools. Across the way, a trash can has tipped over, leaving spilled garbage strewn across the verdant lawn. The mud in the ditch looks thick, and I wonder how close one could get to the other side before sinking in completely.

I decide to investigate the famous Woodbridge lakes. I walk around North Lake, following a scenic pedestrian pathway that abuts the lake on one side and nicely landscaped homes on the other. There is a perceptible tranquillity in the air, and as birds sing, it is not hard to imagine I am miles and miles away from a sprawling metropolis. The lake is perfectly still. A group of teenagers plays volleyball in a fenced-off sand court. I am impressed, as it is still fairly early for a Saturday. A slight breeze picks up from the west. It feels very idyllic.

I continue down the path to an enclosed beach area. Dozens of lounge chairs are set up in meticulous rows, all standing at attention, facing a drained white concrete lake. The sign on the gate says, "Closed for Maintenance." This, I learn, is part of the private North Beach Club. The fence encloses a small stretch of sandy shoreline. But it is the drained lake that stands out most. An empty lifeguard tower rises from the center. I imagine the lazy summers spent by the pool, the fountains in full bloom, and the deck chairs full of sunning bodies. I imagine the smell of barbecued corn and chicken, the laughter of giddy sunbathers, and the soft shouts of "Marco Polo" ricocheting around the area. I hear beer cans cracking open and the soft whir of Frisbees sailing through the air. This seems to be it—the apotheosis of the "recreationally themed" life Irvine's marketers had long been touting.

Despite the admittedly pleasant setting of Irvine, I cannot help but think of something art historian Karal Ann Marling once said about Disneyland, about the "architecture of reassurance" it embodies. Such architecture, she argued, espouses a highly "domestic" aesthetic, garnered by "smallish, pinkish, safe, and comfy spaces," an aesthetic that inspires "not the big, histrionic emotions appropriate to public life: righteous anger, heated passion, the soaring elation of victory . . . [but rather] mild contentment and the overarching reassurance that there is an order governing the disposition of things."[50] Although Woodbridge is a residential neighborhood and not necessarily meant to be the seat of Irvine's public life, its aesthetic of comfort seems to have been one of the dominant messages of the city itself. Perhaps Irvine and other postwar master-planned cities have settled a bit too handily into that mold, which makes me wonder: Can such places ever shake their "landscape-of-reassurance" image, and can large "histrionic emotions" ever be staged in settings that largely deny the presence of struggle and imperfection? In what urban future will grassy walkways and planned open spaces move beyond the semiotics of privilege?

Conclusion

Promising potential residents a strong sense of community, an "old-neighborhood" feel where shopkeepers know your name and children and families can "walk barefooted over lawns to their neighborhood swimming pool," Irvine's master plan is, in some ways, a stroke of genius, claiming to subtly soothe away the postwar suburban problems of social isolation and monotony of design while incorporating in industry and a university a way for people to attain a more centralized way of life within a suburban setting. But, as with any article of faith, there are those who believe and those who do not. And to those who do not believe in the Irvine Company's version of city life, Irvine has become just too much studied flawlessness and exclusivity, as one is left longing for the happenstance mistakes and democratic blunders of a far messier world.

The marketed image of Irvine bespeaks a modernist planning ideal rooted in attempts to blend both city and country. By relying heavily on the imagery of both wild and cultivated nature, the promoters of Irvine created a portrait of the new city as a thoroughly modern, technologically sound place still strongly connected to the natural world. The image makers of communities like Irvine have, by integrating the holy trinity of master-planned community marketing—nature, balanced living, and familiarity—emphasized many desired values of suburbia while attempting to erase design features that seemed to foster isolation and ennui. In this way, developers hoped to sculpt a master-planned new city on a metropolitan scale that maintained both a "small-town" feeling and a sense of pioneering individualism. In weaving together the classic ideals of the garden and of the frontier, Irvine's marketers spun a tale of capitalistic utopia, hoping to inspire faith in better living through corporate-run community planning, while avoiding the "ugly" chaos of a less planned world.

In constructing an Edenic future in which the new city can rise sparkling and clean amid open spaces, fountains, and tastefully landscaped villages, the new city, speckled with pods of industry and commerce, can emerge as a paean to a particular brand of planning, a monument to a corporate vision of what the good life means to some in twentieth-century America. The question remains as to whether newer planned cities such as Irvine will actually prove to be any more or less "authentic" to their inhabitants than other built forms. Just as postwar tract suburbs were criticized as "scamscapes" that failed to deliver on their advertised promise of a better life, the next phase of large-scale suburban-tinged development is in turn criticized for its shunning of a grittier reality and its disturbing homogeneity and elitism. What the *idea* of Irvine represents is the culmination of a corporatized California Dream that believes it is possible to "start over"—while picking and choosing desirable bits from the past—and try again, to overlay yet another version of the good life onto the not-yet-cold ashes of the past. It was another attempt to remake California in the image of its creators.

Notes

I am grateful to Michael Steiner, Pamela Steinle, and Terri Snyder of the American Studies Department at California State University, Fullerton, for their insight, guidance, and encouragement; to Jeni Rohlin, Alex Bundy, Kristin Hargrove, Simon Atkinson, and Steve Hoelscher for their critical readings of various drafts; and to Amy Scott and Kathy Brosnan for their feedback and suggestions.

1. For an examination of the role of developers as "community builders," see Edward P. Eichler and Marshall Kaplan, *The Community Builders* (Berkeley and Los Angeles: University of California Press, 1967).

2. With respect to antiurban and antisuburban feelings, see John Keats, *The Crack in the Picture Window* (New York: Ballantine Books, 1956); William H. Whyte, *The Organization*

Man (New York: Doubleday Anchor Books, 1956); Sloan Wilson, *The Man in the Gray Flannel Suit* (New York: Simon and Schuster, 1955); Lewis Mumford, *The City in History: Its Origins, Its Transformations, and Its Prospects* (New York: Harcourt, Brace, and World, 1961); Betty Friedan, *The Feminine Mystique* (New York: Dell, 1963); and Morton White and Lucia White, *The Intellectual Versus the City* (New York: Mentor Books, 1964).

3. Advertisement, new City of Irvine, Don Meadows Collection, Regional History Collection, Special Collections and Archives, Langson Library, University of California, Irvine (hereafter cited as Meadows Collection), n.d., approx. 1971–72; "Staff Report on the Proposed City of Irvine General Plan," prepared by the Orange County Planning Department for submission to the Orange County Planning Commission, Special Collections, Local History Ephemera, Pollack Library, California State University, Fullerton (hereafter cited as Ephemera Collection), November 12, 1970, 7; Robert Fishman, *Bourgeois Utopias: The Rise and Fall of Suburbia* (New York: Basic Books, 1987), xi, 183; William Sharp and Leonard Wallock, "Bold New City or Built-Up 'Burb? Redefining Contemporary Suburbia," *American Quarterly* 46 (March 1994): 1–30. As of 2005 the city of Irvine had a population of 175,000.

4. Leo Marx, *The Machine in the Garden: Technology and the Pastoral Ideal in America* (New York: Galaxy Books, 1967), 6; Lisa McGirr, *Suburban Warriors: The Origins of the New American Right* (Princeton: Princeton University Press, 2001), 94–95.

5. T. J. Jackson Lears, *No Place of Grace: Antimodernism and the Transformation of American Culture, 1880–1920* (Chicago: University of Chicago Press, 1981), 300.

6. According to the Irvine Company Web site, "Through the years, the company's land holdings have diminished as homes have been sold and as land deemed sensitive for environmental or public recreational uses has been conveyed to governmental agencies to ensure preservation and public access. Today, approximately 44,000 acres remain under the company's stewardship" (http://www.irvinecompany.com/aboutus/News.asp?type=factsheet1#The%20Ranch).

7. Martin J. Schiesl, "Designing the Model Community: The Irvine Company and Suburban Development, 1950–88," in *Postsuburban California: The Transformation of Orange County Since World War II*, edited by Rob Kling, Spencer Olin, and Mark Poster (Berkeley and Los Angeles: University of California Press, 1991), 56.

8. Raymond J. Burby III and Shirley F. Weiss, *New Communities U.S.A.* (Lexington, Mass.: Lexington Books, 1976), 89.

9. Schiesl, "Designing the Model Community," 57, 58.

10. Ibid., 59. See also Scott Donaldson, "City and Country: Marriage Proposals," *American Quarterly* 20 (Fall 1968); Kenneth T. Jackson, *Crabgrass Frontier: The Suburbanization of the United States* (New York: Oxford University Press, 1985); and Burby and Weiss, *New Communities U.S.A.*

11. Ebenezer Howard, *Garden Cities of To-Morrow*, edited and with a preface by F. J. Osborn and with an introductory essay by Lewis Mumford (1902; reprint, Cambridge: MIT Press, 1965), 35.

12. William Pereira quoted in "The Man with the Plan," *Time*, September 6, 1963, 69–70. "By 1960, approximately two-thirds of the land in metropolitan Southern California supported car-related needs: highways, roads, driveways, freeways, parking lots, service stations, and car lots" (Kirse Granat May, *Golden State, Golden Youth: The California Image in Popular Culture, 1955–1965* [Chapel Hill: University of North Carolina Press, 2002], 13).

13. "Highlights of the History of the Irvine Ranch," Irvine Company, n.d., approx. 1965, California Index, Los Angeles Public Library, Los Angeles; James Steele, ed., *William Pereira* (Los Angeles: Architectural Guild Press, 2002), 19.

14. "Planning Ahead," February 1999, http://www.irvinecompany.com/aboutus.pa0299/page7.htm.

15. "University Park Gets Under Way This Year," *Orange County: Newsmagazine of Life, Business, and Industry*, reprint of a Feature Section in the September 1964 issue of *Orange County Newsmagazine*, 3.

16. Myron Roberts, "The Making of a City," *Saturday Review*, September 23, 1967, 72; May, *Golden State, Golden Youth*, 26.

17. Helen Johnson, "UC Irvine to Foster City," *Los Angeles Times*, December 13, 1964, OC1; David Shaw, "Irvine—City or Super Subdivision?" *Los Angeles Times*, June 14, 1970.

18. "Staff Report on the Proposed City of Irvine General Plan," prepared by the Orange County Planning Department for submission to the Orange County Planning Commission, Ephemera Collection, November 12, 1970, 7.

19. "Products and Procedures," Section VI, 1973, Ray Watson Papers, Special Collections and Archives, Langson Library, University of California, Irvine.

20. Schiesl, "Designing the Model Community," 63, 65, 75. Although initially Irvine was largely white, today it is more diverse. As of the 2000 census, the City of Irvine was 61 percent white, 29 percent Asian and Pacific Islander, 7 percent Hispanic, 2 percent Black, and 1 percent "Other" (http://www.cityofirvine.org/about/demographics.asp).

21. Shaw, "Irvine—City or Super Subdivision?" Watson also served as president of the Irvine Company from 1973 to 1977. In 1977 Donald Bren, a wealthy real estate developer and founder of the upscale Mission Viejo community in Orange County, became the largest shareholder with 34 percent of the stock in a reorganized Irvine Company. By 1983 he secured 92 percent of the shares and was elected chairman of the board. In 1996 Bren became the single shareholder. See the company Web site at http://www.irvinecompany.com. See also Schiesl, "Designing the Model Community," 75.

22. Numerous articles cited Irvine as a model of successful planning, such as Norris Leap, "Irvine Plan, a Dream of Future—Thomas Set to Bring It True," *Los Angeles Times*, March 5, 1961; and Don Smith, "Irvine Master Plan Unveiled," *Los Angeles Times*, January 19, 1964.

23. Jim Sleeper, "James Irvine—the Man: Prunes for Breakfast, a Love for Dogs," in [publication title unknown] (1964). Jim Sleeper was the Irvine Company's historian.

24. "60 Second Radio Spots," Irvine Company, 1966–67, Ephemera Collection; Kevin Starr, *Americans and the California Dream, 1850–1914* (New York: Oxford University Press,

1973), 126; Nicolas Dagen Bloom, *Suburban Alchemy: 1960s New Towns and the Transformation of the American Dream* (Columbus: Ohio State University Press, 2001).

25. Adam Rome, *The Bulldozer in the Countryside: Suburban Sprawl and the Rise of American Environmentalism* (New York: Cambridge University Press, 2001), 8 (quote), 119–52 (regarding open space).

26. Mike Davis, *City of Quartz: Excavating the Future in Los Angeles* (1990; reprint, New York: Vintage Books, 1992), esp. 170–80.

27. "60 Second Radio Spots."

28. McGirr, *Suburban Warriors*, 28. Los Angeles County grew from 2,786,000 in 1940 to 6,039,000 in 1960, a growth of 217 percent. From 1960 to 1970 Orange County's growth slowed slightly, though the population more than doubled, growing from 704,000 to 1,420,386 (http://www.census.gov/population/cencounts/ca190090.txt).

29. Such language perhaps echoes the rapid growth of the defense industry in Orange County that McGirr outlined (*Suburban Warriors*, chap. 1, esp. 25–29).

30. "An Introduction to the Irvine Ranch and an Explanation of Its Participation in the Orderly Development of Orange County," supplement of the *Orange County Register*, February 2, 1969, Special Collections, Local History Collection, Pollack Library, California State University, Fullerton. See also Greg Hise, *Magnetic Los Angeles: Planning the Twentieth-Century Metropolis* (Baltimore: Johns Hopkins University Press, 1997).

31. "Welcome Home," 1973, Meadows Collection

32. "Progress, 1970: The Irvine Company," Meadows Collection.

33. For a history of sylvan-themed advertising in the United States, see Stephen V. Ward, *Selling Places: The Marketing and Promotion of Towns and Cities, 1850–2000* (New York: Routledge, 1998).

34. "The Village," Meadows Collection, n.d., although it appears to be preincorporation, sometime in the mid-1960s; *Voice of the Turtle*, Spring 1968, Meadows Collection.

35. "Irvine: Builders of Tomorrow's Cities . . . Today," the Irvine Company, *Los Angeles Times Home Magazine*, June 28, 1970.

36. "Irvine Ranch: Road Map and Visitor's Guide," April 21, 1971, Special Collections, Pollack Library, California State University, Fullerton.

37. Rome, *Bulldozer in the Countryside*, 129–31.

38. "Welcome Home," 22; [untitled], Meadows Collection, n.d., approx. 1972; "Welcome Home," 22; advertisement, *Irvine World News*, July 4, 1974, 15. Irvine's first bar, the Trocadero, did not open until 1988. Its owner, Mark Holochek, observed, "They [The Irvine Company] were really careful about opening their first bar. We were handpicked, and they didn't want a sleaze bar" (Maria L. Ganga, "Mixing It Up in Irvine," *Los Angeles Times*, November 5, 1988).

39. "Welcome Home," 13; [untitled], Meadows Collection, n.d., approx. 1971–72.

40. "It Will Be a City of Villages," n.d., approx. 1973, Ray Watson Papers, Special Collections and Archives, Langson Library, University of California, Irvine. Special thanks to the UCI Special Collections staff for allowing me to utilize this newly acquired source.

41. Others have argued for a different approach to the planning of *urban* space. For a classic take on this, see Jane Jacobs, *The Death and Life of Great American Cities* (New York: Random House, 1961). See also Richard Sennett, *The Uses of Disorder: Personal Identity and City Life* (Vintage Books: New York, 1970), 9.

42. Amos Rapoport, *The Meaning of the Built Environment: A Nonverbal Communication Approach* (1982; reprint, Tucson: University of Arizona Press, 1990), esp. 156–72.

43. Norman Sklarewitz, "Irvine Ranch: Master-Planned Living," *Christian Science Monitor*, September 14, 1982; "25th Anniversary Article," Woodbridge Village Association Web site, http://www.wva.org/news/news-009.htm. Watson left the Irvine Company in the mid-1970s to work for Disney.

44. *Woodbridge Village Association Membership Manual*, 1984.

45. Kevin Chudy, Woodbridge Village Community Relations Manager, telephone interview by author, May 2, 2005.

46. Virginia Postrel, *The Substance of Style: How the Rise of Aesthetic Value Is Remaking Commerce, Culture, and Consciousness* (2003; reprint, New York: Perennial, 2004). For an examination of the "search for community" as related to a search for "niceness," see Setha Low, *Behind the Gates: Life, Security, and the Pursuit of Happiness in Fortress America* (New York: Routledge, 2003).

47. James S. Duncan and Nancy G. Duncan, *Landscapes of Privilege: The Politics of the Aesthetic in an American Suburb* (New York: Routledge, 2004), 3, 4.

48. *Reflections: A Monthly Reflection of Life Within Woodbridge*, November 2004.

49. *Reflections: A Monthly Reflection of Life Within Woodbridge*, February 2005.

50. Karal Ann Marling, *Designing Disney's Theme Parks: The Architecture of Reassurance* (Montreal: Canadian Centre for Architecture, 1997), 83.

Open-Space Politics in Boulder, Colorado

AMY L. SCOTT

For many decades, residents of Boulder, Colorado, tried to balance two competing visions for their city. The town's founders believed that Boulder had to grow—both economically and in population—to be a viable community capable of competing with other regional towns and cities. At the same time, many had moved to the Rocky Mountain town for its breathtaking vistas and proximity to the mountains; they envisioned the foothills to the west of Boulder as the centerpiece of the town's parks and recreation system, and they wanted Boulder to remain small. From the 1890s through World War II, the progrowth vision of town boosters and promoters coexisted uneasily with constervationists' plans to maintain the town's natural beauty.

In nineteenth-century Boulder, mountain parkland conservation was influenced by the "multiple resource usage" policies of conservationist Gifford Pinchot, who formed the U.S. Forest Service during Theodore Roosevelt's administration, and by wilderness preservationists' desire to protect irreplaceable wild landscapes.[1] It was also connected to a nineteenth-century urban planning tradition that emphasized the role of nature in creating public spaces in which the native-born middle class could model civic culture and appropriate social behavior for the immigrant occupants of America's densely populated industrial cities. Landscape architects and community planners like Frederick Law Olmsted and Ebenezer Howard had responded to the social problems that accompanied rapid industrialization and urbanization by planning urban park systems and garden cities. These men imagined cities ordered by nature. Believing that modern urbanites had harnessed the technology of the Industrial Revolution to build cities that existed independently of nature, Olmsted and Howard designed public spaces and communities that would bring nature back into the city. Notably, Olmsted's Central Park was designed to soften the social and environmental inequalities that defined industrial New York City and foster pedestrian democracy by reintroducing nature into the heart of the city. New York elites believed that the city's poor, uneducated immigrants could witness examples of civilized interactions with nature by observing their social betters in Central Park. As historian Dolores Hayden writes, these planners also believed that "a model community in a natural setting led to the reform of society."[2] In England, Howard intended for his garden cities to remove middle-class citizens from the class conflict and environmental degradation of London's industrial neighborhoods, restore them to the land, and reconnect them to nature. Applying the skills of the landscape architect to utopian community planning, Olmsted designed "picturesque enclaves" such as Llewellyn Park, New Jersey, and Riverside, Illinois.

In the twentieth century, to those who were making homes in the growing cities of the American West, it was not the centralized, industrial city that was transforming their relationship to nature but rather the decentralizing effect of mass suburbia. Local responses to the bulldozing of open spaces and the technological problems that accompanied suburban developments contributed to the growth of the environmental movement regionally and nationally.[3] Unlike nineteenth-century planners who sought to use nature to order centralized, industrial cities, postwar planners who were influenced by the emerging environmental movement developed planning theories in response to decentralized suburban growth and operated within a system of regional-metropolitan politics in which cities and suburbs competed for resources and power.[4]

In response to the rise of suburbia, environmental activists began to influence urban planning.[5] They thought about land use, density, and urban design with one goal in mind: balancing economic viability and environmental sustainability.[6] They argued that cities and suburbs did not exist independently of nature; sprawling development was costly to cities, and it destroyed the countryside. The physical shape and size of the city, they continued, determined its social organization, its effect on the landscape, and its relationship to local ecosystems. Believing that the very survival of a city and the health of its citizens depended on land-use decisions and development patterns, environmental activists concluded that they could no longer defer to property owners and market trends. Instead, ecologically minded citizens and activists sought to use municipal regulations to build into their urban landscape an acknowledgment of the connection between city and nature and a recognition of environmental limits.[7]

After World War II, as Boulder developers began to bulldoze pine trees and build access roads to subdivided lots in the foothills, more and more people began to rethink the traditional hierarchy of city promotion, local economy, and environment that had defined the pace of the city's growth. Activists in Boulder, Colorado, tried to steer the city away from the national trends of suburbanization and privatization by imagining collective solutions to urban and environmental problems. A coalition of university scholars, wilderness preservationists, recreational enthusiasts, and home owners insisted that to maintain Boulder's beauty, growth had to be controlled. Their desire to protect their perceived quality of life gave rise to a local environmental movement and politics of lifestyle, through which they imagined a different kind of urban living. Through grassroots organizing and referendum elections, coalition members demanded public open-space purchases that would limit Boulder's footprint on the land. They argued that conserving the forests and rural lands that bordered the city was a logical and necessary first step toward creating a compact, dense city edged by mountain parklands and surrounded by prairie open spaces that could be enjoyed by a physically active citizenry. After winning control of local planning boards, activists designed systematic programs that used natural features to shape, define, and limit the size of their city. Furthermore, Boulder's urban environmentalists made open space central to both the physical design of the city and the culture that developed within its borders. Boulder activists pressed city planners to think critically about the connections among environment, economy, population, and sustainability and to adopt an ecosystem-management approach to urban planning. In the process, they transformed the nature and intent of urban planning in Boulder. By the 1970s older planning practices had given way to citizens' demands for responsible stewardship of the environment and an urban model that fostered sustainability.[8] By demanding a voice in decisions about land use and economic growth, Boulder's postwar environmental coalition imagined a spatial fix to suburban growth that has continued to influence urban development in the West and throughout the United States.

Promoting Boulder: Selling Blue Sky

Drawn by the Colorado gold rush, American settlers incorporated the City of Boulder in 1858. Having reluctantly visited Boulder in the 1870s, English traveler Isabella Bird later noted, "Boulder is a hideous collection of frame houses on the burning plain, but it aspires to be a 'city' in virtue of being a 'distributing point' for the settlements up the Boulder Canyon, and of the discovery of a coal seam."[9] Although the extractive industry's influence continued into the twentieth century, higher education, rather than mining, would become the answer to Boulder's urban aspirations. Town boosters secured a state contract for Colorado's land-grant university in lieu of a state prison. Although many townspeople believed that Boulder's boosters had jeopardized their town's future by betting on the university instead of a prison, they welcomed the University of Colorado's first faculty members and students in 1898.

City leaders hoped to insulate their community from the boom-and-bust cycle of economic development that defined urban life on the edge of the Rocky Mountain mining frontier. As T. V. Wilson wrote in 1909, "We must be careful not to attempt to sell 'blue sky' at too great a price. Other places have tried this and failed.... It is safe to say that not one businessman or property holder in five hundred of the fifteen thousand people in and around the city, tributary to it, wants a 'boom.' We want a good live town, not only this year, but throughout the years to come."[10] By platting unusually large residential lots, municipal leaders purposefully curtailed real estate speculation and residential population. Town fathers also understood that the West's itinerant, sometimes radical, and always undesirable working class—hard-rock miners, railroad workers, agricultural laborers, and sex workers—could not afford to purchase large residential lots.

Fostering social stability required the proper mix of enterprising people. Boulder boosters traveled to cities in the South and Midwest, heartily promoting the town to potential migrants. They touted Boulder's benefits as an educational center, a gateway to Rocky Mountain adventure, and a respite for those who had tired of the pace and environment of modern industrial cities. The Seventh-Day Adventist Sanitarium, located at the foot of Mount Sanitas, offered health retreats and Progressive Era medical treatments. Advertisements for guided adventures with the Colorado Mountain Club (CMC) enticed middle-class tourists from the Midwest.[11] Publications by the Chamber of Commerce featured articles about Boulder's natural resources such as the city's glacial-fed water supply. A 1920s advertisement, for instance, depicted businessman Eben Fine explaining Boulder's proximity to the glacier to a cartoon caricature of the world. Standing before a map of Colorado that was titled "The Switzerland of America," Fine proposes a scenic road between Boulder and the Arapahoe Glacier. The world responds, "It's up to you citizens to finish the road and I'll come and spend millions." Clearly, town boosters envisioned Boulder as a resort destination that could rival the finest resorts in the Swiss Alps.[12]

Across the West, boosters were trying to capitalize on the region's natural splendor. Railroads promoted the natural wonders of Yellowstone and the Grand Canyon. Colorado Springs and other nearby towns promoted the restorative powers of their locations and the sublimity of wilderness. Influenced by trends in nature tourism, Boulder's residents worked to preserve the incomparable vistas of their mountain location. In 1898, Boulder citizens passed a seventy-five thousand-dollar bond issue to buy a Chautauqua campground, seventy-five acres of land in the foothills west of town where gold miners gathered for social and cultural activities. Chautauqua became the foundation of the Boulder mountain parks system. The city also purchased eighty acres of federal land on Flagstaff Mountain to prevent clear-cutting by private lumber companies. To permanently prohibit the harvesting of other forests within sight of Boulder, officials requested that Congress set aside all of Flagstaff Mountain. The U.S. Forest Service, already engaged in setting aside millions of forestlands in the West, responded by donating eighteen hundred acres of land on Flagstaff Mountain to Boulder's Parks and Recreation Department.[13]

Progressive Era civic organizations in Boulder—such as the Boulder Improvement Association, which was founded in 1903—were also influenced by the ideas of the City Beautiful movement, whose architects and planners premised their grand regional plans on the belief that cities could be at once profitable, functional, and beautiful.[14] Such groups pressured the city council to limit the size of the town by vigorously acquiring parkland. In 1908 the Boulder Improvement Association also commissioned nationally renowned landscape architect Frederick Law Olmsted Jr. to plan a system of city parks and open spaces for Boulder. Although the city did not follow Olmsted's recommendation to purchase the Boulder Creek floodplain for urban parkland, it continued to add mountain land to the holdings of the city's Parks and Recreation Department.[15]

From the town's founding through the Progressive Era, a conservationist ethic had developed in Boulder. Still, town leaders, familiar with the cyclical nature of the West's agricultural and extractive economy, also adhered to a primary belief of frontier boosters: Communities must either grow or die. Most Progressive Era conservationists were not interested in limiting growth; rather, they hoped to increase their town's stability, attractiveness, and marketability to middle-class migrants. The activism of conservationists shaped boosters' promotional materials on Boulder as well as the types of businesses the Chamber of Commerce courted. During Boulder's early history, it was possible to be both a conservationist and a booster, working to protect nearby forests from industrial uses by setting aside mountain parks while simultaneously luring seemingly benign economic activities, such as higher education and tourism. In the Progressive Era, tensions between growth and environmental preservation were manageable. The astounding growth of Denver and its suburbs after World War II, however, ended Boulder's isolation from the capital city and provided a tipping point at which growth and environmental preservation became mutually exclusive in the minds of many Boulder residents.

Front Range Metropolis Rising

In many ways the history of the modern American West is defined by westerners' response to massive urban migration and the reorganization of metropolitan areas during World War II.[16] After 1941 federal defense spending transformed the economic, physical, and human landscapes of the West and "shifted the American center of gravity westward." Eight million Americans migrated to the West during the war, and twenty-two million arrived over the next twenty-five years. More than 90 percent of these migrants chose to live in towns, cities, and suburbs.[17] While drawing people to Colorado, wartime mobilization also integrated local economies along the Front Range of the Rocky Mountains from Colorado Springs to Boulder into a 160-mile linear regional economy centered on the rapidly growing metropolis of Denver. Within this emerging spatial and economic structure, Denver became Colorado's model city for economic expansion and diversification, postwar population growth, and suburban development.

In addition to its role as the capital city of Colorado, Denver was an important regional distribution center and headquarters for Rocky Mountain mining companies. After World War II, city leaders hatched a plan to modernize the city's economy and remake downtown by securing military installations, technology-based jobs, and educated workers. During the cold war Denver mayors secured millions of federal dollars, constructing a regional scientific-research-military network of military installations, businesses, and research centers that stretched from Colorado Springs to Fort Collins. Federal defense contracts were lucrative economic gems for Colorado cities. From 1952 to 1962, 20 percent of Coloradans' income could be traced to the Department of Defense.[18]

Most newcomers to Colorado moved to the suburbs. Postwar suburbanization in metropolitan Denver was part of a national trend. As Liz Cohen writes, "Between 1947 and 1952 the suburban population increased by 43 percent, in contrast to the general population increase of only 11 percent; over the course of the 1950s, in the twenty largest metropolitan areas, cities would grow by only .1 percent, their suburbs by an explosive 45 percent."[19] Housing construction expenditures rose commensurately, and with increasing frequency, the bulldozer entered the countryside to make way for suburbia. "Every year," writes historian Adam Rome, "a territory roughly the size of Rhode Island was bulldozed for metropolitan development."[20]

The rate at which people moved into newly constructed Front Range suburbs was astounding. During the 1940s Colorado's population increased by 200,000, with 78 percent of newcomers settling in Denver and its suburban counties of Adams, Arapahoe, and Jefferson. By 1950 these four counties held 42.5 percent of the state's population. Between 1950 and 1970 Colorado's population nearly doubled from 1,325,089 to 2,207,000.[21] The city of Denver grew by nearly 100,000, while the population of the Denver Metropolitan Statistical Area exploded from 563,832 to 1,227,529.[22] Suburbanization altered the physical landscape and transformed Denver's social demographic. Denver, writes historian Carl Abbott, "became an island of old, poor, minority peoples surrounded by middle-class affluence."[23] In Denver's growing suburbs and surrounding cities, people began to fear the loss of open spaces, ranches, and farmland.

Postwar Planning in Boulder

Looking to Denver's burgeoning cold war economy as an example of peacetime prosperity, Boulder's post–World War II leaders schemed to extract their next mother lode not from the gold mines and glacial waters of the Rockies but from Uncle Sam. Businessmen, government leaders, and University of Colorado administrators believed that Boulder could prosper by attracting federal government research laboratories and private defense contractors who would collaborate on high-tech projects with research scientists at the university. In 1950 town lobbyists convinced the state legislature to build a turnpike—Highway 36—between Denver and Boulder, which made commuting possible.[24] The construction of Highway 36 provided a greater incentive for the development of rural land between Denver and Boulder. Tract housing, strip malls, and business parks soon replaced ranches and farms. Additionally, the federal government located several high-tech research agencies and strategic military operations in or near Boulder, such as the Rocky Flats nuclear facility and the National Center for Atmospheric Research. Companies engaged in high-technology research and production, such as Ball Brothers Research, Beech Aircraft, and IBM, selected Boulder for branch plants and regional offices. To most Boulder residents, economic growth was necessary and beneficial. New industry provided high-income jobs, the city's tax base was expanding, and middle-class migrants were creating more cosmopolitan spaces in Boulder.

To manage its postwar building boom, Boulder hired Trafton Bean as the city's first planning director in 1951. Pragmatic conservatism, articulated in the *Guide for Growth* planning document, characterized Bean's approach. The planning director believed that low-density suburban development was Boulder's future; he also thought that the city had the right to profit from the construction of suburbs. Bean oversaw the revision of the city's subdivision laws, establishing a "pay as you go" system in which the city awarded building permits to developers who agreed to fund infrastructural improvements. Additionally, the revised regulations required developers to set aside land for public schools and parks. Not surprisingly, developers opposed tougher regulations on suburban development. Developer Allen Lefferdink asked, "What if a merchant was told to give the city 4 per cent of his merchandise when he went into business?"[25]

While the planning director was merely anticipating suburban growth in the Boulder Valley, by 1958 landowners began to bulldoze and subdivide mountain properties. Boulder's business-friendly, politically moderate city council encouraged such construction, expecting an economic infusion from the well-off residents who would occupy new mountain homes. The city council extended utility services to housing sites in the foothills. Providing water to mountain homes at higher elevations was a more difficult challenge. As part of a larger plan to improve Boulder's waterworks, the city council proposed the construction of a water-treatment plant, pumping station, and pipeline on Boulder Creek, three miles west of the city in scenic Boulder Canyon. Developer contributions and the city's capital improvement budget did not cover the cost of these major structural improvements. Consequently, the city council called a July 1958 bond issue election. In part the provision asked Boulder voters to fund a water system for mountain developments.[26]

The Blue Line Campaign

In the 1950s the University of Colorado, competing with other institutions for federal research dollars, had assembled a brain trust of research scientists and intellectuals. Academicians like Albert Bartlett and Robert McKelvey moved to Boulder, in part, for its college-town atmosphere and mountain scenery, and they appreciated the legacy—thousands of acres of mountain parklands—left by nineteenth-century preservationists. When Boulder's population doubled between 1950 and 1958, many residents, particularly recently arrived University of Colorado professors, complained that Denver's expanding residential developments threatened to trap their community within an indistinct suburban web. By 1958 citizen concerns about mass suburbanization and diminishing open-space land on the urban fringe were garnering national attention. William Whyte popularized the term *sprawl* in a 1958 *Fortune* magazine article about suburban development between Los Angeles and San Bernardino. Describing his view from an airplane as "an unnerving lesson in man's infinite capacity to mess up his environment," Whyte wrote, "The traveler can see a legion of bulldozers zoning in on the last remaining tract of green."[27] Similar perceived threats to Boulder's livability—low-density suburbs and highways supplanting agricultural lands between Boulder and Denver, loss of wilderness and mountain views, a decline in community identity and autonomy—sparked a grassroots environmental movement. At first environmentalists were small in number, and most were affiliated with the University of Colorado or the Colorado Mountain Club, an organization dedicated to the preservation of wilderness areas for individual recreation and Boulder's oldest environmental organization. In the hallways of classroom buildings at the University of Colorado and at Colorado Mountain Club meetings, people began to talk about countering regional growth. They discussed the consequences of suburban development in the foothills and began to question the city's responsibilities to developers.

At stake for Bartlett, McKelvey, and an emerging cohort of environmental activists were intact ecosystems and beautiful views of the foothills that bordered Roosevelt National Forest and what is now the Indian Peaks Wilderness. They believed that the loss of forestland and the transformation of the landscape far outweighed any economic benefits of development. With a topographical map, the mathematicians hiked the area where the city was considering an extension of utilities and calculated the cost and logistics of a public commitment to foothills development. Given the location of Boulder's existing water facilities, they estimated that the city would have to pump water uphill to supply houses at elevations higher than 5,750 feet. To the two professors, such an expenditure of public funds seemed like an unfair subsidy to developers whose projects would wreck the view for those who lived in the valley. Drilling private water wells and installing septic tanks at this altitude would be expensive, impractical, and unreliable. They reasoned that if the city refused to provide utilities above this elevation, marked on their map with a bold "blue line," developers could not build in the foothills. They took the issue to the city council, demanding a revision to the city charter that prevented development above 5,750 feet.

The citizen proposal for a Blue Line Charter Amendment received a cool reception. Comments by Councilman James Hickman recalled the traditional balancing act between boosters and conservationists that had tempered development in Boulder from the 1890s through World War II. "I do not want to see the beauty of the mountains marred," said Hickman, "but this resolution would eliminate one of Boulder's advantages—choice home sites." To the majority of the council, who voted against amending the city charter, drawing a line on a map and declaring an area off-limits to development was an academic exercise that did not reflect economic realities. "A blue line based on elevation," claimed Councilman Abram McCoy, "is a poor substitute for good planning. There is room for some acceptable development to the west." Additionally, in the cold war climate of the late 1950s, the city council probably agreed with leading economists that "the suburbanite is tomorrow's best customer and a firm foundation for future national prosperity."[28] Not only were Blue Line advocates criticizing suburban development, but they were also advocating government controls on the uses of private property.

Bartlett, McKelvey, and a growing number of supporters no longer trusted Boulder's planning experts or city council to protect community interests. They believed that planning regulations were imperative to maintain quality of life in Boulder and wanted a guarantee against foothills development written into the city charter. In 1958 Bartlett and McKelvey formed "Citizens for the Blue Line." Working with a local attorney, the professors drafted a "Blue Line Amendment" to the city charter. To publicize the charter amendment, they recruited quality-of-life foot soldiers from the Colorado Mountain Club. CMC members, some of whom were University of Colorado professors, knocked on doors and passed out fliers on street corners. Those who were avid hikers led organized hikes into the foothills. Sometimes adopting a populist strategy, they situated themselves as the people's spokesmen and targeted real and imagined developers. Despite the populist language of Blue Line campaigners, many potential developers, in fact, were individual home owners who wanted to secure their economic future by selling their mountain properties in a hot real estate market.[29]

To sway Boulder residents, Blue Line supporters wrote editorials that offered an alternative understanding of the relationship among private landownership, property values, and community responsibility:

> We recognize that the owners of high land have certain property rights. But these rights do not include charging the taxpayers as a whole to enhance private profit. They do not include charging the taxpayers to create blight, and we think the great majority of local citizens consider developments scarring the mountain backdrop as blight.... In Boulder, there is a sort of "unwritten right" of the public to enjoy the mountain beauty that has created a large measure of the real and esthetic value of local property. There is an unmistakable degree of community responsibility resting in ownership of this land. After all, it would have scant value if the community had not first built up below it and

created the municipal services that theoretically might make high-land development feasible.³⁰

They also argued that community needs took precedence over the property rights of individuals who had bet on the rising value of mountain land. "Often a man cannot use his land the way he would like," wrote Wheeler, "if such use is not in the best interests of the community."³¹

By July 1958 Citizens for the Blue Line had gathered enough signatures to force a citywide vote. In the November 1958 election, 76 percent of the voters approved the Blue Line Charter Amendment, prohibiting city officials from granting water service to mountain properties above 5,750 feet and preventing suburban development in the foothills.³² The Blue Line campaign created a community of urban environmentalists who demanded that the city adopt planning practices that privileged environmental protection over economic growth.

The urban environmentalism of the Boulder coalition was inspired by immediate community concerns, but it was connected to a broad critique of how liberals' policy ideas for national economic growth were affecting local communities and environments. Some of the leaders of Boulder's environmental movement were already active in national social movements, and they had criticized federal inaction on African American civil rights and global peace initiatives. To them, the "grow or die" paradigm, which had long sustained local boosters' vision of urban development, was magnified in national policies that privileged economic growth and cold war militarism over human rights, the health of American citizens, and the beauty of American landscapes. As they developed a politics based on protecting quality of life, Boulder environmentalists turned away from a national political model whose leaders, they believed, had failed to reconcile the economic imperatives of growth liberalism with residents' desire for environmental protection of natural resources and human health. At both the local and the national levels, governments' position on the relationship among growth, the economy, and the environment provided a target for collective political action by environmentalists who insisted on policies that protected quality of life. To Boulder environmentalists, the question was no longer whether government should stimulate the economy or protect the natural environment. Rather, Blue Line activists argued, the environment and the economy were intimately connected, and it was imperative to do both.

The position of Boulder environmentalists—which raised questions about the difficulty of balancing economic growth with environmental preservation—foreshadowed the programmatic contradictions that confronted liberal technocrats during the 1960s: Could government address simultaneously Americans' desire for economic abundance and lives of individual meaning and qualitative value? Liberal policy makers tried to capture middle-class discontent about environmental change by layering government programs that promoted economic prosperity through state-managed growth with "qualitative liberalism." Consequently, liberals experimented with federal programs and policies aimed at improving Americans' quality of life. Stalwarts of the Democratic Party, such as historian Arthur Schlesinger Jr. and economist John Kenneth Galbraith, pondered how to implement liberal programs for aggregate growth and national prosperity while ameliorating the environmental consequences of that growth. During the 1960s Presidents John F. Kennedy and Lyndon B. Johnson institutionalized these debates by putting environmental preservation at the center of their legislative programs.[33]

PLAN-Boulder and the Language of Landscape

The veterans of the Blue Line campaign established a permanent environmental organization called PLAN-Boulder: The People's League for Action Now.[34] The main goals of the organization were to prevent sprawl and foothills development. To achieve these goals, the organization needed to persuade residents that their vision of a new land-use ethic based on environmental preservation was economically viable. McKelvey wrote, "To resist urban sprawl, a community must first develop the will to resist unrestrained development. It must become conscious of the seriousness of its plight. And it must disabuse itself of the notion that unrestrained development is synonymous with progress and prosperity."[35] Appealing to a traditional booster strategy—capitalization and commoditization of the western landscape as an amenity and selling point—local environmentalists argued that wilderness access determined residents' quality of life and, therefore, Boulder's economic future.[36] Yet, flipping the script on this traditional free-market strategy, urban environmentalists argued that livability, and, therefore, economic success, depended on the local government's ability to safeguard Boulder's most important commodity: a view of the mountains and access to forests unmolested by suburbia. This could be achieved, activists argued, by limiting the physical size of the city and confining growth to developed areas. As activists were trying to develop the tools and language of a new ecological planning tradition, they discovered that the community-wide recognition of environmental limits actually resulted in different and more rewarding kinds of economic opportunities.

During the Blue Line campaign, environmentalists had begun to develop a scenic aesthetic and cultural landscape language in which access to unspoiled western lands, particularly mountain wilderness, was central to "the good life." PLAN-Boulder became a vehicle for environmentalists to promote and institutionalize this new way of thinking about their urban lives in relation to the landscape. PLAN-Boulder's first newsletter explained the group's *aesthetically based* environmentalism, or the basic desire of urban residents to preserve the region's distinguishing landmarks and scenic beauty: "We are for green belts, floodplain zoning, natural and developed parklands, underground utilities—in essence, a beautiful, well-planned community with special emphasis on retaining those characteristics which make Boulder unique. We are against haphazard growth, unsightliness, and ugliness in any form."[37]

Consequently, PLAN-Boulder worked to convince residents that the geographical features of the surrounding forests and countryside constituted the natural infrastructure of the city. This green infrastructure made their mountain enclave uniquely attractive, and it was the primary ingredient of quality of life in Boulder. The "mountain backdrop" was the central element of PLAN-Boulder's aesthetically based environmentalism.[38] This phrase, frequently used to describe western foothills visible from most of Boulder, portrayed the mountains as the backdrop for an urban stage that created a unique living experience. Echoing the language of 1950s urban renewal policies, which had allocated federal dollars to urban slum clearance, environmentalists described foothills development as "blight" that ruined the view for everyone who lived in the valley. PLAN-Boulder also argued that the preservation of the Boulder Creek floodplain and the prairie, rural, and agricultural land surrounding the city contributed to the natural infrastructure as well. In the group's new landscape language, the geography of the Boulder Valley was transformed into "gateways," "buffers," "visual corridors," and "viewsheds" that insulated the city from suburban growth. As early as 1959 PLAN-Boulder members were imagining a comprehensive open-space policy that would eventually envelop Boulder within a landscape of interconnected ecosystems.

After 1960 PLAN-Boulder members looked vigilantly over the shoulder of the city council, making it clear that city bureaucrats had to listen to PLAN-Boulder, lest the organization press their agenda with petitions and referendums. In a letter to Bartlett, city manager E. Robert Turner observed that PLAN-Boulder liked "keeping things hot for the group at City Hall."[39] Members attended every meeting of city council, the planning board, and the Boulder County commissioners. PLAN-Boulder members proposed environmentally focused planning programs and lobbied the city council with letters and speeches. Before every election the organization hosted debates and endorsed a slate of candidates. By 1968 candidates for the city council coveted PLAN-Boulder's endorsement.

PLAN-Boulder's first chance to mobilize citizen support for a permanent open-space policy came in 1963. A few years earlier Kenneth Mirise, a Colorado Springs businessman, announced a plan to develop a 155-acre tract of land known by locals as the Enchanted Mesa. Mirise planned to construct a hotel and tourist shops and divide the remaining property into residential lots for mountain homes.

According to PLAN-Boulder's vision, the Enchanted Mesa was a valuable element of Boulder's environmental infrastructure. Along with Chautauqua Park, Flagstaff Mountain, and the Dakota Ridge, the mesa was a part of Boulder's mountain backdrop. PLAN-Boulder members organized a campaign to oppose Mirise's proposed development. Dr. Herbert Mason of the Nature Conservancy in Berkeley, California, joined the campaign, explaining to the city council that the Enchanted Mesa's significance to the community rested in its "complete naturalness." Mason wrote, "Buildings and even roads would nullify the complete naturalness in depth that meets the beholder from the point where he stands all the way to the craggy skyline. This is the quality that even bits of man-made rubbish in immediate view will vitiate."[40] Echoing PLAN-Boulder's claims that individual property owners must be held accountable to community needs, Mason asserted that development decreased the value of mountain property in the long term because it decreased the attractiveness of the community. Influenced by Boulder's environmental movement, the city council proposed a $105,000 bond issue to buy 155 acres on the Enchanted Mesa. Boulder residents passed the bond issue, and the city condemned the land for purchase, abruptly halting Mirise's development plans.[41]

Protecting the Boulder Valley:
Satellite Communities or a Greenbelt Plan for Boulder?

By the midsixties environmentalists had slowed development in the foothills. Preventing suburban development in the Boulder Valley was another matter. Acquiring open space and protecting rural areas of Boulder County promised to be controversial since they would place the city in direct competition with private investors and developers who intended to purchase land for suburban and commercial development. Although most Boulderites favored protecting their mountain views, not nearly so many supported government restrictions on productive agricultural land and rural land.

By 1965 the city could not build streets and extend services fast enough to accommodate development in the valley. Observing the accelerating pace of suburban construction along the Front Range, newly elected city manager E. Robert Turner had concluded that suburbanization on the city's edge was inevitable. If the city refused to pay for water lines, sewer lines, and streets, as growth-control advocates insisted, developers would install septic tanks and water wells on county properties outside of Boulder's jurisdiction. To prevent such independent developments, Turner decided to use traditional land-use planning and selective placement of capital improvements to direct growth on the urban fringe. By providing city services and annexing developments, however, the Boulder Planning Department could enforce density and design standards while adding productive properties to the city's tax rolls.[42] Studying Boulder's neighbor to the south, Turner learned that the powerful Denver Water Board had tried to control the cost of suburbanization by forcing suburban developers and home owners to pay extra for water and sewer services before allowing them to apply for annexation. Turner liked the economics of this approach, and he worked it into a program for planned development.[43]

Turner's Planning Department worried about more than the financial cost of suburban infrastructure. Influenced by two successful preservation campaigns, Boulder's professional planners wanted to avoid sprawl and maintain Boulder's identity. Planning Department officials wrote, "If growth takes place in a manner which results in a direct expansion of the city to a size in excess of 50,000 in population, personal values may very easily be lost. But if it takes place in a manner which results in the development of identifiable subcommunities around the central city, then the human scale will be retained."[44] Accordingly, in the *Spokes of the Wheel Plan,* Boulder tried to maintain the city's human scale by defining an urban boundary beyond which the city would not provide utilities. To satisfy developers the city would extend utilities, radiating outward, like the "spokes of a wheel," to separate satellite communities. At the end of each extension, the city also zoned land for industrial parks, employment centers, and residential neighborhoods. Turner and the city council did not intend to restrict growth. Rather, government leaders hoped to eliminate sprawling developments on rural and agricultural land. Mindful of the city budget, they intended to control public expenditures by requiring suburban developers to pay a percentage of the cost of building roads and installing utilities on undeveloped land. According to Turner's vision, land between the satellite developments and Boulder city limits would eventually be developed and annexed, creating continuity and infill. Boulder's officials employed the rhetoric of preservation, but growth was still desirable to them as long as developers and future suburban home owners footed the bill instead of Boulder taxpayers.[45]

The first extension under the Spokes of the Wheel plan stretched northeast of Boulder toward a site that IBM was considering for a new plant and the nearby subdivision of Gunbarrel. The city extended a second line east along Arapahoe Avenue toward the Ball Brothers industrial site. The first two extensions benefited high-technology firms that locals considered "clean industries," and there was measured response from PLAN-Boulder. When developer Sam Rudd proposed a third extension of utilities to the south—over Davidson Mesa toward Denver—a murmur of discontent turned into outright revolt against the city's development policies. For environmentalists who had been working on an antidote to suburbanization, a plan that encouraged suburbanization in the direction of Denver was unacceptable. In 1965 PLAN-Boulder organized yet another referendum, and voters rejected overwhelmingly the city manager's plan to accommodate suburbanization through satellite developments and eventual annexation.[46]

After voters rejected the Spokes of the Wheel plan, PLAN-Boulder worked to popularize its vision for a city surrounded by open space. In 1967 PLAN-Boulder hosted a conference called "Greenbelts: Why and How?" For the first time the conference gathered scholars, activists, Boulder planning officials, city council members, and Boulder County commissioners for a public discussion on land-use planning, greenbelts, and open space. PLAN-Boulder made it clear that saving the mountain backdrop remained priority number one, but also argued that wilderness preservation did not constitute a comprehensive plan for urban shaping and growth management. One had only to look at the growing footprint of Denver's suburbs to recognize that the ranches, farms, and open spaces of Boulder County represented the largest potential for suburbanization in the Boulder Valley. PLAN-Boulder activists suggested that the only way to prevent sprawl on rural land in the Boulder Valley was to purchase it with public funds and permanently zone it as open space.[47]

What emerged from the conference was yet another ballot measure—"Greenbelts and Major Thoroughfares"—sponsored by founding PLAN-Boulder member and city councilwoman Ruth Wright. City manager Ted Tedesco had suggested the city fund its greenbelt program with a 1 percent sales tax: The city would use 40 percent of the revenues from the sales tax to purchase open space and 60 percent for street construction. As Al Bartlett recalls, "This was a marriage of convenience."[48] Including thoroughfares in the provision gave it broad appeal because most Boulder residents relied on cars for transportation and were willing to pay for well-maintained streets. At the time, few people saw a contradiction in a sales tax that paid for pavement and purchased open space at the same time.

In November 1967 some 61 percent of Boulder citizens voted to adopt the Open Space Sales Tax Amendment.[49] Residents gave institutional power to PLAN-Boulder's plan for compact development, levying a tax for the purchase of rural and agricultural land in Boulder County and its designation as permanently protected open space. By creating a plan for a contiguous greenbelt of land around the city, voters rejected growth advocates' master plan for a decentralized city based on "scatteration development" of satellite suburbs.[50] Instead, voters agreed to limit Boulder's physical size by restricting suburban development sites on the city's fringe. Contained development, urban infill, and greater density had become the operative planning principles of Boulder's human-scale model of urban development.

Institutionalizing Open Space: The Boulder Valley Comprehensive Plan

Voters had funded a basic program to shape the city through open-space acquisitions. Planners still needed to complete the details of open-space policy, and a number of questions remained unanswered: How much land was necessary to insulate Boulder from Front Range sprawl? Which parcels of land belonged in the greenbelt? What kinds of procedures were necessary for purchasing land outside city limits? The City of Boulder had officially entered the real estate business, but with inverse intentions from private players who wanted to develop real property and from neighboring cities that wanted to grow. Without jurisdiction and the powers of eminent domain and condemnation, the city could be forced into a bidding war over desirable pieces of property with private developers. Annexation was a possible but problematic solution. Boulder risked starting annexation wars with surrounding communities. Some of Boulder's neighboring communities already resented the city's growth-management policies and frowned on efforts to designate the county's rural areas as open space. Towns such as Longmont, Louisville, Broomfield, and Superior wanted to grow, and their leaders looked skeptically on Boulder's plans to acquire open space in Boulder County. By early 1968, less than a year after the creation of the greenbelt program, Boulder officials concluded that their greenbelt plan for urban shaping would fail without the cooperation of the Boulder County commissioners, who oversaw development requests in rural areas of Boulder County. Growth-management advocates from the city would have to either get elected to the county commission or convince county officials to adopt the city's philosophy.

In 1968 city and county planners drafted the Boulder Valley Comprehensive Plan (BVCP), an enforceable land-management agreement between the two governments. After two years of public input and planning, both governments adopted the plan. The plan seemed simple and straightforward. It was one page in length, accompanied by a map of designated land uses on one side and explanatory text on the other.[51] Most important, the 1970 BVCP defined an urban service-area boundary that governed development in Boulder County. Lands beyond the urban service-area boundary were to remain rural until Boulder City and Boulder County jointly agreed to extend urban services. The BVCP gave the city more power to review development plans and start condemnation proceedings.[52]

By the late 1970s the city had established two primary methods for preserving Boulder's green infrastructure: policing fringe development in Boulder County with open-space purchases and setting up a system for core development and sustainable design. Meanwhile, a third component of the infrastructure, a management system that balanced growth and sustainability, had also been nurtured. City planners and advocates of growth control understood the three parts of the system to be self-reinforcing, but a board entrusted with the responsibility for enforcing the first two tenets would be key to sustainability in Boulder's vision for a green infrastructure. The task of protecting the open spaces on the city's fringe while planners crafted policies that promoted infill development in the core area of the city fell to the Open Space Board of Trustees (OSBT). This committee of five Boulder residents appointed by the city manager developed philosophies and rules that governed the acquisition, management, and use of open space. The committee's makeup and its duties reflected the political power that environmental activists had gained in Boulder since 1958. The director of Open Space and Real Estate, the Department of Planning, and the city's legal department provided support and expertise and advised the Open Space Board on which pieces of property contributed to Boulder's urban-shaping goals.

As implied by its name, the Open Space Board of Trustees played the role of protector. The OSBT's rationale for acquiring certain properties indicated a defensive posture against other communities and developers, and the trustees approved purchases in order to "protect Boulder's flanks."[53] Until the passage of the Danish Plan in 1976, which limited growth in Boulder to 2 percent each year by controlling the number of building permits that developers received, the OSBT viewed itself as the first and last line of defense against developers. To achieve the landscape aesthetic that environmentalists had been promoting in Boulder since 1958, the OSBT prioritized open-space purchases based on topographical features, eventually creating a series of open-space zones tied to the distinct landscapes of the Boulder Valley. The mountains formed a "backdrop" to the west. Prairie lands, farms, and ranches were envisioned as "gateways" along the highways that entered Boulder from the north, south, and east. Undeveloped parcels of land in the valley were also labeled as "visual corridors" and "viewsheds" that buffered Boulder from suburban sprawl on the southeastern and southern boundaries of the city where development pressures were the strongest. The OSBT did not prioritize the acquisition of open space on the northern edge of the city where development pressures were less intense. Since some development already existed along Boulder's northern border—a trailer park, the Elks Club, a few warehouses—the city treated North Boulder as a zone of sacrifice in comparison to the city's other boundaries.[54]

By 1978 a clear shift had occurred in the way that the OSBT described open space in the Boulder Valley. With views and lands to the west legislatively safeguarded from development, planners and residents began to argue that protecting the natural ecosystems of the Boulder Valley was central to greening Boulder's urban infrastructure and economy. As it intervened in the development of rural land, the OSBT still talked about protecting Boulder's viewsheds, corridors, and gateways, but it also increasingly spoke of protecting environmental preservation areas that consisted of threatened wetland, prairie, and forest ecosystems. As ecosystems management became the primary justification for purchasing land in the Boulder Valley, the OSBT shifted its strategy to the acquisition of contiguous lands that could support a viable native-grassland ecosystem—*native* being generally defined as the state of the prairie prior to the arrival of white settlers in Boulder. Rather than referring to desirable properties as farms, ranches, or agricultural land, the OSBT was more likely to call these agriculturally productive parcels "prairie" land.

The trustees also experimented with new management techniques. They studied the Nature Conservancy's efforts to preserve prairie ecosystems in the western United States and worked with local scientists to monitor human use on open space. They also wanted to encourage an appropriate balance of plant and animal life on open space. For instance, they studied prairie-dog populations, eventually setting aside preserves for the prairie dogs and controlling their numbers through environmentally safe extermination practices. Ecosystem-management principles required that the human footprint be reasonably eliminated in certain areas. Consequently, the city banned motorized vehicles, bicycles, and dogs on large sections of open space.

Open-space advocates had to come to terms with a central question: If ecosystem management requires maintaining open space in a natural state, how should humans act on open space, in what ways should they influence open space, and how should people manage open space? In *The Organic Machine*, environmental historian Richard White explains how people with different social, cultural, and political interests "literally and conceptually disassembled" the Columbia River: "People with quite specific social and economic interests are not just fighting over ownership of a piece of nature. They are fighting over something they in part create but which contains within it, at its heart, something they have not made. This unmade world is what we call nature. . . . There is no easy way to disentangle the natural and cultural here. What is real is the mixture, and we seem unable to come to terms with this even though we have created it."[55] Boulder environmentalists achieved a similar reconstruction of geographical space, reassembling an imagined natural historic landscape through open-space acquisition and ecosystem management. Similar to the physical rearrangements of the Columbia River, open space in Boulder County became a puzzle of sorts: The Open Space Department pieced together parcels of land and managed its return to a "natural" state. In the ecosystem approach, people acted on and managed nature, but natural ecosystems maintained their integrity, uninterrupted by productive uses or the built landscape. After the 1970s philosophical disagreements about how to construct and manage the city's open-space lands played out in policy debates over who had the right to access open space and determine how the land would be used by both people and animals. By the 1990s both prairie dogs (native species) and dogs (nonnative species) became iconic symbols in Boulder residents' efforts to define their relationship to open-space land and nature.[56]

The Open Space Board of Trustees and the director of Open Space and Real Estate enforced the city's urban infill–greenbelt strategy for population control and environmental sustainability. The OSBT acquired open space to influence land use and promote a dense, human-scale city. This new goal of balancing the relationship among city, suburb, and countryside meant acquiring an enormous amount of connected open-space land in the Boulder Valley. In the process the city of Boulder became one ecosystem among the others.

With a planning vision for a centralized city surrounded by public open space and a funding mechanism in place, Boulder's newest bureaucracy, the Open Space Department, shaped the city with elements of three iconic American landscapes: the wilderness (mountain parklands), the pastoral "middle landscape" of small farms and ranches (prairie open space), and the pedestrian village (growth focused around the city center).[57] Moving beyond the language of planning—visual corridors, viewsheds, and gateways—people in Boulder began to develop a cultural landscape language to justify open-space purchases and create a new urban aesthetic and culture. Since 1967 residents of Boulder have spent $180 million to purchase thirty-nine thousand acres of open space and seven thousand acres of mountain parkland. By 2000 Boulder's environmental coalition included aesthetic preservationists, nuclear freeze activists, dog owners and "guardians," endurance athletes, animal rights activists, and deep ecologists. All claimed an interest in determining human use and access to Boulder's public lands.

Conclusion

Boulder's environmental activists had discovered the powerful possibilities of drawing lines on a map, and they had created a model of urbanism in which public ownership of open space was central to the physical design of the city and the culture developing within its borders. Environmentalists and planners influenced by the postwar environmental movement were reacting to the growth of standardized, decentralized suburban communities and to a new system of regional-metropolitan politics in which central cities and suburbs competed for resources and power. Urban planners and environmentalists who took the ecological turn began to view decisions about land use, density, and urban design through the framework of community sustainability. Under a postsixties model for community planning, the public, as well as property owners and developers, would have a say in determining the built environment and the social organization of their city.

Boulder had arrived at a spatial fix within which activists could work out a social agenda for a new kind of city. By limiting suburban development, urban environmentalists in Boulder offered an alternative path to city building, rethinking the relationship among density, social organization, and community definition. Arguments in Boulder over population control, city oversight of urban design, and the proper management of public open space symbolized larger questions on the minds of Americans in the postwar years: Was it possible to build an economically viable and environmentally sustainable city? If so, what role should government and activists play in building such a city? By the late 1960s plenty of Americans agreed that development patterns determined quality of life, but a state of confusion existed about the proper relationship among city, suburb, and environment. After 1968 Boulder environmentalists tried to solve that problem by setting up a system for core development and sustainable design, policing fringe development in Boulder County with open-space purchases, and developing an ecosystem approach to the management of open space.

Eventually, Boulder's commitment to open-space preservation, central-city development, human-powered and public transportation, and sustainability formed the core of Boulder's political identity. In the postwar years Boulder's environmentally focused planning tradition contributed to the city's reputation as a liberal enclave in a region dominated by conservative politics. Positioning their city as a laboratory for sustainable urban living, Boulder environmentalists tried to create a system that might be exported to "Boulder and beyond."

Notes

Many thanks to David Hays at the University of Colorado Archives and Wendy Hall at the Carnegie Branch Library for Local History in Boulder, Colorado, for their expert assistance with historical sources.

1. Mark Hamilton Lytle, *The Gentle Subversive: Rachel Carson, Silent Spring, and the Rise of the Environmental Movement* (New York: Oxford University Press, 2007), 200.

2. Frederick Law Olmsted, "Public Parks in the Enlargement of Towns," in *The City Reader*, edited by Richard T. LeGates and Frederic Stout, 3rd ed. (New York: Routledge, 2003), 307; Ebenezer Howard, "'The Town-Country Magnet' from *Garden Cities of To-Morrow* [1902]," in *The City Reader*, edited by LeGates and Stout, 312; Dolores Hayden, *Building Suburbia: Green Fields and Urban Growth, 1890–2000* (New York: Vintage, 2004), 45.

3. Adam Rome, "'Give Earth a Chance': The Environmental Movement and the Sixties," *Journal of American History* 90, no. 2 (2003): 525–54; Adam Rome, *Bulldozer in the Countryside: Suburban Sprawl and the Rise of American Environmentalism* (New York: Cambridge University Press, 2001); Samuel P. Hays, *Beauty, Health, and Permanence: Environmental Politics in the United States, 1955–1985* (New York: Cambridge University Press, 1987).

4. Carl Abbott, *The New Urban America: Growth and Politics in Sunbelt Cities* (Chapel Hill: University of North Carolina Press, 1981), 14; Robert O. Self, *American Babylon: Race and the Struggle for Postwar Oakland* (Princeton: Princeton University Press), 27, 33.

5. Greg Hise and William Deverell Hise, *Eden by Design: The 1930 Olmsted-Bartholomew Plan for the Los Angeles Region* (Berkeley and Los Angeles: University of California Press, 2000), 11.

6. Timothy Beatley, "Green Urbanism in the Lessons of European Cities," in *The City Reader*, edited by LeGates and Stout, 399–408; Stephen Wheeler, "Planning Sustainable and Livable Cities," in *The City Reader*, edited by LeGates and Stout, 486–96.

7. Peter Hall, *Cities of Tomorrow: An Intellectual History of Urban Planning and Design in the 20th Century*, 3rd ed. (New York: Blackwell, 2001).

8. Peter Calthorpe writes, "Against this modern alliance of specialization, standardization, and mass production stands a set of principles rooted more in ecology than in mechanics. They are the principles of diversity, conservation, and human scale" ("Designing the Region Is Designing the Neighborhood," from *The Regional City: Planning for the End of Sprawl*, by Peter Calthorpe and William Fulton [Washington, D.C.: Island Press, 2001], in *The City Reader*, edited by LeGates and Stout, 333).

9. Isabella Bird, *A Lady's Life in the Rocky Mountains*, rev. ed. (Norman: University of Oklahoma Press, 1999), 197.

10. T. V. Wilson, "Real Estate Values," A. A. Paddock Collection, Real Estate Printed Materials, 1909–1955, Carnegie Branch Library for Local History.

11. Glenda Riley, *Women and Nature: Saving the "Wild" West* (Lincoln: University of Nebraska Press, 1999), 123.

12. Chamber of Commerce advertisement, Promotional Materials Collection, Carnegie Branch Library for Local History.

13. *Highlights of PLAN-Boulder County, 1959–1986*, Boulder Public Library, Municipal Government Reference Center, Vertical File: Associations, PLAN-Boulder, 10.

14. Carl Smith, *The Plan of Chicago: Daniel Burnham and the Remaking of the American City* (Chicago: University of Chicago Press, 2007), 19, 31.

15. Stephen J. Leonard and Thomas J. Noel, *Denver: Mining Camp to Metropolis* (Niwot: University Press of Colorado, 1990), 339; *Highlights of PLAN-Boulder County*, 10–11.

16. Self, *American Babylon*, 27, 334.

17. Carl Abbott, *The Metropolitan Frontier: Cities in the Modern American West* (Tucson: University of Arizona Press, 1993), 26; Gerald D. Nash, *The American West in the Twentieth Century: A Short History of an Urban Oasis* (Englewood Cliffs, N.J.: Prentice-Hall, 1973), 198.

18. Abbott, *Metropolitan Frontier*, 45; Carl Abbott, "The Metropolitan Region: Western Cities in the New Urban Era," in *The Twentieth-Century West*, edited by Gerald Nash and Richard Etulain (Albuquerque: University of New Mexico Press, 1989), 82; Abbott, *New Urban America*, 40; Carl Abbott, Stephen J. Leonard, and Thomas Noel, *Colorado: A History of the Centennial State*, 3rd ed. (Boulder: University of Colorado Press, 1994), 312.

19. Lizabeth Cohen, *A Consumers' Republic: The Politics of Mass Consumption in Postwar America* (New York: Alfred A. Knopf, 2003), 195, 122. From 1950 to 1970 central cities grew by 10 million; suburbs grew by 85 million.

20. Rome, *Bulldozer in the Countryside*, 8.

21. Abbott, Leonard, and Noel, *Colorado*, 323, 324, 301. In 1980 Colorado's population was 2,888,834. By 1990 the population of Colorado was 3,294,394 (Carl Ubbelohde, Maxine Benson, and Duane A. Smith, *A Colorado History*, 7th ed. [Boulder: Pruett Publishing, 1995], 346). The population of Colorado in 2000 was 4,301,261; in 2009 Colorado's population was estimated at 5,024,748 (*State and County QuickFacts*, http://quickfacts.census.gov/qfd/states/08000.html).

22. Denver's population increased from 415,786 in 1950 to 514,678 in 1970 (Ubbelohde, Benson, and Smith, *A Colorado History*, 346).

23. Abbott, Leonard, and Noel, *Colorado*, 310.

24. By September 1967 tolls had paid for turnpike construction costs, and the state removed tollbooths ahead of schedule (Leonard and Noel, *Denver*, 272).

25. "Rules Drawn for New Subdivisions in City, County," *Boulder Daily Camera*, April

24, 1951, Trafton H. Bean Printed Material, 1954–1979, Carnegie Branch Library for Local History; Trafton Bean, "How Cooperative Planning Works," *Colorado Municipalities* (March 1953): 44–45; "Subdivision Law Is Debated at Council Hearing," *Boulder Daily Camera*, August 8, 1951, Trafton H. Bean Printed Material, 1954–1979, Carnegie Branch Library for Local History.

26. *Highlights of PLAN-Boulder County*, 3.

27. Whyte quoted in Mike Davis, *New Cities* (New York: New Press, 2002), 92.

28. "City Council Votes to Bar Water Services in Foothills; Misinformation on Plan Charged," *Boulder Daily Camera*, February 18, 1959, Blue Line Papers, Carnegie Branch Library for Local History; "Council Decides Against Election on 'Blue Line,'" *Boulder Daily Camera*, March 11, 1959, Boulder Blue Line, Vertical File, City of Boulder, Central Records, Boulder, Colorado; "Suburban Customers—Sometimes Strange, Indeed . . . but They Promise Prosperity," *Newsweek*, April 1, 1957, quoted in Cohen, *Consumers' Republic*, 195.

29. Albert Bartlett, interview by author, November 10, 2003, Boulder; Caroline Hoyt, interview by author, December 7, 2003, Boulder.

30. James Corriell, "Let's Draw the Line," *Boulder Daily Camera*, February 5, 1959, 4; James D. Corriell, "Waterworks Expansion and Mountainside Blight," *Boulder Daily Camera*, January 17, 1959, 4.

31. H. N. Wheeler, "Open Forum: Blue Line Should Vary in Elevation," *Boulder Daily Camera*, March 21, 1959.

32. Mark Stoddar, "PLAN-Boulder Still Vigilant at 25 Years," *Boulder County Courant*, January 25, 1984, 1.

33. Rome, "Give Earth a Chance." Environmental legislation included the Open Space Land Program (1961), Clean Air Act (1963), Land and Water Conservation Fund Act (1964), Wilderness Act (1964), Water Quality Act (1965), Highway Beautification Act (1965), Fish and Wildlife Conservation Protection Act (1966), Endangered Species Act (1966), National Trails System (1967), and National Wild and Scenic Rivers System (1967).

34. PLAN-Boulder, "Letter of Invitation," September 3, 1959, Associations: PLAN-Boulder, Municipal Government Reference Center, Boulder Public Library.

35. *Highlights of PLAN-Boulder County*, 45.

36. On boosters and capitalization of the western landscape, see Mike Davis, "Sunshine and the Open Shop: Ford and Darwin in 1920s Los Angeles," in *Metropolis in the Making: Los Angeles in the 1920s*, edited by Tom Sitton and William Deverell (Berkeley and Los Angeles: University of California Press, 2001), 115; and Michael Logan, *Resistance to Urban Growth in the Southwest* (Tucson: University of Arizona Press, 1995), 147–48.

37. *Highlights of PLAN-Boulder County*, 45.

38. PLAN-Boulder, *Newsletter*, October 1959, 1, Associations: PLAN-Boulder, Municipal Government Reference Center, Boulder Public Library.

39. E. Robert Turner to Al Bartlett, January 23, March 22, 1961, Albert Bartlett Papers, University of Colorado Archives, Boulder.

40. Herbert L. Mason, "The Enchantment of the Mesa: A Statement of Values in the Flatirons-Mesa Trail, 1963, Boulder, Colorado," Bartlett Papers.

41. Bartlett, interview by author, November 13, 2003, Boulder.

42. As Dolores Hayden explains, once developers closed their books on a suburban development, the investment process was just beginning for the neighboring municipal government. "However badly they were built, however lonely their locations, these new houses and raw neighborhoods could always be upgraded. And this is what the residents did, pouring time and money into creating schools, civic organizations, and town committees to make public improvements and generate a sense of community" (*Building Suburbia*, 152, 153).

43. James Bowers, Tom Pugh, and Trafton Bean, *Boulder's Fringe Area Objectives* (Boulder: Boulder Planning Department, 1964), Trafton H. Bean Printed Material, 1954–1979, Carnegie Branch Library for Local History; City of Boulder Planning Department, *The Service Area Concept: A Program for Boulder's Planned Development*, 2, Bartlett Papers.

44. Bowers, Pugh, and Bean, *Boulder's Fringe Area Objectives*, 1, 2.

45. City of Boulder Planning Department, *Service Area Concept*, 3–4; Bowers, Pugh, and Bean, *Boulder's Fringe Area Objectives*, 6.

46. League of Women Voters, "Growth in Boulder: The Gunbarrel Story," *Boulder Sunday Camera*, September 21, 1997, E4.

47. Daniel McLoughlin, "In Pursuit of the Common Green," *Colorado Daily* (1974), Vertical File: "Blue Line," City of Boulder, Central Records, Boulder, 16.

48. Bartlett interview, November 13, 2003.

49. McLoughlin, "In Pursuit of the Common Green," 17.

50. For a description of "scatteration development," see Bowers, Pugh, and Bean, *Boulder's Fringe Area Objectives*.

51. *Highlights of PLAN-Boulder County*, 25.

52. Peter Pollack, "Controlling Sprawl in Boulder: Benefits and Pitfalls," *Land Lines* 10, no. 1 (1998), http://www.lincolninst.edu/pubs/435_Controlling-Sprawl-in-Boulder---Benefits-and-Pitfalls.

53. Roger Cracraft, Open Space Board of Trustees, Minutes, March 7, 1979, Carnegie Branch Library for Local History.

54. Open Space Board of Trustees, Minutes, June 2, 1976.

55. Richard White, *The Organic Machine: The Remaking of the Columbia River* (New York: Hill and Wang, 1996), 110–11.

56. Richard White has written about how salmon became "repositories of meaning" that "symbolize nature" in the West (ibid., 90–91).

57. Oliver Gillham, *The Limitless City: A Primer on the Urban Sprawl Debate* (Washington, D.C.: Island Press, 2002), 144.

Wilderburbs and Rocky Mountain Development

LINCOLN BRAMWELL

Nestled high in the Rocky Mountains, Park City, Utah's prosperity has always been firmly linked to its rich natural resources. Over the past century, Park City's environment shaped two major transitions in the town's development. The city began as a mining boomtown, creating vast fortunes from its ore-rich mountains. After mining declined and almost disappeared from the city, the last remaining mining company converted the hills that housed its mines into ski slopes. Beginning in the 1960s the town wholeheartedly converted to a western-style ski town with an economy built on the tourism and service industries. In the two decades after its first ski resorts opened, Park City's population exploded, as many people moved into the area on a permanent basis, inaugurating the second transition. The population soared between 1980 and 2000, leaving the small city incapable of meeting newcomers' demands for housing. New subdivisions subsequently flowed into the unincorporated areas of Summit County. This second transition ushered in an era of residential development on the hilltops and ridges in the surrounding rural county. Although the new housing developments were outside of the city, they relied on the amenities and recreation lifestyle that made Park City famous. New arrivals in Summit County came looking for fresh air and beautiful vistas, but often they did not bargain for the environmental realities their choice of home sites entailed. On the surface, the two transitions from failed boomtown to ski town and ski town to bedroom community might seem unrelated. However, they both reflect the town's capitalizing on its environment for its livelihood. Both transformations are shifts in the way the town used its environment. Exploring these two conversions, particularly the recent environmental interactions between new exurban residents and their surroundings, gives historians of the urban West a new model to understand how the environment shaped rural development taking place across the region.

Over the past half century, new trends in home ownership and economic development, as well as an evolution in American attitudes toward the natural world, fueled a demographic shift into previously undeveloped rural areas across the American West. This vignette of Park City's history illustrates how these new rural subdivisions balanced developers' and home owners' ideals of suburban security and form with their natural surroundings. Three types of stakeholders operated within these rural subdivisions: real estate developers seeking profit through home sales, home owners searching for a sylvan retreat from the city, and government officials trying to regulate orderly land use in rural areas. Each group experienced obstacles to achieving its goal. Developers had difficulties bringing suburban services and security to mountain landscapes, while government officials struggled to enforce outmoded land-use statutes and regulations. Home owners ran into unforeseen environmental problems such as unpredictable water supplies, threats from wildfires, and haphazard encounters with wildlife around their homes. It is important to understand rural developments because they are transforming more undeveloped land than any other industry in the Rocky Mountain West. But more important, residential subdivisions reflect the changing demographics and attitudes about consuming nature throughout the West.

Transforming mining and ranching towns into recreational tourist destinations is big business in the Rocky Mountains. Over the past forty years, several towns poor in economic opportunities but rich in scenic beauty capitalized on their environment. Park City, Utah, is one such town. Nestled in a long valley at the base of the Wasatch Mountains, Park City began as a mining boomtown. Although there is no definitive proof as to who first discovered silver in the 1860s in Park City, it is certain that by 1872 a boom was in full swing. That year prospectors discovered a huge silver vein that became the Ontario Mine, one of Park City's longest-operating and most productive mines. Miners poured into the tiny valley, staking claims in the four narrow, steep-sided gulches that cut the gradually descending slope of the ridge overlooking the valley.[1] A typical mining town instantly germinated in the tiny valley, complete with numerous saloons and brothels that the church-run territory tolerated and regulated with a special tax. In nearby Salt Lake City, Brigham Young forbade members of the Church of Jesus Christ of Latter-day Saints from mining. Thereafter, by Utah's standards, Park City developed a unique non-Mormon population.[2]

Eventually, more than one hundred mining operations extracted wealth from Park City's hills. Silver, gold, lead, iron, zinc, antimony, arsenic, bismuth, and manganese were among the metals pulled from the district's mines. By 1960 Park City mines had produced 250 million ounces of silver, 900,000 ounces of gold, 1.3 million tons of lead, and 600,000 tons of zinc with a total value estimated at $500 million. The mining boom, however, did not last.[3]

After declining in the early twentieth century and nearly collapsing during the Great Depression, Park City did not fare well after World War II. Labor disputes and falling lead and zinc prices forced mines to operate well under capacity. The population started to decline as miners lost their jobs and simply moved on. Between 1930 and 1950 the city's population fell from 4,281 to 2,254 residents. School enrollment fell as well, indicating that the exodus involved more than single male miners. In 1941–42, 1,052 children enrolled in Park City schools; by 1953–54, only 449 reported for class. As the number continued to decline, the residents that remained in the city braced for bad times. As one writer explained, "The community was given over to a few stalwart old-timers who neighbored among boarded-up buildings and weed filled lots."[4]

Fearing they had mined all the land's wealth, miners and their families left Park City, leaving the mining companies scrambling to keep their operations afloat. Park City lost half its population during the 1950s, and one Utah guidebook even started listing the city as a ghost town.[5] In order to survive, the two largest mining operations in town, the Park Utah Consolidated Mining Company and the Silver King Coalition, merged, forming the United Park City Mines Company. The UPCMC remained open, but it was certainly not thriving. The company shut down its venerable Silver King mine shaft and cut its workforce to a skeleton crew of 200 men. The UPCMC hunkered down and tried to wait out the economic downturn.[6]

To most mining company executives, miners, and residents, the natural resources that appeared most profitable had run out. The UPCMC's directors knew they had to search for other alternatives. As it turned out, the company sat in the alternative's shadow. The forested hills surrounding Park City offered perfect winter skiing terrain. Park City locals had been taking advantage of the hills for years, holding an annual winter festival that featured skiing.[7] However, hundreds of separate mining claims blanketed the land surrounding Park City, making any large-scale development difficult—that is, until the remaining mining companies consolidated into the United Park City Mine Company. Once again, nature was about to offer Park City new wealth.

With barely any economic activity taking place in Park City, the UPCMC acquired the land at rock-bottom prices: five dollars for hillside lots and sixteen dollars for regular lots. Quietly, the company increased its surface and mineral holdings to ten thousand acres by the late 1950s.[8] The land acquisition drew little attention due to the essentially nonexistent planning oversight in Summit County at the time. Following the UPCMC's leadership, Park City was poised to move into a new relationship with its environment, one that would capitalize on the topographic, climatic, and aesthetic features of the landscape instead of extracting its mineral wealth. From the first discussions about building a ski resort, Park City's mountains, valleys, cirques, and hills impressed the UPCMC's board of directors. The topographic and social similarities between Park City, Sun Valley, Idaho, and Aspen, Colorado were striking. The latter two resorts built their tourist destinations in small, economically depressed Rocky Mountain towns. Because both towns sat right against large mountain ranges, visitors had easy access to the slopes. Both Sun Valley and Aspen also enjoyed the profits associated with the increasingly popular ski industry. The mining company saw silver in the hills once again.[9]

Park City shared key topographic and geographic characteristics with Sun Valley and Aspen. Park City is located at the intersection of the Uinta and Wasatch mountain ranges. As the mountains form a T intersection, Park City sits on the northern slopes of the Uinta Mountains, east of the Wasatch Front. Above the town a ten thousand-foot ridge forms a north-south dividing line between Salt Lake and Summit counties and then gradually descends to the valley floor. The ridge also protects several natural bowls, or cirques, from the high winds associated with the westerly flowing storm systems.

Because it is much higher in elevation than nearby Salt Lake City, Park City enjoys a cooler and wetter climate. Seasonal temperatures average ten to twenty-five degrees cooler. The Sierra Nevada in eastern California cast a rain shadow over Utah and Nevada's Great Basin, but the Wasatch Mountains run perpendicular to the prevailing winds, producing an orographic barrier that induces precipitation. A narrow zone at the Wasatch's base receives thirteen to eighteen inches of precipitation, while the higher elevations typically receive more than fifty. The higher elevations receive the majority of their precipitation in snow, with the peaks surrounding Park City accumulating between one and two hundred inches of snow each winter.[10] Because the Wasatch and Uinta mountains rise in the middle of an arid desert, the snow that falls during the winter is incredibly dry and light. The light, powdery snow provides skiers an experience similar to surfing. Gliding through knee- and sometimes waist-deep powder, the friction between the skis and the ground decreases, and the soft snow supports the skier, taking pressure off the knees and hips.[11]

Amazingly, the UPCMC's Treasure Mountains ski resort opened for business on December 21, 1963, only one year after the start of construction. Treasure Mountains featured a gondola, a double chairlift, and two J-bars that carried skiers to the top of three thousand acres of terrain cut by eighteen miles of ski runs. Cognizant of Park City's mining past and its new relationship with the environment, a 1963 Treasure Mountains press release declared, "The bonanza has climbed out of the shafts, tunnels and slopes to the placid, pine-clad hills, and a new chapter is being written in the 100 year history of this town that refuses to join the ghost parade of western mining camps."[12]

Despite its pioneering effort to begin the modern era of skiing in Park City, the UPCMC could not support both the ski resort and its declining mining operation. In 1971 the mine sold its interest in the ski operation to a New Orleans development corporation that changed the ski area's name to Park City Resort and began an ambitious plan to expand daily skier capacity and resort facilities surrounding the ski area. The 1970s national recession triggered by the 1973–74 Arab oil embargo struck Park City's ski industry and the resort's owners in particular. In 1975 Park City Resort changed hands once again, this time to Alpine Meadows of Tahoe, Inc. Over the next two decades, the Alpine Meadows group focused on Park City Ski Area's skiing facilities and left the real estate end of the business alone.[13]

Notwithstanding the mining company's demise, Park City's nascent ski industry benefited from its geographic location near Utah's largest metropolitan area, the Wasatch Front. Stretching eighty miles from Ogden in the North to Provo in the South, 90 percent of the state's population lives along the western slope of the Wasatch Mountains. Interstates linked Park City to the Wasatch Front before the mines suspended operations. A fleet of Utah Department of Transportation snowplows kept the interstates open during the winter, enabling more than seven hundred thousand potential customers to drive to Park City. Interstate 80 eventually connected Park City to Salt Lake Municipal Airport, making the drive to the ski resort a straight shot. This proved crucial to marketing the ski resort; campaigns could advertise nationally as well as internationally, attracting a clientele with enough disposable income to fly to the resort and ski for several days.[14]

During the winter of 1976–77, Park City experienced a severe winter drought.

The lack of snow compelled the Alpine Meadows group to invest in state-of-the-art snowmaking equipment. The investment paid huge dividends in the future. Now with an ensured snow supply, Alpine Meadows chairman Nick Badami and his son Craig led the effort to place their Park City Resort on the World Cup ski tour. They also expanded the resort to twenty-two hundred skiable acres with eighty-two runs on a thirty-one hundred–foot vertical drop. The resort's size dwarfed Alta and Brighton ski resorts in nearby Salt Lake City. When representatives of the international tour visited Park City Resort, the resort's snowmaking capabilities impressed them. The tour held its first event at Park City Resort in 1985 and has remained a regular stop on the World Cup tour ever since. By this time, Park City Resort was not the only ski resort in town.[15]

Two more ski resorts opened in Park City by 1981. Developers established the pair on either side of Park City Resort and at opposite sides of the ski-resort spectrum. The earlier of the two resorts, Park West, was the brainchild of California developer Robert Major. He, along with his local partner, Robert Ensign, raised enough capital by 1968 to begin construction of a two thousand–acre ski area that featured three chairlifts and a day lodge. The same 1970s recession that affected Park City Resort impacted the newer Park West as well. Park West's owners habitually underfunded the ski area, leaving destination skiers with few resort amenities to heighten their ski experience.[16] At least twice, once in the early 1980s and again in the early 1990s, Park West came close to insolvency. Each time a group of long-term employees raised funds to keep the ski operation afloat. The lack of financial solvency led to the resort's sale twice in the 1990s. In 1994 a Salt Lake City financier bought the resort, changed the name to Wolf Mountain, and announced significant construction plans to improve the poor base facilities. Nothing came of the plans, however, and the financier sold Wolf Mountain in 1997 to the American Skiing Company, a corporation with deep pockets that owned several high-profile ski destination resorts across the country.[17] That same year the company renamed the resort "The Canyons" and began constructing a new gondola, five new lifts, and an eight thousand–square-foot midmountain lodge.[18]

The new ski resort on the east side of Park City Resort lay physically close but stood qualitatively miles from the financially insecure Park West. When Deer Valley opened for business in December 1981, the resort was unlike anything Park City had ever seen. From his experience in the luxury hotel business in San Francisco, owner Edgar Stern designed Deer Valley as a first-class ski-resort destination. The original plans included a six-phase construction project with seventeen hundred residential units and a resort capable of accommodating twelve thousand skiers.

From the start Stern wanted to create one of the most exclusive ski areas in the country. "Nobody was doing it," Stern remembered in 1991. "We had been in the high end of the hotel business and had been very successful at that. I thought that same pattern would work in the ski business." When skiers arrived at the forty-eight thousand–square-foot Snow Park lodge at the bottom of the ski hills, valets removed skis from patrons' car racks and held them until a parking lot shuttle returned skiers to the base of the ski hill. Deer Valley ski runs spanned three mountains, with a daily skier capacity of more than eight thousand. The resort commissioned former Olympic champion Stein Eriksen to develop and operate its nationally ranked ski school. After expanding onto a fourth mountain, by 1997 Deer Valley had a skier capacity of twenty-five thousand skiers an hour. Deer Valley's emphasis, however, remained as always on dining and guest service. Between the Snow Park lodge and the twenty-seven thousand–square-foot midmountain Silver Lake lodge, Deer Valley was home to three five-star restaurants, including the Seafood Buffet, a fresh seafood restaurant made possible in such a landlocked location through two daily direct flights from West Coast seafood suppliers.[19]

The penultimate measure of Park City ski area's success came when Park City Mountain Resort and Deer Valley hosted several events for the 2002 Winter Olympic Games. Planning for the event began in 1989 when Utah voters dedicated a small portion of the state sales tax to building facilities in several locations. The Olympic planning committee chose Deer Valley as the site for the slalom, moguls, and aerial events and Park City to host the giant slalom and snowboarding competitions. In addition to these two venues, the Salt Lake Olympic Committee built the Utah Olympic Park to hold the games' ski-jumping and sliding sports of bobsled, skeleton, and luge in Park City. The Nordic jumps are the highest in the world at 7,310 feet, and the fifteen-curve track is one of only three refrigerated competition-certified tracks in North America. For Park City to host the majority of the ski and sliding sports events at the Olympic Games is particularly significant because the city beat out the four Salt Lake City–based ski areas that consistently rank near the top in annual surveys of the best ski resorts in North America. The 2002 Olympics provided a window for the world to view Park City as more than a tourist town. The games also showcased Park City as one of the West's elite upscale real estate markets.[20]

Park City's world-class ski resorts came a long way from their humble beginnings in the 1960s. By the 1990s Deer Valley and Park City Mountain Resort became the county's top employers in terms of both number of employees and total payroll.[21] Parallel to the ski resorts' growth, commercial and residential real estate boomed in the surrounding unincorporated Snyderville Basin. A number of medium-size yet nationally recognized companies moved to the basin. Mrs. Field's Cookies and Black Diamond Equipment joined the U.S. Ski Team, U.S. Ski and Snowboard Associations, and the U.S. Speed Skating Federation in making Park City their headquarters. In the late 1980s Delta Airlines chose Salt Lake City as its national hub, adding more than three hundred "Delta families" that earned "a lot more than the median income" to the Park City area, according to the city's public relations director.[22] As the ski resorts expanded their operations, including amenities and condominium construction around their bases, visitors and area residents sought less expensive dwellings away from the ski hills. Park City's geography always limited its growth potential. The city proper rests in a tight valley that allowed very little room to grow, especially once ski resorts claimed the hills directly surrounding the city. Residential development consequently flowed into the unincorporated area of Summit County directly north of Park City named Snyderville Basin.

Just as the quality and quantity of skiing increased dramatically during the 1980s and 1990s, so did the populations of Park City and Summit County. Between 1990 and 1995 Park City's permanent population swelled from 4,468 to 6,323. Enrollments in the Park City School District, which includes the surrounding Snyderville Basin, rose from 1,700 to 3,000 students during the same period. Since the 1980s Summit County led Utah's counties in growth. In the 1990 census Summit County claimed 15,518 residents; just three years later the figure jumped to 19,724. The majority of these new residents invested in residential real estate. The assessed value of private property rose 80 percent in Park City, from $1 billion to $1.8 billion during the same period.[23] The approval of the first subdivision in the basin in 1950 set a precedent for this future development. Named Summit Park, the subdivision marked the beginning of Park City's second transition from a strictly resort-based economy to a bedroom community that catered to Salt Lake City's metro-area commuters. The trend took off, and Dick Wilde, president of Silver King State Bank in Park City, correctly predicted in the 1970s that the ski resorts were a "blinder" to the town's future as a suburb.[24]

The same environmental amenities that brought skiers to Park City also brought home owners seeking outdoor recreation and scenic amenities. Beginning in the 1950s developers in the Rocky Mountain West capitalized on relatively isolated areas of scenic beauty by designing what I term *wilderburbs*—clusters of homes in rural valleys and up mountain slopes that lay within commuting distance to metropolitan centers. People moved to these new developments to live amid the beauty and freedom of wild surroundings while striving to maintain suburban security, protection of their investment, and control over their environment. The resulting wilderburbs were a new middle landscape where the middle to upper classes lived beyond the urban fringe amid a beautiful "untamed" landscape, while feeling safe from threats from the natural environment. These wilderburbs are neither wild nor completely suburban; instead, they function as a new kind of low-density residential development in which people feel they can live in a proximate wilderness while maintaining a level of personal security, control of their surroundings, and accessibility to the city like that available in the suburbs.[25] Despite the amenities that these developments offer, home owners are subject to often-unforeseen interactions with their environment. Examining the history of a specific subdivision named Summit Park helps us understand the environmental interactions taking place at the suburban fringe. Summit Park's travails with water in particular expose the vulnerability inherent with living at the forest edge.

Following World War II, the first mass-produced city-size suburbs such as Levittown attracted millions of Americans with single-family dwellings, grass yards, and the promise of an easy commute by car to a job in the city. Thus began the great post–World War II exodus of urban workers to the suburbs. Aided by the dramatic increase in federal highway construction, suburbs spread farther outward from the urban core and grew in size. By the 1980s residential development shifted once again. Many businesses chose to locate themselves in rural areas to reduce capital expenditures and obtain tax incentives, taking their employees with them. Later, with the invention of the Internet and wireless technology, capital and information became more mobile, freeing Americans to work farther from the urban core in wilderburbs. These new developments did more than just leapfrog over the outer ring of planned suburbs; wilderburbs leaped beyond the suburban fringe and climbed up the hills, completely separating themselves from previous residential developments.

In the arid West, when residents move beyond suburbia's borders, the reality of living in the forest brings many new interactions with their physical surroundings. One of the most fundamental and problematic interactions exurbanites face is with water. Residents face the obstacle of mountain geology and lack of laws governing water use, which combine to create varied and problematic water delivery and disposal systems. In most traditional suburbs built just beyond the boundaries of any city edge, obtaining water was as easy as paying an extension fee for extending the city's water lines. In the wilderburbs, the problem was much more complex than in areas of the West that have garnered historians' attention.[26] Providing water to residents required overcoming topographic and geologic features that make locating and maintaining a water source very different from and much more difficult than in traditional suburbs. Wilderburbs that provided the fewest amenities placed the burden of water procurement on the home owners, requiring them to drill their own wells. More sophisticated and generally more expensive developments built community water systems that removed the burden of water procurement from the home owners, but these water systems also gave residents a false sense of security that their water supply was safe and would last the lifetime of their homes.

Wilderburbs like Summit Park are noteworthy places because before the 1950s people never lived on mountaintops and slopes in great numbers in the arid West. One reason they did not was the lack of available water. Surface water ran off too quickly, and downslope users already appropriated it.[27] Groundwater seemed to be too expensive or too unpredictable a proposition for large-scale subdivisions for many years. In the early 1950s a developer outside Park City, Utah, took a chance at overcoming the water problems posed in mountaintop developments. The developer was at his most creative and at times most negligent when it came to overcoming the lack of a permanent water supply.

Summit Park overlooks the Snyderville Basin that surrounds Park City. Located at the intersection of two Rocky Mountain ranges, the development sits on the northern slopes of the east-to-west-oriented Uinta Mountains right where the range intersects with the Wasatch Front section of the north-to-south-oriented Rockies. The Wasatch-Cache National Forest surrounds the subdivision in three directions. This shared boundary with public lands protects the subdivision from future development along most of its border.

According to Summit County, Utah's official history, "No subdivision has been more haunted by water problems than Summit Park."[28] Summit County approved the 850-lot subdivision in the late 1950s when the county zoning regulations consisted of one eight-and-a-half-by-eleven-inch piece of paper tacked to the planning office's wall.[29] The lack of planning oversight at the time became manifest when an 850-lot subdivision adjacent to a city with a population of just over twenty-two hundred residents received little scrutiny from county planners. Summit Park represents some of the worst aspects of planning and development in the county. Developer Sam Soter platted many lots on such steep terrain that they remain unoccupied to this day. Steep, treacherous roads wind along the hillsides, creating hazards for motorists during the winter. However, Soter did not build or advertise Summit Park as a year-round development; instead, he intended Summit Park as a summertime retreat from nearby Salt Lake Valley's heat.[30] From the late 1950s, when the development began, until the late 1970s, the two hundred summer homes in Summit Park relied on individual wells for their water.[31]

Summit County, Utah, is an example of how lax a rural western county's oversight of water system standards and requirements could be, particularly when economic growth was the county commission's priority. Although the county regulations have historically required developers to obtain water rights to ostensibly provide water to their new subdivisions, long ago developers figured out how to evade the rules. They devised a shell game that used "paper" water rights to avoid providing on-site "wet" water.[32] Such shenanigans existed in large part because the Summit County water system had no expert oversight. Years later a Summit County planner remarked that this type of arrangement took place at a time "when the county thought that engineers were guys who drove trains."[33]

This shell game of paper and wet-water rights continued in Summit County for the next thirty years. Developers gained approval for many projects without actually obtaining water on-site. The system created problems as more people moved to the Snyderville Basin. The fractured geology compartmentalized the problems to individual developments so the whole basin was not under stress. The geology made drilling for water in the mountains surrounding the basin a crapshoot. Some developments had an abundance of water; others ran into severe shortages, and numerous wells failed. Unpredictable water sources created a Las Vegas casino atmosphere that made instant water winners and losers. Enough people won to keep the system running.

Using groundwater for domestic use in mountain communities historically fell into a legal gray area that allowed developers and residents to circumvent the institutions that govern water use in both rural and agricultural areas. Before World War II the story of water in the West was the story of surface-water rights, use, and fights. Normally, the fight for surface water was between urban areas and agriculture. Groundwater never figured into this fight. In the 1950s and 1960s there were no groundwater laws because no urban population wanted the water. There was no constituency for the resource. Water laws on the books adjudicated surface water alone. As far as states were concerned, rivers, streams, and lakes were state business; wells were an individual's business in the eyes of the law. When the first waves of wilderburbs rose in the West, they came at a time when neither urban nor rural forces were dominant in terms of water. Wilderburbs were outside the urban areas but were not in the rural areas, either. They existed in a water borderland no one could control. Until very recently wilderburbs were able to circumvent the institutions that dealt with water because they were outside of areas people cared about. States institutionalized water use because a sizable population with a thirst for water moved into the mountains by the late 1980s.

Both developers and residents exploited the lack of state laws adjudicating groundwater use. The Snyderville Basin developments fell geographically into areas that were to their builders' advantage. Summit Park lay outside city limits, but it also fell outside the river basins where the state engineer regulated and apportioned surface water for urban and agricultural uses. Developer Sam Soter was thus able to avoid the city's infrastructural requirements but also avoid regulation by state engineers. Most rural developments were the responsibility of the rural county. Usually underfunded and overworked, the rural counties typically had to play catch-up with development. This left the earliest wilderburb residents vulnerable to the developer's whims when it came to water, creating arrangements that naturally led to problems. Patricia Nelson Limerick's characterization of the nineteenth-century West's foibles with water is equally appropriate for twentieth-century wilderburbs: "When it came to producing a mess, Western aridity gave humans and nature their prime opportunity to work as a team."[34]

Summit Park was one of the first developments in the basin to build a community water system connecting each home to the same water delivery lines and sewer treatment facilities. To attract more buyers, Sam Soter installed a primitive water and sewer system. The system had problems from the start. The problems so affected one Summit Park resident that she made it her crusade to improve the subdivision's water quality and ensure a reliable supply. Marti Gee moved to Summit Park in 1980 and built her own home. In February 1984 Marti gave birth to twins but lost one during delivery. Her surviving baby girl was very small and weak and struggled for survival as she suffered from recurring illnesses for the better part of a year. After many visits to pediatricians searching for hereditary or genetic causes for her daughter's poor health, Marti began searching for environmental causes. Living in the high mountains where the air was much cleaner, she focused her attention on her water. She was well aware of the subdivision's water problems. Like many of the residents in Summit Park, Marti and her family endured interrupted water delivery for days at a time while breaks in the water lines required repair. When she approached the county Board of Health for information about her water, she was shocked to find the board never approved her water because it did not regulate private systems. The news horrified Gee. She determined to make the water quality in her subdivision her cause.[35]

When Gee learned that the Board of Health had not approved the water system in Summit Park, she thought of selling the home and moving to a different location. However, this was in the mid-1980s when the national recession was still in full swing and the real estate market was stagnant. To make matters worse, home owners in Summit Park could not get loans to refinance their mortgages because the water system was unapproved. Without the ability to sell or refinance, many like Marti were stuck paying mortgage interest rates at 17 percent and above. Marti dug in her heels and decided to make the subdivision's series of wells, old pumps, and crumbling water lines work.

Marti Gee and the rest of the residents faced an uphill battle. The water system in Summit Park was a mess. Developer Sam Soter and his son Greg acted as the Summit Park Water Company, a developer-owned, for-profit entity. It is impossible to know if Soter did not plan or simply tried to save money, but the construction specifications and materials he installed were woefully inadequate. Summit Park Water Company originally installed cast-iron water lines less than twelve inches underground. At such a high altitude, the ground freezes each winter often below twelve inches. Cast iron becomes very brittle when cold. According to Gee, "It's as fragile as egg shells." After Soter hired Gee as the subdivision's water manager, she often dealt with more than twenty-five simultaneous breaks in the system.

The steep, narrow roads within the subdivision made repairing the underground water lines very difficult. The roads were so narrow that any attempt to repair the water system blocked the roads. When Soter decided to install a sewer and water system, he set aside money to pave the roads at the same time. Soter hired one contractor for both jobs, but residents recalled that the ground was so rocky and hard, the contractor used the project's entire budget installing the water and sewer lines, leaving the roads unpaved. The roads' steep grade and narrow dimensions made them nearly impassable during the wet fall, winter, and spring months, so leaving them unpaved was not an option. The developer was either not able or unwilling to commit more funds for the project, which forced residents to appeal for help to the Summit County Commission. The commission voted to create a special service area and adopt the subdivision's roads as county roads. This vote committed the county not only to repaving the roads but also to expensive and hazardous snow removal and repairs each year.[36]

After the developer-owned water company installed a community water and sewer system, development sped up and the 850-lot subdivision began to fill. Problems with the water system, however, continued as well. The crude water system suffered over the years from chronic problems with frozen and broken pipes, leaking storage containers, and water contaminated with dirt and other debris. Despite the prodigious efforts of Marti Gee acting as Summit Park Water Company's field operator, the development's water system desperately needed repairs and overhaul. Soter never committed the funds to make the necessary upgrades. Years later, after Marti Gee ascended to the management of a Snyderville Basin–wide water conglomerate, she said that Soter's reluctance to commit money for the upgrades was typical of her experience with developer-owned water companies. She found over the years that developers made poor water managers and were always reluctant to commit funds to projects that would reduce their profits. For the developers, she conjectured, there was little incentive to spend their own money for the good of the development.

Soter was in deep trouble by the mid-1980s. The national recession affected development throughout the state. His water company was unable to keep pace with the improvements necessary to maintain the water and sewer system. In 1986 residents took their grievances with Soter before the Utah Public Service Commission, which oversees public and private utilities. The commission ruled that the developer must repair the water system. Almost immediately after the ruling, Soter's water company filed for bankruptcy, leaving Summit Park subdivision without a water company.[37]

Led by Marti Gee, Summit Park residents approached Summit County in 1987 and asked the county commission to create a special improvement district and a special services district in Summit Park. This legal maneuver allowed the Summit Park residents to apply for low-interest bank loans to purchase Soter's water company and make the necessary improvements. The special improvement district allowed the residents to use the county as a cosigner to their loan. The county in turn used the 850 lots as collateral on the loan. The agreement gave power to the county to auction off lots in the subdivision if the residents defaulted on the loan. In 1988 the residents obtained a four million–dollar loan to purchase the water company from the bankruptcy court and make improvements.[38]

At this point it seemed that Summit Park's water trials were over; unfortunately, they were not. In the winter of 1988–89, Summit Park's wells failed, leaving the entire development without water. The intrepid Marti Gee managed to meet with Utah governor Norman Bangerter and persuaded him to declare Summit Park in a state of emergency. The governor agreed and called on the U.S. Army Corps of Engineers to deliver water by truck from a neighboring subdivision. This arrangement lasted through the winter, a total of eight months, at a cost of nearly forty thousand dollars a month. The state-of-emergency declaration allowed Summit

Park residents to shirk their water-delivery costs onto the rest of Utah's taxpayers. In the spring of 1989 Summit County placed a moratorium on new housing starts within the subdivision.[39]

During the next two years Summit Park replaced miles of water and sewer lines and had their entire system telemetered, or completely monitored electronically. With Marti Gee still at the helm of their now resident-owned water company, the subdivision built a large storage tank and drilled two new wells in nearby Toll Canyon. A March 1991 article in the *Salt Lake Tribune* declared the subdivision's water travails over. The paper spoke too soon. Later that year the second well Summit Park had just drilled was contaminated. The little water company began a search for new sources of water.[40]

Summit Park's solution to its water problems came with the help of two neighboring subdivisions, which lie on the slopes below Summit Park. Pinebrook sits near the bottom of the hill, covering Eckert Hill, site of several of the first U.S. ski-jumping championships in the 1930s. Pinebrook is a very well-to-do master-planned community with stringently enforced covenants. The development features a resident-owned water co-op named Gorgoza Water Company. Between Pinebrook and Summit Park lies the tiny Timberline subdivision. Timberline is a contrast in style to Pinebrook. Timberline residents voted to keep their roads unpaved and to keep the traffic speeds down to allow dogs and children to safely roam the subdivision's roads. The residents in Timberline also formed a small water co-op. As Summit County residents balked at the idea of creating a county-owned water company designed to link the dozens of private water companies in the Snyderville Basin in the early 1990s, the Summit Park, Timberline, and Pinebrook water co-ops agreed to connect their water systems.[41]

Pinebrook subdivision enjoys an abundance of groundwater compared to Summit Park. Even though Pinebrook and Summit Park are very close to one another, the geography underneath each subdivision made a tremendous difference in obtaining water. Pinebrook found plenty of water for its needs in the bedrock aquifers below the subdivision. In a 2006 survey the U.S. Bureau of Reclamation found that Pinebrook used eight wells to supply its domestic water needs.[42] What the company did not have, however, was much storage space to reserve water. Summit Park, on the other hand, had difficulty obtaining reliable wells within its boundaries. The difference was in the geology. Most wells in Summit Park have to pierce a limestone formation below just a few feet of dirt on many lots. Marti Gee explained to the *Salt Lake Tribune* how unpredictable even new wells were in Summit Park: "We will not know that until we test pump it, find out what we can actually pump out of that well. We're in a hard place to drill wells." Summit Park did have one asset that interested Pinebrook. During its first phase of improvements after buying their water company from the bankruptcy court, Summit Park residents built a seven hundred thousand-gallon underground concrete reservoir in 1989. In 1990 the two subdivisions, along with their neighbor Timberline, joined their water systems. The agreement gave Summit Park access to Pinebrook's abundant water supply, while Pinebrook used Summit Park's storage facilities to guard against well failures and to have enough water on hand in case of a wildfire.[43]

The very different experiences of Summit Park and Pinebrook illustrate the difference geology makes for mountain developments. The geology is so difficult a factor because developers and residents cannot predict what lies beneath their property in terms of geologic formations and groundwater. Unpredictable geology causes situations similar to Pinebrook and Summit Park: close neighbors whose ability to find water is vastly different. The Summit County Commission decided against a countywide water system and instead required developers to form their own water companies. The county's decision created dozens of independent water companies that experienced troubles similar to Summit Park's. As late as 2000 two developments in the Snyderville Basin ran into major well failures and contaminations. Former Summit County commissioner Pat Cone explained what these two failures signified for the county: "One of the problems we found with these water companies is that your neighbor could be in trouble and you couldn't help them. . . . Before others ran out of water, we decided to go in there and help them." In 2000 Summit County attempted to regionalize all the water companies in the Snyderville Basin under the Mountain Regional Water Special Service District. The new water company combined more than a half-dozen troubled delivery systems, including Summit Park and Pinebrook, and connected them. The connection allowed water to move from one development to another. For Marti Gee, then manager of the Summit Park Water Special Service District, the Mountain Regional District was a godsend for her subdivision. It meant that Summit Park will always have a reliable source of water and that the other taxpayers will subsidize the water delivered to her subdivision.[44]

These recent improvements to Summit Park's water system are encouraging for residents. However, potential trouble may affect the subdivision in a far more malignant fashion in the future. Park City's past as a mining town left another environmental legacy besides undeveloped terrain perfect for skiing and rural developments. The subdivisions surrounding Park City have a much more toxic past to manage. The Summit Park subdivision endured many well failures, broken water lines, and water so contaminated with simple sediment that residents remembered that it seemed like mud poured out of their faucets. The potential for more serious contamination is possible for the water throughout the Snyderville Basin. Most visitors know Park City today as a former mining town–turned–ski town that hosted the 2002 Winter Olympics and hosts the annual Sundance Film Festival. Few today dare recognize Park City as a Superfund site.

The city's mining legacy left enormous amounts of toxic mining waste throughout the city and its waterways. Environmental scientists estimate the mining companies dumped more than seven hundred thousand tons of mill tailings into Silver Creek, which runs through the city center, by 1930. Even before the turn of the twentieth century, the downstream town of Wanship abandoned its use of Silver Creek for irrigation because the water was contaminated. In 1983 the Utah Geological and Mineral Survey conducted a soil survey around the creek that found dangerously high levels of lead, arsenic, cadmium, and mercury, all by-products of the mining process. Later that year the investigation widened as the state Health Department ordered soil tests, water sample tests of Silver Creek, and tests of household dust in the homes around the creek. The Health Department found elevated levels of lead and cadmium in both the water and the household dust around Silver Creek. The state took its findings to the U.S. Environmental Protection Agency, which subsequently investigated and recommended listing the Prospector Park Condominiums and Business Park as a Superfund site. Boosters for Park City's tourist industry successfully lobbied to remove Park City from the Superfund list, effectively burying the story for more than fifteen years.[45] Most of the searches to identify cases of mining's toxic legacy occurred within Park City's boundaries. However, mining was not contained within the city limits. There is the ominous specter of contaminated groundwater in the Snyderville Basin, particularly since 2000, when Summit County created basinwide water systems.[46]

The variety of experience with water systems in Summit County was determined much more by geology than by residents' desires. Historian Mark Fiege wrote about similar human relations with nature in the southern Idaho farming country, in particular how residents imagined the countryside they farmed as an "irrigated Eden" that they could shape through technology and ingenuity. The residents commonly could not imprint all their desires onto the landscape; they had to compromise with their environment.[47] Summit Park and other wilderburbs too are places where people brought their dreams and hopes of living beyond the urban fringe, while still maintaining a level of security, control, and accessibility to the city that is available in suburbs. In mountain developments residents brought their own ideas and imagined landscapes as they tried to settle the undeveloped hillsides and ridgetops throughout the Rocky Mountain West. Standing in their way to achieving many of their mountain retreats is the fractured geology below. The geology is often an impediment to development. The creative and sometimes negligent solutions developers created to overcome this impediment are some of the key examples of the unique mountain development phenomenon.

Looking at western towns and cities through the lens of environmental history gives historians a new model to understand the history of place. Cities in the West, like Park City, often grow because of their environment and sometimes in spite of it. Fortune seekers established Park City as a mining town in hopes of extracting a fortune from its hills. The transition from mining town to ski town was a new way the town capitalized on its environment. Park City's latest transition to a Salt Lake City bedroom community featuring mountaintop subdivisions is an iteration of this trend. The history of Park City is the story of a town inseparably reliant upon its landscape. Understanding the environment of western cities allows us to appreciate what attracts residents yet sometimes deters them from living in formerly rural areas. Without this appreciation, we would understand only a portion of Park City's history.

Notes

1. John Mason Boutwell, *Geology and Ore Deposits of the Park City District, Utah*, U.S. Geological Survey, Professional Paper No. 77 (Washington, D.C.: Government Printing Office, 1912), 15–16.

2. Marie Ross Peterson, *Echoes of Yesterday: Summit County Centennial History* (Salt Lake City: Mountain States Bindery, 1947), 316–29; David Hampshire, Martha S. Bradley, and Allen Roberts, *A History of Summit County* (Salt Lake City: Utah Historical Society, 1998), 96–103; Heather Lockman, "Park City, Utah: A Ski Resort's Days of Ore," *Travel Holiday* (June 1988): 48–53; Nancy Volmer and Tom Roberts, "History of Park City," *Rangelands* 14, no. 2 (April 1992): 60–63.

3. Richard W. Sadler, "The Impact of Mining on Salt Lake City," *Utah Historical Quarterly* 47 (Summer 1979): 248; William M. McPhee, "Vignettes of Park City," *Utah Historical Quarterly* 28 (April 1960): 137–53.

4. Raye C. Ringholz, *Paradise Paved: The Challenge of Growth in the New West* (Salt Lake City: University of Utah Press, 1996), 2; Hampshire, Bradley, and Roberts, *History of Summit County*, 306; United States Census Office, *Census Bulletin* (Washington, D.C.: Government Printing Office, 1930–50).

5. Stephen L. Carr, *The Historic Guide to Utah Ghost Towns* (Salt Lake City: Western Epics, 1973), 53–54.

6. Cont L. Jones, "The Study of a Redevelopment Program: Its Political and Economic Effect on Park City, Utah" (master's thesis, Brigham Young University, 1967), 18, 29; James Tedford, "Park City, Utah: Yesterday, Today, Tomorrow" (master's thesis, University of Utah, 1970), 32–35; Hampshire, Bradley, and Roberts, *History of Summit County*, 306–7.

7. During much of the 1930s, Ecker Hill outside Park City hosted the annual U.S. ski-jumping competition.

8. Raye Ringholz, *Diggings and Doings in Park City* (Park City: Ringholz, 1983), 105; "New Bonanza at Park City!" Ski Utah Associates Collection, Special Collections, Marriott Library, University of Utah, Salt Lake City.

9. Hal Rothman, *Devil's Bargains: Tourism in the Twentieth-Century American West* (Lawrence: University Press of Kansas, 1998), chaps. 7, 8.

10. Dan Flores, "Zion in Eden: Phases of the Environmental History of Utah," *Environmental Review* 7 (1983): 327–28; Walter F. Holmes, Kendall R. Thompson, and Michael Enright, *Water Resources of the Park City Area, Utah, With Emphasis on Ground Water*, State of Utah Department of Natural Resources Technical Publication No. 85 (Salt Lake City: Utah State Department of Natural Resources, 1986).

11. "New Bonanza at Park City!" 3–4; Flores, "Zion in Eden," 328; Claire Walter, "Bright Lights, Park City," *Skiing* (Spring 1988): 34–35.

12. Park City Ski Corporation Records, Woody Anderson Papers, 1956–1991, Special Collections, Marriott Library, University of Utah, Salt Lake City; Janice Peck-Sansom, "Park City's Painful Prosperity," *Utah Holiday* (May 1979): 65.

13. Tedford, "Park City, Utah," 40–44; Mark Menlove, "The Grandfather," *Park City Lodestar* 20 (Winter 1997): 28; Hampshire, Bradley, and Roberts, *History of Summit County*, 322–23.

14. "New Bonanza at Park City!" 6.

15. "Park City Ski Area 1990–91 Information Guide," Park City Ski Corporation, 1990; Walter, "Bright Lights, Park City," 32–38; Richard J. Pietschmann, "At Their Peak," *Westerner's World* (December 1985): 37–57.

16. Walter, "Bright Lights, Park City," 38.

17. The American Skiing Company owns Killington in Vermont, Sugarloaf and Sunday River in Maine, Steamboat Springs in Colorado, and Heavenly Valley in California, among others.

18. Tedford, "Park City, Utah," 44–46; Hampshire, Bradley, and Roberts, *History of Summit County*, 322–26.

19. Kurt Repanshek, "Expanding Into Empire," *Park City Lodestar* 18 (Winter 1995): 64; Hampshire, Bradley, and Roberts, *History of Summit County*, 324–25; Stern quoted in Alan Horowitz, "Moguls Behind the Moguls: Utah's Ski Resort Owners," *Utah Business* 5, no. 11

(1991–92): 13–14; Mike Korologos, "From Neon to Crystal Chandeliers," *Westways* 74, no. 11 (1982): 50–53; Pietschmann, "At Their Peak," 37–57.

20. Cheryl Smith, "Preparing for the Olympics: Building World Class Facilities for Winter Sports," *Utah Highways* 2, no. 3 (1994): 18–19; Jeff Phillips and Linda Hays, "Go for the Gold—and the Food," *Sunset*, February 1998, 42–44.

21. Utah Department of Employment Security, *Summit County, Utah, Selected Demographic, Labor Market, and Economic Characteristics* (Salt Lake City: Utah Department of Employment Security, November 1994), 27.

22. Miles Rademan, telephone interview, June 20, 2006; "Park City: Utah's Summer Playground," *Utah Business* 5, no. 3 (1991): 58–60.

23. Park City Planning Department, Draft Growth Management Element, *Park City General Plan Update* (Park City: Park City Planning Department, August 1995); Utah Department of Employment Security, *Summit County, Utah*, 37; Jordan Bonfante, "Sky's the Limit," *Time*, September 6, 1993, 23.

24. Peck-Sansom, "Park City's Painful Prosperity," 72.

25. Physically, rural developments are disconnected from the metro areas, but residents are still connected culturally to suburban norms. Residents want to live in areas free from suburban pressures and as much human artifice as possible, but they still expect suburban amenities such as reliable water and protection from fire and wild animals.

26. Most of the major works on water in the West are too broad in their attempts to represent the entire region. Typically, historians focused their research on one particular area and attempted to extrapolate their findings upon the entire region. This is certainly true for Donald Worster's *Rivers of Empire: Water, Aridity, and the Growth of the American West* (New York: Oxford University Press, 1985), but it is also true for earlier works such as Walter Prescott Webb and his student W. Eugene Hollon. Even one of the most prescient studies, Donald J. Pisani's *To Reclaim a Divided West: Water, Law, and Public Policy, 1848–1902*, mischaracterizes the water availability in mountainous areas.

27. Many of the best works on water deal exclusively with surface water. See Marc Reisner, *Cadillac Desert: The American West and Its Disappearing Water* (New York: Viking Penguin, 1986); Mark Fiege, *Irrigated Eden: The Making of an Agricultural Landscape in the American West* (Seattle: University of Washington Press, 1999); and Richard White, *The Organic Machine: The Remaking of the Columbia River* (New York: Hill and Wang, 1995).

28. Hampshire, Bradley, and Roberts, *History of Summit County*, 256.

29. Don Sargent, interview by author, March 23, 2006, Coalville, Utah; Peck-Sansom, "Park City's Painful Prosperity," 65–74.

30. Summit Park sales brochure, 1955, in possession of the author.

31. Marti Gee, tape-recorded interview, June 10, 2004, Park City, Utah; Hampshire, Bradley, and Roberts, *History of Summit County*, 256.

32. Pat Cone, tape-recorded interview, June 11, 2004, Oakley, Utah.

33. *Park City Newspaper,* June 12, 1980.

34. Patricia Nelson Limerick, *The Legacy of Conquest: The Unbroken Past of the American West* (New York: W. W. Norton, 1987), 318.

35. Gee interview; Sena Taylor, "Construction of Homes OK'd in Summit Park," *Salt Lake Tribune,* March 20, 1990, B7.

36. Hampshire, Bradley, and Roberts, *History of Summit County,* 256.

37. Bureau of Reclamation, *Park City and Snyderville Basin Water Supply Study Special Report* (Provo: Bureau of Reclamation, Upper Colorado Region, 2006), sec. 2, p. 1.

38. Taylor, "Construction of Homes."

39. Hampshire, Bradley, and Roberts, *History of Summit County,* 96–103; David Hampshire and Elliott W. Evans Jr., tape-recorded interview, June 6, 2005, Park City, Utah.

40. *Salt Lake Tribune,* March 20, 1991.

41. Hampshire, Bradley, and Roberts, *History of Summit County,* 257.

42. Bureau of Reclamation, *Park City and Snyderville Basin,* 2–4.

43. Kurt Repanshek, "Summit Park Lot Owners Are Left High, Dry Lot Owners at Summit Park Sit High, Dry, and Fighting to Build," *Salt Lake Tribune,* October 22, 1994, B1; Taylor, "Construction of Homes."

44. Cone interview; Christopher Smart, "Summit County Awash in Water Problems," *Salt Lake Tribune,* September 28, 2003, A16.

45. Jay D. Stannard, "Irrigation in the Weber Valley," in *Report of Irrigation Investigations in Utah* (Washington, D.C.: Government Printing Office, 1903), 173–74; David Hampshire, "Mining Leaves Its Mark on Park City," *Beehive History* 26 (2000): 19.

46. Elise M. Giddings, Michelle I. Hornberger, and Heidi K. Hadley, *Trace-Metal Concentrations in Sediment and Water and Health of Aquatic Macroinvertebrate Communities of Streams Near Park City, Summit County, Utah* (Salt Lake City: U.S. Geological Survey, 2001).

47. Fiege, *Irrigated Eden.*

Middle–Class Migration and Rural Gentrification in Western Montana

RINA GHOSE

A newcomer to Missoula made an interesting observation about her neighbors and, in doing so, captured a profound change in community in western Montana. She noted, "Yeah, they moved from Billings, but they were in Chicago before that. And those people are from Florida and Texas. They're from California. And, next door, they're from New Mexico. I think I've only met, you know, had a long conversation with one person from Missoula."[1] In the past decade the Rocky Mountain region of the United States experienced a remarkable 25.4 percent increase in population growth, the largest percentage change among all the regions defined by the U.S. Bureau of the Census. Such rapid growth has occurred primarily through the migration of residents from urban areas across the United States. The most dramatic changes occurred in the nonmetropolitan rural counties of the Rocky Mountains, where population growth has either influenced or been accompanied by economic restructuring, increased urbanization, sprawl, and a reallocation of resources.[2]

Past studies regarding this phenomenon have reinforced the notion that an amenity–driven migration is under way in the Rocky Mountain region, appealing to highly skilled laborers, entrepreneurs, equity–rich households, and retirees.[3] However, while these studies identified "equity–rich migrants" and "entrepreneurs" as key agents in this rural restructuring process, the demographics of and motivations behind this migration remain less explored, in part due to the macroscale examinations of the migration process. Addressing this omission is important, as the motivations of these middle–class migrants have borne significant implications for the changing landscapes of the western communities they joined and now call home.

Through the processes of migration and consumption, middle-class newcomers acted as the principal agents of change in the rural restructuring process. The migration of relatively affluent "service-class" or "new middle-class" newcomers employed in the professional or service sector profoundly changed the landscape, beginning a process of "rural gentrification." British geographers coined this term to describe the profound changes in the English countryside, caused by the arrival of white-collar middle-class newcomers from urban areas, with occupations in professional, executive, administrative, managerial, and various other services. A range of motivations inspired this migration and similar migrations in the United States, but one major cause was the migrants' perception of the countryside as the ideal place to live and raise a family. Owing to their greater purchasing power, these newcomers greatly influenced the physical and social environments of the countryside through conspicuous consumption.[4]

The transposed trappings of the culture of consumption brought and continue to bring many changes to the Missoula community, particularly within the local economy, culture, and politics. Community identities were reshaped and resources reallocated. The countryside has become commodified, inspiring a privatization of resources that has often become too expensive for the original residents, leading to their marginalization. Conflicts have arisen between the newcomers and established residents regarding this privatization, housing affordability, and issues of environmental conservation. Rural gentrification has transformed the landscape of Missoula, Montana, and the surrounding region.

Population Growth and Rural Gentrification in Missoula

The rural restructuring process in the Rocky Mountain region has attracted attention both in popular media and in scholarly research. However, other than a few studies,[5] little notice has been paid to the changes in Montana. The state population grew from 799,065 in 1990 to 902,195 in 2000, a 12.9 percent growth. This growth occurred mainly in the thirteen counties located in the splendor of Rocky Mountains in western Montana, while the state's other twenty-three counties experienced either no growth or a population decline.

Among the most affected counties was Missoula County. Its population boomed from 58,263 in 1970 to 96,303 in 2002. Standing at an elevation of 3,205 feet above sea level, the Missoula valley is surrounded by the majestic Rocky Mountains. The town of Missoula is the county seat, the home of the University of Montana, and the regional center of population. Missoula is well known for its gorgeous scenery, small-town charm, and liberal politics, all captured by Missoula native and author Norman Maclean in his famous novella, *A River Runs Through It*. Recreational opportunities abound year-round in Missoula. It offers skiing, rafting, hiking, and hang gliding in addition to hunting and fishing. The city of Missoula grew from a population of 42,918 in 1990 to 57,053 in 2000, earning metropolitan status. The adjacent rural county of Ravalli became a bedroom community for Missoula commuters, with a population increase of 10,314 people, or 44 percent, in the last decade of the twentieth century.[6] Historically, Missoula's economy was based on extractive industries (primarily wood and paper products) and farming. However, as a nationwide decline in these industries in the past thirty years resulted in a rise in service-sector activities such as education, medicine, recreation, forest products, and retailing, Missoula emerged as the primary service provider for western Montana. Despite this economic restructuring, incomes remained low in the region, with the average wage in Missoula County reaching only $29,635 by the year 2005.[7]

The number of newcomers and the fact that most of them earned more than the county's average income have helped change Missoula. Its physical and social landscapes soon depicted the powerful consequences of population growth and rural gentrification, including escalating real estate values, the emergence of prestigious neighborhoods and new housing tastes, the creation of "western living" as a positional good, conspicuous consumption, the privatization of open space, and the emergence of new cultural institutions and events. All of these changes have sparked community debates. Housing has been one of the most affected areas, marked by both a boom in housing construction and a steep rise in prices. In 1989, for example, the median sale price of homes in Missoula was $54,965, a price within the reach of most Missoulians, who earned an average annual wage of $17,454 at the time.[8] By 2006, however, the median selling price of homes in less desirable neighborhoods was $218,000. The cost of a new house of high-quality construction that boasted a good location reached $350,000.[9] Both planners and real estate agents attributed this rapid escalation of house prices to the increasing demand and the purchasing power of affluent newcomers.[10] By 1999 some 75 percent of Missoula households lacked adequate income to meet purchase prices, placing home ownership out of the reach of many native Missoulians.[11]

With greater purchasing power than many of Missoula's longtime residents, newcomers commodified more and more open space, transforming it into expensive low-density subdivisions with homes that differed in style, size, and price from prior construction. Some homes were four to five thousand square feet.[12] Traditionally, housing in Missoula has tended to be plain and compact, located mainly in the heart of the town, on smaller lots. In contrast, new houses were large, located on the mountain slopes or open farmlands, commanded the best views of the surrounding mountains, and offered easy access to recreational opportunities, many practically in their backyards. New consumption tastes are also reflected in the construction of new log homes, large barn-style houses, and houses with large verandas, brass carriage lanterns, and partial rock facades that evoke the theme of leisurely country living. The interiors of these homes are frequently decorated in country styles and in distinct western themes. These stylish new constructions situated on the best locations are a powerful "positional good."[13] A positional good is a commodity in short supply, the access to which is dependent on a person's economic and cultural capital.[14]

Fieldwork reveals that an overwhelming number of newcomers lived in new subdivisions, despite a new city ordinance promoting urban infill development. In fact, most new construction has occurred beyond the city limits, where developers bought tracts of vacant, inexpensive farmland and transformed it into new housing. As noted above, Missoula County has grown more rapidly than the city of Missoula. Preexisting subdivision regulations had designated these areas for low-density rural development. Taking advantage of low-density development clauses, developers built houses on large lots, ranging anywhere from two to twenty acres, increasingly in gated communities in the countryside of Missoula and Ravalli counties. Despite their rural locations, these neighborhoods are well connected to the city proper through major roads, allowing residents to reach the city in twenty minutes or less, although demands for new secondary roads, libraries, schools, and emergency response systems to serve these new subdivisions considerably stressed the city and county budgets. These new neighborhoods repackaged a Rocky Mountain lifestyle with quick access to modern city amenities.

Developers and real estate agents have played a critical role in shaping the new residential landscape of the Missoula region and promoting rural gentrification. As the planning staff of Missoula County noted, "There are plenty of opportunities to provide lower end market rate housing in this town . . . but of the total developers only a few do it . . . because they can make a lot more profit per unit on custom houses."[15] As such, the developers and real estate agents have catered to consumer preferences for elite landscapes that generate the largest profit margins. This pattern of development illustrates the linkages between the production side and the consumption side of rural gentrification.[16]

As the Missoula region's elite migrants transformed the landscape, they also transformed consumption patterns in the city of Missoula. By 2000 trendy boutiques, shopping malls, gourmet restaurants, and designer sports and recreation stores were found all across the town. Missoula's new sites of consumption and leisure displayed an urban sophistication in stark contrast to the town's working-class past.[17] Other institutions changed the city's cultural landscape. It now boasts of having the Montana Repertory Theater, String Orchestra of the Rockies, and Garden City Ballet Company. Missoula also hosts a number of international events, such as the International Choral Festival and International Wild Life Film Festival. In addition to several art museums, some fifteen art galleries grace the city's streets, offering many evening events. Regional artists and craftspeople market expensive handmaid articles at frequent bazaars.

The changing community, in its transition from a blue-collar mill town to an elite landscape of urbane sophistication, is perhaps best exemplified by downtown Missoula. This district experienced a steady decline even in the 1980s, as regional industries failed. Retail businesses left the downtown, and many old buildings fell into states of disinvestment, disrepair, and abandonment. By the twenty-first century, historic buildings have been renovated and restored to house art galleries, pricey boutiques, expensive antique stores, and gourmet food stores. The eating establishments of the downtown changed as well. Working-class bars and cheap restaurants that dotted downtown Missoula until the early 1990s have been slowly edged out through high rents, giving way to the establishment of upscale pubs and stylish restaurants. The new residents brought new consumer tastes and interjected them into their new community, helping to commodify the downtown landscape. It became a "positional good" that claimed the newcomers' greater wealth.[18] The historic downtown now acted as a fashionable playground whose charming ambience projected a sophistication that the newcomers understood. It provided them with a familiar cultural playground akin to what they left behind in the cities from which they had migrated. Perhaps the transformation is best observed in a recent trend—the widespread proliferation of stylish coffeehouses throughout the town.

Past research has revealed that the lifestyle choices and consumption patterns of the service class and new middle class, reflected in housing, shopping centers, eateries, and recreational centers, have been central to the process of urban gentrification.[19] A similar culture of consumption has also occurred in other towns and regions undergoing rural gentrification. In the case of Missoula, the emergence of a more cosmopolitan eating arena has been welcomed and readily utilized by the newcomers, many of whom complained about the lack of variety among restaurants when they first arrived in Missoula.[20] Such shifting landscape tastes have become crucial positional goods that serve as a form of cultural capital for the newcomers.[21] The process of gentrification in Missoula introduced a wealthier class of population, and with their greater economic and cultural capital, they, in turn, influenced the creation of new landscapes while erasing older, established ones.[22]

Escalating housing prices, the growth of gated communities, and the gentrification of Missoula's leisure spaces have not pleased many of the city's long-term residents.[23] The changes in the housing market, for instance, have created significant tension among those long-term residents who are unable to afford the "new Missoula" owing to their lower salaries and increasingly face displacement.[24] In *Collapse*, Pulitzer Prize–winning author Jared Diamond addresses the changes in western Montana, observing that polarization has occurred along different axes: "rich versus poor, old-timers versus newcomers, those clinging to a traditional lifestyle versus other welcoming change, pro-growth versus anti-growth voices, those for and against governmental planning, and those with and without school-age children. Fueling these disagreements are Montana's paradoxes . . . a state with poor residents attracting rich newcomers, even while the state's own children are deserting Montana upon graduating high school."[25]

The long-term residents have reacted with anger at the consumption of slopes, hilltops, and open land for housing, fearing environmental damage and the loss of habitat for wildlife. The changes in the cultural landscapes are equally jarring to long-term residents, who find Missoula to be a "yuppie town," different from its historic "down-to-earth" identity. In June 2008, for example, Eric Hurd complained about efforts to build more of the local economy around the arts. In a letter ("Artsy City Doesn't Benefit Working Class") to the *Missoulian*, Hurd spoke to an underlying tension: "The arts market is unstable. In Missoula, as elsewhere, the arts market is sustained in the main by gentrifiers (nonnative, land-owning elites intent on building 'culture' in their novel communities). They buy the art. . . . What is good for gentrifiers is bad for the rest of us. . . . Not only are many locals displaced by the influx of gentrifiers, so too are their institutions."[26] Overall, many long-term residents perceive that Missoula has been gentrified at their expense to cater to the tastes of more affluent newcomers.

Community conflicts over issues of rapid growth, affordable housing, and environmental protection have led to the implementation of significant growth-management policies in Montana, a state reputed for its antiregulatory attitude and fierce independence. Over the past decade Missoula's city government has enacted an urban-growth boundary and passed ordinances that encourage infill housing and assess impact fees for new subdivisions to the developers. However, the outcomes of such planning regulations have been uneven and have failed to curb the ongoing gentrification process.[27]

Migration Patterns in Missoula

Counterurbanization and rural-gentrification processes are marked by strong urban-to-rural migration trends, in which migrants increasingly choose to live in rural locations that offer high amenities. An examination of county-to-county migration data sets between 1985–90 and 1995–2000 has revealed four critical patterns about the process of migration to Missoula. First, the data indicate that the migration to Missoula has been and remains predominantly urban to rural. Between 1985 and 1990 seven states acted as the primary sources of migrants to Missoula. Ranked in the order of their importance, these states are California, Washington, Idaho, Utah, Texas, Oregon, and Colorado. These seven continued to act as the primary sources of migrants to Missoula between 1995 and 2000, but their ranking order changed: Washington, followed by California, Utah, Oregon, Idaho, Colorado, and Texas. Moreover, the majority of migrants from all of these states, except Idaho, come from counties containing large metropolitan areas or bordering such metropolitan areas. Thus, metropolitan regions such as Los Angeles–Riverside–Orange County, San Francisco–Oakland–San Jose, and Sacramento in California; Seattle–Tacoma–Bremerton and Spokane in Washington; Salt Lake City–Ogden–Provo in Utah; Portland–Vancouver and Eugene–Springfield in Oregon; and Denver–Boulder in Colorado have been the major sources of newcomers to Missoula. The big cities of Texas—San Antonio, Houston, and Dallas–Fort Worth—have also sent migrants to western Montana.[28]

Second, the data show that a significant number of Missoula newcomers are from high-immigration states. Among all states, California and Texas, for instance, ranked first and third in terms of the number of immigrants from outside the United States. As previous studies have shown, Americans have sometime perceived immigrants as contributing to a "variety of social costs including higher crime rates, reduced services or increased taxes which imply greater out-of-pocket expenses for middle class residents." Perceptions of these social costs, whether accurate or not, have in some cases combined with racial and ethnic prejudice to prompt migrations to Missoula.[29] This author's survey of newcomers to the region unearthed such concerns. Thus, the large influx of immigrants in some source states has acted as a push factor, motivating newcomers to migrate to Montana, a low-immigration state with a nearly homogeneous white population.

Third, a significant number of migrants to Missoula have arrived from states, such as Washington, Colorado, and Arizona, and metropolitan areas, such as Seattle, Portland, and Denver, that experienced high rates of internal migration. Viewed as desirable places to live, these areas, for example, ranked in the top-ten listings for the years 1985 to 1995. With this internal migration, some residents of these western states and cities perceived a decline in their standards of living, prompting flight to places with similar lifestyle amenities but lower costs and fewer crowds. Newcomers to Missoula, as revealed in the author's survey, corroborate this trend.

Fourth, while Missoula migrants fall within a range of demographic characteristics, a subsection clearly fit the profile of rural gentrifiers. The identification of this subset of migrants is important, as these migrants have created profound changes in the landscapes and social fabrics of western Montana. Gentrification (in both urban and rural contexts) has been broadly defined "as an upward movement in the social status of a census tract." In the context of urban gentrification, scholars have identified the gentrifiers as belonging to the "new middle class" or the "service class" in which income, occupation, and education act as indicators of social status.[30] Extending this concept, the British rural–gentrification literature has identified the rural gentrifiers as newcomers from urban areas who belong to the service class and actively transform the English countryside. The concept of a "service class" used in the rural–gentrification process is practically interchangeable with that of the "new middle class" defined by geographer David Ley in discussing the urban–gentrification process. "Service-class" newcomers are typically white family households with higher educational attainment and higher income levels than the average Missoula resident. They tend to enjoy white-collar occupations.[31] Rural gentrification has become a process of "class colonization" in which the economic affluence of the newcomers enables them to impose a degree of hegemony through their consumption patterns. With this power, they greatly alter existing land use, housing, and retail activities. Consequently, newcomers have reshaped the identity of affected communities such as Missoula.

Migration data derived from the U.S. Census clearly reveal that a significant subsection of newcomers to Missoula belonged to the service class. This group is composed of predominantly white family households, in which nearly 29 percent have an annual income between fifty and one hundred thousand dollars (with 1.25 percent earning two hundred thousand dollars or more). Some 67 percent have occupations that fall within the service sector, and 36 percent have college degrees.

Another 2002 study on Montana's migration similarly shows that a sufficient number of the migrants fit the socioeconomic profile of a rural gentrifier.[32] Local real estate data also demonstrate that a majority of home buyers in Missoula fit this profile.[33] The forty-six newcomers who participated in my survey and interviews confirm this pattern as well.

The demographics reveal that the newcomers' impact has been greater than their mere numbers. First, many newcomers were primarily in the middle stages of their life cycles, engaged in raising children and forming a stable family life. There were, however, older newcomers in the later stages of their life cycles, generally free of child-raising responsibilities and either retired or contemplating retirement. In both groups, men were primarily the wage earners, while the women were engaged in homemaking and child-rearing activities. British rural-gentrification studies similarly noted that rural gentrifiers tended to be overwhelmingly married family households, in which women mainly focused on raising children and being homemakers while men acted as the wage earners.[34] This pattern of asymmetrical class positions within the households in rural gentrification is directly opposite the urban-gentrification scenario, where symmetrical class positions within a household are common and contribute directly to the decision to live at the heart of the city, as such a location allows for the best management of paid and unpaid labor.[35]

Second, the majority of the newcomers in the author's Missoula study earned incomes that are greater than the average Missoula salary. Others were equity rich from the sale of their prior homes.

These facts corroborated the local community's belief that newcomers were wealthy gentrifiers. Furthermore, many newcomers circumvented the problems of Missoula's weak local economy because they arrived with a good professional position in hand or were semiretired or self-employed. The male newcomers who were employed locally were well educated and employed in well-paying professional occupations. Most of these men arrived in Missoula with a good local career position in hand and overcame Missoula's well-known problems of underemployment and low salaries.[36] This group again involved two segments, the first representing men who came with a new job in town and the other representing those who took a job transfer. For both, Missoula was one among several places in the Rocky Mountains region where they had found a good employment position or had the opportunity to be transferred. Some men experienced a salary reduction as a result of their moves, but the relatively lower cost of living in Missoula (in comparison to their prior residential locations in California or Washington State, for example) somewhat compensated for it.

The men who were self-employed (and owned or co-owned successful businesses) utilized different strategies. Some relocated their business in order to move to Missoula. Others conducted their business from afar, with clients that were located in the large cities of the West, Midwest, or Northeast. These newcomers were frequent fliers, usually traveling out of town for at least two weeks of the month to visit client sites. As they explained in their interviews, one reason for their selection of Missoula as their residence over other places in Montana was the availability of a good-size airport as well as other business infrastructure that enabled them to conduct their business from afar. Thus, these men were able to circumvent the less prosperous local economy and maintain their business and income standards, all while living in their ideal location. Such cases were observed in another study as well, indicating that economic restructuring, information technology, and footloose employment have indeed facilitated such people to relocate to amenity-rich western Montana. For both the business owners and the salaried professionals, Missoula represented an ideal choice owing to its combination of strong lifestyle amenities, cultural provisions, and business and transportation infrastructures.[37]

Overall, employment was not a primary motivation pulling migrants to Missoula. Instead, many brought their work with them. Their class positions enabled them to control their choice of location and circumvent a weak local economy in order to live their preferred lifestyle. An array of other factors shaped their migratory decisions and, in turn, reshaped the landscapes and community identities of Missoula.

Migration Motivations Among Middle-Class Newcomers

"Life is more exciting in Montana," or so proclaimed a Montana Pontiac minivan advertisement slogan in 1997. Past studies on the changing Rocky Mountain region have noted that the beauty of the natural landscape, recreational opportunities, proximity to wilderness, reasonable living costs, and the "western lifestyle" emerged as powerful motivations for migration for highly skilled labor, entrepreneurs, and retirees. Christiane Von Reichert, in her 2002 study on Montana migration, found that "the environmental quality and the rural character of Montana attract nearly one in five [newcomers]." Another survey on Montana's migration has noted such factors as "outdoors, scenery, less congestion, hunting and fishing, pace of life, less expensive to live, fewer people."[38] The dominance of the "quality-of-life" factor as motivation behind migration has also been noted in the real estate data on home buyers. Yet few scholars have unpacked this "quality-of-life" motivation or considered its various layers.

The desire to live a Rocky Mountain lifestyle set within the majestic mountains and wide-open spaces undoubtedly has been a critical motivation behind the migration of middle-class newcomers to Missoula. Newcomers identified "beautiful landscape, scenery, and environment," "access to varieties of recreation," the "slower pace of living," and "rural lifestyle/country living" as the most important pull factors that attracted them to Missoula. Even those newcomers who had moved from relatively scenic areas felt that western Montana's beauty far outranked their previous places of residence. For instance, one former Minnesotan who arrived as a faculty member at the University of Montana acknowledged the beauty of Minnesota but added that it "didn't have the mountains. There weren't elk, there weren't deer." Other newcomers who moved from high-amenity cities such as Seattle or Boulder believed that such places had lost their appeal due to overcrowding caused by high internal migration rates. One newcomer from Seattle, an information technology professional formerly employed at Microsoft, observed, "[In Seattle] there are now houses everywhere. There's very little open space.... I think people have this internal need to be with nature. And, when it's not there ... after a while it just starts to drive you crazy." Many of the male newcomers also saw "hunting and fishing opportunities" in Missoula as added attractions. For these newcomers, life was indeed "more exciting in Montana." The allure of a "western lifestyle" matched the magnificent landscape of the Rocky Mountains in attracting new residents.

However, newcomers also selected Missoula because it fitted their concept of a "rural idyll" that would provide a safe, friendly, and attractive place to raise their children. In essence, it represented the "idyllic vision of a healthy, peaceful, and natural way of life" that rejected the urban life in favor of the rural one, as noted in past British studies.[39] In this American case study, newcomers voiced a strong reaction against the chaos of urban life, showing a preference for a simpler rural one. Most of them had moved not only from highly urbanized regions of the nation but also from regions experiencing heightened social tensions as a result of high rates of immigration and other issues. In discussing their former residences, newcomers frequently voiced complaints of "crowds, crime, congestion, endless subdivisions, bumper-to-bumper traffic, long commutes, and a hectic life." Such feelings betrayed a historical rejection and fear of the city by Americans, in which a crowd represented "a fear of organized insurrection, the explosive riots of the marginalized, the crime and random violence of the dispossessed."[40] Indeed, the talk of crowds and congestion they left behind produced visceral reactions among the newcomers. One newcomer family from New Jersey concluded, "We really wanted to get away from people.... Back East there's still a lot of people ... [and we left] because it's deteriorated. I mean, the place got more congested, more traffic, dirtier. You know, people who got more unfriendly." A transplanted Californian summed up his feelings: "Work was only about thirty miles away, but it took me sometimes an hour and a half to get there. . . . The crowd of traffic . . . it's pretty, pretty stressful." In contrast, he added, "when you come here [to Missoula], you think, God, it's beautiful here. Open spaces and you can breathe."

Life in western Montana provided not only a lifestyle free of crowds and congestion but also one of amity and security. For instance, the same newcomers from New Jersey said, "We like the small-town effect. . . . People are friendly [and trusting]. When you offer them your identification when you cash a check they say, 'No, you don't need it.'" Most newcomers described Missoula as a "friendly, safe town," compelling attributes that drew them to the region. This is unsurprising, as newcomers also frequently cited fear of crime as a push factor that caused them to leave highly urbanized areas, even though none of them had personally experienced any violent crime in their former residences. Indeed, they admitted that their suburban homes had been perfectly safe. However, the larger metropolises to which those suburbs were attached represented a threat to them. Historically, Americans have perceived the city to be "a den of crime and lawlessness."[41] In particular, the proximity of their children's lives to the dangers of the city made them fearful as parents. Influenced by the strong pastoral myth that is entrenched in the American psyche and glorifies the bucolic lifestyle, the newcomers have found Missoula to be a safe haven, which they described as a "great place to raise children." As one newcomer stated, "I would say having kids made me more want to live in a place like this. If I was, you know, single or married without children, I would probably want a more active city life." Thus, parental perceptions of children's safety have acted as a major motivating factor behind urban-to-rural migration in Missoula, as it had been in migrations to the British countryside.[42]

In some instances, the high rates of foreign immigration in certain cities have also added to some parents' perception of the city as a social threat, causing some newcomers to Missoula to seek out its more homogeneous setting. For instance, one newcomer interviewee complained of the increasing number of Hispanic immigrants in Southern California, her former place of residence. This woman believed that California has incurred heavy social costs as a result, such as causing cutbacks in her young daughter's art classes in order to pay for the English lessons for the children of illegal immigrants. She felt relieved to have escaped such problems in Missoula. Thus, places such as Missoula also provide an idyllic vision of a predominantly white rural community where the old American traditions of home and hearth were still maintained—a suitable place to live and raise children.

Simultaneously, however, the newcomers also desired a place that contained a certain array of urban amenities in order to satisfy their consumer lifestyles. Thus, most newcomers since 1995 believed that Missoula had obtained the right combination of a small-town setting with certain big-city attributes. In their interviews, newcomers admitted that they were essentially urbanized people who would feel lost in a truly rural environment. To them, Missoula was large enough in size to have an adequate number of urban amenities but small enough to provide a friendly, safe, small-town atmosphere. One newcomer from Phoenix, Arizona, recounted the tale of friends who had moved to a rural part of the Rocky Mountain region to pursue ranching: "It was exciting in the first year; now they have gone back. It's a very drastic lifestyle change, you know. You can do it for a month on vacation, but for a permanent lifestyle, you have to know what you are comfortable with. We knew that we would be lost in a completely rural farming community. That's why we chose Missoula." Another newcomer said, "I like the idea of being close to town and yet almost feeling like you are in the mountains. I wanted the views and a little bit of elbow room." Here is once again the voice of ambivalence in reference to attitudes concerning the city and the country. The urban infrastructures, cosmopolitan qualities, and cultural experiences are all aspects of the city that the newcomers had enjoyed in the past and were unwilling to renounce. Many of the newcomers said they selected Missoula because the presence of the University of Montana "provides diversity" and "brings in young people." "The university," one man stated, "has made the town liberal and progressive in its thinking." As well, the newcomers found, "there are a lot of cultural amenities here" because of the town's growing community of artists and writers. Missoula's beautifully preserved historic downtown, with an ever-growing array of gourmet restaurants, coffee shops, galleries, and boutiques, filled the consumption needs of these newcomers, who confessed that they found the downtown charming and its shops enticing. British scholars have noted that rural gentrifiers in England have been similarly drawn to "various theatres of consumption, especially to small towns with historic cores" that legitimize "service-class consumption lifestyles."[43] Missoula's location in a scenic valley surrounded by the Rockies and its proximity to wilderness and recreational areas (within ten minutes from most parts of the city) provided the opportunity for the newcomers to appropriate the countryside as their playground, while continuing to enjoy urban amenities. One newcomer family in Missoula perfectly captured this balance of city and country. The family purchased two homes, a ranch in the outskirts of Missoula where the husband landed his plane and practiced shooting in the backyard and a house in the city of Missoula where his wife and children fulfilled their social and educational needs.

Missoula's continuing role as a major service provider for the western Montana and northern Idaho region also meant that the town offered other important assets. A good business and commercial infrastructure with a good airport and other reliable transportation and communication services appealed to newcomer professionals whose careers required such facilities. For many, this existing infrastructure proved very influential in their final choice of Missoula as home. Missoula has also grown as a significant medical–services provider to the region, perhaps as a result of the many doctors relocating their practices to the town. The retiree migrants perceived such medical facilities as an important asset and a contributing factor in their locational decision. Missoula thus contains the right set of attributes and represented to the newcomers "the ideal middle landscape between the rough wilderness of nature and the smooth artificiality of the town." Americans historically have sought middle landscapes that combine the best elements of nature and culture.[44]

At the same time, economic factors, such as real estate prices in Missoula, also shaped migration choices. Although Missoula's housing prices have risen sharply in the past decade, they have remained quite affordable to newcomers from the West and East coasts, regions where land and homes are more expensive. The sale of their former homes provided most newcomers with considerable equity. The realization that the equivalent sum of money bought them much larger properties in the choicest locations in Missoula strongly influenced their migration decisions as well. Many purchased or built homes in Missoula at equivalent prices in order to avoid capital gains tax, which, in turn, meant a significant rise in the quality and size of their homes. For instance, one couple moved from Boulder, where the cost of living had become too high because of its popularity as an internal migration destination. They went online to compare Missoula to Boulder and discovered that a person needs to earn 15 percent more income in Boulder than in Missoula to maintain the same standard of living. In Missoula, they were able to buy a large house on the slopes of the prestigious Rattlesnake area of Missoula. For them, "Missoula is where Boulder was thirty years ago." Like other newcomers, these migrants from Boulder had purchased a particular lifestyle at a more reasonable price. This purchase was made possible by the uneven circulation of capital, leading middle–class newcomers to act as capitalists. The gentrifiers consciously chose to buy homes as good investments in what they consider to be cheaper housing markets.[45]

A final factor affecting the migration process of middle-class newcomers is the role of their family and friends. During interviews a surprisingly high number of newcomers claimed friends and relatives living in this region. In fact, many newcomers were introduced to the beauty of western Montana during their visits with family and friends. After multiple visits as tourists, they decided to relocate to Missoula. And, in turn, the migration of these newcomer families to Missoula prompted another phase of migration to Missoula (or adjacent areas) among their family members. There were several instances of chain migration where brothers and sisters (along with their families) had followed each other to Missoula. Similarly, retired parents had followed their adult children to the region, or the adult children and their families had followed their parents. Thus, the desire to live close to friends and family members provided a final motivation for migration.

Conclusion

Rural restructuring in the Rocky Mountains has led to significant growth and change in the region's small towns. Newcomers belonging to the service class or new middle class have acted as important agents of change, migrating from the urban areas across the nation to seek out their rural idyll. The interviews in this case study indicate that such a group has moved from highly diverse, increasingly chaotic urban landscapes to the inner "heartland" of the Rocky Mountain. The motivations behind their migration are complex and involve pursuing an idyllic lifestyle in small and friendly towns containing an ideal combination of urban amenities, packaged in an attractive wilderness setting. Development of speedy transportation and technological innovations such as computers, fax modems, and the Internet has certainly enabled this group of migrants to become more footloose regarding their location decisions. As employment has become more mobile and culture more portable, increasing numbers of middle-class professionals are opting to pull up stakes and move to the relatively unspoiled and beautiful small towns of western Montana. Although aware of the problems of the weak local economy, newcomers have navigated it in various ways so as to avoid compromising their class positions. Moreover, most newcomers had arrived with good savings and equity; these independent sources of income allowed them more flexibility in their lifestyle choices. As one newcomer from California put it, it is almost inevitable that such moves attract moneyed people: "If a man's going to move a long ways, he's going to be coming from the upper salary bracket. You're not going to find somebody that's been working at the service station and can't afford to move a long ways. So, I think you would find that the people in general that move into Missoula have money and find the prices of houses and food and so on and so forth are at a level that they like. So, they feel comfortable and are moving in and settling down."

As middle-class newcomers have continued to settle in their new destinations, their consumption needs have critically shaped the local landscapes and community identities. Upscale retail services have sprung up to cater to the newcomers, as have expensive low-density subdivisions created in the choicest locations in what once was open farmland or unspoiled mountain slopes. Such subdivisions are almost inevitably occupied by various newcomers. Although the newcomers' infusion of money created high-wage construction and service jobs that fed the overall economy and increased the property tax base, these new developments also fragmented open space, converted working forests and farms into homes, increased the price of land, degraded water sources, increased sprawl, eliminated wildlife habitats, and drained tax dollars for far-flung services.[46]

Open space and mountain views became commodified and privatized and are now positional goods that only the wealthy can afford. The consumption and privatization of open space and escalating real estate prices coupled with underemployment and low salaries among longtime residents have created tremendous tensions in Missoula, as few Montanans can now afford to live in western Montana.[47] The newcomers are well aware of these issues. As one newcomer noted, "I would feel a little bit like that if it were my hometown that was being invaded." Moreover, once they were established, newcomers also expressed their own concerns about the impacts of further growth, as it would then affect the quality of life that they value. Thus, most of these newcomers strongly supported the implementation of growth-management policies and wanted strict regulations to check unplanned growth. For example, after he retired Jim Glidden and his wife, Sarah, moved from New Hampshire in 2000 to a home on Deschamps Lane, where zoning limited construction to one house per five acres. In 2005, to their dismay and over their objections, the Missoula County commissioners approved developers' request for a zoning change that allowed them to build a new subdivision of twenty-one homes on forty-six acres of neighboring land.[48]

In many ways the Montana experience is similar to the rural-gentrification process in Britain, where migrants from the new middle class or service class left their city lives and moved into the English countryside, attracted by a vision of the rural idyll. In both the United States and England, people viewed the countryside

TABLE 5.1
Socioeconomic Characteristics of Migrants

Category	New Migrants (%)
Age	
5–19 years	22.07
20–29 years	37.57
30–39 years	16.26
40–49 years	10.94
50–64 years	8.06
70 years and older	5.09
Education	
Less than 9th grade	1.79
9th–12th grade, no diploma	5.11
High school graduate	24.11
Some college, no degree	25.72
Associate degree	6.91
Bachelor's degree	25.78
Graduate or professional degree	10.58
Occupation	
Management, business, financial	8.94
Professional and related	22.05
Protective or other service	21.33
Sales and related	14.81
Office and administrative support	15.29
Farming, fishing, forestry	0.96
Construction, extraction	5.08
Installation, maintenance, repair	2.97
Production	3.56
Transportation, material moving	5.01
Household Income	
Under $25,000	37.48
$25,000–$49,999	32.43
$50,000–$74,999	17.51
$75,000–$99,999	6.92
$100,000–$199,999	4.41
$200,000 or more	1.25
Industry	
Agriculture, forestry, fishing, hunting	2.49
Mining	0.04
Construction	6.02
Manufacturing	4.71
Wholesale trade	2.48
Retail trade	15.37
Transportation, warehousing, utilities	4.23
Information	3.17
Finance, insurance, real estate, rental, leasing	4.85
Professional, scientific, management, administrative, waste-management services	9.14
Educational, health, social services	23.83
Arts, entertainment, recreation, accommodation, food services	16.21
Other services	5.12
Public administration	2.36

Source: County-to-County Migration Data, 1995–2000

TABLE 5.2
Socioeconomic Characteristics of Newcomers

Category	Newcomers Male (%)	Newcomers Female (%)
Education		
Less than high school	0	0
High school graduate	13	17
Some college, no degree	13	30
Associate degree	4	0
Bachelor's degree	35	26
Graduate or professional degree	35	27
Occupation		
Executive, administrative, managerial, and professional	79	58
Technicians and related support	—	17
Sales/clerical service	11	8
Service	5	—
Operatives	5	—
Industry		
Agriculture, forestry, fishing, hunting	5	—
Construction (company owned by newcomers)	16	8
Finance, insurance, real estate	21	—
Professional–health	—	8
professional–education	21	25
Other services	21	58
Public administration	11	—

Source: Survey of newcomers by author

TABLE 5.3
Salary Distribution of Newcomers

Newcomer Household Income Levels	Percent of Households
Under $25,000	0
$35,000	4
$35,000–$45,999	19
$50,000–$74,999	43
$75,000–$100,000	19
$100,000 or more	15

Source: Survey of newcomers by author

as a healthy, tranquil area with a friendly community. They perceived the countryside as the ideal place to live and raise children, a perfect escape from the violent and chaotic urban environment. But their very migration has changed the idyll they sought, prompting spiraling real estate prices, privatization and commodification of open land, changing consumption patterns, and the marginalization of original residents who can no longer afford that place. Community conflicts have ensued, leading to enactment of strict land-use regulations. Most newcomers have supported such policy enactments, in order to prevent further growth that would spoil their rural idyll. The process of rural gentrification has been enacted in the American countryside. In the case of western Montana, it is clear that the good life in this "last best place" is increasingly available only to the privileged.

Notes

1. I conducted case-study research in Missoula from 1996 to 2005. I also examined county-to-county migration data sets (1985-90, 1995-2000) provided by the U.S. Bureau of Census and migration data from Missoula's real estate and planning reports (1996-2002). I conducted questionnaire surveys followed by semistructured interviews among forty-six newcomers and thirty long-term residents in Missoula, all middle-class home owners. Unless otherwise noted, all quotations are from these interviews. I also interviewed the mayor, members of the planning department and city council, developers, real estate agents, and community activists.

2. Michael Elliott et al., "The West at War," *Newsweek,* July 17, 1995, 24–28; Christopher Farley, "Sorry No Vacancies: Worried That Their Way of Life Is Threatened, Rocky Mountain Residents Fight Growth," *Time,* August 7, 1995, 34–35; Rina Ghose, "'A Realtor Runs Through It': Rural Gentrification and the Changing Cultural Landscape of Missoula, Montana" (Ph.D. diss., University of Wisconsin-Milwaukee, 1998); Peter B. Nelson, "Rural Restructuring in the American West: Land Use, Family, and Class Discourses," *Journal of Rural Studies* 17 (2001): 395–407.

3. J. Matthew Shumway and James A. Davis, "Nonmetropolitan Population Change in the Mountain West, 1970-1995," *Rural Sociology* 61 (1996): 513–29; Alexander C. Vias, "Jobs Follow People in the Rural Rocky Mountain West," *Rural Development Perspectives* 14 (1999): 14–23; Christiane Von Reichert and Jim Sylvester, "Motives for Migration: A Study of Montana Newcomers," *Montana Business Quarterly* (Winter 1998): 15–19; Christiane Von Reichert and Jim Sylvester, "Returning and New Montana Migrants: Socio-economic and Motivational Differences," *Growth and Change* 33 (2002): 133–51; Gundars Rudzitis, "Migration, Sense of Place, and Nonmetropolitan Vitality," *Urban Geography* 12 (1991): 80–88, and *Wilderness and the Changing American West* (New York: John Wiley and Sons, 1996)

4. Brian P. McLaughlin, "Rural Policy in the 1980s: The Revival of the Rural Idyll," *Journal of Rural Studies* 2 (1986): 81–90; Jo Little, "Gender Relations in Rural Areas: The Importance of Women's Domestic Role," *Journal of Rural Studies* 3 (1987): 335–42, and "Gentrification and the Influence of Local Level Planning," in *Rural Planning: Policy Into Action?* edited by Paul Cloke (London: Harper and Row, 1987), 185–99; Howard Newby, *Country Life: A Social History of Rural England* (London: Weidenfield and Nicholson, 1987); S. Harper, "People Mov-

ing Into the Countryside: Case Studies of Decision Making," in *People in the Countryside: Studies of Social Change in Rural Britain*, edited by Tony Champion and Charles Watkins (London: Paul Chapman, 1991), 22–37.

5. Von Reichert and Sylvester, "Motives for Migration"; Jim Sylvester et al., "Montana Migration Patterns," *Montana Business Quarterly* 33 (1995): 2–13; Von Reichert and Sylvester, "Returning and New Montana Migrants."

6. U.S. Bureau of the Census, 2001, http://www.census.gov. Moreover, continued growth is anticipated; the projected population of the county in the year 2010 is 107,000 (Missoula Area Economic Development Corporation, *Missoula Community Profile, 1986–2000* [Missoula: Missoula Area Economic Development Corporation, 2000]).

7. Missoula Area Economic Development Corporation, 2007.

8. Missoula Housing Authority, 1989.

9. Missoula Area Economic Development Corporation, 2007. By 2006 the average monthly rent reached $679 as well.

10. Missoula County Board of Realtors 1993, 2001; City of Milwaukee, 2000.

11. Missoula Housing Authority, 1999.

12. Rina Ghose, "Big Sky or Big Sprawl? Rural Gentrification and the Changing Cultural Landscape of Missoula, Montana," *Urban Geography* 25 (2004): 528–49.

13. Fred Hirsch, *Social Limits to Growth* (Cambridge: Harvard University Press, 1976); Paul Cloke and Nigel Thrift, "Class and Change in Rural Britain," in *Rural Restructuring: Global Processes and Their Responses*, edited by Terry Marsden, Philip Lowe, and Sarah Whatmore (London: David Fulton Publishers, 1990), 165–81; Martin Phillips, "Rural Gentrification and the Processes of Class Colonization," *Journal of Rural Studies* 9 (1993): 123–40.

14. Pierre Bourdieu, *Distinction: A Social Critique of the Judgment of Taste* (London: Routledge, 1984).

15. Interviews with staff, Office of Planning and Grants, 2001.

16. Phillips, "Rural Gentrification."

17. Ghose, "Big Sky or Big Sprawl?"

18. Hirsch, *Social Limits to Growth*; Newby, *Country Life*; Cloke and Thrift, "Class and Change in Rural Britain," 170–72.

19. Sharon Zukin, *Loft Living: Culture and Capital in Urban Change* (Baltimore: Johns Hopkins University Press, 1982); Mike Featherstone, *Consumer Culture and Postmodernism* (London: Sage, 1991).

20. Ghose, "'A Realtor Runs Through It'" and "Big Sky or Big Sprawl?"

21. James S. Duncan and Nancy G. Duncan, "The Aestheticization of the Politics of Landscape Preservation," *Annals of the Association of American Geographers* 91 (2001): 387–409; David Ley, "Past Elites, Present Gentry: Neighborhoods of Privilege in Canadian Cities," in *The Changing Social Geography of Canadian Cities*, edited by Larry S. Bourne and David F. Ley (Montreal: McGill–Queens University Press, 1993).

22. Bourdieu, *Distinction*.

23. For a detailed analysis of the community changes and individuals' responses, see Ghose, "Big Sky or Big Sprawl?"

24. Missoula consolidated plan for federal fiscal years 1999-2003 in Missoula Area Economic Development Corporation, *Missoula Community Profile, 1986-2000*; and Ghose, "'A Realtor Runs Through It.'"

25. Jared Diamond, *Collapse: How Societies Choose to Fail or Succeed* (New York: Viking, 2005), 56.

26. Letter to the editor, *Missoulian*, June 8, 2008.

27. Ghose, "'A Realtor Runs Through It.'"

28. U.S. Bureau of the Census, 2001, http://www.census.gov. These migration patterns were confirmed by my own surveys as well as other sources mentioned in note 1.

29. William H. Frey, *Immigration, Internal Out-movement, and Demographic Balkanization in America: New Evidence for the 1990s*, PSC Research Reports No. 96-364 (Ann Arbor: Population Studies Center, University of Michigan, 1996), 7.

30. Ley, "Past Elites, Present Gentry," 232.

31. David F. Ley, "Gentrification and the Politics of the New Middle Class," *Environment and Planning D: Society and Space* 12 (1994): 54-56.

32. According to this study, some 39.5 percent of newcomers are college graduates, 17.3 percent have an annual income between fifty and one hundred thousand dollars, while 4 percent have incomes of one hundred thousand dollars or more (Von Reichert and Sylvester, "Returning and New Montana Migrants").

33. Lambros Real Estate, Missoula, Montana, Real Estate Records, 1993-2001; personal interviews, 1996, 2001.

34. Little, "Gender Relations in Rural Areas"; Phillips, "Rural Gentrification"; Gill Valentine, "A Safe Place to Grow Up? Parenting Perceptions of Children's Safety and the Rural Idyll," *Journal of Rural Studies* 13 (1997): 137-48.

35. Damaris Rose, "A Feminist Perspective of Employment Restructuring and Gentrification," in *The Power of Geography: How Territory Shapes Social Life*, edited by Michael Dear and Jennifer Wolch (Boston: Unwin Hyman, 1989), 118-35; A. Warde, "Gentrification as Consumption: Issues of Class and Gender," *Environment and Planning D: Society and Space* 9 (1991): 223-32; Phillips, "Rural Gentrification."

36. Diamond, *Collapse*, 60.

37. Shannon H. Jahrig, "Have Computer and Fax Modem, Will Travel: NY City Analyst Becomes Montana Lone Eagle," *Montana Business Quarterly* (Summer 1995): 12-16.

38. Rudzitis, "Migration, Sense of Place, and Nonmetropolitan Vitality" and *Wilderness and the Changing American West*; Von Reichert and Sylvester, "Returning and New Montana Migrants," 143; Sylvester et al., "Montana Migration Patterns," 5.

39. Little, "Gentrification and Local Level Planning," 186.

40. John R. Short, *Imagined Country: Society, Culture, and Environment* (London: Routledge, 1991), 45.

41. Ibid., 46.

42. Paul Cloke and Nigel Thrift, "Intra-class Conflict in Rural Areas," *Journal of Rural Studies* 3 (1987): 321–33; Cloke and Thrift, "Class and Change in Rural Britain"; Little, "Gender Relations in Rural Areas" and "Gentrification and Local Level Planning"; Valentine, "A Safe Place to Grow Up?"

43. Cloke and Thrift, "Intra-class Conflict," 327.

44. Short, *Imagined Country*, 35; Robert A. Beauregard, *Voices of Decline: The Postwar Fate of the U.S. Cities* (Oxford: Blackwell, 1993).

45. Again, this is similar to the findings in British rural gentrification studies, such as Phillips, "Rural Gentrification."

46. Michael Jamison, "Montana Is the Hot Spot, Planners Say," *Missoulian*, October 8, 2005.

47. Ghose, "Big Sky or Big Sprawl?"

48. Ginny Merriman, "Residents of Rural Area West of Missoula Band Together to Protest 21-Unit Subdivision," *Missoulian*, February 11, 2005.

Part II

TOURISM, MEMORY, AND WESTERN URBAN IDENTITIES

By the late nineteenth century, cities were the dominant organizers of community and environment. "No environment," writes Philip Dreyfus, "could really escape the grasp of an increasingly dominant urban civilization."[1] Certainly, this was true of Napa County, California, as well as the national parks. Essays by Kathleen Brosnan and Susan Rugh explore the ways in which tourist demands led to the development of getaway destinations: rural or wilderness places in the hinterlands near western cities that offered urban and suburban amenities to vacationers. In the 1960s Napa County supervisors designated their famous valley an agricultural preserve, rejecting the sprawl that otherwise defined the San Francisco Bay Area. Kathleen Brosnan argues, however, that sustaining the preserve depended, in part, on molding a wine tourist culture that mixed the bucolic with urbane accoutrements at a price tag for wealthier American vacationers. Napa's reputation as a resort destination attracted an elite population that matched the reputation of rarity and prestige that regional businessmen cultivated for their increasingly popular commodity.

A similar phenomenon occurred in the West's national parks where less affluent but still middle-class visitors escaped the cities and suburbia, hoping to encounter nature on the utopian family vacation. What they created, however, was a civilized wilderness, as Susan Rugh demonstrates. Visitors and park officials adapted the landscape to meet the needs and desires of tourists. Far from roughing it in an unadulterated natural setting, visitors brought with them many of the amenities of home, patronized the parks' grocery stores, and took advantage of amenities such as laundry services. Tourism created artificial and temporary communities in which people reinforced cultural identities through the acquisition of and experience in nature.

As places of intersecting cultural geographies and diverse populations, western cities were also sites of struggles over whose narrative of the past would dominate community culture and civic identity. In cities such as Santa Fe, Monterey, and Seattle, some westerners looked to revitalize downtowns, neighborhoods, and entertainment districts by constructing and marketing an idyllic past that ignored their communities' multilayered histories. In the 1920s, as Jeffrey Sanders discusses, a debate over public art revealed a community competition over which historical memory of New Mexico's frontier and territorial history—one defined by the Camino Real or one defined by the Santa Fe Trail—would give Santa Fe its identity.

Residents of other western cities had few illusions that those places were or could be Edenic gardens. Nonetheless, they still hope to improve their communities by idealizing important parts of their histories. In Monterey, California, Connie Chiang tells us, the city and private groups have restored Cannery Row and made it a viable tourist attraction. Their image of a workers' utopia depends, as it did in John Steinbeck's novel, on overlooking the labor disputes and ethnic conflicts that frequently defined the sardine industry. In Seattle post-1960s downtown redevelopment was influenced by residents' determination to re-create a small-scale neighborhood market. When urban renewal threatened Pike Place Market, a grassroots movement thwarted redevelopment plans, hoping to restore a historical moment when Seattle residents of all classes and ethnicities mingled among European and Japanese farmers selling their wares. Judy Mattivi Morley argues that in the end, however, the market has succeeded as a tourist haven where paintings of vegetable stands sell more frequently than vegetables themselves.

Note

1. Philip Dreyfus, *Our Better Nature: Environment and the Making of San Francisco* (Norman: University of Oklahoma Press, 2008), 96.

Urbanity and Pastoralism in Napa Tourism

KATHLEEN A. BROSNAN

Decked out in red, white, and blue bunting, the pavilion of the Napa County fairgrounds provided the setting in 1952 when the Napa Valley Vintners Association (NVVA) greeted two thousand representatives of the General Electric (GE) Company. The event afforded the winemakers an opportunity to introduce the visitors to the products of Napa Valley. Formed during World War II, the NVVA initiated a long-range public relations campaign to distinguish Napa's best wines from inferior California vintages and to establish new markets for them. Hoping to lure sophisticated consumers and to educate them in the finer aspects of wine, the vintners invited San Francisco conventioneers such as the American Medical Association, the Western Conference of Bankers, and the Associated Harvard Clubs, arranging winery tours and a luncheon for six hundred alumni of the Ivy League standard-bearer. The General Electric gathering stands out for neither its logistics nor its size, although it was the largest event in the NVVA's first decade. In retrospect, it captures our attention because of the nature of the affair—an old-fashioned, western-style barbecue. With neither artifice nor pretension, vintners and guests donned cowboy hats, spangled shirts, bolo ties, and kerchiefs to dine at the plebeian fairgrounds. Napa Valley wines accompanied grub reminiscent of the greater American West.[1]

Some fifty years later, the NVVA hosted a strikingly different gala at the Meadowood resort. The twentieth Napa Valley Wine Auction, held in 2000, attracted more than eighteen hundred guests who paid $2,500 per couple and one thousand volunteers who offered their services to rub elbows with the elite, all while raising $9.5 million for local charities. A retired Silicon Valley executive and first-time participant spent $1.7 million in bids on five auction lots, perhaps buying prestige as much as fermented grape juice. His single largest purchase, $500,000 for an imperial (six liters) of 1992 Screaming Eagle Cabernet Sauvignon, constituted a record for a single bottle of wine. Another guest, a ten-year auction veteran, bid $700,000 for a vertical vintage, or ten 1.5-liter bottles spanning the first decade of the Harlan Estate. Over time, the auction had become part of a larger phenomenon. Festivities covered four days and involved more than one hundred events that by 2003 required patrons to wear "supper club swank" or "Academy-award glamorous."[2]

Life in Napa Valley had moved far away from bolo ties and kerchiefs in that half century. Visitors who wandered across the Golden Gate Bridge in the 1950s found a picturesque rural place. At that time, as local vintners urged Americans to adopt wine as part of daily gracious living, Napa remained home to diversified agriculture that included orchards, dairy farms, and cattle ranches as well as vineyards. Beef generated more profits than grapes. Wine-industry participants, as evidenced by the GE barbecue, seemed to revel in their rural western roots. With changing consumption patterns and greater national affluence, however, U.S. sales of dry table wines rose steadily and finally surpassed those of fortified dessert wines in 1967.[3] Through tours in the valley and tastings across the country, Napa vintners helped lead this transition, but to compete with larger vineyards in California's Central Valley, they sought a more lucrative niche in super- and ultrapremium wines.[4] To support that market position, vintners joined other Napans, tourism entrepreneurs, and the large corporations that purchased some Napa wineries in consciously changing the image the valley presented to travelers seeking sophisticated consumer experiences. Other agricultural activities faded in the wake of new wineries, roadside tasting rooms, and a multitude of restaurants, hotels, and shops catering to wealthy "guests." As Napa wine grew in popularity, it centered its own tourism. Wine and tourism existed in symbiosis.

Designed to attract visitors to the San Francisco region and residents from Northern California cities, Napa tourism offered the pastoral and the urbane in a paradoxical mixture. A trek through the vineyards differed from a walk along Fisherman's Wharf, but also stood in sharp contrast to a visit to an Iowa cornfield. Unlike many Bay Area communities, Napa still contained large open spaces. Prosperous vineyards spread from the valley floor to the hillsides. Large-scale suburban development, for the most part, had been avoided.[5] With the exception of the city of Napa, the valley lacked the population density that typically defined urban living. Yet the valley no longer constituted unaffected countryside. Wine-culture appurtenances promised an urbanity found in few locations. The monocultural land-use and technical systems of postwar viticulture mimicked industrial agribusiness more than traditional agriculture. Connections to the global marketplace for wine and the annual presence of millions of outsiders removed Napa from the isolation that, in part and in the past, determined rurality. Residents and tourists alike began to transmute the Napa landscape into their utopian vision of a cultured pastoral idyll that superseded the realities of place.

This type of tourism was not new to Napa. People had traveled there a century earlier seeking a similar social affirmation. Like the larger West, Napa possessed a long history of tourism. Visitors had flocked to the West for undisturbed wilderness, majestic vistas, and the emblems of a "Wild West" that the NVVA exploited at its 1952 barbecue. In the latter half of the nineteenth century, California became many things to many people: an immense garden, a pastoral enclave, a cosmopolitan place.[6] Napa garnered a small share of this tourism by wedding aspects of these simulacra. Within years of the Gold Rush, visitors came to appreciate its Mediterranean climate and mineral waters. Just north of the San Francisco Bay, Napa County's genteel beauty implied refinement. The Mayacamas Mountains divide Napa County from Sonoma County on the west; the Vaca Mountains rise on its eastern edges. Ensconced between the mountains and carved prehistorically by the Napa River, the Napa Valley has been the county's preeminent geographic feature and economic breadbasket. The valley begins narrowly at the base of Mount St. Helena on the north and opens fanlike into the marshy delta of the Bay. In the mid-nineteenth century, Napa was home to wheat farms, cattle ranches, orchards, and nascent vineyards.[7] Others envisioned tourism possibilities.

Napa County first emerged in the 1860s as an "urban getaway" for prominent San Franciscans hoping to escape the cold summer winds that braced their city. Imitating their eastern counterparts, resorts sprang up around the mineral springs scattered across Napa County. Mineral springs were a marketable commodity, and summering at such spas carried a European tone. Visitors spoke of living like the English aristocracy. Napa, of course, was not the first place to occupy such a niche. Urban elites have used rural areas for leisure as long as there have been cities. In connotations deeply entrenched in Anglo-American traditions, the country offered health, simple virtues, and a more natural way of living, while artificiality, filth, and baser human traits like greed and ambition ruled the city. Wealthy urbanites in the industrial era sought a mythic rurality that romantically placed man and nature in harmony and created an enduring demand for access to the country. "What is idealised is not the rural economy, past or present," Raymond Williams argues, "but a purchased freehold house in the country, or a 'charming coastal retreat,' or even a 'barren offshore island.'"[8]

White Sulphur Springs was the first Napa resort to offer an idealized rurality. Under the guidance of Sven Alstrom, an experienced San Francisco hotelier, it became "the fashionable resort of San Franciscans during the summer." Visitors, including Ambrose Bierce, Hubert Howe Bancroft, and Leland Stanford, made the one-day journey by boat from San Francisco to Vallejo and from there by stagecoach to the springs. Some guests, enamored of the resort, leased land for permanent cottages.[9] Sam Brannan hoped to copy this success. The expelled Mormon made fortunes in Sacramento mercantile and realty during the Gold Rush and later in San Francisco banking, publishing, and railroads, but many viewed him as a reprobate who swindled miners and led the lawless vigilantes. He pursued a European-style resort that might redeem him in their eyes and renamed upvalley land "Calistoga," combining California and Saratoga. His Hot Springs Hotel cost a half-million dollars, but Brannan discovered that his luxuries, including a racetrack, drew a sporting crowd rather than the respectable San Franciscans who frequented White Sulphur Springs. The key to success, he concluded, lay in the construction of a railroad, so that guests could skip long, dusty stagecoach rides, but even with its completion in 1866, elites avoided his resort, especially after Brannan began a well-publicized tryst with Lola Montez. His business struggled and his marriage failed. While evicting a tenant, and perhaps inebriated, Brannan charged the house and was shot. He recovered, but soon leased his resort and left the valley.[10]

A new venture in the 1870s at the southern end of the valley, Napa Soda Springs, eclipsed Calistoga Hot Springs and White Sulphur Springs, proving the fashionable crowd's favorite because of its greater accessibility. "The nearest watering places and summer resort to the metropolis," it allowed businessmen to spend the week in the city and rejoin wives, children, and governesses for the weekend.[11] In describing Napa Soda Springs, Dr. Winslow Anderson emphasized the attributes of the countryside: "One feels envious of the quiet and peaceful rural life when thus contrasted to the busy whirl of the western metropolis." Adding a European element, he compared the resort to "an ancient fortress along the Rhine." The Rotunda Hotel reached seventy-five feet skyward toward a large glass cupola. Guests enjoyed mineral springs, billiards, bagatelle, tennis, and hikes among groves of oak, eucalyptus, and orange trees.[12]

Despite isolated successes, tourism remained a tertiary interest. Napa County was known for agriculture, and viticulture became its centerpiece. Americans, who settled in the valley while it was still part of Mexico, had planted a few Mission grapes that produced musty-tasting wines. Napans began selling commercial wine only after 1860 with the arrivals of German immigrant Charles Krug, American George Crane, and others who introduced vinifera viticulture (European vines). By 1880 Napa was a premium grape-growing region. Oenophiles stressed the quality of the valley's best vintages, although local viticulturalists still produced large quantities of jug wine. Beautiful stone wineries, some like the Beringer Brothers still famous today, became part of the landscape, but in this earlier era, tourism and wine were not intertwined. The realities of the rural economy, which might have included wineries, rarely were part of tourists' agendas.[13]

By the 1910s Napa's luster as a place for summering faded for many San Franciscans. The advent of the automobile age made it easier to travel to distant locales, but there was still no direct access to Napa from San Francisco by car. Napa had rarely attracted great numbers from beyond California in its first tourist incarnation, and changes in fashion from rural to urban entertainment left few Americans interested in this small enclave. In literature and popular culture, the countryside had become the habitat of ignorance and backwardness, while the metropolis housed illumination and sophistication. Only a few small Napa hotels continued. Fires destroyed some major resorts; others crumbled to the ground. Prohibition also undermined Napa tourism as the city of Sausalito and neighboring Sonoma County developed reputations as illegal hideaways that attracted the Bay Area's more adventurous travelers.[14]

Prohibition, of course, proved even more damaging to the wine business. The Volstead Act arrived just as Napa vintners overcame an ecological disaster. In the 1890s some ten thousand acres of Napa vines died due to a phylloxera infestation.[15] After a long debate about resistant rootstocks, vineyards began to reappear in the northern end of the valley. In the southern half, however, fewer new vineyards mixed with fruit and nut orchards, fodder crops, and cow pastures, and in the Carneros area, just above the Bay, viticulture disappeared. The new vineyards contained better grapes, and Napa wines regularly received awards at national and international expositions in the 1910s, although most wineries, even those with premium products, still produced large quantities of inexpensive jug wine as well. The future looked bright until 1919. With Prohibition, more than one hundred Napa wineries closed their doors. Under federal law only wineries producing religious or medicinal wines, such as Beringer Brothers, Christian Brothers, and Beaulieu in Napa, remained open. Yet the acres dedicated to grapes grew because the law allowed Americans to make two hundred gallons of wine a year at home. Napa growers turned vineyards over to inferior varieties, such as the Green Hungarian, that traveled well due to thick skins but were inappropriate to the fine wines Napans saw as their signature. After Prohibition's repeal, wineries reopened in anticipation of a new demand for wine, but demand did not rise immediately and overproduction with poorer grapes contributed to a statewide glut. Substandard surpluses exacerbated the weak reputation of most California vintages, and their distillation into highly alcoholic dessert wines seemed to confirm the association Prohibitionists made between wine consumption and alcohol abuse. Shortages of materials and labor during World War II further stalled a return to premium wine production and its extension across the valley.[16]

The Great Depression and World War II also afforded few opportunities for Napa tourism to recover the prominence it once enjoyed among San Franciscans. Guidebooks suggested few reasons for travelers to visit. Mineral waters no longer appealed to most tourists. One 1937 volume identified five hundred interesting, historical, or unusual places in California but included only two Napa sights: Mount St. Helena and the Petrified Forest five miles west of Calistoga. A decade later things were not much better. California guidebooks still had scant few pages on Napa, often pointing people toward Mount St. Helena as the gateway to Lake County amusements. Yet the kernels of future tourism can be gleaned. Fred Abruzzini, winemaker and general manager at Beringer Brothers, began inviting famous guests, such as Tom Mix, Clark Gable, Edgar Bergen, and Jack Dempsey, for well-publicized tours in the 1930s and 1940s. He opened Beringer's grounds for the filming of *They Knew What They Wanted* with Charles Laughton and Carole Lombard. Linking Napa to Hollywood and celebrity culture, Abruzzini's promotions created an image of Napa as a rising star in California's growing constellation of urbane sophisticates. Following a tradition established by Napa vintners at early expositions, Abruzzini and others organized a wine temple at San Francisco's Treasure Island Fair in 1939, but added something new. A map guided visitors across the newly constructed Golden Gate and Oakland Bay bridges to the valley. And by 1947, drawing upon European images, travelers read that "many wineries in [the valley's] towns and vineyards welcome visitors." A year later tourists learned how appealing visits might be. "You'll hear the soft syllables and staccato sentences of Mediterranean-born citizens on the streets if you stop long, and each fall they have a gala festival just as they do in Old World wine districts."[17]

Abruzzini had anticipated the future. In the Napa Valley vintners would profit by introducing tourists to their wines, and tourism would experience its resurgence by tying itself to wine. Wrapping this merger in a veil of European historicity enhanced both. If, as Raymond Williams suggests, the countryside was increasingly perceived as an ignorant backwoods, then wine tourism provided a means to overcome the negative aspects of rurality. Poets had long evoked the mysterious power of wine. John Gay wrote, "Fill ev'ry glass, for wine inspires us, and fires us with courage, love, and joy."[18] As strategies slowly developed, Napans hoped to evoke similar passions. Vineyards, they told consumers, combined the lure of a pastoral idyll with the romantic cosmopolitanism of wine. Napa, over time, offered urban consumers a unique, if only temporary, escape; they seemingly left the city behind but did so for a particular rural landscape increasingly defined by its urbanity.

First launched on a small scale in nineteenth-century Europe, wine tourism became an essential part of the global grape business after World War II. Napans played a major role in developing American wine tourism. In the most basic sense, tourism is a form of consumer behavior. Internal motives drive consumer choices. As historian Hal Rothman concludes, "Tourism, through which people acquire intangibles—experience, cachet, proximity to celebrity—became the successor to industrial capitalism, the endpoint in a process that transcended consumption and made living a function of accoutrements." Tourists shaped self-identities by visiting places that offered social affirmation. Nowhere was this truer than in the world of wine tourism. As other scholars have noted, "Tourism is fundamentally about the difference of place, while wine is one of those rare commodities which is branded on the basis of its geographical origin."[19] Napans promoted their wine and their region in equal measure, projecting the sensuous imagery that began to dominate travel guides and food books in the postwar era. Organized tourism became a regular part of winery operations. It took time for Napa wine to be perceived as a sophisticated beverage and time for Napa tourism to experience a rebirth, but as they developed in a mutually beneficial relationship, both were pitched by their promoters (often the same promoters) to people with the greatest disposable income and the greatest disposition to dispose of it.

Isolated activities gradually cohered into a comprehensive public relations campaign. In the late 1940s the Charles Krug Winery began a monthly newsletter, *Bottles and Bins,* and hosted concerts with tastings. One newsletter captured what vintners perhaps perceived as their marketing challenge: "Contrariwise Americans are rather ashamed of the undeniable national backwardness in the social arts and graces. They shrink from exposure to this lack of savoir-faire, and by thinking of wine in terms of sophistication, they are inclined to develop a phobia toward it." It became the task of Napans to educate people such as San Francisco's conventioneers. The NVVA sponsored a cable car in that city to advertise its wines and to lure visitors to Napa. In a 1954 display of the showmanship that defined his career, Robert Mondavi, then president of the NVVA, prepared a good-natured declaration in response to a fictional work in the *Saturday Evening Post*. In that story, the Duchy of Grand Fenwick asserts that Napa's ignoble wines badly imitate the Duchy's vintages. "With humble recognition of the happiness and touch of ceremony that Napa wines add to dinners and good living throughout America," Mondavi proclaimed Napa wines to be unique. He volunteered "the men and resources of Napa Valley in the defense of the republic and the glory of our American wines."[20] The NVVA wooed travel and wine writers as well. Articles focused on the European romance of the local wine industry. One 1952 story noted, "Touring the countryside, over the back roads and the main highways, the tourist is literally fascinated by the picturesque old stone wineries, nestling against the wooded hillsides—reminiscent of the age-old wineries of Germany, France and Switzerland." Another article that same year in *Holiday* offered the first of many "lifestyle" pieces on the valley. By 1957 Napa and Sonoma wineries centered an essay on the North Bay region in *Motorland*: "The feature of the region which makes the greatest impression on the visitor, however, is the wine country."[21] Napans were slowly reaching their prospective consumers.

They did so just as Americans entered an unprecedented era of widespread affluence that changed consumption patterns. Wine commentators point to various factors that coalesced in a growing demand for table wines as the United States entered the 1960s. The middle class grew larger and its members wealthier. More Americans traveled abroad and discovered wine as a courtly aspect of daily life rather than a pompous display of snobbery or a cheap skid-row binge. The Kennedys evoked a continental timbre at the White House. At the same time, changes in production made domestic vintages more palatable. Better grape varieties and technological improvements in fermentation ensured that tasty and stable wines were regularly available. California vintners developed new products with low-tannin levels or added fruit flavors that helped consumers gradually grow accustomed to higher-caliber wines.[22] Nonetheless, it took time for California wines to overcome their poor reputation. Even as the NVVA distinguished its premium products from those of other regions, many Napa vineyards remained in inferior grapes and sold their harvest to large corporate entities for the manufacture of jug wine.

The comprehensive transition to more noble grapes across Napa and the final transformation to near-universal grape production in the valley required a few more decades, but one international event in 1976 solidified Napa's leadership in

U.S. viticulture. At a blind tasting in Paris, and to many observers' surprise, French judges selected two Napa Valley vintages as the best. The results conveyed to consumers that superlative Napa wines merited inclusion with the world's best. The chair of the Napa County Board of Supervisors observed, "We represent the only County in the United States which has within its boundaries an internationally recognized wine industry." With American notions of affluence increasingly tied to conspicuous consumption, Napa winegrowers promoted their superior wine and its romantic culture.[23] Elite and middle-class consumers, searching for experiences and goods that bolstered their status, readily accepted such conceits.

In the 1960s Napa's tourism numbers jumped significantly. By 1968 the Christian Brothers' Greystone Winery alone welcomed 150,000 visitors annually. In Napa tourists found a seemingly authentic country experience. As the county's orchards and pastures gave way to vineyards, visitors experienced a pastoral idyll through vines rather than prunes and cows. The profitability of other agricultural activities matched or surpassed viticulture's until the late 1960s, but their commodities were not branded with a regional identity as wines were. Travel books increased both the pages dedicated to the "Wine Country" and the loquaciousness of their descriptions. In its 1959 edition, for example, one guidebook provided a brief matter-of-fact depiction of Napa and Sonoma counties with directions. Five years later, in a more poetic version, Northern California visitors learned that the wine trail to these counties had "begun in the Middle East long before the Greeks." And as a result of the NVVA efforts at home and in tastings across the country, the Napa Valley was raised above other California regions in the minds of writers and consumers. By the 1970s it dominated media coverage and guidebooks. *The Wine Bibber's Bible* (1975), for example, identified fifty-one wineries in nine North Coast counties. Only Napa County merited a separate map, and its wineries constituted 37 percent of all selected. Other Northern California districts produced varietals of equal quality, but in wine and tourism, perception was everything. One author noted, "To wine snobs, California vintages grown outside the Napa Valley rank somewhere below Pepsi-Cola."[24]

Although Robert Mondavi was not singularly responsible for the changes in tourism and the wine industry or for the elevated position of Napa in both, his career is particularly instructive on such issues. His father, Cesare, had profited during the 1920s and 1930s by selling Central Valley grapes for home production. Eager to move into the premium-wine business, Robert and his brother, Peter, joined Cesare in 1943 in purchasing the Charles Krug Winery at St. Helena. Peter guided winemaking at Krug, and Robert took over marketing and distribution. In addition to the newsletter and concerts, Robert opened one of the valley's earliest public tasting rooms at Krug in the 1950s. After their father died, Robert and Peter disagreed about Krug's direction. When his mother sided with Peter following a heated debate, Robert left the family business in the mid-1960s. He soon opened the Robert Mondavi Winery, one of the first major new operations since the repeal of Prohibition. His winery stood close to the county's main traffic artery and included small tasting rooms for consumers, retailers, and restaurateurs. More than that, he intrinsically understood the romance and geographic uniqueness of wine tourism. Mondavi later said, "I wanted to have a place where I could hold some cultural events, such as art shows, pop concerts, plays or jazz festivals. . . . We were trying to combine winemaking with the cultural aspects of life. . . . I also believed very strongly in the association of fine wines with elegant cuisine."[25] Mondavi and his staff introduced visitors to their wines, and when those same visitors later purchased a Mondavi wine at home, it reinforced their experience in the valley. The front label carried a representation of the distinctive winery, and the back label held this winemaker's relentless message: "At the Robert Mondavi Winery, we view wine as an integral part of our culture, heritage and the gracious way of life. We believe that wine is the temperate, civilized, sacred, romantic mealtime beverage recommended by the Bible. Wine has been praised for centuries by rulers, philosophers, poets and scholars. Wine has been with us since the beginning of civilization and will be with us indefinitely. Share a glass of wine with us: to good friends, good food and good wine—those things which make life worth living."[26]

Mondavi gave his new winery greater European authenticity through its design. Many nineteenth-century architectural influences in valley wineries, such as Krug and Beringer Brothers, had been vaguely Germanic. Mondavi sought a more specific comparison. Historian Kevin Starr explains that Americans since John Charles Frémont analogized California to the Mediterranean because of similarities in climate and terrain. Bay-region vines brought to mind southern France, Italy, or Spain.[27] In the postwar era new wineries grasped, through architecture, a historicity they otherwise lacked. Mondavi's mission-style winery utilized a "history" with some fact since Napa had once been a distant part of the Spanish empire in the Americas. Nineteenth-century Americans disdained Mexican culture in California but romanticized the mission era whose images Mondavi recaptured in his building.

Another new winery celebrated a Greece of blue skies and whitewashed buildings, art and ancient pageantry, and mythic divinity. Sterling Vineyards played it to the hilt. Opened to the public in 1973 on a hill that bisected the northern valley, Sterling's stone-white winery stood like "an Orthodox monastery on an Aegean island." Its owners eventually planned to produce fine vintages, but the winery seemed to cater foremost to visitors who took a tram to the top for the view.

Across the valley, established surnames like Mondavi and Martini or the seemingly leisurely pace of the evolving Napa lifestyle suggested to visitors a Mediterranean luminescence, but it was another newcomer who most blatantly exploited the imagery of rustic Italy. In 1976 Dominic Sattui built a pseudo-Italian villa and named it for his grandfather Vittorio, a San Francisco winemaker at the turn of the century. More of a delicatessen and picnic grounds, the V. Sattui "winery" initially made no wine and owned no vineyards.[28] Some Napans lamented the "Disneyland" effect of the accoutrements at Sterling, V. Sattui, and other wineries that seemed unrelated to wine production, but these facilities drew new tourists and introduced them to local vintages.

As the symbiotic relation of tourism and wine grew stronger, two threats to their union emerged in the 1960s. First, Napa was the nation's best-known viticultural area, but it produced a very small percentage of California's total wine output. Napa's narrow valley covered only thirty miles with a smattering of hillside vineyards. The broader Central Valley stretched for hundreds of miles and produced millions of tons more than Napa. Second, a trend toward greater urbanization led to the loss of agricultural land in the San Francisco area. For example, farms once filled the Santa Clara Valley, which produced many fruits, including wine grapes and a third of the world's prunes at one time. One writer observed in 1945, "It is a sight to see in the spring, when the whole valley is softly blanketed with blossoms." Another added that "nature intended the Santa Clara Valley to be covered with trees." Instead, by the 1960s, tract houses filled the area that came be known as Silicon Valley. This moniker, perhaps along with the name Levittown, seemed to encapsulate for many all that was wrong with modern suburbia. Examining trends in their own county in 1966, Napa planners envisioned a similar growth pattern, estimating that the population might reach 213,000 by the year 2000—a 223 percent increase over the 1960 figure.[29] Such growth would choke the viticulture that increasingly defined Napa.

Napans found one solution to halt both threats and to secure the agricultural character of their home. That solution—an agricultural preserve—ultimately benefited wine tourism as well. Statewide concerns over the loss of agricultural lands led to the California Land Conservation Act (1965), which allowed counties to tax farms at lower rates than residences. In 1968, with the growing strength of the wine industry, Napa County supervisors went a step further, designating the valley floor a preserve. Zoning laws prevented building on lots of fewer than twenty acres within the preserve.[30] The preserve, as initially instituted, was a backward-looking measure designed to halt Silicon Valley–type suburban growth. Over time, motives changed, and residents expanded and renewed the preserve to sustain the local environment, open space, and the illusion of rurality.

The preserve, which was defined in large part by the Napa River watershed, encompassed primarily private property within unincorporated county lands. The preserve, over time, enforced scarcity. Even allowing for inflation, property values increased substantially as the premium-wine industry experienced unprecedented growth in the last three decades of the twentieth century. And, as intended, the preserve staved off sprawl; Napa County's population teetered just below 125,000 by the year 2000.[31] By strengthening viticulture, the preserve facilitated tourism. Moreover, it seemed to offer visitors to and residents of the Bay Area an alternative to the urban worlds they regularly inhabited. Napa contained accessible open spaces.

The supposedly bucolic character that the preserve seemed to enhance was one of the factors that contributed to Napa's always-growing popularity. By the early 1980s an estimated two million people visited Napa Valley annually and spent $136 million. Many Napans celebrated tourism's contribution to the local economy, but others grew wary of its impacts, as studies of tourism solicited by the city of St. Helena (1983) and the Napa Valley Foundation (1984) revealed. Businesses that served locals closed, and "new establishments on or near Main Street in St. Helena seem more oriented to tourist tastes: four expensive French restaurants, jewelry stores, art galleries, a quality housewares shop, additional delicatessens, a specialty women's lingerie boutique, and a wine-tasting bar." The meaning of these changes was a subject of debate among residents. Some complained about higher rents, the difficulty in finding "necessities," and the expulsion of "oldtimers." Others argued that locals constituted the majority of customers at new shops and restaurants and believed that St. Helena was "too rooted" to lose its "small town character." The mere presence of such businesses, however, demonstrated how well valley entrepreneurs had exploited the balance between tourism and wine. In the early 1970s more than one observer echoed Jefferson Morgan, who noted, "A gourmet in search of a leisurely meal could starve to death in the Napa Valley. . . . For an area that plays host to tens of thousands of tourists, first-rate accommodations and places to dine are sparse."[32] Yet, within a decade, Napans developed entertainments that appealed to such urbane consumers. Vintners proposed combining winemaking with the cultural aspects of life. The restaurants and stores in St. Helena and other valley communities filled that niche for a growing number of tourists.

Equally significant from the perspective of the valley's wine-industry participants was the demographic character of Napa's tourists. Vintners tapped a key group: baby boomers with disposable income. A subsequent study prepared for the Napa County Board of Supervisors disclosed that 56 percent of visitors to Napa County earned more than $50,000 in 1988; the median U.S. family income at the time was $42,200. Moreover, almost two-thirds of the pleasure seekers surveyed had no children, suggesting fewer demands on their wealth.[33] Napans in the tourist trade did not try to be all things to all people. Napa's wine producers had increasingly positioned themselves in the superpremium and ultrapremium market. They expanded their own tourist operations, hoping to attract consumers who would purchase expensive wines once they returned home. The price tags attached to those wines, as well as the gourmet restaurants, Calistoga spas, or hot air–balloon rides, were often beyond the reach of the casual visitor.

These various studies on tourism, however, exposed additional concerns about the more discreet costs to the valley. Residents worried that the changes related to wine tourism might undermine the agricultural activities and small-town character that defined Napa. As the 1983 study observed, "The future of St. Helena is inextricably intertwined with that of the wineries. Quaint as the town may be, the main reason tourists travel through it on Highway 29 (at least initially) is to visit the wineries. It is hard to predict any decline in the steadily increasing flow of visitors to the Napa Valley." In a pattern consistent throughout the valley, 28 percent of St. Helena's employed residents worked in agriculture (almost all viticulture by this time) or wine production (which included guest services at wineries). Another 15 percent held jobs in the retail sector. Although this percentage was comparable to other California areas, it is doubtful that a small town such as St. Helena would have supported a booming retail trade without tourism. Throughout the 1980s and 1990s, tourism remained the fastest-growing sector of the local economy. These jobs had a "multiplier effect" when employees spent their money locally.[34] Many people in Napa Valley had promoted wine tourism, but it began to create a dependency that now seemed to threaten their way of life.

Wine tourism also brought an urbanity to the Napa Valley that seemed antithetical to traditional country living. Napa vintners had married the rural and urban idylls, simultaneously selling the quaint and the sophisticated. And at times it appeared as if the very problems associated with city living followed wine tourists there. Most complaints by residents and visitors surrounded traffic. In 1966 a state proposal to build a freeway through the Napa Valley was one factor that had helped trigger the creation of the agricultural preserve. Given the preserve and in the absence of significant population growth, the state abandoned its highway plan. Consequently, the narrow valley possessed only two north-south arteries, and both, for most of their length, were only two lanes wide. Between 1977 and 1986 daily traffic across the valley increased 34 percent overall, and at certain intersections it almost doubled. Weekends presented the worst problems. Most visitors came by private vehicle for one day only. Traffic jams reminiscent of a big city's rush hour regularly occurred. The St. Helena police hired extra staff for traffic control, and while transiency taxes and sales taxes covered these costs, they did not leave the city with additional revenue. Traffic was particularly problematic during harvests. As the valley entered each autumn and grapes reached full, beautiful ripeness, tourists flocked to Napa to taste wine and watch the crush. Slow-moving gondolas carried the grapes necessary to these activities, but they also inhibited visitors' ability to flit from winery to winery. Tourists, who had anticipated the romance of wine and its consumption in an idealized pastoral idyll, seemed surprised by the noise, dust, chemicals, and pace of real agricultural activity.[35]

Local residents employed in wine and tourism contributed to the congestion. They traveled to and from their jobs alone in private cars because the valley lacked adequate public transportation. By the 1980s the negative implications of the preserve for workers became apparent. As intended, the preserve stalled urban sprawl, slowed population growth, maintained viticulture's primacy, and, in turn, ensured the expansion of tourism. Zoning laws, however, limited building within the preserve to lots in excess of twenty acres (and later laws increased the minimum acreage), forcing most new home construction into the valley's four cities: Calistoga, St. Helena, Yountville, and the city of Napa. Across the rest of the valley, and to the chagrin of many local residents, "McMansions" began to dot the hills on twenty-plus-acre lots. Some newcomers brought the wealth of Silicon Valley and other businesses to "country living" in the Napa Valley and began to dabble in the wine industry. Housing costs escalated beyond the means of many Napa workers. Some lived at the valley's southern end in the more plebeian city of Napa, which received fewer visitors and was 30 percent Hispanic by the year 2000. Other workers increasingly lived outside the county. In the 1960s almost all persons working in Napa County had lived there. In 1980 some 87 percent still resided there. A decade later the number declined to 80 percent. By the turn of the twenty-first century county officials estimated 30 percent of Napa workers commuted from other counties, and they expected the trend to continue. Thus, the value of the multiplier effect associated with the tourist trade diminished over time. James Conaway describes locals' resentment: "They felt it while sitting in a long line of cars on Highway 29, looking up at once pristine slopes dense with conifers and chaparral, studded now with 'steroid houses,' 'muscle houses,' 'McMansions,' all contemptuous names for places built not to live in but as monuments to finance, visited by absentee owners."[36]

Agricultural workers represented a disproportionately large share of these commuters, and agricultural workers were disproportionately Hispanic. One industry participant observed in 1984, "Our cellarmen and laborers may be the family's major breadwinners; they cannot compete with young restaurant and retail workers, who may combine two to three workers per household." The 1990 study of tourism commissioned by the Napa County supervisors, however, suggested that visitor-related employees also struggled to live inside the valley. Much of the work was seasonal. Vineyards and wineries experienced peak employment during the fall harvest and crush. In accommodations the greatest variation—a 40 percent decline—occurred between summer highs and winter lows. Given the nature and seasonality of their work, these employees earned substantially less than the consumers they served. In 1987, while the nation's median income hovered near forty-two thousand dollars, local hotel and restaurant workers made less than one-fourth of that figure (not including tips). Historian David Wrobel has appropriately suggested that scholars "move beyond the 'visited as victims' model in studying the 'toured upon.'" Clearly, Napan entrepreneurs and the large corporations that increasingly bought into the valley had purposefully sought a tourist economy both for its own benefits and to enhance the wine industry. Yet even with the great profits tourism secured, other realities persisted. The same costs commonly attributed to other tourist locales in the West—inflated real estate values, seasonal work, low-paying jobs, increased congestion, interference with daily routines—proliferated within Napa as well.[37] Vintners reaped large benefits from wine tourism, but their workers and other residents often bore its burdens.

The convergence of wine and tourism also had unexpected effects on the agricultural preserve that had enhanced their spectacular growth. Through public relations that targeted wealthier consumers, by establishing a niche in the super-premium and ultrapremium markets, and by adopting the technical advances proffered by the University of California, Davis, Napans emerged as U.S. viticultural leaders despite the comparatively small size of their annual harvests. The growing strength of wine and tourism in the 1960s made it possible for county supervisors to create the preserve. Their ongoing success allowed the preserve to continue. Oenophiles argued that Napa grapes produced superior wines because of their unique terroir—the climate, soils, water, and culture that distinguish vineyards and the wines they produce. Napa grapes, like those from other premium areas, drew hundreds more dollars per ton each year. Such prices gave local growers substantial profits while vintners (often a grower and a vintner were one in the same) sold high-priced wines. As table-wine sales began to stagnate by the mid-1980s, the only market segment that continued to boom was the one in which Napans had situated themselves. Given the potential for profit associated with the Napa Valley appellation, an explosion of wineries and vineyards followed. Newcomers hoped to capture the valley's magic and its commensurately lofty prices. In 1966, when Robert Mondavi opened his new facility, the number of Napa wineries could be counted with one's fingers. By 1988 there were 164 wineries under the Napa Valley appellation. Twelve years later nearly 300 littered the landscape.[38]

With the introduction of more wineries and vineyards, land-use patterns changed. Since the phylloxera outbreak in the late nineteenth century, Napa acreage in wine grapes had never exceeded twelve thousand acres, even during Prohibition. By the year 2000 some forty thousand acres were in grapes. These acres represented more land under cultivation than in any previous year under mixed agriculture. Wine grapes accounted for 98 percent of the county's gross agricultural production.[39] Where were the new vineyards planted? Grape growers turned to the surrounding mountains. Hillside vineyards had been a part of Napa viticulture before Prohibition, but after repeal they had remained relatively ignored until 1970. After that, with the valley floor fully planted, the pace of hillside expansion increased. Those who wanted the cachet of the Napa sobriquet needed the hills. And, for those eager to produce the "cult" vintages that reaped high prices and greater prestige, studies showed that the quality of wine produced from hillsides was superior due to thinner, better-drained soils.[40] Deforestation followed in certain areas, although large strands of trees are still found in Napa County. In 1971, for example, Stuart Smith purchased forested land on Spring Mountain that had been home to a small nineteenth-century vineyard. Smith logged 250,000 board feet of timber and 500 firewood cords from thirty-eight acres.[41]

Many of the hillside operations that followed Smith's over the next thirty years were larger. Expansion caused many problems. In 1980 heavy rains on a newly deforested hill drove an avalanche of silt to the valley floor, blocking the main traffic artery. During a 1989 rainstorm two thousand tons of sediment from a cleared hillside flowed into the Bell Canyon reservoir that supplies the city of St. Helena, turning the water red. Thin soils that stressed the vines and produced superior grapes were especially susceptible to erosion. By 1987 the California Water Quality Control Board identified the Napa River as an "impaired" water body. Sediment filled gravel beds, smothered fish eggs, and changed water temperature and oxygen content. Diversions and road crossings hampered steelhead-trout migrations. The explosion of vineyards contributed to a loss of biodiversity. A third of Napa's native species were rare or endangered. Clear-cutting threatened oak woodlands. Remaining trees competed with grapes for soil moisture. Regeneration became difficult because of fire-suppression methods where vineyards mingled with forests.[42] The dedication of more acres to grapes, by diminishing biodiversity, contributed to pest infestations. Phylloxera returned in the late 1980s and forced the replanting of nearly half of Napa vineyards, although the infestation was attributable to historical choices about rootstock as well as the wall-to-wall planting of vines.[43]

This singular agricultural devotion to grape production led sociologist William H. Friedland to question Napa Valley's rurality. Traditionally and legally, winemaking has been considered "agriculture because the juice, transformed into wine, is biologically active. When aged and bottled, wine continues to 'live' and to be transformed." Serried vines, changing color with the seasons, contrasted sharply with suburban tract housing and minivans, but, Friedland argues, the production systems and the density of winery development transformed Napa into an urban place. In his eyes, "Wineries, storage facilities, bottling operations, and the like resemble factories." Friedland's assessment echoed concerns raised by Napans in the late 1980s. Worries about tourism's impact led to questions about the relationship of agriculture to the plethora of new wineries. To many, the V. Sattui Winery seemed to start a questionable trend in 1974 when it opened a winery within the preserve that, at the time, offered picnic grounds and a deli but produced no wine. To attract more tourists, other wineries reinforced the image of gracious living by offering much more than wine. Cultural amenities included restaurants, cooking classes with renowned chefs, art exhibits, and summer concerts. Urban visitors were confident that they would find the conveniences and amusements of the city in this countryside. Retail stores within wineries sold chocolates, olive oil, and pasta bowls, items at least tangentially related to the idea of wine as "the temperate, civilized, sacred, romantic mealtime beverage," but others included everything from T-shirts and golf hats to binoculars and boccie balls, where the connection to grapes seemed tenuous at best.[44] Eventually, the Napa County Board of Supervisors took up the question of how to define a winery. A compromised ordinance allowed established wineries to maintain existing activities, but by 1990 this included some

164 wineries. Concerts at Krug and Mondavi continued, and V. Sattui still sold cheese and cold cuts. At new operations retail activities were more limited.[45] In the end the ordinance did nothing to slow the waves of tourists—4.5 million annually by 2000—who found an abundance of wine and urbanity.

In the postwar West, Rothman argues, tourism generally served as a replacement economy. This was not case in the Napa Valley. Tourism formed a symbiotic relation with the wine industry. Viticulture dominated the valley, but tourism facilitated its growth. And in the process these activities had transformed the predominantly rural Napa Valley into an urbane enclave defined by participation in an idealized wine culture. That culture and the agribusiness-type production systems employed in the valley removed it from traditional rurality, while also protecting it from uncontrolled suburban development. Visitors identified the bucolic scenery as one of the main attractions of the valley, but the pastoral idyll it suggested competed with highly refined retailing, chic restaurants, wall-to-wall "industrial" vineyards, and endless traffic jams. In the Napa Valley wine and tourism created an economy that employed thousands, albeit many on a seasonal basis and on salaries that denied them access to local housing. Few tourists looked beyond the roadside tasting rooms to notice erosion and diminishing biodiversity or to question how viticultural expansion had altered the valley's character. Napa has proved less an urban getaway or rural retreat and more of a hybrid destination that offered consumers utopian visions of social affirmation, agriculture without dirt, and urbanity without skyscrapers.

In the end Napa Valley's wine tourism had promoted an image of living that combined those aspects of the country and the city most appealing to affluent consumers or those who sought self-identity through consumption and travel. The valley also provided—to those who could afford it—great wine, sumptuous food, stunning scenery, and a respite from the everyday world. Wine tourism proved successful, offering an image of Napa that tried to supersede the underlying, sometimes harsh, realities of its mixed landscape. NapaStyle, a local retail store, selling food, wine, and housewares in the valley and on the Internet, captured in its name the ethereal yet carefully crafted style that had come to distinguish the valley. Perhaps only a handful of the world's wealthiest could afford to bid at the annual Napa Valley Wine Auction, but NapaStyle, just like the wineries in the valley, offered the same vision of pastoral urbanity to many more consumers.

Notes

The author wishes to thank Bruce Wheeler for his comments; the American Historical Association for its Littleton-Griswold Grant; the University of Tennessee for its Professional Development, EPPE, and SARIF grants; and Joe Pratt and Marty Melosi at the University of Houston.

1. "Napa Valley Vintners: The Early Years, 1943 to 1958," album, St. Helena Public Library, Napa Valley Wine Library Association (NVWLA); James T. Lapsley, *Bottled Poetry: Napa Winemaking From Prohibition to the Modern Era* (Berkeley and Los Angeles: University of California Press, 1996), 147.

2. Some 85 percent of the $9.5 million went to charities. Between 1981 to 2002 auctions raised $42 million. Press releases of June 4, 2000, June 11, 2001, and June 10, 2002, http://www.napavintners.com.

3. Regarding profits from crops and beef, see Napa County Department of Agriculture, *Crop Reports*, 1967, 1971, and 2001. Regarding wine sales, see "California Wine Outlook," Bank of America, September 1973, 6–7.

4. *Napa County: Wine Industry Growth*, Master Environmental Assessment, Part 3: Economic Model (Larkspur and Berkeley, Calif.: Agland Investment Services and Economic and Planning Systems for the County of Napa, October 1989), 4.

5. For a comparison of postwar suburban sprawl, see maps 14 (Napa) and 19–20 (Santa Clara) in Robert C. Berlo, *Population History Maps of California Places, 1770–1998* (Livermore, Calif.: Robert C. Berlo, 1998).

6. John A. Jakle, *The Tourist: Travel in Twentieth-Century North America* (Lincoln: University of Nebraska Press, 1985), 240–41.

7. *History of Napa County* (Oakland: Enquirer Print, 1901), 5–6.

8. *Napa Valley Tourism Project*, prepared for the Napa Valley Foundation (San Francisco: Environmental Science Associates, 1984), 9; Raymond Williams, *The Country and the City* (London: Chatto and Windus, 1973), 1, 47.

9. Ben C. Truman, *Tourists' Illustrated Guide to the Celebrated Summer and Winter Resorts of California* (San Francisco: H. S. Crocker, 1883), 205.

10. Campbell A. Menefee, *A Historical and Descriptive Sketch Book of Napa, Sonoma, Lake, and Mendocino Counties* (Napa: Reporter Publishing House, 1873), 179–85.

11. *Napa Soda Springs, California's Famous Mountain Spa* (San Francisco: E. D. Taylor, n.d.). See also *San Francisco Chronicle*, August 3, 1901, 1.

12. Winslow Anderson, M.D., *Mineral Springs and Health Resorts of California* (San Francisco: Bancroft, 1892), 201, 207.

13. Charles L. Sullivan, *Napa Wine: A History from Mission Days to Present* (San Francisco: Wine Appreciation Guild, 1994), 30–70, 103; William F. Heintz, *California's Napa Valley: One Hundred Sixty Years of Wine Making* (San Francisco: Scotwall Associates, 1999), 43–105.

14. Patricia Cooper and Laurel Cook, *Hot Springs and Spas of California* (San Francisco: 101 Productions, 1978).

15. Phylloxera, a louse native to the Mississippi Valley, feeds on fluid in rootstock to destroy vines. It traveled on cuttings to France around 1860, destroying 75 percent of its vineyards, and spread across Europe. The French found a solution by grafting European vines onto resistant American rootstocks. Californians believed that the *Vitis californica* rootstock was immune but soon discovered otherwise. See *Report of the Board of State Viticultural Commissioners for 1889-1890* (Sacramento: J. D. Young, 1890), 6-7, 22; and Sullivan, *Napa Wine*, 61-62.

16. Sullivan, *Napa Wine*, 84-85, 116-23; James Morgan Bray, "The Impact of Prohibition on Napa Valley Viticulture, 1919-1933" (master's thesis, California State University, San Jose, 1974), 63-163; *California Grape Acreage* (California Crop and Livestock Reporting Service, 1979), 8; interviews of Frank Pocai by Irene Haynes, January 9, 1975, and Jerome Draper by Gunther Detert, May 15, 1976, 2:93, 303, NVWLA.

17. *The Chapter in Your Life Entitled San Francisco and the California It Centers* (San Francisco: Californians, 1947), 48; Blair Tavenner, *Seeing California: A Guide to the State* (Boston: Little, Brown, 1948), 429. See also interview of Fred Abruzzini by Nancy Haven, July 11, 1975, 1:51-55, NVWLA; Bert Van Tuyle, *Know Your California: Interesting, Historical, Odd, and Unusual Places in the State* (Los Angeles: E. F. Wallace Press, 1937), 42, 47; and Denzil Verardo and Jennie Dennis Verardo, *Napa Valley: From Golden Fields to Purple Harvest* (Chatsworth, Calif.: Windsor Publications, 1986), 91.

18. John Gay, *The Beggar's Opera* (1725); Williams, *The Country and the City*, 1.

19. Hal K. Rothman, *Devil's Bargain: Tourism in the Twentieth-Century American West* (Lawrence: University Press of Kansas, 1998), 15; C. Michael Hall, Gary Johnson, and Richard Mitchell, "Wine Tourism and Regional Development," in *Wine Tourism Around the World: Development, Management and Markets*, edited by C. Michael Hall et al. (Oxford: Butterworth-Heinemann, 2000), 196.

20. *Bottles and Bins*, July 1953; Robert Mondavi et al., letter to the editor, *Saturday Evening Post*, December 30, 1954.

21. Alice Fisher Simpson, "Trails of Romance: Springtime Tour in Historic Napa County," *California Highway Patrolman* 16 (March 1952): 94; Frank Schoonmaker, "California's Vintage Vale," *Holiday*, August 1952, 103-7; D. R. Lane, "The Unique North Bay Region," *Motorland* 78 (March-April 1957): 5.

22. Improvements in quality are attributable to growers, vintners, and the Viticulture and Enology Department at the University of California, Davis (Lapsley, *Bottled Poetry*, 137).

23. Testimony, John Tuteur, Chairman of the Board of Supervisors of Napa County, Bureau of Alcohol, Tobacco, and Firearms, Meeting in the Matter of Proposed Regulatory Definitions of Appellation of Origin, San Francisco, Calif., transcript, 228; "Cabernet Sauvignon: An Assessment of Supply and Demand," Grape Intelligence Report, George M. Schofield, St. Helena, July 1989, 1-2, NVWLA; *Time*, June 7, 1976, 58. Joseph Epstein suggests that it

is the very "Europeaness" of wine that appeals to American snobs (*Snobbery: The American Version* [Boston: Houghton Mifflin, 2002], 224–26).

24. *Northern California, a Sunset Travel Book* (Menlo Park, Calif.: Lane, 1959), 24–27; *Northern California, a Sunset Travel Book* (Menlo Park, Calif.: Lane, 1964), 47–59, quote on 55; James Norwood Pratt, *The Wine Bibber's Bible* (San Francisco: 101 Productions, 1975), 136; Stuart Nixon, "Wine Country 1974: Would You Believe Counties, Sonoma, Mendocino . . . and Lake?" *Golden Gate North*, Summer 1974, 13.

25. Mondavi received a substantial award from the Charles Krug Winery, privately owned by his family, following extended litigation (Robert Mondavi, interview by Ina Hart and T. E. Wilde, December 29, 1978, 3:212–13, NVWLA). The major wineries in 1966 were Charles Krug, Beringer Brothers, Inglenook, Freemark Abbey, Hanns Kornell Cellars, Louis M. Martini, Napa Valley Co-operative Winery, and the St. Helena Co-operative Winery. Lawrence Kinnard, *History of the Greater San Francisco Bay Region* (New York and West Palm Beach: Lewis Historical Publishing, 1966), 556.

26. Label, 1987 Robert Mondavi Napa Valley Pinot Noir, Burt Wuttken Collection, NVWLA.

27. Kevin Starr, *Americans and the California Dream* (New York: Oxford University Press, 1973), 372–403.

28. In another example, Clos Pegase premiered across the street from Sterling a decade later. Named for the mythic winged horse that released the waters for Bacchus's vineyard, the Aegean-style winery was conceived by its owner as a "marriage of art and wine" (Sullivan, *Napa Wine*, 268–69, 316, 343–44).

29. *Chapter in Your Life Entitled San Francisco*, 35; Tavenner, *Seeing California*, 307; "Population Data of Napa County," Napa County Planning Department, November 28, 1966. Regarding Bay Area urbanization, see "Draft Environmental Management Plan for the San Francisco Bay Region" (Association of Bay Area Governments, December 1977), 2:3.

30. Ralph B. Hutchinson and Sidney M. Blumner, *The Williamson Act and Wine Growing in the Napa Valley* (San Luis Obispo: California State Polytechnic College, [1970]), 1–23; Volker Eisele, "Twenty-five Years of Farmland Protection in Napa County," in *California Farmland and Urban Pressure: Statewide and Regional Perceptions*, edited by Albert G. Medvitz, Alvin D. Sokolow, and Cathy Lemp (Davis: Agricultural Issues Center, Division of Agricultural and Natural Resources, University of California, 1999), 103–23.

31. In 1967 some Napa vineyards sold for three thousand dollars per acre; by 2000 prices regularly exceeded two hundred thousand dollars. See Irving Hoch and Nickolas Tryphonopoulos, *A Study of the Economy of Napa County, California*, Giannini Foundation Research Report No. 303 (n.p.: California Agricultural Experiment Station, August 1969), 36; and *Projections and Planning Information: 2001 Updates for Napa County"* ([San Francisco]: Employment Development Department, 2001), A2.

32. *Study of Tourism in St. Helena*, prepared for the City of St. Helena, California ([San Francisco]: Environmental Science Associates, December 1983), 11–12; *Napa Valley Tourism*

Project, prepared for the Napa Valley Foundation (San Francisco: ESA Planning and Environmental Services, November 1984), 5, 14–18; Jefferson Morgan, *Adventures in the Wine Country* (San Francisco: Chronicle Books, 1971), 53–54.

33. *Planning for Travel and Tourism in Napa County*, prepared for the Napa County Board of Supervisors (Portland, Ore.: Dean Runyan Associates, February 1990), 65–67. The Napa Valley Conference and Visitors Bureau (NVCVB) unapologetically attempts to identify and cater to the very wealthiest consumers (*Annual Report*, 2000–2001).

34. *Study of Tourism in St. Helena*, 1, 3–5, 22. See also, for example, *Annual Planning Information: Napa County, 1984–1985, 1988–1989, and 1994* (San Francisco: State of California, Employment Development Department); and *Projections and Planning Information, 2001*, 6.

35. *Study of Tourism in St. Helena*, 17; *Planning for Travel and Tourism in Napa County*, 19, 82; *Napa Valley Tourism Project*, 10, 25–29; *Annual Report, 2000*, NVCVB; Hutchinson and Blumner, *Williamson Act*, 3–5. The 1984 tourism study, noting local resistance to public authority, recommended private solutions for tourism's ills, and although county officials contended that the visitors had a negligible impact on air and water quality, no viable remedy for ongoing traffic problems has been found.

36. *Napa Valley Tourism Project*, 24; *Annual Planning Information, 1984–1985*, 5; *Annual Planning Information, 1994*, 14; *Projections and Planning Information, 2001 Updates*, A2; *New York Times*, December 12, 2001, E1, 14; James Conaway, *The Far Side of Eden: New Money, Old Land, and the Battle for Napa Valley* (Boston: Houghton Mifflin, 2002), 7.

37. *Napa Valley Tourism Project*, 30; *Planning for Travel and Tourism in Napa County*, 101–4; David M. Wrobel, "Introduction: Tourists, Tourism, and the Toured Upon," in *Seeing and Being Seen: Tourism in the American West*, edited by David M. Wrobel and Patrick T. Long (Lawrence: University Press of Kansas, 2001), 21.

38. *Wineries of Napa Valley*, survey compiled by Irene W. Haynes, NVWLA; *Napa County: Wine Industry Growth*, 4; Mondavi interview, 209–11.

39. In 2001 the gross value of Napa grapes exceeded $354 million. Only four other much larger counties had more acres in grapes. See Napa County Department of Agriculture, *Crop Reports*, 1967, 1971, and 2001; reports on *California Fruit and Nut Acreage, 1919–1953, 1971, 1981, and 2001* (Sacramento: California Agricultural Statistics Service); and Hoch and Tryphonopoulos, *Economy of Napa County*, 31, 35.

40. Napa River Watershed Task Force, *Phase II, Final Report*, prepared for the Napa County Board of Supervisors (Berkeley: Moore Iacofano Goltsman, September 2000), 1–3.

41. The county subsequently placed a moratorium on timber sales in hopes of slowing growth. It did not stop prospective vineyardists from cutting trees. With profits to be made in grapes, they burned timber they could not sell (Stewart [sic] Smith, interview by Gunther Detert, March 9, 1985, 4:249–54, NVWLA).

42. Napa County enacted a zoning law to limit erosion from hillside vineyards, but the local Sierra Club successfully sued to force the county to improve its enforcement of the law. See Napa River Watershed Task Force, *Phase II, Final Report*, 4; and Juliane Poirier Locke,

Vineyards in the Watershed: Sustainable Winegrowing in Napa County (Napa: Napa Sustainable Winegrowing Group, 2002), 32–36, 47, 51.

43. *Integrated Pest Management: Field Handbook for Napa County* (Napa: Napa Sustainable Winegrowing Group, 1997), 2; Napa County Department of Agriculture, *Crop Report*, 1999; "Cabernet Sauvignon: An Assessment of Supply and Demand," Grape Intelligence Report, George M. Schofield, St. Helena, August, 1998, 2, NVWLA.

44. William H. Friedland, "Agriculture and Rurality: Beginning the 'Final Separation'?" *Rural Sociology* 67 (2002): 358, 357; Conaway, *Far Side of Eden*, 369; Sullivan, *Napa Wine*, 349.

45. Napa County Winery Definition Ordinance, *Environmental Impact Report*, prepared for the County of Napa (Point Richmond, Calif.: LSA Associates, December 1989); Friedland, "Agriculture and Rurality," 357; Sullivan, *Napa Wine*, 351–52.

Family Travel, National Parks, and the Cold War West

SUSAN S. RUGH

For Americans ready to tour the country after World War II, the West was the prime vacation destination. In 1949 those who responded to the Gallup Poll's question asking what was the most desirable place to visit if one could go anywhere in the world (all expenses paid) listed California as their top choice, with Colorado second. Yellowstone National Park and the Grand Canyon were ranked fifth and sixth as choice destinations, and the western states of Arizona, Washington, and New Mexico were all in the top twenty.[1] A specialized literature catered to western tourists, explaining how to survive desert driving or how to find scenic sites for snapshots.[2] The increase in paid vacation benefits, the expansion of car travel on the new interstates, and the popularization of the national parks helped create the postwar tourism boom in the West.[3]

The lure of the West can also be explained by Americans' increased desire to participate in outdoor activities or enjoy scenery rather than visit cities on vacation. About one-third of those who took vacations in 1962 visited a federal or state park; of those, three-fourths stated that "being outdoors close to nature" was the reason they visited the park. The western population boom also contributed to nature tourism, since nearly half of those who visited national parks lived in the West. Furthermore, westerners were two or three times as likely to camp outdoors as people from other regions. The rest of the country viewed the West as the national playground with its grand and scenic national parks.[4]

After World War II (during which the parks were essentially mothballed), the national parks offered a utopian alternative to the West's expensive dude ranches and commercialized amusement parks. The leading women's magazine, *Ladies'*

Home Journal, promoted the park as an idyllic retreat from the pressures of modern life. "Today the parks hold for you a promise of release from the tensions of modern living. They do not stress the latest in manmade diversion (tile-lined swimming pools, dance pavilions, movies around the corner) but rather its antidote, untouched nature, with the hope that you may gain from it serenity and knowledge."[5]

Not only did a visit to the parks promise "untouched nature," but it also offered a chance to return to the democracy of the frontier West. "In the lure of their rivers, in steep-walled glacier valleys, the parks hold our tradition of westering. Theirs are the stories our fathers fashioned of pioneers. Of women in bonnets and men in buckskins." Going to the parks was thus a western adventure all in itself, where "this wilderness, this grandeur still await discovery in the national parks system." And because it was "free to all, preserved for all," visiting a national park was a good choice for budget-minded families on summer vacations. Indeed, the parks provided a wilderness utopia, "a magic haven from the traffic and tension of everyday routine."[6]

Those who promoted camping in the national parks might have toned down their rhetoric if they had been among the millions who visited the parks after the war. Caught off-guard by the flood of campers, in 1956 the National Park Service (NPS) undertook Mission 66, a ten-year program to improve their facilities, while the U.S. Forest Service launched Operation Outdoors to increase the number of its campsites from 41,000 to 125,000.[7] Complaint letters from visitors to Yellowstone National Park reveal the reality of camping, with crowded campgrounds, stinking toilets, cafeteria lines, bear attacks, and even death. The tension between preservation and use—preserving wilderness and serving the needs of visitors—made visiting the national parks far from idyllic for many American families in search of a western vacation utopia.

Utopian Visions

In July 1954 the *Ladies' Home Journal* featured a story about how a fireman's family was able to afford a two-week vacation camping in Yosemite National Park in California. Dick and Geegee Williams took their two children, Dickie (age five) and Leslie (age seven), on their first vacation in six years. The story highlighted the vacation as well deserved after "six years filled with important job and financial decisions, an attack of polio, the only big fights of their marriage, and plenty of growing up." During the war Dick served in the navy, and Geegee married him on leave in 1944. Typical of other young couples, they started their life together with little money. He built their house with his father's help; when little Leslie suffered an attack of polio, the National Foundation for Infantile Paralysis paid the bills. On his salary and with a mortgage and car payments, vacations "just don't exist, unless they're inexpensive."

Camping was the perfect solution to vacationing on a tight budget for the family of the young veteran. The drive north from Los Angeles to Yosemite took all day, and when they arrived, they found a spot with a view across the river and a nearby play area for children. They had rented a trailer tent from a fellow fireman, and they had also rented a gasoline stove and a portable icebox. Geegee immediately set up house. She unpacked the four wooden boxes and "set the boxes upright to make shelves, and reorganized everything—food and eating equipment on the shelves, pots and pans on an old card table." They used the camp's picnic table for eating a simple supper, "canned pork and beans, fruit and coffee." The children were in their sleeping bags by eight o'clock, their parents by eight thirty. The first night's sleep was interrupted by a bear that ate the food in a pack they failed to hang high enough; while Dick and Geegee cowered in their tent, a nearby camper scared the bear away by beating a dishpan with a wooden spoon. In the bear attack they lost two pounds of bacon, a jar of blackberry jam, cheese, eggs, and two boxes of chocolate chip cookies.

Dick was the veteran camper, but Geegee was a complete novice. By seven fifteen the next morning, Dick, "who does not cook at home—had pancakes, bacon and coffee going strong." He relished the delights of camping: "M'm-m," he said. "That's camping—a great big breakfast and lots of time to lie down afterward." The family ate heartily, and Geegee washed up the breakfast dishes in water heated on the stove. Dick readied the campfire pit with fuel, put up a clothesline, swept out the tent, "and stretched out on the ground under a shady tree, his day's chores done." Both Dick and Geegee were happy with the change in their routine. "'You can't beat this for living,' he said dreamily." She liked the fact that camping was less housework. "Ideal," she said, "just wash the dishes, fold the pajamas into the sleeping bags, and close the flap on the tent." Freed from her housework at home, Geegee agreed, "It's a vacation for me all the way."

Even cooking was easier while camping. Geegee learned how to broil steak over the fire and "discovered to her delight how really simple it is." Her "boldest experiment" was to wrap "individual portions of lamb stew in aluminum foil" and cook them over the coals. She regarded the results as "absolutely delicious. You get a flavor cooking this way you just don't get at home." The park made it easy for her to do her shopping. Four general stores in the park sold fresh food, ice, and wood for campfires. Stores rented a variety of equipment for camping families, "cooking utensils, towels, tents, even a children's crib." Twice a day a truck visited the campsites carrying milk, eggs, and bread, and a mobile "laundrecar" meant she could do the laundry and ironing any day of the week. Yosemite catered to camping families like the Williamses. "Pretty civilized camping," Geegee said, "but a big help when you go with children."

Camping provided opportunities for family togetherness. Their days were spent visiting Yosemite highlights like Happy Isles Rapids and Vernal Falls and the giant redwoods forty miles away where they drove through the Wawona Tunnel Tree. They fished in the river and floated downstream on air mattresses. After morning activities, they lunched on peanut butter sandwiches and took short naps; later, Dick took the children for a swim or a hike. The park offered evening entertainment: campfire lectures on the plants and animals in the park, sing-alongs, and square dancing. They stayed up late to see the famous Firefall, "a mass of glowing coals, pushed over the cliff at Glacier Point each night down a thousand feet in a stream of living fire." The Williamses, however, "discovered that they much preferred sitting quietly by their own evening fire." Camping in Yosemite even rekindled their romance. "Honey girl," Dick said, taking Geegee's hand, "we sure are lucky." At the end of the two weeks, they were pleased with their choice to take a camping vacation. It was inexpensive (less than two hundred dollars) and offered a change of routine, and the family had fun together outdoors.[8]

The Williamses were typical of the families who contributed to a huge boom in family camping in the 1940s and 1950s. In a time of tight budgets for young families, the camping explosion was fueled by its affordability. A minimum of equipment was required to camp out, and camping equipment was improved to make it easier to use. Advancing technologies attracted more women to camping by making it more comfortable and less like roughing it in the woods. New types of vehicles made camping easier as well. Families slept in station wagons or bought tent trailers, and campers, trailers, and recreational vehicles (RVs) allowed families to take their homes with them. Family magazines such as *Better Homes and Gardens,* map companies such as Rand McNally, and camping equipment manufacturers published camping guides that advised campers on every detail, from how to buy a tent to making foil-wrapped dinners in the campfire. Buying the right equipment, choosing the right place to camp, and taking the right food would mean the family could have the comforts of home in the outdoors.

The rise of enthusiasm for camping was linked to Americans' desire to leave the pressures of civilization behind to relive America's pioneering past. Motoring magazines cited the advice of sociologists and psychologists to "escape from mass-induced conformity, high-strung urbanized living in the asphalt jungle, smog and noises." Escaping modern life was made easier by "increased mobility, intensified interest in family-orientated activities, shorter work week, more leisure time, more money." Camping guides argued that "a camping vacation is probably the most relaxing type of vacation" a family could take; "no schedules have to be met, no need to lay out large amounts of money for accommodations." Camping allowed families "a chance to enjoy nature to any degree wanted, from the rustic forest campsite to the seashore recreation area."[9]

People went back to nature because nature was made more accessible to them. The federal government built new western dams with attractive reservoirs for boating and fishing. States opened new campgrounds and refurbished old ones after the war to meet the needs of the waves of campers that overran their sites. State parks hosted more than 215 million visitors in 1958, with 15 million overnight stays in park campgrounds.[10] The groundswell of enthusiasm for camping surged throughout the decade; camper registration totaled 10 million in 1950 and tripled to 30 million by 1960.[11]

Parents took their children camping to acquaint them with nature. American parents who had grown up in rural America's wide-open spaces wanted their children to know the pleasures of being outdoors, away from the cul-de-sacs of suburbia or the blacktop playgrounds of the city. Children were thought to be natural campers, curious explorers who needed to take only a few precautions for their own safety. Fishing, boating, hiking, and swimming drew children away from the campsite to a more immediate experience with nature. Children "might be following the campsite's nature trails, or 'exploring' by themselves." Park rangers provided nature talks and walks to entertain and inform the children. The point was to get children closer to nature, to have a fresh glimpse of the flora and fauna of their setting. A motoring magazine promised exciting outdoor entertainment: "Trails close to camp tempt hikers; a fresh-water stream provides an always-changing spectacle to watch; and the more fortunate of the small fry find excitement with a glimpse of a wild animal or a bird that's new to them."[12]

Camping together appealed to family vacationers because it was seen as inexpensive, fun, and wholesome to be outdoors. A family magazine proclaimed, "Camping, today, is for everyone. Your family can pack up for a weekend—or a month—in state and national parks across the land. It's an inexpensive, carefree way to have fun together." In an era of family togetherness, "camping brings the family together in the clean, wholesome outdoors." Once limited to men's hunting and fishing trips, camping became a common family vacation choice. It was an all-American family vacation with baby carriages and a station wagon and a carload of camping equipment to make a home in the outdoors.[13]

The idea that camping was a home away from home propelled the manufacture of wheeled camping vehicles. Although trailers and "house cars" had long been available, the 1950s saw the invention of portable camper shells mounted on the backs of pickup trucks, and in the 1960s manufacturers began to sell motor homes, fully self-contained vehicles, now called RVs, about triple the cost of a travel trailer. For families, the increasing affordability of manufactured campers and trailers meant they could be, as historian Roger White suggests, "at home on the road."[14]

In 1961 Keith Brown of Villa Park, Illinois, told how he took "seven kids, the wife, and myself" in a camper to see the "entire West." They covered a lot of ground in their trailer, and no place was off-limits. "Nine thousand miles in five weeks. All through Yosemite, Yellowstone, Jackson Hole. Grand Canyon—you name it. We were there." It was cheaper than staying in motels. "It cost us $300, maybe $350. Without the camper, we'd have spent $50 or $60 a day just for food and a place to stay." They had no trouble finding a place for everyone to sleep, but "we had to eat in shifts because we couldn't fit everybody at the table at once!" Brown promoted trailers as doing double duty as a fallout shelter for the family. "Since a trailer or camper is designed for extended family living, it makes a good basic unit for a home fallout shelter."[15] The cold war fears of the bomb were calmed by the purchase of the same camper that would allow them to escape civilization by going back to nature.

Because of their lower cost, travel trailers were the mainstay of the wheeled camping vehicle market. From 28,000 units in 1961, sales of travel trailers rose to 76,600 units in 1965. Because the trailer was lightweight, it could be pulled by a station wagon, although some owners found that they needed to buy a new car to pull the load. Because the owners did not have to worry about finding a motel or paying for lodging on the road, "It's the ideal family summer home." Travel trailers provided the comforts of home in the outdoors: "After a day's hiking in the woods or trolling out on the lake, there's nothing like pulling off your boots and sinking into those easy chairs in your travel trailer!"[16] Motoring magazines saw trailers as proof of the persistence of the pioneering spirit: "Today's nomad sits at the wheel of the station wagon; the prairie schooner spirit sails the highways on the wheels of a house trailer."[17] Words such as *escape* and *nomadic* assured consumers they could have home and wilderness all at once.

Ironically, the popularity of trailers and RVs made it even more difficult to "get away from it all" because "popular campgrounds are jammed on weekends, and people trying to get away from it all are taking it all with them." To accommodate the demands for campgrounds, the American Automobile Association reported "federal and state recreational areas are being opened up to lure campers away from some of the state and national parks that are suffering environmental damage through overuse." Private campgrounds provided a deluxe alternative to public campgrounds. Rand McNally combined its camping guidebook and travel trail guide in 1971, and it listed more than seventeen thousand campgrounds and RV parks, including eight thousand private facilities, more than three thousand national forest campgrounds, plus national parks, state parks and forests, and city, county, and civic areas.[18] It was such a popular guide that regional editions were issued for travelers.

Like Dick and Geegee Williams, Americans discovered camping was the ideal choice for the family vacation because it was an affordable way to get away from it all, even if they had to bring it all with them. Advertised as a vacation that was as cheap as staying at home, it was made possible by the family car or wheeled vehicle that had room for the whole family; all its equipment created a temporary home in the outdoors. Improved equipment like gas stoves made camping more attractive to women, and camping offered parents an opportunity to introduce their children to the wonders of nature. Weekends might find the family at a nearby state park or reservoir, but to really get back to nature, families chose the national parks.

Camping in Yellowstone National Park

The reopening of national parks at war's end in 1945 opened the floodgates to American tourists. Yellowstone National Park officials reported that with the end of gasoline rationing, "thousands of persons who had occasion to move across the country were able to make side trips to the park and enjoy the scenery, fishing and other recreation offered."[19] The first surge of visitors turned into a flood of campers. The total number of visits to national parks rose from 21.7 million in 1946 to 61.6 million in 1956, the year Mission 66 was announced. Under Mission 66, an ambitious program to upgrade park facilities to meet the needs of tourists, the government spent more than a billion dollars. By the time Mission 66 was complete, ten years later, visitation exceeded 133 million. By 1970 visitation soared to 172 million, but in the early 1970s, it decreased, and not until 1974 did it recover. By 1976 visitation reached 216.5 million.[20]

The NPS, and the private concessioners that operated the lodging and dining facilities in the parks, struggled to provide for the explosion of visitors. In 1958 the director of the NPS reported, "Campgrounds have been burdened beyond capacities, but this appropriate and beneficial experience in the parks brings enjoyment to many that could be provided in no other way." The problem of accommodating the crowds while preserving the wilderness was compounded by the fact that parks were owned by the NPS (and thus all American citizens) but operated by park concessioners—private companies with a profit motive. Historian Mark Daniel Barringer argues that concessioners were in the business of "selling nature, recreation and frontier history to Americans" to attract them to the parks. Furthermore, NPS officials were divided about how to meet visitor needs without threatening park ecologies. The expansion of the family vacation as national summer ritual meant that parks had to contend with an invasion of small children for whom they were unprepared, with sometimes tragic results.[21]

To understand the experience of the visitors, we can read their letters about the flagship park of the NPS: Yellowstone National Park, where park facilities were strained beyond their limits. Complaint letters from park visitors open a window into the experiences of tourists in the parks, and replies by park officials help us understand how they justified park policies. Each national park kept track of all complaints made about concessioner services and assigned them to various categories, where they were tallied. For example, in 1951 Yellowstone reported a total of fifty-one complaints about the concessioners: thirteen complaints about the "unsatisfactory condition of Accommodations," seven about the high rate for the cabins, seven about reservations not being held, two for the lack of bathing facilities, and one about the condition of the "comfort stations" (toilets). A separate tally was made of the thirty-three complaints about services provided by the government: Four complained about the camping facilities, four about inadequate sanitation. The primitive state of park roads generated eight complaints about the road conditions and three about road signs. One person complained that the bears were a nuisance.[22]

Ironically, visitors who went to the national parks to "escape civilization" seemed surprised to encounter inconveniences in the wilderness. They complained about having to wait in line for meals in the cafeterias, about not finding a place to stay, about the poor quality of the primitive toilets, or about the noise of other visitors. Visitors grounded their complaints in the expectation that these were *their* parks and that as American citizens, they were entitled to enjoy them in the way they had expected. Tourists saw themselves as consumers of park services, and they expected a return on their fees and on the investment they made in time and effort to arrive at the park. In reply, the park superintendent reminded them that they would expect a wait if they were at a city cafeteria, or a ticket if they disobeyed parking regulations in the city, and that regulations were necessary to maintain order. Park officials apologized but explained that the number of visitors had exceeded all expectations and that they simply were overwhelmed and short-staffed.[23]

Most complaints related to accommodations. Families on a budget tended to stay in the cheaper tourist cabins, where the facilities were most primitive. Tourists complained that the cabins were small and dirty, or that they lacked essentials for camping. Mr. and Mrs. Phillips from Pennsylvania arrived at Yellowstone late one afternoon in May 1952 at the Fishing Bridge Campground, where they rented a furnished cabin for the night. Phillips wrote, "We went to [the] cabin and found only a bed and a leaky wash basin and a battered up pitcher two towels and a piece of soap a wood stove and a pile of wood in the corner. All we had to set on was our suit cases." He returned immediately to the office to complain and waited an hour for benches to be delivered. They gave up and went to dinner. After dinner at the cafeteria, they went back to the office to complain, and the manager "spoke to my wife roughly and said to her if you don't like it we will return your money." Finally, at about seven o'clock, "a young man came with a wheel cart and brought two old benches," but Phillips complained they did not have a table to write on. He wrote, "[I] Don't believe they should rent to people this way and take their good money and return so little." Phillips thought that the public was entitled to better treatment at their national parks; he had made considerable sacrifices to visit.[24]

Others visitors wrote to complain that they could not find accommodations in the park. A man who was turned away from the park in July 1952 wrote a complaint to suggest that park rangers "advise tourists regarding the availability of overnight accommodations when entering the park." In his reply, the superintendent admitted, "It is a serious problem for which we do not entirely have the answer." In his defense, Rogers cited the fact that on July 24, the day Waldman entered the park, sixteen thousand persons had entered the park. Because eighty-three hundred could be accommodated in the hotels, lodges, and tourist cabins, and another three to four thousand in the campgrounds, "it is apparent that not all visitors could be accommodated and this same situation exists almost daily throughout July and August." He warned, "Unless people make reservations in advance it is very difficult for some of them to obtain accommodations in view of the unprecedented travel since the war."[25]

Overcrowding in the parks resulted not only from the crush of human visitors but also from cars and camping vehicles that filled the parking lots and caused "bear jams" on park roadways. More than 98 percent of visitors to Yellowstone in 1950 arrived by automobile. NPS historian David Louter argues that "Americans in the twentieth century would encounter parks primarily through autos; they would interpret the park landscape from a road and through the windshield." Camping vacationers experienced parks as "places of windshield wilderness." A man from Montana asked, "Will my little daughter be unable to know this pleasure because people are so crowded into restricted camping areas that we leave in disgust because it is impossible to get away from it all? Please, God, No."[26]

Even though visitors intended to escape civilization, the crowds meant that its evils followed them to the park. For example, in July 1956, six-year-old Betty Jane Laird of Orem, Utah, was fatally struck by a car, which was only one of seventy-four automobile accidents reported that month at Yellowstone. The overflow of cars in the national parks meant that park rangers became traffic cops regulating visitors who thought that they were on vacation from the rules of the road. In 1953 a man from Kansas was ticketed for violating parking regulations, and a park ranger warned him that a second ticket would result in his being required to appear before an officer of the local court at nearby Mammoth. Wary of unwittingly committing a second offense, their vacation was spoiled. His complaint letter compared being in the park to living in a communist country: "When we finally drove out of the gate we felt we knew how the Iron Curtain people must feel when escaping from Soviet Zones." He accused the park officials of maintaining the rules of a totalitarian state, terrorizing American citizens on vacation.[27]

By the late 1950s campers began to clearly favor travel trailers to tents, but without sufficient funds, parks were behind the curve on trailer facilities. In 1954 officials of the Department of the Interior began studying the possibility of adding trailer courts to the national parks. A 1962 survey showed that "camping is no longer the nearly exclusive preserve of the family under a canvas tent on the ground." Just over 50 percent used wheeled camp vehicles. "Nineteen camped in house-trailers, seven in tents erected on trailers, six in camper-coaches, six in station wagons or specially equipped buses, three in tiny sleeping trailers, and eight utilized more unusual equipment—or none at all." Use of tents in Yellowstone National Park declined 11 percent in the 1960s; in the same period, wheel-mounted equipment rose 14 percent. But despite the increase in use of trailers and campers, the Fishing Bridge Trailer Court was only 77 percent occupied. RVs dominated the other campgrounds, at 69 percent, with only 27 percent in tents.[28]

The increasing use of trailers and campers prompted complaints. As trailers and truck-mounted campers became more popular, it became clear that friction resulted from the mix of tents and trailers. A couple from Pennsylvania wrote in June 1952 to complain about the nuisance of motor-driven electric generators used by trailer owners: "The noise and fumes spoil for the majority the pleasures provided by the Park and nullify thereby the primary reason for the setting aside of the Park." They suggested the park prohibit the use of such generators in the park or "segregate owners of engine drive generators so that they might suffer together their own nuisance." In that way they could help visitors "enjoy the quietness and beauty of the Park."[29]

The park service carried out an exhaustive survey of its park campgrounds in 1966 and reported that campgrounds at the largest parks were overoccupied every day of the two-week study. The campgrounds accommodated huge numbers of persons. For example, Yellowstone's Grant Village had 399 campsites, but it was occupied by an average of 484 camping parties—on the highest day, 620 camping parties! Rangers were working six days a week to cope with the overcrowding in the park in August. In response to the crowding and mechanization of camping, more visitors chose to camp in the backcountry, where there were no facilities. At Yellowstone rangers reported in 1962 that "back country use continued to be excellent," but the total of 962 visitors undertaking hiking-fishing trips "to the more remote areas" was a mere fraction of the visitors to the park.[30] Most visitors congregated in the busy campgrounds and cafeterias of the metropolitan areas of the parks.

Frustrated park visitors wrote complaint letters to their congressmen. Tattling on the parks to elected officials upped the ante, and park officials found themselves in the unenviable position of explaining their position to those who decided their annual budgets.[31] Park officials' reply letters blamed their problems on postwar shortages or lack of funds; after Mission 66 was launched in 1956, they promised that the problems would be solved by the ambitious park-building program. Superintendent Rogers responded to a visitor complaint about the poor state of the cabins in October 1956 with enthusiasm about the improvements undertaken as a result of the Mission 66 program. Five hundred "modern cottage rooms, all with bath and heated," were being built in the new Canyon Village area by the Yellowstone Park Company. Rogers boasted that the new rooms were "comparable to those better motels found outside the park" and were costing the Yellowstone Park Company five million dollars. Dwight Pitcaithley, historian of the NPS, explained, "By 1966 the National Park Service had increased the number of parking lots fivefold; created 1,197 miles of new roads; added 575 new campgrounds and 742 new picnic areas; constructed 535 additional water systems, 521 new sewer systems, and 271 new power systems; developed 50 marinas; and constructed or rehabilitated 584 new comfort stations (the service's term for toilets)."[32] Despite the added improvements, the parks remained crowded, spoiling hopes of a utopian vacation in the wilderness.

The packaging of nature of the national parks did not mean that parks were safe places for families with young children. Park operators feared that if nature was fenced in and roped off, made safe for visitors, tourists would not come to the parks and profits would fall. The NPS, which had conservation as one of its goals, likewise opposed making a Disneyland out of the national parks. The tensions between preservation and profits meant that family vacationers experienced the national wilderness with all its hazards, including boiling thermal features, steep canyons, swift-moving rivers, and hungry bears.

The parks established programs and museums to educate the tourists about the local environment and its hazards. Thousands of tourists attended the nighttime campfire programs with slides at Yellowstone every night, where they were taught about the history, plants, geology, and wildlife at the park. Crowds gathered at designated viewing platforms at spectacular park features to listen to rangers point out the features. The educational programs were popular with tourists, but children paid little heed to the lectures in the museums and were more engaged out-of-doors on nature walks. The park established a junior nature program as early as 1947 for children aged six to fourteen years. Led by a park ranger, it met every weekday in the afternoon and "consist[ed] of special exploring trips for the youngsters and a treatment of nature lore with some work being done on nature craft." Children clustered around the rangers as they pointed out the wild grasses and other environmental features, accompanied by only a few adults. Photographs demonstrate that most attentively listened to the ranger, and one curious boy leaned down to inspect the grass himself.[33]

More likely, children accompanied their parents as they took in the sights. Photographs of children in the parks demonstrate the absence of barriers between tourists and the sights. Parents held their small children, but older ones sat on the edge of the boardwalks or stood at the edge of the pools, heedless of the rangers' warnings. Tourists in cars were free to pull up alongside Yellowstone's thermal features like Beryl Springs, where a rushing stream of thermal waters coursed a few feet from the road. Children stood at the edge of hissing Roaring Mountain and played on the banks of the Firehole River while watching Riverside Geyser erupt. There was nothing to keep children from harm's way except their parents' vigilance or their own sense of self-preservation.

Children liked to explore and often wandered away from their parents, distracted by sightseeing or unaware of the hazards in the park. Twelve-year-old Allis Lovel fell 130 feet into Yellowstone Canyon when "she followed what she thought was an established trail along the rim," but she took a wrong path. Luckily, she was "pulled to safety by members of the ranger force and suffered only minor bruises and scratches." The rushing rivers and falls also posed a hazard to children. In July 1955 twelve-year-old David Gaskill was swept off his feet by the current while fishing with his father in the Yellowstone; "his father was unable to reach him." The next month a seven-year-old boy fishing with his grandfather drowned in the Yellowstone River when he "slipped from the rocks into the swift current and attempts to rescue by his grandfather were unsuccessful." A father and son out fishing on Lewis Lake were caught in a storm and presumed lost after weeks of searching for their bodies.[34] A simple fishing trip could quickly turn to tragedy in the park.

The thermal features that attracted visitors to Yellowstone could be perilous to children who could not read the signs and were unaware of the dangers surrounding them. In 1949 two children died in the same season, prompting the NPS to reconsider its policies. NPS director Newton B. Drury replied in detail to Senator Hubert Humphrey's inquiry prompted by a letter from a constituent who had been visiting the park. On July 14, 1949, Mr. and Mrs. Philip Kasik sent their two sons, Robert (age five) and Phil (age ten), to Hamilton's store for groceries. The boys mistakenly headed for the park cafeteria, where two employees saw them round the corner and approach hot pools east of the cafeteria building. The park official reported that the employees "heard one of the boys yelling and they immediately ran in the direction of the yelling and found that the younger boy had fallen into one of the hot pools. They pulled the boy from the pool. Apparently, he had stepped on slippery ground and had slid into the pool." The boy was given first aid while park officials found his parents, and he was taken to the hospital in Mammoth, where he died the next morning.[35]

The second victim was Karen Lee Anderson, who was four and a half years old at the time of her death on September 13, 1949. Mr. and Mrs. Theodore Anderson, Karen, and a younger brother had parked near the Emerald Pool in the Upper Geyser Basin "to sightsee and take pictures." The report continues:

> Apparently, the family did not stay on the board walks which are provided for safe travel over geyser formations. The son called to his mother, saying that he was going to try to find the Emerald Pool. Karen Lee turned away from a point near her mother and walked toward her brother, apparently with the intention of following him. She had only pro-

gressed about twenty-five feet when her mother saw that she was walking toward one of the hot pools in the area. Mrs. Anderson called to Karen Lee to attempt to warn her, but the girl walked straight into the pool.

The pool was only a few feet wide and two feet deep, but its sudden vertical drop trapped little Karen Lee in two feet of "violently" boiling water. Unable to lift her daughter out of the pool, Mrs. Anderson "called her husband and he removed the girl from the pool as quickly as possible." The doctor and nurse on duty "wrapped the girl's body in Vaseline soaked gauze and administered a hypodermic to lessen the pain." Karen Lee suffered third-degree burns over 90 percent of her body, and despite being given emergency treatment and rushed by patrol car to the nearest hospital at Livingston, she died just over three hours after the accident.[36]

With two deaths in close succession, and a higher than usual number of injuries occurring in the thermal pools, park officials admitted that "it may be necessary to restrict somewhat the freedom that people now enjoy in seeing the geyser basins." But, as Drury told Humphrey, "with limited funds, it is quite impossible to fence or otherwise guard all of the potentially dangerous places in the park, and there may be some question as to the desirability of doing so." Indeed, it "may not be practicable to protect all of the dangerous areas in the park." Furthermore, they were "reluctant" to fence off the dangerous pools, because "it is desirable that people be permitted to enjoy the parks fully, with a minimum of restrictions."[37] Park officials adamantly maintained that if they had the resources to protect all visitors from the hazards of the park, the park would no longer give visitors the sense that they were in the wilderness.

Do Not Feed the Bears

The biggest draw of Yellowstone National Park was its bears, and they posed one of the greatest dangers to tourists. Tourists insisted not only on seeing the bears but also on feeding them and posing for pictures next to them. And although visitors wanted to go back to nature, they imposed their own views of a benevolent nature on a place that was more dangerous than they could have imagined. Some may have been genuinely ignorant of the hazards bears posed to the safety of them and their children. Camping manuals downplayed the danger of bears in camp, saying they would cause "little trouble" if "food has been stowed correctly and campers avoid irritating the animals." It cautioned campers, "Remember, these are wild animals," but it did not specify the dangers of an encounter with bears. Children's books portrayed the bears as lovable cubs "who play all day" and "sleep so peacefully the whole night through."[38]

Visitors seemed unable (or unwilling) to comprehend the warnings about bears and resented the park rangers' admonitions. Forest Sweet from Battle Creek, Michigan, who had taken his family in a house trailer to Yellowstone in August, wrote a letter in October 1950 that exemplifies the problem. Sweet suggested that they build playgrounds for the children where "you might provide children's swings, slides and climbing bars like most elementary rural schools provide." He also thought the park could be made safer for children by building handrails on the paths to Tower Falls and mud pots. And he was very tired of hearing about the dangers of bears. "We attended twenty campfire meetings and resented the harping on bears, even tho' most of the rangers tried hard to vary the story. We recognize bears for dangerous wild animals and also for perhaps the most attractive single feature of the Park."

In reply, the NPS official stated that they had avoided installing playgrounds because "we believe it would attract many campers purely for the play opportunities provided for the children rather than for a visit to the parks for the enjoyment of the inherent values." As for the bears, he insisted that it was necessary to overemphasize the bear issue because it was one of the main safety problems.[39] The NPS refused to construct playgrounds in the parks and install fences around every possible danger, so the safety and welfare of children were left to parents.

Despite park policies, visitors continued to feed the bears, and in the 1950s injuries and damages from bears spiraled out of control. From 40 incidents during 1952, reported injuries rose to 70 in 1955 and 109 in 1956. In 1956 park officials analyzed the figures and reported, "18 victims were feeding bears which bit them and in an equal number of cases nearby people were feeding the bears. Thirty of the visitors who were bitten knowingly approached bears or permitted bears to come too close to them." Furthermore, the bears were endangered by the visitors. Park officials responded by removing dangerous bears and destroying eight bears. "Four additional bears were killed by traffic, one was destroyed because it had a tin can lodged in its throat." Because of the danger they posed to park visitors, park officials destroyed approximately forty bears yearly in the latter half of the 1950s.[40]

Park officials reasoned that the injuries to humans resulted from visitors disobeying park rules or knowingly placing themselves in dangerous situations. Despite warnings to keep their food away from bears, "Food probably tempted the bears in 81, or 67% of the incidents." Since campers usually carried in their own food, the problem seemed insurmountable. A man from Alabama wrote in 1966 about the difficulty of keeping food away from the bears. He and his wife and three children had stayed in their Apache camper trailer for a few days in the Fishing Bridge campground, where "the bears were allowed to invade our campsite at their pleasure and much to our dismay." The bears were ruthless: "They pawed and clawed our rig in broad daylight although there was no food in it, nor had there been any." Campers *with* food endured worse fates: "In the camp next to ours a bear wrested an ice-box right out of the arms of a woman carrying it. He opened it easily without unlatching it and feasted on its contents." Frightened by the incident, they decided to pack up and leave. "After witnessing this, you can be sure that we lost all heart for preparing our breakfast or for staying in that park for another moment." His suggestion was to "put stout electric fences around each campground to keep bears out, and to keep people out of bears." The fact that this man claimed the bear invaded *his* space in Yellowstone suggests that campers had little understanding of the park as a home to wildlife. He saw his claims to the park's nature as superior to those of the bear, who lived there year-round.[41]

Accident reports reveal an astonishing number of injuries inflicted on children by bears as a result of parental carelessness. Visitors seem to have lost all sense of judgment when given the chance to see a bear. Most injuries occurred, oddly enough, while the children were still in the family car. Because air-conditioning was not available in cars, tourists drove through the park in the hot summer months with their windows down. Bears reached into car windows and clawed or scratched children sitting by the rear windows. A three-year-old girl was bitten on the wrist when her parents stopped the car to watch a tourist feed a bear. One can only imagine the skepticism of the nurse who treated a three-year-old boy bitten by a bear, teeth marks visible on his hand. His parents protested that they were not feeding the bears, but said that before they realized what was happening, a bear had climbed into the backseat to take a bite of the cookie that the boy was eating! When the Hendrickson family car stopped to observe a bear, six-year-old Nancy reached out to "pet" it and suffered a deep bite that required five stitches. Accustomed to cartoon bears like Yogi the Bear or the firefighting Smokey the Bear, neither parents nor children were prepared for the savagery of real bears in the park.[42]

Park visitors were more likely to suffer severe injuries if they got out of their cars to observe the wild animals. When the Brittendall family stopped in September 1956 to watch a group of people take pictures of a coyote, four-year-old Gale Lee got out of the car with her parents to take a closer look. The coyote was going from person to person, begging for food, and when it came to her, she became frightened. When she turned and ran, the coyote nipped her in the behind, resulting in three small puncture wounds "on the child's posterior." When a woman from Georgia got out of the family car to feed a bear, the bear bit her three-year-old son on the neck. And despite park literature that prohibited feeding bears and verbal warnings from rangers, a visitor from Sacramento was feeding cookies to a bear when it bit her on the right wrist.[43]

The number of injuries slowly declined after the institution of a new bear-management plan in the 1960s, including removing dangerous bears and fining visitors who fed them. In 1962 the superintendent reported, "13 cases of bear feeding have been brought before the U.S. Commissioner to date, with a total of $110 in fines." Only by slapping stiff fines on visitors who were caught feeding bears were park officials able to reduce the incidence of violence.[44]

Conclusion

In light of the complaints by park visitors, one has to consider the irony of the 1963 NPS report's statement that the park system "affords Americans opportunities to enjoy great scenic and inspirational areas of their country in a natural, unspoiled condition and the rare quality of the primitive wilderness that was America before it was touched by civilization."[45] Yellowstone, with its parking lots, cafeterias, lodges, and trailer parks, was hardly untouched by civilization. However, it was as close as many families in America would get to what was regarded as wilderness, and it was wilderness at a price they could afford. Best of all, they could get there in the family car or camper, even if it could not protect them from the bears they had come all that way to see.

In the postwar era, camping seemed to offer a utopian family vacation for penny-wise parents who loaded up their station wagons with coolers and tents and went off with their children. Visitors to the national parks demanded the comfort and safety of civilization that put distance between them and the natural wonders, resulting in a mediated experience of nature. Campers who could afford to escape the crowded campgrounds retreated to the privacy of their recreational vehicles or trailers. The camping boom grew into a mass movement that resulted in overcrowding, making getting back to nature more and more difficult.

By the early 1960s conservationists alleged that park overuse endangered wilderness preservation. In 1962 the director of the NPS reported, "Today, Americans are crowding the highways and visiting the parks and recreational areas of the country as never before in history. Yearly visits to the national parks have leaped from 22 million only 15 years ago to more than 80 million last year." That same year the park service welcomed its one billionth visitor with public hoopla. Secretary of the Interior Stewart Udall acknowledged the concerns of conservationists, but he declared, "Preservation is combined with use, not alienated from it." Sensitive to the criticism that Mission 66 had paved over the parks, Udall defended the NPS: "The wilderness character of the System has not been sacrificed to mission 66, but saved by it."[46]

Within the decade the NPS faced another set of critics. On July 4, 1970, a counterculture group of long-haired hippies rioted in Stoneman Meadow in Yosemite National Park, a confrontation between generations. The riot between the young people and the "establishment" marked the end of an era of family camping in the park. In part as a result of the oil crisis, visitation dropped in the early 1970s, and park rangers were more occupied with law enforcement than making visitors feel welcome in their parks.[47]

In its democratic policy of access to the American public, the national parks that had offered access to the wilderness for war veterans and their children had become so crowded that the only way to escape civilization was to set off on foot. Backpacking offered the hiker freedom to "wander as far as his legs can carry him, away from hotels, roads, campgrounds, commerce and other people. He has the satisfaction of knowing he is in a place that is seen only by those who have the energy and love of wilderness to come on their own feet." The Sierra Club and the Wilderness Society promoted wilderness preservation, and manufacturers developed lightweight camping equipment that could fit in a backpack, not the back of the station wagon. The same people who as children had slept in the back of the station wagon now claimed the wilderness as their own, rejecting the car-oriented consumerism of their parents who took them to the parks in the first place. They shouldered backpacks full of lightweight camping gear and walked into the backcountry in search of not nature but wilderness. In their quest, they redefined western utopia and helped launch a powerful political movement.[48]

Ultimately, seeking western utopias in the parks helped raise a consciousness of the environment that laid the foundation for movements to set aside federal lands as wilderness, to implement regulation to reduce industrial air and water pollution, and later to reduce the consumption of energy. Camping offered Americans with children a closer experience with the natural environment through recreation. Being in the woods fostered an expanded appreciation for the environment that motivated many to political action.[49] The child campers of the postwar era were among those who turned out en masse for Earth Day in April 1970—twenty million persons who had somehow come by an environmental sensibility, maybe in a tent by a river on a family vacation in the West.

Notes

1. Gallup Poll [computer file], *Public Opinion, 1935-1997* (Wilmington, Del.: Scholarly Resources, 2000), 1949: 822; 1950: 904; 1953: 1166; 1961: 1718; 1963: 1800–1801.

2. Kent Ruth, *How to Enjoy Your Western Vacations* (Norman: University of Oklahoma Press, 1956); *Where to Go in the Western States* (Chicago: Chicago Motor Club, [1940?]); Fred Bond, *Westward How, Through the Scenic West* (San Francisco: Camera Craft Publishing, 1947). Popular magazines also catered to the western tourist: *Sunset Magazine,* founded by the Southern Pacific Railway; *Westways* (the magazine of the California State Automobile Association), the venerable *Arizona Highways,* and the short-lived *Desert Magazine* (Palm Desert, Calif.).

3. Susan S. Rugh, *Are We There Yet? The Golden Age of American Family Vacations* (Lawrence: University Press of Kansas, 2008).

4. Outdoor Recreation Resources Review Commission, *National Recreation Survey* (Washington, D.C.: Outdoor Recreation Resources Review Commission, 1962), 46, 56, 57, 67, 71; Gallup Poll, 1963: 1821. Westerners were far more likely than those in other regions to take a summer vacation, 48 percent compared to 39 percent in the East and Midwest, and 43 percent in the South. For the importance of the West as a symbol of national unity, see Marguerite S. Shaffer, *See America First: Tourism and National Identity, 1880-1940* (Washington, D.C.: Smithsonian Institution Press, 2001).

5. "How to See a National Park," *Ladies' Home Journal,* June 1947, 185.

6. "Your America," *Ladies' Home Journal,* June 1947, 48–55.

7. "Camping," *Motorland,* July–August 1960, 12.

8. Jan Weyl, "Time of Our Lives," *Ladies' Home Journal,* July 1954, 91–120.

9. Ibid., 14; *Rand McNally Campground Guide: A Family Camping Directory* (Chicago: Rand McNally, 1963), vol. 1.

10. *Annual Report of the Director, National Park Service to the Secretary of the Interior, 1958,* 313; William D. Rowley, *The Bureau of Reclamation: Origins and Growth to 1945* (Washington, D.C.: U.S. Department of the Interior, 2006).

11. *National Recreation Survey,* 56, 57.

12. "Camping," 12.

13. Neil R. Kuehnl, "The How-To of Family Camping," *Better Homes and Gardens,* May 1958, 156; *Rand McNally Campground Guide,* vol. 1.

14. Roger B. White, *Home on the Road: The Motor Home in America* (Washington, D.C.: Smithsonian Institution Press, 2000), 153–54.

15. Ibid.

16. Ibid., 154; John Gartner, "How Big a Trailer?" *Westways,* April 1950, 10; *Life,* June 8, 1959, 119; *Westways,* June 1959, 42.

17. *Motorland,* March–April 1964, 30s; Rand McNally, *Rand McNally Western Campground and Trailering Guide* (Chicago: Rand McNally, 1970), n.p.; "Camping," 14.

18. "Recreational Vehicles: The Great Turtle Syndrome," *Motorland*, March–April 1973, 54–55; *Rand McNally Campground and Trailer Park Guide* (Chicago: Rand McNally, 1971), ii.

19. U.S. Department of the Interior, NPS, *Annual Report, 1946: Yellowstone*, 1–2, *Annual Report, 1947: Yellowstone*, 2, Box 1707, Record Group 79, National Park Service Administrative Files (1949–71), hereafter cited as RG 79.

20. NPS Public Use Statistics Office, *Decade Report, 1941–1950, 1951–1960, 1961–1970, 1971–1980*, available at http://www2.nature.nps.gov/stats/. Historians of the park service often see the park visitor as the problem to be solved. See Dwight T. Pitcaithley, "A Dignified Exploitation: The Growth of Tourism in the National Parks," in *Seeing and Being Seen: Tourism in the American West*, edited by David M. Wrobel and Patrick T. Long (Lawrence: University Press of Kansas, 2001), 299–312. John Ise, *Our National Park Policy: A Critical History* (Baltimore: Johns Hopkins University Press, 1961), 458, compares the visitors to an infestation of insects.

21. *Annual Report of the Director, National Park Service, to the Secretary of the Interior, 1959*, 341; Mark Daniel Barringer, *Selling Yellowstone: Capitalism and the Construction of Nature* (Lawrence: University Press of Kansas, 2002), 12, 173–74; Richard West Sellars, *Preserving Nature in the National Parks: A History* (New Haven: Yale University Press, 1997), 5.

22. Report 4a3, "Annual Summary of Written Complaints Concerning Facilities and Services of the Government in Yellowstone National Park," September 30, 1951, Folder A3615, Box 382, RG 79.

23. Edmund B. Rogers to Regional Director, Region Two, August 17, 1951, ibid.

24. Drucilla C. Planson to U.S. Department of the Interior, August 10, 1956; H. G. Phillips to "The Ranger in Charge at Fishing Bridge, Yellowstone Nat'l Park, Wyoming," June 5, 1952, ibid.

25. Superintendent Edmund B. Rogers to Regional Director, Region Two, September 18, 1952, ibid.

26. American Automobile Association, "Travel Trends," May 1951, 1, Folder A88, Box 714, RG 79; David Louter, "Glaciers and Gasoline: The Making of a Windshield Wilderness," in *Seeing and Being Seen*, edited by Wrobel and Long, 250; D. S. Martin, to the NPS, attached to Fred M. Packard to "Connie," April 21, 1955, and R. K. MacDonald to Elmer F. Bennett, August 25, 1959, both in Folder A3615, Box 382, RG 79.

27. "NPS Monthly Narrative Report, Yellowstone," July 1956, 8, Folder A2823, Box 320, RG 79; O. E. Hemphill to Superintendent of Rangers, August 31, 1953, Folder A3615, Box 382, RG 79.

28. *Annual Report of the Director, National Park Service to the Secretary of the Interior, 1959*, 341; Ernest A. Welch to Department of the Interior, June 14, 1954; Thomas C. Vint to Ernest A. Welch, June 23, 1954, Folder A3615, Box 382, RG 79; *Annual Report of the Director, National Park Service to the Secretary of the Interior, 1963*, 81, 95–96, 98; Camping Committee of the National Park Service, "Compilation of Campground Data Collected in the 1966 Camping Survey" and "A Summary Report of 17 Parks in the Campground Survey, 1966," 68, Folder L3415 WASO, Box 119, RG 79.

29. Mr. and Mrs. Leslie C. Mackrill to the National Park Service, June 29, 1952, Folder A3615 YELL, Complaints Box 382, RG 79.

30. "Summary Report," 2; "Compilation," 23–24.

31. Ronald F. Lee, Acting Director, to Senator Everett M. Dirksen, September 7, 1951, Folder A3615 YELL, Box 382, RG 79.

32. Edmund B. Rogers to E. K. Campbell, October 23, 1956, Folder A3619-B, Box 382, RG 79; Pitcaithley, "Dignified Exploitation."

33. Photographs found in Historic Photograph File, Records of the National Park Service, RG 79; *Annual Report, 1947,* 11, Box 1707, RG 79.

34. *Superintendent's Monthly Narrative Report, Yellowstone,* July 1956, 9, 17, Folder A2823, Box 320, RG 79.

35. Newton B. Drury to Senator Hubert H. Humphrey, October 17, 1949, Folder A3615, Box 382, RG 79.

36. Ibid.; Lee H. Whittlesey, *Death in Yellowstone: Accidents and Foolhardiness in the First National Park* (Boulder: Roberts Rinehart, 1995), 14.

37. Drury to Humphrey, October 17, 1949.

38. Better Homes and Gardens, *Family Camping* (Des Moines: Better Homes and Gardens, 1961), 115; Dr. and Mrs. N. W. Christiansen, *A Trip Through Yellowstone Park: Interesting Events Portrayed in Music* (Long Island: Belwin, 1953), 15, in author's possession.

39. Forest H. Sweet to Drury, October 10, 1950; Paul R. Franke to Sweet, October 19, 1950, Folder A3615, Box 382, RG 79.

40. Memorandum, Superintendent of Yellowstone National Park to the National Park Service Director, June 16, 1959, Folder A26, Box 79, RG 79; *Superintendent's Monthly Narrative Report, Yellowstone,* August 1955, Folder A2823, Box 320, RG 79; Alice Wondrak Biel, *Do (Not) Feed the Bears: The Fitful History and Wildlife and Tourists in Yellowstone* (Lawrence: University Press of Kansas, 2006).

41. *Superintendent's Monthly Narrative Report, Yellowstone,* August 1955, Folder A2823, Box 320; Samuel E. McCrary to Stewart L. Udall, June 22, 1966, Complaints Box 383, RG79.

42. *Superintendent's Monthly Narrative Report, Yellowstone,* June 1955, Folder A2823, Box 320, RG 79; "Report of Personal Injuries for Eugene Nayes, Ann Boutte, Daughter of Robert Gloyd, Paul Brown, Nancy Hendrickson," Folder A7623, Box 624, RG 79; Biel, *Do (Not) Feed the Bears,* 68–71.

43. "Report of Personal Injuries for Gale Lee Brittendall, James Applewhite, Mrs. Robert Thomas," Folder A7623, Box 624, RG 79.

44. *Superintendent's Monthly Narrative Report, Yellowstone,* August 1962, 8, Folder A2823, Box 320, RG 79; Biel, *Do (Not) Feed the Bears.*

45. *Annual Report of the Director, National Park Service to the Secretary of the Interior, 1962,* 111–12; *Annual Report of the Director, 1963,* 95.

46. *Annual Report of the Commissioner, National Park Service, to the Secretary of the Inte-*

rior, Reprinted From the Annual Report of the Secretary of the Interior, for the Fiscal Year Ending June 30, 1961,* 357, 360.

47. Jack Hope, "Hassles in the Park," *Natural History,* May 1971.

48. "Carrying Everything He Needs to Survive, the Backpacker Is One of the Freest People on Earth," *Motorland,* March 1969, 20; Sellars, *Preserving Nature,* 338n5.

49. Samuel P. Hays, *Beauty, Health, and Permanence: Environmental Policies in the United States, 1955–1985* (New York: Cambridge University Press, 1987), 54, 115.

Public Art, Memory, and Mobility in 1920s New Mexico

JEFFREY C. SANDERS

Longtime Santa Fe resident and archaeologist Jesse Nusbaum recalled the day Harry Truman arrived "at the corner of Shelby and San Francisco on the Plaza" bearing a gift for the city.

> As the truck came to a stop, the Santa Fe group there to meet it immediately expressed refusal and loudly ordered the truck to move on. Someone shouted that life was not lived merely consisting of breathing but in acting and the controversy raged loud and heated, as the Pioneer Mother was unwrapped by the equally determined men on the truck. When an attempt was made to move the sculpture, Mary Austin, known to all of us as a lady of great literary brilliance and independence, and a formidable and large lady of stature, stepped forward and with no offense to modesty began to kick Harry Truman on the shins. The Pioneer Mother never left the truck. She was hastily rewrapped and taken to grace the little park on Fourth Street in Albuquerque.[1]

Truman came to Santa Fe in the autumn of 1927 to present the city with a heavy pink-hued statue called the *Pioneer Mother* (or *Madonna of the Trail*). The Santa Fe press at the time described the piece as "imposing."[2] The sculpture depicts a sunbonneted, rifle-toting, big-boot-wearing pioneer woman with a child gripping her skirts and another in one of her big arms. Despite Truman's good intention to bestow a new piece of public art upon Santa Fe, he and the statue stepped into an artistic and cultural ambush. Mary Austin led the attack, and she certainly kicked him in the shins, if only metaphorically. Nusbaum's story, told years after the actual events, is more legend than truth. But his tale of confrontation on the plaza conveys the heat of a very real early-twentieth-century battle over public art in New

Mexico. Santa Feans rejected the *Madonna of the Trail*. She found an end to her restless journey in Albuquerque rather than the utopian "Capital to the North." In the meantime, she had raised the hackles of Santa Fe residents, posing interesting questions about the role of public art and taste in the urban landscape. More important, the dispute over the statue revealed divergent usable pasts and hopes for the future within the contested cultural atmosphere of the 1920s. Truman did come to Santa Fe, and the tastemakers of Santa Fe did believe that he was trying to "unload" a statue of questionable quality and historical merit on their plaza.[3] Yet the scene that Nusbaum describes is fantasy. In order to get to the truth of the story, we have to know what Harry Truman, an up-and-coming judge from Missouri, was doing in Santa Fe with a statue of a pioneer woman in the first place. We must also know from where this *Madonna of the Trail* statue came, why it created such a stir, and how it finally came to rest in Albuquerque's McClellan Park.

At the beginning of an illustrious political career that would propel him from senator to vice president to president of the United States, Truman worked hard to build a name for himself in Missouri politics. Enlarging his public persona, Truman became the president of the National Old Trails Road Association in 1924, a Missouri group comprising concerned citizens, patriotic organizations, and businesspeople who wanted to create "the Great Historic Highway of America."[4] By the 1920s this historic highway and the *Madonna of the Trail* statues formed a grand project that would take Truman and controversy to Santa Fe. Highway booster projects proliferated across the United States after the turn of the century as Americans increased their automobile use. Organizations sprang up around the country with fantastic plans to improve haphazard systems of muddy, local wagon roads. In the Progressive spirit of the time, groups similar to Truman's, and part of the broader Good Roads movement, envisioned great and historically resonant monuments in the form of federally supported asphalt highways. They envisioned safe and efficient roads that would tie the nation together, celebrate the past, and attract a growing tourist industry and dollars.[5]

Even before statehood the New Mexico Territory shared this nationwide enthusiasm for the road and had begun to develop its own vision of a landscape of cars, roads, and bridges that would bind the future state from north to south. In 1904 territorial governor Miguel Otero purchased the first automobile in the territory. As more wealthy and prominent people began using the new technology, drivers eventually demanded better roads. Significantly, as early as 1905 the territorial legislature decided to designate the historic Camino Real as the Camino Real

Highway, making it the major north-south car route in the state. One of the early stretches of this gravel highway for cars was meant to connect Raton with Santa Fe. Early on, car owners and boosters in New Mexico saw the benefit of good roads for the state's burgeoning tourist economy. By 1913 the new state had a highway commission and a state engineer that set about designating and building NM 1, again following the same north-to-south trajectory of the Camino Real and part of the Santa Fe Trail. The highway would later become U.S. 85 when the federal government assigned its own numbers to roads. These increased efforts by new state agencies and "Good Roads" groups set in motion more local efforts and eventually garnered federal assistance for road building throughout the state. By 1926 New Mexicans had begun to form a clear vision of their future landscape and economy that partly revolved around the automobile. With national auto registration rising from 1,258,062 in 1913 to 7,565,446 in 1919, the spirit of mobility gripped locals in New Mexico and Missouri, along with the entire nation. Long dependent on the railroad for out-of-town travel, people began to push into the countryside in new gas- and electric-powered automobiles. These modern pioneers formed social groups of like-minded auto enthusiasts such as the Automobile Association of America and the Automobile Club of Southern California. They also created activist road-lobbying organizations. One of these groups, the American Road Builders Association, held its first annual meeting in 1903 in Atlantic City, New Jersey, hosted by Woodrow Wilson, then the state's governor.[6]

By 1912, responding to the growing movement, Congress created an act supporting the mission of Truman's Missouri-based Old Trails Road Association. The following year the House of Representatives created a new Committee on Roads, and a Missouri congressman sought to chair it. In the 1910s and 1920s Missouri had become one of the hotbeds of this growing highway movement. As head of the growing local group and part of this larger national effort, Truman derived increasing public exposure from the popular roads issue.[7] However, men such as Truman were mere ornaments on the hood of this gathering movement—women were the drivers.

Well-to-do and middle-class women in Missouri turned highway boosterism into a patriotic cause. With more women driving every year and carmakers marketing the convenience of electric cars to them, women's activities on behalf of old roads in Missouri revealed a dual motivation. The original idea of a National Old Trails Road Association began in 1909 when a group of Missouri women decided to mark the fading traces of the Santa Fe Trail through their state. At first their concerns were purely patriotic and provincial. But soon after, in 1912, the Daughters of the American Revolution, a group with national scope dedicated to historical commemoration, joined the cause and helped to formulate a more elaborate plan for the transcontinental highway that would follow various old roads and historical trails from coast to coast. Throughout Missouri and the nation, the DAR installed heavy chunks of granite along historical trails, bearing plaques to the memory of pioneers and patriots or commemorating events or sites they deemed significant. Each month the DAR magazine published photographs submitted by chapters around the country that featured proud groups of conservatively dressed women clutching their purses in front of newly dedicated stone monuments. The DAR's official constitution described the group's mission to "perpetuate the memory and spirit of the men and women who achieved American Independence—the acquisition and protection of historical spots—and the erection of monuments."[8]

The DAR's plan for a memorial highway seemed a natural extension of their disparate, local monument-building mission. When Congress supported the DAR's effort to create a national highway, these patriotic activities took on more significance. But facing the daunting task of building a national highway in 1912, the groups of women realized they would require male assistance to complete the project. Although women drivers would benefit directly from better highways, the DAR kept their arguments for highway building within the "proper" feminine realm of maintaining historical memory. To this end, the women who supported the national highway emphasized nationalistic fervor in their quest to establish their monumental road.

A highway would bind the country together, they argued. And they found historical precedents for the idea of a linked road system as far back as the Revolutionary War and George Washington's desire to see a national thoroughfare. They traced out a national road that moved steadily West, beginning with the old Cumberland Road from Maryland to West Virginia, then with trails extending toward Missouri, and eventually the trail through Missouri to Santa Fe.[9] From Santa Fe they connected their road to the Old Spanish Trail and to California. The road itself embodied the DAR's belief in the spirit of Manifest Destiny and the country's apparently inevitable westward expansion. In 1912, the year Arizona and New Mexico achieved statehood and Congress approved the national road system, Manifest Destiny was not an idle historical thought but an active reality for the DAR—an organization preoccupied with assimilating immigrants and inculcating proper notions of citizenship.[10] Putting a road from the East to the West coasts through New Mexico and Arizona, all the way to the coast of California, would symbolically complete the project of national expansion and cement the nation. The road would stand as a monument to past American achievements and more recent triumphs—a history remembered and reinforced in the ritual act of driving.

Well after planning their patriotic highway, these women brought men into the endeavor. The National Old Trails Road Association formed explicitly "to assist the Daughters of the American Revolution in marking the Old Trails and to promote the construction of an Ocean-to-Ocean Highway of a modern type worthy of its memorial character."[11] The DAR required the male-counterpart organization to do the political and business promotion for the project, or so it seemed. The DAR, however, did much of the work, while the male organization, led by Truman in the 1920s, legitimated their endeavor. Arlene B. Nichols Moss, a teacher in a school for the deaf in St. Louis and the chair of the National Old Trails Committee of the DAR, described the relationship of the male and female trail groups:

> These two patriotic groups . . . have had much in common, and while our DAR Committee gave the first organized impetus to this plan of a Pioneer Mother Highway across the Continent, and issued the first map, named the road, originated the first road sign, and painted it on telegraph poles and introduced a bill in Congress calling upon the Government to build the road, we Daughters most gratefully acknowledge the impetus and far-reaching power, the able assistance, and never-ceasing cooperation given to this movement by the splendid men of the National Old Trails Road Association.[12]

The DAR needed men's "far reaching power," but only because of gender restrictions of the time. In the teens and twenties citizens could not take roads for granted. Men in the National Old Roads Trail Association built on the women's case. They argued that creating a national highway would create more efficient travel, and it would supplement already existing rail routes. In his 1925 history of the movement, J. M. Lowe related common Progressive Era justifications for the road: "We have fallen upon a time when the insignificant wagon roads of the country demand a place on the stage of progress. Where improved, they carry six times as many passengers, daily, as the railroads and steam boats combined, and 80 percent of the freight."[13] According to Lowe, progress and road improvement went together and helped further streamline the nation. With a potent mix of patriotic, moral, and progressive zeal, concerned state officials, businesspeople, and the DAR combined forces to build such roads. A national highway was their noble project, and by 1927 Harry Truman and Arlene Moss were their fearless leaders.

With the combined efforts of the male and female organizations, the practical highway that taught patriotic lessons about the country was well on the way to becoming a reality. With the assistance of the federal government and the expansion of road construction during World War I, the group's monument to western expansion created an asphalt vein from Washington, D.C., to Los Angeles, California, in the 1920s. Once the road itself became a reality, the DAR began more elaborate plans to properly memorialize the new highway. Instead of the standard granite blocks and plaques that they used on earlier trail markings, the group envisioned a more substantial set of statues to mark out the path of historical memory. The women of the DAR, and in particular Arlene Moss, chose a monument in their own image—the "pioneer woman." Moss, who accompanied Truman to Santa Fe for the showdown on the plaza that fateful day, was the mastermind behind the *Madonna of the Trail* statue—"erected by state societies to mark the Ocean-to-Ocean Highway in honor of the pioneer mothers of the covered wagon days."[14] The design for the *Madonna* was unveiled at the Lewis and Clark Exposition held in Portland, Oregon, in 1905. Moss hired August Leimbach, a German American architectural sculptor from St. Louis, to execute the design. It is rumored that Moss used one of her young children as a model for the pioneer children depicted in the statue. Needless to say, she was very proud of the design and appeared in several promotional photographs hovering near Leimbach as he worked on the statue. The sculptures stand ten feet tall on top of six-foot bases. Each sculpture, with base, weighs a substantial seventeen tons. They were all cast in concrete from the original, using an aggregate made of Missouri granite called algonite—giving the monuments a warm, pink shade.[15] The DAR placed these identical statues in twelve states at various significant points along the "Pioneer Memorial Highway." The *Madonna* commemorated the role of women in settling the West, but it was also clearly a monument to the work of women such as Moss and organizations such as the DAR who sought expanding influence in public life and a role in shaping their preferred version of national memory.

Since the early days when Missouri women retraced and memorialized their state's trails, the terminus of the Santa Fe Trail was one of the most important sites on the historical road that Moss and the DAR subsequently mapped. The DAR placed its first statue in Springfield, Ohio, on July 4, 1928, with successive statues erected in West Virginia, Kansas, Missouri, Colorado, New Mexico, Arizona, Illinois, Indiana, Pennsylvania, California, and Maryland. From Santa Fe the DAR chose a route that would follow the Old Spanish Trail west through Arizona on the way to California.[16] Each significant point on this somewhat arbitrary mapping of historical routes deserved a monument. With its special meaning to the women of Missouri, the city at the end of the Santa Fe Trail, they believed, needed to have a *Madonna*.

After the fifteen-year effort to construct a great highway, and with twelve new monuments to install, Truman and a very proud Moss made their way toward Albuquerque in early October 1927, perhaps by highway but more likely by train. They headed off to the ninth annual state conference of the New Mexico DAR. Albuquerque's Lew Wallace chapter hosted the conference at the Art Deco Spanish Pueblo Revival Franciscan Hotel downtown. The *Santa Fe New Mexican* society page devoted a large section to the event, describing it in detail. The Albuquerque chapter decorated the hotel's Spanish Room with patriotic flourish, including "blue candies tied with red and white tulle," "dainty place cards" embossed with the DAR emblem, and a "large blue Wedgwood bowl filled with red and white flowers."[17]

According to the *New Mexican,* more than one hundred women planned to attend the conference, many of whom would also attend the seventy-person luncheon. The meeting was the largest gathering "at any state conference of the Daughters so far held." The *Pioneer Mother* was the primary focus of the meeting and the reason that Moss and Truman attended. The DAR, an organization dedicated to commemorating an Anglo-American history that did not include Hispanics or immigrants, planned to put their statue in New Mexico. On the day of the conference, the *New Mexican* described the conference's primary purpose as a "meeting to decide on the location of an historical marker, a statue of 'The Pioneer Woman,' in the state in pursuance of the program of the national organization for a marker in each state."[18]

Throughout the conference days, Moss and Truman actively pursued the statue issue in private meetings and public addresses. Santa Fe, the terminus of the western trade route from Missouri, was Moss and Truman's favored site. But the actual decision had yet to be made. During the two-day conference, Truman and Moss worked the Albuquerque crowd, which included many representatives from the Santa Fe DAR. At the Monday luncheon, after various speeches and "several pleasing vocal selections," the "toastmistress" from the Lew Wallace chapter introduced the main speaker and main subject of the afternoon: Moss and the *Madonna.* At the reception that evening, with guests including University of New Mexico president J. F. Zimmerman, Truman also spoke about the significance of the road and the monument. During the Tuesday-morning session the Albuquerque newspapers reported that the DAR passed resolutions to "stimulate renewed interests in the Bible" (a "defensive measure aimed at the American Association for the Advancement of Atheism"), they reaffirmed various patriotic and nationalistic "creeds," and they voted that "a silk flag be purchased and placed in Valley Forge Memorial Chapel." That morning Moss and Truman held a meeting with the Albuquerque Chamber of Commerce to discuss possibly placing the statue in the city. The *New Mexican* reported that the "members of the National Old Trails Committee left for Santa Fe before deciding on the erection of the Pioneer Mother's memorial monument in either place."[19] Despite Nusbaum's recollections, the pair brought only photographs with them to Santa Fe.

Moss and Truman drove up the Rio Grande valley on Tuesday afternoon to meet with the Santa Fe Chamber of Commerce and concerned citizens. Instead of meeting in broad daylight on the plaza, as Nusbaum suggested, the delegation of DAR women and Old Trails men, emboldened by the festivities in Albuquerque, hoped for a cordial meeting at a Kiwanis Club luncheon in the De Vargas Hotel. According to the *Santa Fe New Mexican,* Moss and Truman were the main presenters at the luncheon, where they described their gift to the city and the plan to place the *Madonna* on the plaza. In brief remarks the two leaders and some local historical society members described "Santa Fe's historic fame," and then the group led the Kiwanis Club in singing "the Old Trail" song. Next, according to journalists present, Moss spoke in "eloquent tribute to the Pioneer Mothers of the West."[20]

Newspapers the following day gave little indication of controversy at the luncheon, much less any shin kicking. The headline read, simply, "Albuquerque Gets Statue." The article stated, "By a vote of 5 to 2 the committee which met here yesterday decided to place New Mexico's statue of the 'Pioneer Woman' at Albuquerque."[21] In the days that followed, the real story of the meeting trickled out. Santa Fe had rejected the *Madonna of the Trail.* The community, especially certain influential artists, decided against the piece on the grounds that it was bad art, that it would cost too much, and that it represented poor historical judgment. The DAR's plan to put a *Pioneer Mother* at every significant point on their map of western movement ran into an adobe wall in Santa Fe. Chief among the critics were artist Frank Applegate and writer Mary Austin.

In the 1910s and 1920s, while Moss and the DAR planted granite monuments to Revolutionary heroes and commemorated old trails of western expansion, Santa Fe residents like Austin and Applegate were busy building an alternative to that history. Joining other artists and intellectuals who admired New Mexican culture, they found in New Mexico in general and Santa Fe in particular an antidote to the uptight Victorian philistinism, racism, and rampant nationalism of the era. The DAR epitomized the very traits that many artists and bohemians found distasteful about American society at the time. Santa Fe also seemed like an escape from the eastern establishment and mass-produced materialism of America.

These bohemians felt soothed by authentic Indian handicrafts and the rounded corners of Hispanic adobe in New Mexico. City-addled Anglos, critical of mainstream America in the 1920s, turned to the romanticized landscapes of New Mexico for relief. Where such cultural landscapes had crumbled or seemed tainted by the American presence during the territorial period, the artists and utopians commenced creation of an idealized Spanish-Pueblo past. These newcomers also saw fit to redefine the public spaces of the city and its contents. They began to reshape Santa Fe to match their desire for organic brown-adobe facades and winding lanes—a relief from the dominating grid patterns of early-twentieth-century cities like Albuquerque to the south. Cultural historian Chris Wilson describes this process of change, which began officially in 1912 when Anglo culture brokers, such as the head of the Museum of New Mexico, Edgar Lee Hewitt, initiated a comprehensive citywide historic preservation plan. Wilson argues that "Santa Fe has methodically transformed itself into a harmonious Pueblo-Spanish fantasy through speculative restorations, the removal of overt signs of Americanization, and historic design review for new buildings." This process, which continues today, is a creation of "selective historic fantasies."[22]

Of course, groups such as the preservationists in Santa Fe, the DAR, and other historically minded people frequently engage in selective histories and often in outright fantasies. In defining a regional identity for Santa Fe focused on a Hispano past, the artists of Santa Fe hoped to create a counternarrative to the DAR's equally selective story of Manifest Destiny. When the DAR delegation and the group of Santa Fe community representatives, including Austin and Applegate, met at the Kiwanis Club luncheon in 1927, they represented two contending histories about one place and, implicitly, two contending visions for the future. Each hoped to control and commemorate a different story about the region's and the nation's past. When Moss and Truman went to Santa Fe, they unknowingly entered a battle. The *Madonna of the Trail*, a piece of public art, stood at the crossroads of these two opposing and selective narratives about the country's past and future.

In more recent and familiar debates over American public history and art—from the Smithsonian Institute's *Enola Gay* exhibit to Maya Lin's *Vietnam War Memorial*—art objects have become lightning rods drawing anger and the positive energy of public debate. These fights, which often mix taste, politics, historical memory, identity, and public money, have been especially pronounced in New Mexico. Diverse cultural histories crisscross the state with often conflicting stories: Native Americans claim varied cultural geographies that reach back beyond written history, Hispanos trace their historical presence to the Spanish explorers and conquerors of the 1500s, some Mexican Americans or Chicanos may see this place as a stolen part of Mexico, and Anglos have claimed a home in the region since the mid-1800s and earlier. Each group remembers different stories or remembers the same stories differently. Creating monuments to any one of these cultural memories, to one idea of New Mexican history—or, in the DAR's case, the story of triumphant American nationalism—can easily be perceived as excluding or even dismissing others. People have literally competed over what meanings or histories they will allow to be presented in public places in the form of murals, statues, parades, and pageants. And like the debates in the past, these public battles over history reveal as much about history as they do about the hopes of communities in the present.

Some conservative critics, especially since the 1980s, saw such debates as simple bouts of so-called political correctness.[23] It may be fair to criticize the impulse to silence certain historical memories and impose others, but more often, debates over public symbols such as the *Madonna of the Trail* reveal moments of flux as communities continually redefine themselves within a democratic and pluralistic society. As more voices are included in the discussion, such contests over public art and collective memory may come closer to acknowledging historical truths about multiple competing narratives, past and present.

Most recently in Albuquerque, just such a public debate grew up around the city's decision to build a *cuarto centenario* memorial in Tiguex Park in Old Town. The memorial would commemorate Don Juan de Oñate and the four hundredth anniversary of the first Spanish settlers in New Mexico. Native American groups opposed the statue because they saw Oñate as a violent oppressor rather than a hero. The public debate grew more heated during a series of city council hearings and what journalists described as "hours of intensely emotional debate." Newspaper coverage at the time also bemoaned the price of the statue, questioning the huge expense for such a controversial piece of public art.[24]

Contests over art and meaning like the *Madonna* have animated the cultural life of contemporary New Mexico. However, it is interesting to place the recent Oñate debate alongside Santa Fe's rejection of the *Madonna of the Trail* in the mid-1920s. Native Americans assert their voices in decisions about monuments to public memory today, but in the past Anglos like Austin and Applegate used their defense of Hispano history as part of their argument to block the DAR monument to Anglo-American history. Mary Austin felt she could speak on behalf of Hispanos in Santa Fe. In their effort to champion an ideal Santa Fe cleansed of the complexity of historical memory that included the Santa Fe Trail and American pioneer mothers (though far more such pioneer mothers lived in Albuquerque),

Austin and her compatriots championed a Hispano past. Unlike the packed city council chambers during the Oñate debate, however, there is little evidence that Hispanos, Native Americans, or anyone except the members of Anglo society in Santa Fe were present at the Kiwanis Club that day in 1927. Such decisions about culture and memory were the privilege of a small group that met behind closed doors.

Austin and Applegate were neighbors who held sway in the preservation movement in Santa Fe, and they felt an urgency to speak on behalf of others. A recent arrival in Santa Fe, Austin in particular quickly possessed influence as a famous writer of novels and works such as *Land of Little Rain* that helped to inspire early-twentieth-century regionalism and environmentalism. In addition, she was well connected and respected among contemporary artists linked to the city, including Ansel Adams. Champions of regional identity, Austin and Applegate helped revive Hispanic crafts in New Mexico. According to historian Suzanne Forrest, Austin saw her preservation efforts as "a means of restoring integrity and self esteem to their cultural practitioners, and she intended to use them as a profound object lesson for her fellow Americans."[25] Both Austin and Applegate saw in New Mexico a preindustrial ideal of village life, a regional character as yet unravaged by the modern American obsessions with mass-produced goods and empty, mechanized lives. Austin was instrumental in preserving the Santuario de Chimayó, an important chapel north of Santa Fe. With visual artist Applegate she also founded the Spanish Colonial Arts Society. The pair used their cultural authority in the community to help foster a market for Hispano handicrafts, defining what they thought should be considered both authentic and high-quality art. In a reactionary decade marked by increased lynching in the South and a strengthened Ku Klux Klan throughout the country, as well as a general nativist tone to politics, Austin and Applegate saw the *Madonna of the Trail* as an extension of such attitudes. The bohemians in Santa Fe had good reason to block the DAR at the gates of their city.

Applegate and Austin also cast themselves as the true representatives of elevated artistic taste in a world full of people such as Arlene Moss. According to J. D. De Huff, secretary of the Santa Fe Chamber of Commerce, the DAR had telegraphed ahead from the Albuquerque conference to invite a number of people to come to the meeting at La Fonda after the Kiwanis Club luncheon. Apparently, the DAR in Santa Fe thought that local artists would support the Santa Fe claim to the statue. But they made a big miscalculation. Only Applegate and Austin showed up, and they probably arrived before the appointed time of "a quarter to two o'clock," for they cooled their heels awaiting the delegation for nearly an hour, according to

Austin.[26] When the committee finally did arrive, Applegate and Austin were prepared to block the statue. In the exchange that followed, the artist and writer clashed with Moss over New Mexican and American history. They faced off over issues of middlebrow and highbrow tastes, and they ultimately decided that the statue would find a more welcoming home in Albuquerque.

The decision was not made in a civil manner. According to De Huff, the meeting "was somewhat discourteously taken out of the chamber's hands by individuals not members" (Applegate and Austin) who attacked the sculpture on artistic grounds. Authentic, tasteful art formed a crucial component of the unique cultural identity that Applegate and Austin hoped to create, preserve, and perpetuate in Santa Fe. Hispanic art and history were entwined in their romance with New Mexico. The handcrafted, one-of-a-kind pieces of folk art that Austin and Applegate promoted represented the cultural antithesis of Moss's twelve mass-produced *Madonna*s, which Applegate described as "near alike as cement blocks." The fight over the statue was first a fight over taste. After canvassing all of the artists in Santa Fe, Applegate said that he had found not one representative who supported the "inartistic," even "atrocious," statue. Applegate claimed sculptural authority, describing his credentials and his knowledge of the casting process that brought the *Madonna of the Trail* to life. He questioned the use of concrete, suggesting that the material was appropriate only for "sidewalks, paving, cellar walls, foundations and many other useful purposes, but is hardly considered suitable for sculpture." Austin volunteered that she came from a long line of pioneer women and that they looked nothing like the *Pioneer Mother* "caricature." According to the Santa Fe newspapers, the pair riffed at length as Mrs. Moss, the *Madonna*'s proud designer, "became furious."[27]

In an editorial published among the flurry of letters and articles in the weeks after the clash at La Fonda, the *New Mexican* suggested, jokingly, that in the future the "best qualified people" should work with the city council on "skyscrapers, trees, architecture, statuary offenses, and beautification in general" as an "unobtrusive way of having the artistic temperament seep through us low brows [sic]."[28] The clash over the statue was also about who held cultural authority in Santa Fe.

As Moss fumed, Austin and Applegate mapped out a very different historical road for the gathering. The mass-produced concrete memorial evoked a story of westward expansion, the standard triumphant narrative of Anglo trails from east to west. In contrast, Austin and Applegate celebrated a Hispano history and artistic tradition that moved from south to north on the Camino Real—a history reenacted annually in the Fiesta de Santa Fe pageant and embodied by New

Mexico Highway 1 (the Camino Real Highway). In a letter published many days after the meeting, Austin responded to her critics, restating the points she made at the meeting. According to Austin, the DAR celebrated the wrong pioneers: "The pioneers of New Mexico are not the pioneers of the D.A.R.; they should have been consulted and that I considered it profoundly discourteous for the D.A.R. to think of setting up one of their monuments in the city of Santa Fe without the widely expressed approbation of the New Mexican Pioneers." Like Moss and the DAR in honoring the Santa Fe Trail, Austin memorialized the Spanish road and argued on behalf of Santa Fe's Hispano pioneer past. The two trails and their opposing memorializing visions clashed like the two strong women at the meeting that day. After a long morning of meetings, Moss simply had enough. Up until the last remarks, according to Applegate, "Mrs. Moss seemed intent on the statue's coming to Santa Fe, but her anger overcoming her she tossed it to Albuquerque."[29]

For obvious reasons, Moss seems to have taken Applegate's criticism of the statue particularly hard. As president of the DAR's national committee she also may not have been accustomed to such public challenges to her own cultural authority and patriotic mission. Austin remembered that Moss rudely interrupted Applegate's critique and that she presided over the meeting with a "general superior manner" that, according to Austin, warranted "an answering rudeness."[30] Moss eventually grew so angry that she asked Applegate to be silent or leave. However, in the press coverage of the meeting, few if any of Moss's own words were quoted. The Chamber, not Moss, according to the *Santa Fe New Mexican,* rejected the statue. But Moss would take it to Albuquerque. The clash over cultural authority that day at the La Fonda Hotel in Santa Fe was not as public or quite as physical as Jesse Nusbaum remembered it, but the showdown was no less dramatic. Two roads of historical memory met at Santa Fe and found no room for each other.

Lost in both of these exclusory stories about the region's past was any sense of what actually occurred in the West—the real story of how these two historic trajectories, the Santa Fe Trail and the Camino Real, intersected and overlapped as routes of trade and exchange. As self-appointed defenders of Hispano culture in New Mexico, the preservationists of Santa Fe told a story of movement from south to north that featured heroic Spanish figures like Oñate and Don Juan de Vargas. There was no place in this selective history for a pioneer woman from Missouri. In their desire to cleanse the city of a middlebrow, mass-produced reminder of Anglo-American history in New Mexico's past and present, Applegate and Austin helped to deprive the city of a more layered history of place. Similarly, the DAR's single-minded, nationalistic, and even racist vision of coast-to-coast expansion mapped over a more complex and multicultural history of the West. And neither of these selective histories included Native Americans.

Soon after this contentious debate, the *Santa Fe New Mexican* offered congratulations to Albuquerque for "landing the pioneer woman statue." Most newspaper coverage in Santa Fe seemed to side with the DAR, and most editorials made comical jabs at the small clique of influential artists. In a more plaintive moment, the *New Mexican* lamented that Santa Fe seemed to be locked on a course to remove the city's Anglo pioneer past. Many of the older buildings in Santa Fe, "over whose doorsills these pioneer women stepped," according to one editorial, "are being thrust out of the way without passing thought."³¹

Indeed, by the mid-1920s Santa Feans were well on their way to re-creating their city to evoke their romance for a Hispano past, often covering over or tearing down evidence of the territorial period. As it turned out, Santa Fe's romantics and Albuquerque's Progressives matched each other in their zeal to manufacture an identity for their respective cities. Just as railroad-era newcomers in Albuquerque eschewed the old plaza, placed a grid atop old farmland, and replaced the adobe and *acequia* past in their rush to construct a thoroughly modern New Town, Santa Fe artists moved in the opposite direction, toward an identity for Santa Fe that carefully edited the American past. These efforts to create a dominant civic facade had as much to do with reverence for the past as they did with the practical requirements of a booming tourist and business economy. And by the late 1920s both cities competed for tourist dollars.³²

With the tourist industry in full swing, Albuquerque took some steps to create an adobe image, but unlike Santa Fe the transition was never so complete or systematic. Albuquerque remained a jumble of old and new. As early as 1908, years before the Spanish Pueblo revival style became codified in the city to the north, Albuquerque flirted with Spanish and Indian architectural styles on the campus of the University of New Mexico. Albuquerque was a main stop along the Fred Harvey Company's tour of the Southwest, and the city saw direct benefits from a tourist economy that exploited Indian and Hispano culture and history. But Albuquerque only slowly began to construct city buildings, such as the Franciscan Hotel, in the stage-set Spanish Pueblo revival style. Albuquerque did not benefit from the money or expertise of City Beautiful plans that helped to lay out Santa Fe's unique character as a re-created Hispano village. Despite the lofty dreams of early city commissioners, Albuquerque never developed one coherent plan—either romantic or classical. By the late 1920s Santa Fe had successfully changed its image to draw tourism. Albuquerque was less romantic, reflecting an air of middle-class practicality and inauthentic Route 66 kitschyness—the kind of town that would welcome the *Madonna*.

The DAR planned their unveiling ceremony to coincide with the First American Celebration, a pageant that preoccupied the headlines and the streets of Albuquerque in the late summer of 1928. The First American Celebration exhibited Albuquerque's own crass version of utopianism, a more blatantly Chamber of Commerce version of a usable past. Yet it too held out a vision of the city's future. Each issue of the *Albuquerque Tribune* and the *Albuquerque Journal* during the September celebration featured pictures of local politicians and businessmen greeting dignitaries from pueblos around the state. One such photograph featured Albuquerque mayor Clyde Tingley standing next to a man in a buckskin outfit and war bonnet. The caption read, "Here is Chief White Hat Tingley, of the Albuquerque tribe, playing host to Chief Big Feather of San Ildefonso." The celebration of first Americans appeared to be a vaguely Wild West Show–like "production"—more tourist spectacle than a celebration of anyone's specific history. In particular the pageant appeared to make fun of local Indians while at the same time showing them off to Route 66 tourists. The pageant was also a strange kind of early multicultural event that made room for the caricatured diversity of "troops, cowboys, Indians, [and] Spanish," as one headline announced. The timing and mood that week in Albuquerque could not have been more appropriate, or more surreal, for the unveiling of the *Pioneer Mother*.[33]

The DAR's own pageant of American nationalism then had to compete with the weeklong parade of spirited events and quasi-historical celebrations that the *Journal* called a "strange mixture of the history of the ancient, the pioneer and the modern southwest." Through the bustling crowds of tourists and New Mexicans from cities, reservations, and pueblos around the state, Clyde Tingley, the Albuquerque fire chief, and Arlene Moss led a group of more than four hundred people on a short parade through downtown, from the Franciscan Hotel to McClellan Park, for the unveiling ceremony at eleven o'clock. The day before, the *Tribune* announced that a genuine "pioneer mother, as yet unidentified," would lead the procession on Thursday morning, but she never materialized in time for the parade or the ceremony. Harry Truman, who appeared on the schedule, also failed to make it. The *Journal* stated that the DAR's aim in placing this statue was to "perpetuate the spirit of the pathfinder and the trailblazer" and commemorate "the advance of civilization over the National Old Trails highway." Such a statement seems nonsensical, made at the very moment when Albuquerque was so busy celebrating the diverse cultural history and present of the region. The words reveal the level of casual disrespect of Native Americans and Hispanics at the time. Yet the First American Celebration, with its swirl of Indian, Spanish, and Anglo cultural representations, could not help but undermine the DAR's stated purpose. The very vibrancy of Indian and Spanish civilization (albeit caricatured) that Albuquerqueans witnessed on the streets that week seemed to belie the DAR's message that Anglo pioneers brought civilization to the West. When watched in relief against the celebration, these pioneers appeared to have added one civilization among many others—each one competing for tourist attention in the streets of Albuquerque.[34]

The clash over cultural authority on Santa Fe's plaza in 1927 was not as public or quite as physical as Jesse Nusbaum had remembered it, but the showdown was no less dramatic. Two roads of historical memory met at Santa Fe and found no room for each other on the map of the West. Lost in either of the exclusory stories about the region's past was any sense of interaction that actually occurred in the West—the real story of how these two historic trajectories, the Santa Fe Trail and the Camino Real, intersected and overlapped as historic routes of trade and exchange.

In the end, the history of these conflicting yet idealized visions of the past has a physical presence in the remains of McClellan Park behind Albuquerque's new federal courthouse. There, in the area once known as New Town, you can still find the *Madonna of the Trail* standing near Fourth Street on a defunct stretch of Route 66. Many also consider Fourth Street the path through Albuquerque that closely follows the route of the old Camino Real. The *Pioneer Mother* now faces West, looking not at the terminus of either the Santa Fe Trail or the Camino Real but more appropriately at a point where trade routes overlapped, where Mexican traders, Indians, Hispano farmers, and pioneering women may have actually passed by each other on their travels in every direction.

Notes

I would like to thank Chris Wilson for his comments on the original manuscript and especially Virginia Scharff for reading drafts, for convening the original conference, and for her early support of my interest in urban environmental and social history. For a related discussion, please refer to my book *McClellan Park: The Life and Death of an Urban Green Space* (2004).

1. Rosemary Nusbaum, *Tierra Dulce: Reminiscences from the Jesse Nusbaum Papers* (Santa Fe: Sun Stone Press, 1980), 59–60.

2. "DAR Delegation Hears Santa Fe's Historic Fame," *Santa Fe New Mexican,* October 4, 1928.

3. "Applegate Voiced Protest Against Statue Immediately," *Santa Fe New Mexican,* October 19, 1927, 3.

4. See Joseph M. Lowe, *National Old Trails Road: The Great Historic Highway of America; A Brief Resume of the Principal Events Connected With the Rebuilding of the Old Cumberland—Now the National Old Trails Road—from Washington and Baltimore to Los Angeles* (Kansas City, Mo.: National Old Trail Road Association, 1925).

5. See Frederic L. Paxson, "The Highway Movement, 1916–1935," *American Historical Review* 51, no. 2 (1946) 236–53. For more about early car culture, see David L. Lewis and Laurence Goldstein, eds., *The Automobile and American Culture* (Ann Arbor: University of Michigan Press, 1980); Martin Wachs and Margaret Crawford, eds., *The Car and the City: The Automobile, the Built Environment, and Daily Urban Life* (Ann Arbor: University of Michigan Press, 1991); and Virginia Scharff, *Taking the Wheel: Women and the Coming of the Motor Age* (Albuquerque: University of New Mexico Press, 1992).

6. See David Kammer, *The Historic and Architectural Resources of Route 66 Through New Mexico,* prepared for the New Mexico Historic Preservation Division (Santa Fe: New Mexico Historic Preservation Division, 1992), and *Historic Highway Bridges of New Mexico: An Historic Context on New Mexico's Highway Bridges* (Santa Fe: New Mexico State Highway and Transportation Department, 1996); Steven R. Rae, *New Mexico Bridge Survey* (Santa Fe: New Mexico State Highway and Transportation Department and the Federal Highway Administration, Region 6, 1987); and Chris Wilson, *Auto-Oriented Commercial Development in Albuquerque, New Mexico, 1916–1956: Multiple Property Documentation Form* (Washington, D.C.: National Register of Historic Places, 1996).

7. Paxson, "Highway Movement," 242; Helen Peters, "Madonna of the Trail," *New Mexico Magazine,* December 1993, 48.

8. "Madonna of the Trail," *Daughters of the American Revolution Magazine,* July 1929, 399.

9. "The Santa Fe Transportation Co.," 1929, Madonna of the Trail, Vertical File, Center for Southwest Research, University of New Mexico.

10. See *D.A.R. Manual for Citizenship* (Washington, D.C.: Judd and Detweiler, 1945); Martha Strayer, *The D.A.R.: An Informal History* (Washington, D.C.: Public Affairs Press, 1958); and Margaret Gibbs, *The DAR* (New York: Holt, Rinehart, and Winston, 1969).

11. "Madonna of the Trail," 402.

12. Ibid.

13. Lowe, *National Old Trails Road,* 11.

14. "Madonna of the Trail," 402.

15. Peters, "Madonna of the Trail," 50.

16. "Santa Fe Transportation Co."

17. "Luncheons and Receptions at D.A.R. State Conference Are Charming Social Features," *Santa Fe New Mexican,* October 8, 1927, 2.

18. Ibid.; "Hundred at D.A.R. Meet," *Santa Fe New Mexican,* October 3, 1927.

19. "Daughters to Fight Atheism and Democracy," *Santa Fe New Mexican*, October 5, 1927, 6.

20. "D.A.R. Delegation Hears Santa Fe's Historic Fame," *Santa Fe New Mexican*, October 4, 1927, 2.

21. "Albuquerque Gets Statue," *Santa Fe New Mexican*, October 5, 1927, 6.

22. Chris Wilson, *The Myth of Santa Fe: Creating a Modern Regional Tradition* (Albuquerque: University of New Mexico Press, 1997), 232.

23. For an excellent discussion of public art in the 1980s, see Casey Nelson Blake, "An Atmosphere of Effrontery: Richard Serra, *Tilted Arc*, and the Crisis of Public Art," in *The Power of Culture: Critical Essays in American History*, edited by Richard Wightman Fox and T. J. Jackson Lears (Chicago: University of Chicago Press, 1993), 247–89; and Erika Doss, *Spirit Poles and Flying Pigs: Public Art and Cultural Democracy in American Communities* (Washington, D.C.: Smithsonian Institution Press, 1995).

24. "Onate Gets His Day," *Albuquerque Tribune*, March 7, 2000, A1; "Time for a Decision on Onate," *Albuquerque Journal*, February 28, 2000, A8.

25. Suzanne Forrest, *The Preservation of the Village: New Mexico's Hispanics and the New Deal* (Albuquerque: University of New Mexico Press, 1989), 53.

26. "Chamber of Commerce Gives Version of Statue Episode," *Santa Fe New Mexican*, October 14, 1927, 5; "Mary Austin Asked for Her Opinion on Statue and Gave It; Mrs. Moss Discourteous," *Santa Fe New Mexican*, October 18, 1927.

27. "Chamber of Commerce"; "Applegate Voiced Protest," 3; "Mary Austin Asked for Her Opinion."

28. "Let Us Forget it," *Santa Fe New Mexican*, October 18, 1927, 4.

29. "Mary Austin Asked for Her Opinion"; "Applegate Voiced Protest."

30. "Mary Austin Asked for Her Opinion."

31. *New Mexico State Tribune*, September 28, 1928.

32. For more on the general history of this period in Albuquerque and the changes in the New Town, see Marc Simmons, *Albuquerque: A Narrative History* (Albuquerque: University of New Mexico Press, 1982). For specifics about the area where the statue found a home, see Jeffrey C. Sanders, *McClellan Park: The Death and Life of an Urban Green Space* (Albuquerque: Albuquerque Museum Press, 2004). For more on the character of Albuquerque and the University of New Mexico's architecture after the turn of the century, see Carleen Lazzell, "From Red Brick to Pueblo Revival: Early Architecture at the University of New Mexico," *New Mexico Historical Review* 64, no. 1 (1989): 1–23.

33. See coverage of the various events in the *Albuquerque Journal*, September 27, 1928, and the *New Mexico State Tribune*, September 19 and 28, 1928.

34. See the original unveiling program in the Madonna of the Trail Vertical File, Center for Southwest Research, University of New Mexico.

Reclaiming Cannery Row's Industrial History

CONNIE Y. CHIANG

John Steinbeck's 1945 novel, *Cannery Row,* brought to life the Monterey, California, waterfront during the sardine industry's heyday. Surrounded by the hustle and bustle of the fish plants, Steinbeck's characters live on the margins of society. Mack and the boys hang out under the black cypress tree, live in a fish-meal storage warehouse, and frequently stock up on alcohol and other goods at Lee Chong's general store. Dora Flood, the neighborhood madam, runs the Bear Flag Restaurant. At the center of the novel is Doc, a wise, kind man who owns the Western Biological Laboratory, which collects and distributes a wide range of marine and terrestrial specimens to schools and supply houses. Doc draws these eccentric individuals together, and the plot revolves around Mack and the boys' attempts to throw him a party as a token of appreciation for his generosity to the community.

Although the novel was based on real people and places—Steinbeck was close friends with Ed Ricketts, the inspiration for Doc, and spent a considerable amount of time at his Cannery Row laboratory in the 1930s—it is a work of fiction and far from a complete portrait of the neighborhood's history. In particular, *Cannery Row* made only brief mention of the individuals who toiled in the fish plants and at sea in the 1930s and 1940s. During the height of the sardine season, which spanned from August until February, roughly two to three thousand people labored in the canneries. Many workers were local residents; several hundred others were migrants who lived in Monterey temporarily, then found work elsewhere after the canneries shut down for the season.[1] They were attracted to Monterey because of the prosperity of Cannery Row, particularly during World War II, when the federal government took over the fishery and demanded peak production. Local fishermen answered the call to duty, landing no fewer than 145,000 tons of sardines and as many as 200,000 tons in a given season from 1940 to 1946.

Cannery Row's meteoric rise preceded a precipitous postwar collapse. A combination of overfishing and environmental conditions caused sardine catches to plunge by the late 1940s. During the 1946–47 season Monterey landed only 31,240 tons of sardines; the figure dropped to 17,630 tons the following season. Canners, desperate to keep their fish factories humming, trucked in sardines from San Pedro and began packing anything that fishermen caught, including squid. Facing barren seas around Monterey, many fishermen headed south to work.[2] These stopgap measures, however, could not see the industry through to better days. The sardine stocks never fully rebounded, and many canners decided to cut their losses. One by one they shut down the fish plants, their contents sold off and their empty shells rented out to new tenants or left vacant.[3]

Art studios, restaurants, retails shops, and light industrial businesses came to occupy some of the former sardine canneries, and curious Steinbeck fans began to visit the neighborhood that had inspired the author. The city even played up these connections by changing the official name of the street from Ocean View Avenue to Cannery Row in 1957. But despite the literary draw and the city's passage of the 1961 Cannery Row Plan, a development scheme for the neighborhood, it suffered from neglect and arson into the 1950s and 1960s.[4] In an effort to further revitalize the neighborhood, planners revised the Cannery Row Plan in 1973, highlighting the picturesque coastline and its ability to punctuate the decaying industrial buildings.[5] These redevelopment plans were not laden with utopian discourse, but they placed confidence in the ability of Steinbeck nostalgia and natural beauty—not Monterey's industrial history—to revive the neighborhood. They paid little attention to the cold and wet working conditions, the long hours, the persistent odors, or the labor disputes, let alone the environmental and human factors that led to the sardine fishery's collapse. As Cannery Row continued to shift to a service economy, a crucial era in Monterey's history was seemingly erased, replaced by Steinbeck's fictional depiction of it.[6]

By the early 1980s, however, historic preservationists along with some city officials, business owners, and local residents began to push for the recovery of the sardine industry's past and its inclusion in the city's historical narrative. Recognizing the incomplete coverage of previous public history efforts, they began to reclaim the labor history of the canneries and attempted to bring the diverse, largely immigrant workforce to the center of the neighborhood's storied history. They began to address the fishery's collapse and Cannery Row's postindustrial transformation.

They no longer focused exclusively on Steinbeck's idealized vision of social outcasts forming an interdependent community in the shadows of the fish factories, with faint mention of the workings of the fishery. Instead, this neighborhood's public image started to include the experiences of the real people who built the sardine industry, struggled to find a place in it, and witnessed its dramatic fall. However, given the dominance of Monterey's tourism industry and the persistent need to attract visitors, these projects were also limited in their scope and continued to exclude the more contentious and unpleasant aspects of Cannery Row's history. Ultimately, an idealized past remained a powerful force that continued to shape the neighborhood's development projects.

"Rebirth" at the Monterey Bay Aquarium

The Monterey Bay Aquarium spearheaded one of the first efforts to reclaim the labor history of Cannery Row. Plans for the institution came to life in the late 1970s, when a group of graduate students—Steve Webster, Chuck Baxter, Robin Burnett, and Nancy Burnett—at Stanford University's Hopkins Marine Station spotted the neighboring Hovden cannery and came up with the idea to transform the site into an aquarium that would display the diversity of Monterey Bay life.[7] Nancy Burnett approached her parents, Lucile Packard and David Packard, of electronic company Hewlett-Packard fame, and they agreed to fund a feasibility study, conducted by the Stanford Research Institute.[8] When the results were favorable, the Packards established the private, nonprofit Monterey Bay Aquarium Foundation in April 1978 and agreed to fund construction.[9]

The aquarium planning group, which included the original group of Hopkins graduate students and Julie Packard, another Packard daughter, wasted little time in getting the aquarium under way. The foundation bought the Hovden property from Stanford University, which had acquired the defunct cannery in 1967 to provide a buffer from future Cannery Row development, for just under one million dollars.[10] In the fall of 1978 it hired Linda Rhodes as project manager and the architectural firm of Esherick, Homsey, Dodge, and Davis, which had designed the Long Marine Laboratory at the University of California at Santa Cruz.[11] By 1979 the planning group had conceived of a 226,000-square-foot building with decks on three levels. Contractors Rudolph and Sletten estimated a period of thirty-one months to build the aquarium at a cost of thirty-one million dollars. The aquarium decided that it would make its own exhibits, bringing the total cost estimate to fifty million dollars.[12]

Before construction could begin, several government agencies had to approve the project. In addition to addressing potential impacts on parking, traffic, and local ecosystems, the aquarium planners also had to attend to concerns about the historical significance of the Hovden building. Charged with keeping navigable waters open, the U.S. Army Corps of Engineers also evaluated cultural resources and determined that the former sardine plant was eligible for the National Register of Historic Places. As part of the required mitigation measures, the aquarium hired Donald Fitzgerald to prepare a historical report on the Hovden cannery. Fitzgerald completed this comprehensive study in November 1979, detailing the evolution of the sardine canning and reduction processes and the history of the building and its numerous renovations and additions.[13]

Fitzgerald also called attention to the Steinbeck nostalgia that pervaded the Cannery Row neighborhood and the discrepancies between fact and fiction. He wrote, "Steinbeck is now firmly linked to the street he made famous, and the public is equally firm in its romanticized version of what Cannery Row was like. Perhaps the old adage is applicable here—Cannery Row isn't like it used to be, and probably never was." With little knowledge of the actual history of Cannery Row, tourists believed that the street they visited was a vestige of Steinbeck's novel. Yet by the late 1970s it stood in stark contrast to *Cannery Row*. He explained: "Strolling down the refurbished Cannery Row, one senses a feeling of affluence . . . which seems paradoxical to the area that Steinbeck called 'a stink, a grating noise' and 'an odor of rotting fish and the indescribable smell of fish meal.' The smell seems to have turned to sweet success."[14]

The aquarium would become central to the continuing growth of Cannery Row's service economy, but planners and designers were mindful of the industrial past. Rather than razing the historic Hovden cannery and putting up a modern structure, Charles Davis and Linda Rhodes were intent on "preserving the form" of the Hovden plant and designing a building that conformed to the surrounding industrial architecture. They believed that the cannery was "a special place . . . filled with history and metaphor that had to be imbedded in the building," and they "savored its mixture of mill construction, white paint and sunlight pouring into the interior through skylights on the roof." As Davis explained, "We held on to the cannery's façade along Cannery Row as a means of welding the building to its past." Their aquarium design replicated the former plant, with exposed pipes, ducts, and framing on the ceiling inside. As one journalist proclaimed, "The aquarium fits right in because, with its plain cement walls and jumble of rooflines, it too looks like, well, a fish cannery."[15]

In addition to "preserving the form" of the Hovden cannery, aquarium designers and planners also decided to restore the former boiler house, which had once supplied steam for heating the cannery and cooking the sardines. Although it would not generate power for the aquarium, it would be "a powerful reminder of the aquarium's first use as an industrial plant," according to Linda Rhodes and Charles Davis. Aquarium technical specialist Maury Cooper elaborated, "The boiler is symbolic of the old cannery. It was the heart of the old cannery. We—especially Mr. Packard—didn't want to cut the heart out." To save the cannery's core, construction crews had to work carefully around the boiler house as they demolished the rest of the fish plant. They then built the new structure around it.[16]

Falling apart and missing several parts, the boiler house could not be restored without the help of those who had once worked in the fish-processing plants. Former cannery worker Dorothy Wheeler and former Hovden manager Anthony Souza introduced Cooper and aquarium staff members John Christiansen and Jody Armstrong to Hovden machinist Frank Bergara. Bergara, in turn, brought in Al Campoy, the last boiler operator at the old Hovden cannery, to help with the project. With his wife, Esther, who had also worked in the cannery, Campoy had saved a few mementos from their time at the plant, including a boiler repair kit. More important, he still remembered how the boilers worked, and he and Bergara helped Cooper and Christiansen redraw the boiler-room plans. Their assistance proved to be indispensable. As Christiansen explained, "You're looking for parts no one has used for forty years. . . . Finally we asked the guys, 'Was there something up there with a spring on it?' and they said 'Oh yeah! We used to have to go jump up and down on it every now and then.'" The plans complete, Cooper compiled a list of one thousand missing parts and launched a statewide search to find them. Although many boiler parts were sold to South American fish plants after the Monterey sardine industry collapsed, he ultimately did not have to look far. The owners of the nearby Monterey Boiler Company, Aubrey and Tom Burris, donated more than twenty thousand dollars' worth of vintage boiler parts. As the pieces of the boiler house came together, the aquarium proclaimed that it was "bringing the past back to life."[17]

To complete the restoration of the boiler house, construction crews installed three fiberglass smokestacks, the tallest towering 120 feet, in October 1983, one year before the aquarium's grand opening. Seven former cannery workers, including Bergara and Campoy, watched. Bergara remarked, "This looks just like it did when we were here." To celebrate the occasion and to thank the workers for their assistance, aquarium director Julie Packard raised a glass of champagne and proposed a toast. "Let's call this a rebirth of the cannery," she exclaimed. According to *Monterey Herald* journalist Kathleen McGuire, the former cannery workers "seemed amused and pleased with the respect they were being accorded." This was a dramatic turnaround from the sardine industry's height, when Dorothy Wheeler remembered, "People didn't like us, we smelled bad," and Bergara recalled being called a "cannery bum."[18]

Once reviled, the former cannery workers played an instrumental role in the aquarium's boiler-house restoration. Although the aquarium displayed the beauty and diversity of Monterey Bay marine life for tourist consumption—a huge shift from what had transpired inside the Hovden cannery—the planners and designers acknowledged the importance of Cannery Row's industrial history and realized that their renovations should include the people who processed thousands of tons of sardines every season. In recognition of the aquarium's efforts to pay homage to the industrial history of its site, the California Historical Society presented it with an Award of Merit for Historical Preservation at its opening-day celebration on October 20, 1984.[19]

However, historic preservation was never central to the Monterey Bay Aquarium's mission, and the cannery workers and the history of the sardine industry were peripheral to its programs. Although the aquarium may have looked like a cannery, former workers like Frank Bergara and Al Campoy enjoyed only a brief moment in the limelight. Enticed by the beautiful displays, most visitors breezed by the restored boiler house that was once the "heart" of the Hovden cannery. Inside the faux-industrial shell was an institution that bore little resemblance to its former life, both in its function and in the type of people who frequented it. The aquarium incorporated and respected the industrial past, but its wild success depended on its stunning sea-life exhibits—not its tributes to the sardine heyday and the people who sustained it.

Reuniting a "Rapidly Diminishing Resource"

Unlike the participants in the Hovden boiler-house restoration, dozens of other former cannery workers and fishermen did not enjoy such interest in their past labor. To remedy this situation, local resident Michael Hemp decided to create a forum to celebrate their experiences. After Hemp moved to the Monterey Peninsula in 1979, he developed a personal interest in the history of Cannery Row, which, at this time, had received little attention from local journalists and the "historical establishment." This oversight developed, Hemp explained, because "Cannery Row was widely viewed as a filthy, smelly, distasteful, immoral blot on the good name of Monterey." To beat "the race against the daily obituaries," he decided to record the memories of the men and women who had fished the bay and toiled in the canneries. Rather than just focusing on John Steinbeck and Edward Ricketts, he wanted to chronicle "the entire human history of Cannery Row."[20]

Hemp's dedication to recovering this "human history" culminated in the establishment of the nonprofit Cannery Row Foundation in 1983. As executive director one of his first projects was organizing the "Great Cannery Row Reunion," a gathering of Cannery Row "alumni," in May 1983. They congregated at the Outrigger Restaurant on Cannery Row, passed around old photos, reconnected with friends, and reminisced about both their labor in the canneries and their leisure time at the end of the workday. As Charlie Nonella, a former worker who was born in the Cannery Row neighborhood, remembered, "We worked hard and played hard." Although alcohol had flowed freely and prostitution was commonplace, the alumni also insisted that Cannery Row was a safe place with "no troubles on the street."[21]

Not surprisingly, nostalgia tinged the alumni's memories, and Nonella and others even claimed that they would return to work in the canneries if they were ever to open again. In particular, Nonella missed the camaraderie, including the sing-alongs that his boss led as a way to get the workers through the "monotonous and tiresome work." Of course, the celebrants were surrounded by changes that made a return to the past untenable. Sara Souza, a former fish packer and wife of former Hovden manager Anthony Souza, called attention to the aquarium under construction down the street. She remarked, "Mr. Hovden would have been very happy to know that an aquarium is being built where his cannery was."[22] Souza seemed to understand that the canneries would not open again and that the evolution of Cannery Row would proceed. The continuing conversion of fish plants into service businesses was the future of Cannery Row, not a revitalization of the sardine industry.

For the next five years the Great Cannery Row Reunion was an annual event that celebrated the former workers and allowed them to express their pride in their industrial labor. Much like the individuals who assisted with the aquarium's boilerhouse restoration, some participants were surprised by the attention to their past lives. As Frank Tanaka, who worked in the canneries for eight years, explained, "It feels kind of strange to be glorified all of a sudden when we were the lowest workers in the community." Antonette Villines recalled how local merchants once turned up their noses at cannery workers' stench, but she also knew that their purchases kept them in business. She had endured dirty, damp, and dangerous working conditions for her money and was proud that it had come from "the sweat of my brow." Charlie Nonella added, "So many people seem to be ashamed to admit that they worked at the cannery, which to me is an honor. The canneries made Monterey and kept the town solid with the payrolls they had."[23]

While local newspaper stories on the reunions and the former cannery workers usually focused on their work and leisure, their connections to John Steinbeck, however tenuous, were also a source of intrigue. Lawrence Nervo recalled coming across the man upon whom Steinbeck based the character of "Mac" in *Cannery Row*. "Mac was a real gentleman. And he was very smart. But he was a wino," he explained. He was also eager to recount how he bought firecrackers from Wing Chong, the inspiration for the "Lee Chong" character, and sold cats to Ed Ricketts. Similarly, Charlie Nonella recalled that Steinbeck was "kinda surly. I got the idea he resented some of us younger kids goin' over to the lab to visit Ricketts. Everybody liked Ed, you see. Ed did that kinda thing to people." He also remembered Mac as a "cagey guy" who "always had a scam of some kind going" and Flora Woods, the madam who was the inspiration for the "Dora Flood" character, as a classy lady.[24]

The annual reunions inspired and supplemented other historical research. By 1985 Hemp had recorded three hundred hours of testimony from one hundred Cannery Row alumni—a "rapidly diminishing resource," in Hemp's mind. Not only was it difficult to locate former workers with whom to speak, but the interviews posed other challenges. As Nonella lamented, "I'm sorry the Cannery Row Foundation didn't start years ago when a lot of these people were younger and it was fresher in their memories. We have a hell of a time dragging the stories out of the people. We do it by bits and pieces." Hemp also authored *Cannery Row: The History of Old Ocean View Avenue*, which was published in 1986. Illustrated with more than one hundred black-and-white photographs, the book traces the history of Cannery Row beginning in the late nineteenth century and includes John Steinbeck's connections to the neighborhood. Despite these accomplishments in recovering Cannery Row's human history, however, a lack of funding forced Hemp to cease the operations of the Cannery Row Foundation in 1988.[25]

After a hiatus the Cannery Row Foundation was revived in 1993, and the Great Cannery Row Reunion enjoyed a comeback. In October 1997 the foundation organized another gathering of about fifty alumni at the Monterey Plaza Hotel on Cannery Row. Michael Hemp returned to address the group, proclaiming, "You folks really are Cannery Row, and that's why we're here today. You represent the time and the toil that went into the epic years of Cannery Row. You are all a part of what we want very much to remember." Monterey mayor Dan Albert concurred: "The stories that you tell here today need to be passed on to other generations.... [I]t's so important for the total history of Monterey." While Albert acknowledged that these stories were central to Monterey's historical identity, Hemp realized that the race against the clock was becoming increasingly difficult to win. At the 1998 reunion, he explained, "The reunion is smaller than it has been in years, and that unfortunately reflects the fact that many of the alumni are no longer with us."[26]

As they had at earlier reunions, the Cannery Row alumni passed around the microphone to share anecdotes from their times in the fish plants. The distinctive whistle of each cannery calling them to work at all hours of the day and the persistent fish odor were common memories. Gordon White remembered how the smell got into his hair, teeth, and clothes, making for an unpleasant and embarrassing bus ride home from work. Lucido Solis recalled how the women tried to mask the fish stench with perfume and talcum powder before they went dancing after work. Others recounted their workplace romances, while many talked about the union, which improved working conditions with overtime pay, regular breaks, and higher wages. Al Campoy, the boiler man who helped with the aquarium project, concluded, "I love these [reunions]. I get to see a lot of old friends. I still have a lot of memories of Cannery Row."[27]

Collectively, the Cannery Row alumni's recollections demonstrated that Steinbeck's novel provided an incomplete snapshot of the neighborhood's history. While the alumni remembered the eccentric individuals who inspired the novel, their memories offered a more comprehensive and complex account of Cannery Row during the height of the sardine industry. Similar to the novel's portrayal of Cannery Row life, they remembered that people got along and had fun together. Yet they also pointed to the drudgery and tedium of cannery work and the scorn they faced from other Montereyans. They remembered the long, irregular hours, sometimes laboring sixteen to eighteen hours in one shift, and balancing their work with family responsibilities. Dorothy Wheeler, for instance, recalled how she got off of work at midnight, picked up her sleeping kids from the babysitter, and then took them home.[28]

But these vivid memories alone did not sustain the reunions. In October 2005 the Cannery Row Foundation organized a reunion that diverged sharply from previous gatherings. Rather than just inviting alumni to converse informally over dinner, it was a full-day event with panels and presentations led by college professors, historians, and other experts on numerous subjects related to Cannery Row, John Steinbeck, and the sardine fishery. Topics included collecting sardine labels, Steinbeck as war propagandist, Steinbeck and Ed Ricketts's journey to the Sea of Cortez in 1940, the Norwegian sardine industry, and Monterey's Japanese and Sicilian communities. True to the spirit of past reunions, there were also panels of former fishermen and cannery workers who spoke about their work on Cannery Row during the sardine heyday. In addition to listening to these presentations, reunion attendants could peruse exhibits of historical photographs and models of the Hovden cannery, Wing Chong's market, Ed Ricketts's laboratory, and the Western Flyer, the purse-seine boat that Steinbeck and Ricketts took on their journey to the Sea of Cortez.[29]

The Great Cannery Row Reunion of 2005 certainly fulfilled the broader mission of the Cannery Row Foundation—"to preserve the historical and literary resources of Cannery Row, Monterey, California, and to research, interpret, educate, disseminate, and celebrate the unique multi-cultural essence of Cannery Row's historic, literary, cultural and ecological legacies"—but it seemed to stray from the original purpose of these gatherings. Presentations on Steinbeck figured prominently, and the collective experience of the Cannery Row alumni was no longer the sole focal point. Instead, the former cannery workers and fishermen had become experts on one of several panels. Local newspaper coverage did not recount their colorful anecdotes, focusing instead on the parallels between the Monterey and Norwegian sardine industries. In fact, Michael Hemp, master of ceremonies and now vice president of the Cannery Row Foundation, explained that the "true theme" of the reunion was to join Monterey and Stavanger, Norway, as the two "sardine capitals" of the world.[30]

Although the success of the reunion spoke to the growing public and scholarly interest in Cannery Row's history, broadly defined, it was not so much a reunion as it was a conference of sorts. The departure from previous reunions suggested that the Cannery Row Foundation had indeed recovered many stories from the alumni and decided to branch out and broaden the scope of the event in order to generate and sustain interest in its projects and mission. The more diverse the offerings, the more people in attendance and the more new members it could attract. The expanded agenda also demonstrated the breadth and depth of Cannery Row's history. Indeed, Cannery Row was much more than just a setting for one of John Steinbeck's novels.

Yet the myriad presentations and panels may have overshadowed some intriguing anecdotes and rich stories—stories like those told by Charlie Nonella, a larger-than-life presence at the first five reunions. Before his death in 1990, Nonella had shared some of the most captivating tales about the hustle and bustle of Monterey's sardine heyday. During one interview he reflected wistfully: "What I miss most are those whistles. I can still hear 'em. They were the voices of The Row. Especially I miss those old train whistles. There are times when I can still hear 'em, right up here, in the night, when everything is quiet."[31] The silencing of the whistles was just one sign of the times. The reunion itself had evolved since 1983, and voices like Nonella's, though still part of the event, were not the featured attraction in 2005.

Saving the "Tarpaper Sentries"

The Cannery Row Foundation helped to reclaim the memories of the former cannery workers and fishermen, but these individuals also left a physical imprint on Cannery Row. During the sardine season, itinerant laborers often rented small one-room shacks conveniently located near the fish-processing plants on Ocean View Avenue. These rudimentary one-room structures, constructed of a single layer of lumber and tarpaper roofs, rented for $5 to $8 per month. As Cannery Row turned into a tourist destination and enjoyed the tremendous success of the Monterey Bay Aquarium, these shacks began to disappear, razed to make way for new development. Unlike the former fish-processing plants and warehouses, they were too small and possessed little of the industrial charm that would have made them candidates for conversion into retail shops or other service businesses. And there were no longer migrant workers who needed cheap, short-term housing.

By 1987 only three shacks remained in the Cannery Row area. Abandoned and vacant for several years, they were located near the aquarium on a fifty-by-eighty-five-foot commercial lot that was for sale, along with a rental house, for $484,000. *Monterey Herald* journalist Thom Akeman called them "tarpaper sentries" standing guard over the neighborhood. However, their future was in question. Real estate agent Richard Foster noted that there was some interest in the lot, but no one had inquired about the shacks. He explained, "I imagine whoever buys that [lot] is just going to blow them away. They're just little shacks." Foster suggested that the Cannery Row real estate market had no place for derelict shanties; it was the land on which they stood that held the real value for investors interested in capitalizing on Cannery Row's service economy.

The Monterey Historic Preservation Commission had different ideas. Toynette Bryan, chairperson of the commission, wanted to research the historical value of the shacks. But even Michael Hemp was not sure they were worth saving from demolition. He noted, "It would be great to save them, but where do we put them? To what use do we put them. . . . We can't save it all. The best thing to do is just come down here with some film. . . . It's the passing of an era. It's sad, but how can you do anything else?"[32] While Hemp was intent on preserving the memories of former cannery workers and fishermen, he was not as sanguine about preserving their former homes.

Despite the shacks' lack of architectural grandeur and their debatable historical significance, historic preservationists prevailed and saved them from demolition. After the Monterey Bay Aquarium bought the property in 1990 for an employee picnic area, the city agreed to move the shacks. Two years later the Monterey City Council approved the expenditure of $10,000 to transport them to a nearby Cannery Row lot. There, the city planned to build a historical park in honor of Monterey's cannery workers and fishermen. Michael Adamson of the Monterey Historic Preservation Committee explained the city's motivation: "[The shacks] are a memorial to the fishermen that once made up the life of Monterey. They are the last ones, and if they go there's nothing left at all."[33] Surrounded by restaurants and souvenir shops, the shacks would demonstrate how some Cannery Row workers once lived.

The next step was to determine the content and design of the exhibit. Local historian Kent Seavey, Jody Armstrong of the Monterey Bay Aquarium, and the Monterey Historic Preservation Committee tackled this task and decided to designate an archetypal resident of a different ethnic background to "live" in each shack: "Manolon," a Spanish cannery worker; "Billy," a Filipino reduction-plant operator; and "Tanaka and Okamoto," two Japanese fishermen. The four workers also represented a different time period in Cannery Row's history; Manolon, Tanaka, and Okamoto inhabited their shacks during the 1930s, whereas Billy lived there in the 1940s.[34]

Inside, the shacks were decorated to appear as they may have during the sardine industry's peak, with period furniture, appliances, equipment, clothing, and periodicals that the residents may have read. For instance, the Tanaka and Okamoto shack was decorated with copper pots and fish boxes donated by the Kodani family, whose patriarch, Gennosuke Kodani, had helped to establish the Japanese abalone industry in the Monterey Bay region. Billy's shack contained a copy of the *Philippines Mail*, which was published in nearby Salinas. Outside each shack an interpretive sign detailed the historical experiences of the given ethnic group. The shacks were too small for visitors to enter, but they could peek inside the windows. As Seavey explained, "The purpose of the exhibit is to give people glimpses into moments in time in Cannery Row's history. The city of Monterey wants to recognize the working people who were so important to the city's once major industry."[35]

Because Cannery Row workers left few written records, Seavey consulted with members of the Spanish, Filipino, and Japanese communities to put together the exhibit and determine the appropriate furnishings. Filipino immigrant Romualdo Vicente, known affectionately as "Papa Vince," proved to be an especially important source of information, as he had actually lived in one of the three shacks as a young cannery worker. He arrived in Monterey during the Great Depression and immediately found work in the canneries. Along with other Filipino cannery workers—all single men—he lived in shacks or rooming houses in the neighborhood. He remembered with fondness his work in the canneries and the camaraderie among the cannery workers. They ate lunch along the railroad tracks; during their spare time, they flew kites or played poker. At the end of the sardine season in February, they headed to Alaska to work in the fish canneries there. When the sardine fishery crashed, Vicente settled in Monterey and began to work in local restaurants, first as a busboy and later as a bartender at the Sardine Factory, a popular Cannery Row eatery.[36]

Visitors could finally learn more about workers such as Papa Vince when the shacks opened to the public in 1996. Located off Cannery Row on Bruce Ariss Way, named in honor of a local artist, the historical park opened in March and was officially dedicated in June. Fully furnished and spruced up with a fresh coat of white paint, the shacks were ready for visitors to peer inside and learn about the diverse workers who sustained the sardine industry.[37] This new park paralleled and built upon other efforts to bring the past back to life, including the aquarium's boilerhouse restoration and the Cannery Row reunions. Like the aquarium, the city restored a physical artifact of the sardine industry and placed great value on ensuring the authenticity of its work. But unlike the boiler house, the shacks interpreted the daily lives of the cannery workers and fishermen and explained the factors that encouraged their immigration and migration to Monterey. Although the historical park did generalize these experiences, omitting the nuances that made the Cannery Row reunions such a success, it brought history into a public space and had the potential to reach an even wider audience.

Sites, Citizens, and the Boiler House Revisited

The restoration of the fishermen's shacks preceded other public history projects and historical exhibits that continued to uncover the industrial and postindustrial history of Cannery Row. The most innovative venture involved a photography exhibit at the Maritime Museum of Monterey. From December 2000 to September 2001, the museum displayed "Sites and Citizens: Cannery Row, 1957–1958," a collection of 109 photographs taken by Robert Lewis, who had lived and worked on Cannery Row during its postwar nadir following the sardine industry's collapse. Attracted to Monterey by Steinbeck and his novel, he lived at the Ocean View Hotel on Cannery Row for thirty dollars a month, picked up odd jobs, and took photographs. By a stroke of good luck, the hotel owners, Menifee and Margaret Logan, offered him another room to use as a darkroom.[38] His stunning black-and-white images included numerous individuals, from bartenders and artists to children playing on the railroad tracks. It also featured the neighborhood's built environment, with its many vacant, decaying fish plants.

As visitors pored over the images, the museum encouraged their involvement. Rather than being "passive observers," they were told to be "active participants." The exhibit brochure read:

> Interactive exhibits are very popular today.... This exhibit... takes this concept one step further. WITHOUT YOUR PARTICIPATION THERE WILL BE NO EXHIBIT! Although the photographs are beautiful to look at and evocative of a special time in Monterey's history, a critical component of this show is to IDENTIFY these scenes. These men and women all had names, families, stories and identities; these buildings housed canneries, restaurants, shops, and businesses. We need you to help us tell their stories.[39]

Linda Jaffe, executive director of the Monterey History and Art Association, which runs the museum, added, "We hope anyone who knew them will help us give them a place in Monterey history." Curators left a logbook where visitors could write down the names of any people that they recognized. Lewis may have captured a particular moment in history, but that history was incomplete without further input from those who lived during this time. Visitors did recognize some of the people in the photographs, but the logbook did not prove to be the best method to gather this information. As Maritime Museum director of exhibit design and education Jeannie Cartibiano explained, "We hadn't counted on the strong oral tradition. People came with scrapbooks and other pictures saying, 'Oh, that's so-and-so,' but they weren't interesting in writing anything down." To collect these stories, a partnership formed between California State University, Monterey Bay history professor Cecilia O'Leary, and the Monterey History and Art Association in the spring of 2001.[40] Students in O'Leary's course California at the Crossroads had the task of conducting oral histories with and about individuals pictured in the Lewis photographs and researching several aspects of Cannery Row's history, including the African American, Asian American, and Mexican American experiences; women and gender; technology and the environment; and the "politics of history and memory," which accounted for Steinbeck's influence on Cannery Row and the "re-creation" of the neighborhood beginning in the 1950s. The resulting essays, along with ninety of Lewis's photographs and full texts of four oral histories, were published on a Web site, "Sites and Citizens: Cannery Row—a Community Memory."[41]

During their interviews students often showed their subjects photographs from the Lewis collection and asked them to identify any familiar "sites and citizens." These insights were included with the caption of the given photograph. For instance, Annie Garmero identified the man in an image titled "Sculptor with Work" as her father, Nicholas Guastella. The caption explained how Guastella, an art student in Florence, Italy, left Sicily in 1938 or 1939 for Monterey, where the Sicilian fishermen revered him because he was an educated man. For the photographs without identification, Web-site visitors were encouraged to contact the Oral History and Community Memory Institute and Archive at California State University, Monterey Bay, with any information. It explained: "Please look through this virtual gallery and let us know if you recognize anyone, have a photograph, souvenir, or clipping of your own from Cannery Row's past, or a memory/story you are willing to share."[42]

The interviews also proved to be an invaluable source of information on the larger history of Cannery Row, both during the height of the sardine industry and during its precipitous decline. Hope Gradis, daughter of a Sicilian reduction-plant and cannery owner, spoke about the good times of the sardine boom and the hardships that her family faced after the fishery collapsed. When the fish were running, "We had everything we wanted. We lived in this big house. . . . Money was rolling in." But when the fish disappeared, her father, facing repossession, had to sell their home in Pacific Grove. Eventually, the family opened a Laundromat and made a "good living." Patricia Ramsey Wester, who ran a dance studio in the Cannery Row area and lived at the Ocean View Hotel in the 1950s, remembered the deserted feel of the neighborhood. Thomas Logan spoke about his grandparents Menifee and Margaret Logan, featured in several Lewis photographs, and the summer of 1960 when, at the age of eighteen, he stayed at the Ocean View Hotel and worked at one of the few canneries trying to survive. Because the fish were so scarce, he worked only a half day or maybe one full day at a time. Logan elaborated, "[Cannery Row] was rundown. We rarely got sardines, and the economy was shot. All the stores around there were facing bankruptcy. . . . I bet you could have bought property down there for almost nothing."[43]

Like O'Leary and the Maritime Museum, the Monterey Bay Aquarium also took an interest in promulgating a more comprehensive history of the sardine industry.[44] Part of a larger renovation that enclosed the entrance and created an indoor ticket lobby, the aquarium's permanent historical exhibit, which opened in 2004, developed in response to a city building-permit requirement to examine the history of the site and the aquarium's desire to "do a better job interpreting the historical boilers." As Jenny Sayre Ramberg, the aquarium's senior exhibit developer and writer, explained, "The boilers were once the heart of the cannery. Now, through the lens of our conservation mission, they're a reminder of what we've learned about overfishing and the need for sustainable fisheries, for the ocean and people."[45] To convey this message, visitors are funneled to the boilers after buying their tickets and immediately learn that the building was once the site of the Hovden cannery. From there, the exhibit details the boom and bust of the sardine fishery, posits that both fishing and oceanic conditions caused its demise, and ultimately couches the collapse as a cautionary tale. It states, "Sardines are back in this building—and more important, they're back in the bay.... But now we know, and maybe we'll heed: there are limits to the stream of silver from the bay."

In addition to detailing the dramatic transition from exploitation to conservation, Ramberg also realized that the aquarium needed to do more to capture the human history of the sardine industry. She noted, "Our previous exhibition included a few of the same pieces of machinery but was primarily short interpretive graphics, words only, around an outdoor exhibit of machinery parts. It worked for visitors who were fascinated with old machinery but it failed to bring the story of the people and the sardines alive to most visitors." Ramberg acknowledged that the experiences of Frank Bergara, Al Campoy, and the other cannery workers who had assisted with the boiler-house restoration and received such positive attention more than twenty years earlier had been lost amid the beautiful exhibits of Monterey Bay marine life. To remedy the omission of this history, the new exhibit provided a "multi-modal experience" with sardine-era memorabilia, photographs, video, text, and sounds—including the unforgettable sound of the cannery whistles. Visitors could learn about John Steinbeck and Ed Ricketts and their trip to the Sea of Cortez and the social and cultural life of Cannery Row, including the sardine canning process and a day in the life of a cannery worker. Quotations from former cannery workers conveyed the long hours and unpleasant working conditions that they endured. For instance, one passage read, "We used to dread getting up in the morning because we worked so hard.... Can you imagine squeezing the guts out of fish at three or four in the morning?" The content and design of the exhibit, developed in conjunction with historians and scientists, attempted "to make the time come alive for visitors," because, Ramberg concluded, "we wanted visitors to be able to imagine what it might have been like to be a worker in a cannery."[46]

While the Monterey Bay Aquarium was still, first and foremost, an aquarium, the history of the Hovden cannery was now more fully integrated into the building.

Whether interpreted by private organizations like the Monterey Bay Aquarium, the Cannery Row Foundation, and the Monterey History and Art Association or the city government, Cannery Row's industrial history has become increasingly important to Monterey's identity. Of course, it is impossible to escape Steinbeck's legacy—the author and the novel continue to shape Cannery Row's public image—and his impact on the region cannot and should not be dismissed. Yet he no longer overpowers the neighborhood, and his presence has become more balanced with historical exhibits and programs about the diverse lot of cannery workers, fishermen, and other individuals who toiled and lived in the former fish-processing center.

This approach is also evident in the city's recent efforts to preserve Cannery Row's cultural resources and built environment. In 2004 it established the Cannery Row Conservation District. Within the district's boundaries, developers are required to abide by specific design principles, consistent with the existing character of Cannery Row, when altering standing structures or constructing new ones. They also have to go through a review process and receive approval from the Historic Preservation Commission for projects involving or adjacent to a historic property. The overarching goal of the conservation district is "to establish a framework for allowing Cannery Row to grow while retaining its ambiance and historical context." In many respects the new conservation district and its accompanying guidelines paralleled previous city plans that tried to maintain the industrial character of the Cannery Row area. Yet the city also rejected the persistent tendency to focus on Steinbeck. The guidelines stated, "The City of Monterey is not proposing to recreate the fictional setting of the novel, *Cannery Row.*" Instead, the city acknowledged that Cannery Row was an attraction for visitors "interested in both the actual history of the area and the fictionalized setting of John Steinbeck's novels." In other words, the historical *and* literary significance of the neighborhood guided the design principles and gave impetus to the creation of the conservation district.[47]

But as much as the city and other private groups have successfully reclaimed the industrial history of Cannery Row and described many of its social and environmental complexities, their depictions of the sardine heyday still lack significant details. In particular, the labor disputes and ethnic and racial conflicts that shaped Cannery Row receive little, if any, mention. The Monterey Bay Aquarium's exhibit suggests what it was like to work in the canneries, but it does not analyze the ethnic, racial, gender, and class divisions on the cannery floor and aboard the fishing boats or the strikes that invariably delayed the opening of each season. While the shack exhibit does touch on the cannery workers' union, the diversity of the labor force, and the forcible evacuation of the Japanese population at the start of World War II, it does not examine the animosity that Filipinos faced when they first began to work in the canneries in the 1930s. The Cannery Row alumni picked up on some of these conflicts at their annual reunions, but their memories were romanticized by the passage of time and rarely interrogated or fully fleshed out. These details are important because they further complicate Steinbeck's picturesque depiction of Cannery Row's past. He did not suggest that it was a utopian community per se, but he did overlook the struggles for power and dominance that defined the sardine industry.

While an idealized past continues to guide visions for future development, Cannery Row's industrial history has assumed a more prominent place in Monterey. Visitors flock to the coastal community to marvel at the beauty of the bay and the intricacies of the aquarium and to take in Steinbeck's former haunts, but its industrial past is no longer completely ignored. It is a matter of pride for many Montereyans that Cannery Row was once the sardine capital of the world—not just the setting for a Steinbeck novel that bore its name. As Joe Bragdon, who ran a sardine cooker for one season, remarked at the 1997 Cannery Row Reunion, "Back then . . . [n]o one ever would have dreamed [Cannery Row] would become one of the most famous streets in the world."[48] Much work remains to be done, but Cannery Row's fame, once primarily a function of its literary notoriety, has at least begun to include the actual people that surrounded Steinbeck as he wandered the neighborhood during the sardine industry's height.

Notes

1. For estimates on the number of cannery workers, see "Cannery Payroll Near Million," *Monterey Peninsula Herald, Sardine Edition No. 2,* February 26, 1937. For migrant workers, see "Sardine Catch Season Ending," *Monterey Labor News,* February 7, 1941; and "Local Sardine Plants Employ Few Filipinos," *Monterey Peninsula Herald,* September 17, 1930.

2. Frances N. Clark, "Review of the California Sardine Fishery," *California Fish and Game* 38, no. 3 (1952): 371. For the trucking of sardines, see George Clemens, "Canners Went South for Fish," *Monterey Peninsula Herald, Sardine Edition No. 13,* April 3, 1948. For canning squid, see W. Gordon Fields, "A Preliminary Report on the Fishery and on the Biology of the Squid, *Loligo Opalescens,*" *California Fish and Game* 36, no. 4 (1950): 368–69. For Monterey fisher-

men who traveled south to work, see "Fishing Fleet Leaves; Season Is Poorest Yet," *Monterey County Labor News*, November 22, 1946.

3. For the fate of the former sardine canneries, see "Monterey Loses More of Its Oldtime Savor," *Monterey Peninsula Herald*, April 20, 1962; "Monterey Cannery Converted," *Monterey Peninsula Herald*, July 1, 1958; and "Cannery Row Plant en Route to Peru," *Monterey Peninsula Herald*, July 1, 1960.

4. For Steinbeck tourists on Cannery Row, see Margaret Hensel, "Cannery Row," *Game and Gossip* 6, no. 1 (1952): 12, 34. For the street renaming, see Mike Thomas, "What Will Emerge From the Cannery Row Cocoon?" *Monterey Peninsula Herald*, April 21, 1959. For arson on Cannery Row, see Tom Mangelsdorf, *A History of Steinbeck's Cannery Row* (Santa Cruz: Western Tanager Press, 1986), 184–85. For the Cannery Row Plan, see Sydney Williams, *Cannery Row Plan* (Monterey: City Planning Commission, 1961).

5. Monterey Department of City Planning, *Cannery Row Plan: An Element of the General Plan* (Monterey: Department of City Planning, 1973).

6. For similar arguments, see Martha Norkunas, *The Politics of Public Memory: Tourism, History, and Ethnicity in Monterey, California* (Albany: State University of New York Press, 1993), 49–73, 95–96; and John Walton, *Storied Land: Community and Memory in Monterey* (Berkeley and Los Angeles: University of California Press, 2001), 234–62. For an overview of Cannery Row's transformation, see James R. Curtis, "The Boutiquing of Cannery Row," *Landscape* 25, no. 1 (1981): 44–48. Regarding postindustrial western tourism, see Hal K. Rothman, *Devil's Bargains: Tourism in the Twentieth-Century American West* (Lawrence: University Press of Kansas, 1998); Bonnie Christensen, *Red Lodge and the Mythic West: From Coal Miners to Cowboys* (Lawrence: University Press of Kansas, 2002); and Connie Y. Chiang, "Novel Tourism: Nature, Industry, and Literature on Monterey's Cannery Row," *Western Historical Quarterly* 35 (Autumn 2004): 309–29.

7. Monterey Bay Aquarium, *Project Status, January 1980* (Monterey: n.p., 1980), copy in Local History Files, Pacific Grove Public Library.

8. Linda Rhodes and Charles Davis, "Preserving the Form, Reversing the Function: From Fish Cannery to Aquarium," *California Historical Society* (September 1984): 6–7; Gail Allison Baxter, "Monterey Bay Aquarium" (master's thesis, University of California, Berkeley, 1986), 3–4.

9. Monterey Bay Aquarium, *Project Status, January 1980*; Ken Peterson, "Monterey's Age of Aquarium Begins Saturday," *Monterey Peninsula Herald*, October 14, 1984; Carleton Knight III, "Purposeful Chaos on Cannery Row," *Architecture* (June 1985): 53; John Boykin, "Monterey Bay Aquarium," *Stanford Magazine*, Winter 1984, 18–21.

10. For Stanford's justifications for buying the Hovden cannery, see L. R. Blinks to Dean Albert H. Bowker, Stanford Graduate Division, March 10, 1961, Box 1, Folder 14; Hubert Heffner to Kenneth M. Cuthbertson, April 5, 1965, Box 2, Folder 1; and John H. Phillips, "Hovden Acquisition—Status Report," July 11, 1967, Box 1, Folder 10, Department of Biology, Division of Systemic Biology Records, Special Collections, Stanford University Libraries. For the

acquisition of the cannery, see Donald Fitzgerald, *The History and Significance of the Hovden Cannery, Cannery Row, Monterey, California, 1914-1973*, submitted by Carroll W. Pursell Jr., principal investigator to the Monterey Bay Aquarium Foundation, November 15, 1979, 13.

11. Knight, "Purposeful Chaos," 53; Baxter, "Monterey Bay Aquarium," 9; Joseph Esherick, "An Architectural Practice in the San Francisco Bay Area, 1938–1996: Oral History Transcript," interviewed by Suzanne B. Riess, Regional Oral History Office, Bancroft Library, University of California, Berkeley, 1996, 314–16.

12. Baxter, "Monterey Bay Aquarium," 4, 33–46; Planning Collaborative, *Environmental Impact Report, Monterey Bay Aquarium, Monterey, California* (San Francisco: Planning Collaborative, 1979), 22; "Proposed Cannery Row Aquarium Costs Jump," *Monterey Peninsula Herald*, January 25, 1979.

13. Abby Ray, "The Creation of Monterey Bay Aquarium," *Coast Gazette*, May 28, 1981; *Environmental Impact Report*, 33–35; *Monterey Bay Aquarium Newsletter*, October 1979.

14. Fitzgerald, *Hovden Cannery*, 13, 15.

15. Rhodes and Davis, "Preserving the Form," 6–7; Charles M. Davis, "Aquarium Architecture: Some Notes on Monterey Bay Aquarium," *Monterey Bay Aquarium Newsletter*, Spring 1985; Boykin, "Monterey Bay Aquarium," 27.

16. Rhodes and Davis, "Preserving the Form," 6–7; Joe Graziano, "Heart of Hovden Cannery Survives at Aquarium," *Monterey Peninsula Herald*, October 14, 1984.

17. "Bringing the Past Back to Life," *Monterey Bay Aquarium Newsletter*, Fall 1983, 3.

18. Kathleen McGuire, "Ex-Workers Toast Aquarium Project's Aquarium Restoration," *Monterey Peninsula Herald*, October 4, 1983.

19. Rhodes and Davis, "Preserving the Form," 7.

20. "Michael K. Hemp, Biographical Profile," http://www.thehistorycompany.com/Services/bio.html.

21. Alex Hulanicki, "'Sardine Chokers' of Yesteryear Swap Yarns at Reunion Party," *Monterey Peninsula Herald*, May 16, 1983.

22. Ibid.; Al Goodman, "Old Friends Get Together Again," *Monterey Peninsula Herald*, May 12, 1985.

23. Goodman, "Old Friends Get Together Again."

24. "Past Wistfully Recalled at Cannery Row Reunion," *Monterey Peninsula Herald*, May 19, 1986; James Kinney and Kathy Lonero, "Down on the Row," *Monterey Peninsula Herald Magazine*, April 26, 1987.

25. "Row Foundation's Aim Is to Preserve an Era," *Monterey Peninsula Herald*, May 12, 1985. Recordings of Hemp's interviews are archived at the National Steinbeck Center in Salinas, California. See also Michael Kenneth Hemp, *Cannery Row: The History of Old Ocean View Avenue* (Pacific Grove, Calif.: History Company, 1986). A revised edition of the book was published in 2003 and curiously renamed *Cannery Row: The History of John Steinbeck's Old Ocean View Avenue*.

26. Michelle Maitre, "Recalling Life on 'the Row,'" *Monterey County Herald*, October 6,

1997; Michael Hemp, e-mail to author, November 30, 2006; Betsy Lordan, "Cannery Workers Revisit History," *Monterey County Herald*, October 26, 1998.

27. Maitre, "Recalling Life"; Lordan, "Cannery Workers Revisit History."

28. "Worker Recalls Heyday of Sardine Industry," *Monterey Peninsula Herald*, December 14, 1987.

29. "A Look at the Great Cannery Row Reunion," http://www.canneryrow.org/reunion.html; "A Photo Summary of the Great Cannery Row Reunion 2005," http://www.canneryrow.org/reunion_summary.html.

30. "Who We Are," http://www.canneryrow.org/Admin/who_we_are.html; Karen Ravn, "Cannery Row Event Packs 'Em in Like, Well, Sardines," *Monterey County Herald*, October 9, 2005.

31. Kinney and Lonero, "Down on the Row."

32. Thom Akeman, "Abandoned Fisherman's Shacks Now Candidates for Demolition," *Monterey Herald*, October 12, 1987.

33. Esther Schrader, "Last 3 Shanties of Cannery Row Headed for Nearby Historical Park," *San Jose Mercury News*, January 9, 1992.

34. Bonnie Gartshore, "Windows to Our Past: Historic Cannery Row Shacks to Be on View at New Park," *Monterey County Herald Alta Vista Magazine*, February 18, 1996.

35. Ibid. For Gennosuke Kodani, see Sandy Lydon, *The Japanese in the Monterey Bay Region: A Brief History* (Capitola, Calif.: Capitola Book, 1997), 34–37, 85, 108.

36. Bonnie Gartshore, "'Papa Vince' Recalls Life in the Shacks," *Monterey County Herald*, June 6, 1996.

37. "Restored Shacks to Be Dedicated," *Monterey County Herald*, June 6, 1996.

38. Mary Barker, "Days of Decay on the Row: Former Resident's Late-'50s Photographs Displayed," *Monterey County Herald*, December 19, 1999; Bonnie Gartshore, "Photo Exhibit Gives a Rare Glimpse of the Row as It Used to Be," *Monterey County Herald*, December 14, 2000.

39. Several of Robert Lewis's images are posted at the "Sites and Citizens: Cannery Row—a Community Memory" Web site, http://home.csumb.edu/o/olearycecilia/world/cannery_row/exhibit/intro.html.

40. Bonnie Gartshore, "Next Step in Photo Identification Project: Class Starts Taping Oral Traditions," *Monterey County Herald*, February 19, 2001. O'Leary's partnership with the Monterey History and Art Association was part of her involvement with the Visible Knowledge Project, a five-year project based at Georgetown University's Center for New Designs in Learning and Scholarship. Funded by the Atlantic Philanthropies, the project "aimed at improving the quality of college and university teaching through a focus on both student learning and faculty development in technology-enhanced environments." See http://crossroads.georgetown.edu/vkp/index.htm and "Cecilia Elizabeth O'Leary Participant Profile," http://lumen.georgetown.edu/vkp/profiles/public/dsp_page.cfm?id=17.

41. "Sites and Citizens"; "Reclaiming the Diverse Voice of Cannery Row's Past," http://home.csumb.edu/o/olearycecilia/world/cannery_row/student_menus/353_menu.html; "Reclaiming the Diverse Voice of Cannery Row's Past, Oral Histories," http://home.csumb.edu/o/olearycecilia/world/cannery_row/oral_histories/menu.html.

42. "Sculptor with Work, Robert Lewis' Photographs of Cannery Row," http://home.csumb.edu/o/olearycecilia/world/cannery_row/exhibit/lewis_images/set_4/pages/sculptor.html.

43. Hope Gradis, interview by Mary Porter, May 2, 2001; Patricia Ramsey Wester, interview by Mary Porter, May 2, 2001; and Thomas J. Logan, interview by Mary Porter, April 4, 2001, http://home.csumb.edu/o/olearycecilia/world/cannery_row/oral_histories/menu.html.

44. A portion of this discussion also appears in the conclusion of Connie Y. Chiang, *Shaping the Shoreline: Fisheries and Tourism on the Monterey Coast* (Seattle: University of Washington Press, 2008), 182–91.

45. Jenny Sayre Ramberg, e-mail to author, March 29, 2006.

46. Ibid.; Sukhjit Purewal, "Whale of a Remodel: Aquarium Unveils Its New Look," *Monterey County Herald*, May 29, 2004; Ramberg e-mail.

47. Winter and Company, *Cannery Row Conservation District, Monterey, California* (Monterey: City of Monterey Design Program, 2004), 1, 11–16.

48. Maitre, "Recalling Life."

Seattle's Pike Place Market

JUDY MATTIVI MORLEY

Clinging to a hillside on the northwestern edge of downtown Seattle, the Pike Place Market has a carnival atmosphere. The smell of fresh seafood, ripe fruits and vegetables, a panoply of floral arrangements, and masses of humanity mingle with the sounds of fishmongers tossing salmon and yelling at passing crowds. Elderly men, suburban housewives, burned-out hippies, and well-dressed businesspeople literally rub elbows as they vie for space in the crowded arcade. Artists and artisans add to the atmosphere, and tourists mill about, taking in the spectacle. The diversity and seeming authenticity of Pike Place Market are the hallmark of Seattle, the city's top tourist attraction.

Like many of the nation's inner-city treasures, the Pike Place Market was threatened in the 1960s by an urban renewal plan that would have surrounded the core of the market with a luxury hotel, convention center, and condominiums.[1] The urban renewal proposal mobilized the citizenry in a campaign to save the market's unique function and atmosphere, although the campaign itself blurred the distinction between "saving" and "destroying." The battle culminated with a citizens' initiative to preserve the market in 1971, which passed with overwhelming support. The struggle over the market, however, was really a battle over utopian aspirations. Two groups, the downtown business elite and an emerging cultural elite, battled over whose vision would ultimately remake the market. Seattle's downtown business elite, embodied by the city council and the Central Association of Seattle, defined utopia as a consumer paradise, including high-end development designed to attract middle-class shoppers. The cultural elite, claiming to speak for "the people," reflected an idealized vision of the market as a working-class icon of Seattle's

Progressive Era labor movement.[2] In the end, the market fulfilled neither utopian vision. Outwardly, it represented a preindustrial form of capitalism that preserved a laissez faire atmosphere, but it took quasi-socialist city controls to maintain a business structure that increasingly depended on the consumerism of tourists.

The market began in 1907, during the Progressive Era, as a reaction to the unscrupulous practices of produce jobbers and wholesalers. Responding to public outcries for control on food prices, the city council formed the public market along narrow Pike Place on August 17, 1907. The Pike Place Market was an overwhelming success. The first day, farmers sold out of their produce before they even had their wagons against the curb. The shoppers were predominantly women from all social classes and all ethnic backgrounds, creating a diversity rarely seen in other parts of the city. The customers' ethnic diversity reflected the diversity of local farmers. King County had more than three thousand farms in 1906, and more than half of the farmers were European and Japanese immigrants. Within the market, patrons heard Norwegian, Swedish, Finnish, German, Italian, Serbo-Croatian, Tagalog, Chinese, Japanese, and even Chinook languages.

A young architect named Frank Goodwin saw a great opportunity in the city's public market. After witnessing the crowds on the first Market Day, Goodwin purchased land along the west side of Pike Place, between First and Second Avenues, north of Pike Street. Goodwin began construction on the Main Arcade building to provide shelter for farmers. The building had seventy-six stalls, and Goodwin gave top priority to farmers and gardeners marketing their own produce. When Goodwin's Main Arcade opened in 1907, the city held a ceremony dedicating the market to the people of Seattle. Between 1911 and 1916 Goodwin added the labyrinth tunneling down to Western Avenue on the waterfront, the Corner Market at First Avenue and Pike Street, and the Economy Market.[3]

When the market celebrated its tenth anniversary in 1917, it was already an important part of Seattle's civic identity. The city had 340,000 people, and at least one-third had been born or immigrated to Seattle after the market's creation. The market's prices on produce became the going rate, limiting what the food vendors in other parts of the city could charge. When the city wanted to remove the farmers from Pike Place in 1920 to make room for cars, citizens fought to save the landmark. The city council suggested another location, but patrons protested. The market's parent organization, the Pike Place Market Company, owned by Frank Goodwin's nephew Arthur, solved the problem by expanding the Main Arcade and donating the added space to the city. This north arcade, known as the Municipal Market Building, opened in 1924.[4]

The 1930s witnessed the market's heyday. The demand for inexpensive produce meant more farmers sold truck crops directly to the public. The increase in consumers and vendors helped the market thrive during the Great Depression. In 1932 the Health Department issued an all-time high number of permits, 628. The inexpensive food made the market a haven for unemployed men who lived in the nearby cheap hotels and sought part-time or seasonal work. Vendors and businesses catering to the single men lined First Avenue, adjacent to the market.[5]

Ownership of the market buildings changed during the 1930s. A decade earlier an Italian immigrant farmer named Joe Desimone signed a long-term lease for space in the Main Arcade building. During the 1930s Desimone began buying shares of stock in the Pike Place Market Company. In 1941 Arthur Goodwin sold out, making Desimone the primary owner of the market. Desimone and his heirs owned the majority of the market buildings until the city purchased them during restoration in the 1970s.

Unlike the rest of the city, the market's economy did not boom during World War II. Japanese Americans were the largest ethnic group among market vendors. The anti-Japanese sentiment at the beginning of the war kept many consumers from purchasing produce from Japanese farmers. The internment of Japanese Americans nearly killed business in the market. Japanese farmers accounted for 60 percent of all farmers in the market, and in their absence, licenses plummeted from 515 in 1939 to merely 196 in 1943.

The market did not rebound after the war. Few Japanese Americans resumed farming after they returned from internment camps, primarily because they no longer owned their land. Suburbanization also reduced the amount of land available for farming, and rezoning claimed former stretches of farmland for commercial or industrial uses. The need for a farmers market decreased also, as suburbanites purchased fresh produce trucked along the new interstate highway system to supermarkets. The Marshall Plan also changed the nature of farming, as the federal government contracted with farmers to grow food to be shipped overseas. Marshall Plan farmers usually grew a single crop, decreasing the diversity of truck crops grown in the region.[6]

In 1963 the Seattle City Council and the Central Association commissioned the *Comprehensive Plan for Downtown Seattle* (known as the Monson Plan) to address "blight" in the market. Buildings badly needed repairs to wiring, plumbing, and facades. The market had ceased to be a moneymaker for the city. Revenue from stall rentals declined 21 percent between 1951 and 1955, while annual expenses for upkeep and sanitation rose 68 percent. The council considered letting the market's lease lapse in 1957, but gave in to public pressure and reluctantly renewed. Stall rentals reached an all-time low of 42 in 1969. The Desimone family could not justify huge investments in upkeep, because of decreasing profits from permit rentals. The neighborhood tax base offered little hope of funding repairs, either. Inhabitants were predominantly elderly, white, working-class single men with no family ties who opted to live near the market because of inexpensive rent and the male-oriented culture of taverns and poolrooms.[7]

Despite dilapidated facilities and neighborhood decline, customers continued to patronize Pike Place Market during the 1960s. Although suburban supermarkets stole some of the market's business, residents throughout Seattle depended on the market for the freshest produce, fish, or specialty items. During the 1960s daily retail sales in the market averaged fifty-five dollars per square foot, and although this amount was much less than the rehabilitated Ghirardelli Square in San Francisco, it was higher than anyone in Seattle's planning department expected. Eighty percent of the market's business came from the neighborhoods closest to downtown, but only 15 percent was within walking distance, meaning most customers could afford to ride a bus or drive. Twenty percent of the clientele shopped there at least once a week.[8]

Steady customers notwithstanding, downtown businesspeople lobbied the city to do something about the deteriorating physical conditions of Pike Place Market. To deal with decaying urban areas, Washington's state legislature passed an urban renewal law in 1957, which extended the power of eminent domain for the city to control and redevelop the area. With this law in mind, the city council and the Central Association commissioned the 1963 Monson Plan, a comprehensive master plan that proposed the total elimination of the market.[9]

Under the provisions of the Monson Plan, the city intended to authorize a private developer to bulldoze 12.5 acres, including the market. In this space, the plan proposed a terraced garage holding three thousand cars, a downtown park, a hotel, and several high-rise office buildings. A new rebuilt market would fit in the park and become, in the words of Central Association president Ben Ehrlichman, "a visitor and tourist attraction quite equal to the Los Angeles Farmer's Market." The city council approved the plan in January 1965. The study called for federal urban renewal funding to support the redevelopment. Following the council's approval, the federal Department of Housing and Urban Development (HUD) granted preliminary funding in December 1966.[10] The new urban renewal project became known as "Pike Plaza."

Before the city could obtain federal urban renewal funds, the city needed to control the market. The city could not purchase it outright because Joe Desimone's will prohibited his heirs from selling the property. Therefore, the city had to make a case for blight, condemn the market, and take control through eminent domain. Structural studies commissioned by the city found that 90 percent of the market buildings warranted clearance, and 89 percent of the structures within the proposed Pike Plaza Project did not comply with health and safety regulations. The Fire Department, the Health Department, and the Planning Department all concluded that the market was a rat-infested, congested, dilapidated fire trap.[11]

The studies also revealed that the market's economy was significantly less dilapidated than its structures. The market functioned as a "strong magnet" for downtown, and newspaper pundits and research analysts suggested keeping the market as the focal point of any urban renewal plan. The market did not necessarily need to be in its original buildings, however. One private firm's study found that "the public" valued the "essence" of the market because of the "atmosphere stimulated by the merchandising methods" and the "personal attributes of the merchants in the area."[12]

In addition to federal urban renewal funding, Seattle mayor J. D. "Dorn" Braman believed the Pike Plaza Project required private capital. Without large investors, he worried that the area would become an "urban renewal wasteland." Braman had witnessed other cities that cleared land to get urban renewal funds, then waited in vain for either private funds or more public funds to develop the area. Braman urged twenty local investors to incorporate as the Central Park Plaza Corporation. The group, which included prominent downtown businessmen, incorporated in April 1966 and immediately began buying property in and around the redevelopment area.[13]

With federal funding and private investors pending, the city's Planning Department, known after 1970 as the Department of Community Development (DCD), began finalizing designs. The main planning goal was to provide amenities to attract affluent suburban residents. Braman argued, "What we are trying to do here is to respond to what is . . . the exodus of people living in the heart and core of our cities. . . . One way or another, we are going to have to encourage these people to come back in Seattle, and one of the ways . . . [is] to redevelop this wonderful, beautiful living property so that people of high income . . . return to Seattle their brains and their money and their tax base."[14]

The design for Pike Plaza proposed clearing the entire area between First and Western avenues and University and Lenora streets. It called for hotels, luxury apartments, expanded parking facilities, open space, and a connection between the central business district and the waterfront in order to bring high-end shoppers and tourists to the area. Since research showed that the market's function still drew visitors, most of the plans featured a retail development where the Main Market stood. High-rise apartments and hotels surrounded the retail area, and the shopping space was glossy, bright, and brand-new.[15]

The grand plans for Pike Plaza, however, faced opposition. Following the lead of internationally recognized artist Mark Tobey, a group of Seattle citizens joined together to try to save the original shabby market. In reaction to the first redevelopment plans in 1964, artists, architects, students, and professionals formed a group called Friends of the Market in 1965. Most of the organizers were members of Allied Arts of Seattle, an organization dedicated to artistic endeavors.[16]

University of Washington architectural professor Victor Steinbrueck emerged as the Friends' undeniable leader. His books *Seattle Cityscape* and *Market Sketchbook* romanticized the working-class atmosphere of the market. Steinbrueck believed in safeguarding the rights of, in his words, "the working man." Steinbrueck's middle name was "Eugene," after famed labor leader Eugene V. Debs. Born in North Dakota, Steinbrueck's family moved to Georgetown, Washington, when he was a child so that his father could work as a machinist during World War I. According to Steinbrueck, "Georgetown was a poor, working-class neighborhood. I was very conscious of the difficulties of working people."[17] Steinbrueck's influence caused the Friends to frame their opposition to the city's Pike Plaza plans as a populist struggle of the "little people" against the "business interests."

Steinbrueck did not oppose progress per se. He had codesigned Seattle's most prominent symbol of progress, the Space Needle. He realized, however, that the addition of affluent tourists and luxury apartment dwellers would irrevocably change the market. He believed that the market was more than the physical structures. According to Steinbrueck, it was "a series of experiences building on each other not limited to just the core."[18]

Ironically, the architects, artists, housing activists, and students who followed Steinbrueck belonged not to the working class but rather to the cultural elite. They opposed the business elite's vision of the market on aesthetic grounds, believing that the market's historic structures contributed authenticity to the shopping experience. The Friends sought to convince the city that the future lay in the seedy remnants of the past. To that end, they wrote letters to local newspapers and talked to the national media about the virtues of the market. They gave tours and promoted the market to the city council, the planning commission, church groups, and service organizations. Their persistence paid off, and they soon persuaded the city council and the Central Association to modify the Pike Plaza design in 1968.

As part of the compromise, the council held a design competition for the Pike Plaza Project. Architects submitted various designs for the area, and the DCD chose one. Although Steinbrueck submitted a plan on the Friends' behalf, the DCD chose a design by architects John Morse and Paul Kirk. Both Morse and Kirk had ties to the downtown business establishment, with Morse belonging to the Central Association. The choice of the Morse-Kirk plan appealed to the downtown interests but immediately made the Friends suspicious.[19]

Unlike earlier plans, the Morse-Kirk plan advocated keeping some of the market's buildings. Morse and Kirk acknowledged that the market should be preserved, not just for sentimental reasons but also because it was economically healthy.[20] The design included rehabilitating the Sanitary Market, Economy Market, and Corner Market structures, all of which had been slated for clearance in previous plans. Additionally, Morse and Kirk kept the Leland and LaSalle hotels, turning them into studio apartments on the upper floors with market functions on the ground level. Signage was to be for "identification and not advertisement," in keeping with market tradition, and the plan kept the famous "Public Market" marquis. Landscaping in the market was to provide public access and easy right-of-way and included public art.

Had this been the entire plan, the Friends might have been satisfied. The rest of the design, however, stipulated that the area around the market be totally rebuilt along the guidelines of the Monson Plan. The market would be nestled within an area accommodating a four thousand–car parking garage, a thirty-two-story apartment building for low-income and elderly residents, four twenty-eight-story luxury apartment buildings, three hundred thousand square feet of office space, and a hockey arena. A pedestrian bridge stretched from First Avenue to the roof of the Main Arcade, providing a view of Elliott Bay.[21]

The Friends feared that the plan was unsympathetic to the spirit of the market and that the farmers would not be able to afford rents in the new upscale area. They also worried that the market would not survive out of context. According to Steinbrueck, "It is most unrealistic to expect a low income market, or anything resembling what we care so much about, to survive under the new elegantized total situation which is quite unsympathetic." An article in the *Seattle Times* captured the market advocates' concerns: "Can the sellers of day-old bread, week-old fruit and economy grade meat keep drawing the urban poor to patronize their stands under the shadow of the first-class, 600-room hotel to be built down the street?"[22] The DCD felt the Morse-Kirk plan was the perfect compromise; the Friends vehemently and vocally disagreed.

The Friends' opposition outraged Mayor Braman, who generally sided with the business interests. Realizing that the Friends would not support the Morse-Kirk design, or "Scheme 23" as it became known, Braman set the antagonistic tone for the remaining debates by belittling Steinbrueck and the Friends. Braman told the city council that he would not let the Friends stand in the way of the eighty million–dollar urban renewal plan. He called the market a "decadent, somnolent, fire trap" and said that the city would relocate the four hundred residents, mostly elderly single men, to other parts of the city. "We don't have to leave these people in the middle of this choice area, and as far as I'm concerned we're not going to leave them there." Braman criticized the Friends for "nitpicking on behalf of people living in unpainted houses, who are not paying taxes and not contributing a thing."[23] Braman's rhetoric mirrored the business interests' vision of a renewed capitalist utopia and reinforced the class overtones prevalent in the debate over the market's future.

Braman's criticism did not deter the Friends, however. In opposition to the Morse-Kirk plan, they gathered fifty-three thousand signatures on petitions to save the market. The city council could not ignore this much opposition. Over six weeks in spring 1969, it held public hearings that unfolded like a courtroom drama. Numerous city experts made the case for clearing as much of the market as possible. Steinbrueck cross-examined each of the city's experts, pointing out that minor repairs like paint and plumbing might change any building's designation from demolition status to merely substandard status, allowing for rehabilitation.

After the city's experts offered their case for demolition, Paul Kirk and John Morse made an extensive presentation of their proposal. Again, Steinbrueck challenged them. Morse's answers suggested that the Friends and city council were not far apart in their goals. When Steinbrueck asked Morse how he reconciled high-income apartments with the low-income environment of the market, Morse replied, "The history of the Market has been a mingling of people from Broadmoor and people from other areas coming down into the Market to shop and we think this is the main thing about the Market. It hasn't been a single structure or a single class that made the Market work." Steinbrueck and Morse disagreed more on which buildings were part of the market than on its essential character.[24]

When the Friends made their formal presentation, they submitted the petition with fifty-three thousand signatures, reinforcing Steinbrueck's familiar framework of competing class interests. The idea that "the people" were fighting "the interests" became the most prevalent interpretation of the struggle to save the market.[25] Steinbrueck claimed that the thrift shops, taverns, and cafés served working people who could not afford to go elsewhere. During the proceedings a low-income resident of the neighborhood, Merle Haug, echoed perfectly the Friends' position. "Is Urban Renewal supposed to be out to get rid of . . . the low income and move in the high income?" he asked. "Now, is that Urban Renewal, or is it just taking the dirt and scraping it away?"[26]

During these city council hearings, the media's editorial opinion changed slightly. In March 1969 the *Seattle Post-Intelligencer* supported the urban renewal plan and claimed that the Friends had taken an "unreasonable position" in opposition to it. By April 28 the newspaper still claimed to support the urban renewal plan overall but urged the city to consider Steinbrueck's and others' suggestions for preserving more of the market.[27]

Despite the media's shift, despite the fifty-three thousand signatures, and despite the Friends' compelling testimony, the city council unanimously approved the Morse-Kirk plan in August 1969, believing it presented a reasonable compromise between preservationists and developers and offered the greatest likelihood for private investment dollars and federal urban renewal funds. The basis for their decision, according to the ordinance, was the evidence that more than 70 percent of the market structures were substandard to the point where rehabilitation was unfeasible. The ordinance also cited inappropriate uses and traffic congestion.[28]

The council did not completely ignore the Friends' concerns. The final wording in the plan showed sensitivity to the impact redevelopment would have on the area. The plan acknowledged that "while the Market itself has deteriorated, it has become institutionalized and remains as a major activity center in the city."[29] The plan conceded that as much as possible would be done to preserve the market's function.

The Friends did not accept defeat, however. Steinbrueck and the Friends accelerated their efforts, trying multiple strategies to prevent the project's implementation. Steinbrueck wrote letters to anyone who would listen to protest the urban renewal plan—the mayor, city council members, the HUD office in Washington, Lady Bird Johnson, and even President Nixon. He also wrote articles in the editorial section of the Seattle daily papers, decrying the city's economic agenda in Pike Plaza. Between November 1970 and May 1971 Steinbrueck and the Friends inundated the media with press releases opposing the Pike Plaza Urban Renewal Plan, calling the city's plan a "big lie" and decrying the expectation of HUD money as a "pathetic hope for survival" for a project the Friends claimed was floundering. Steinbrueck also emphasized that there was no guarantee that the farmers could remain in the market and thus were "cheated out of their way of life."[30]

As part of the crusade Steinbrueck turned to the state and federal historic preservation agencies for help. In 1969 Steinbrueck nominated 7 acres of Pike Place Market to the National Register of Historic Places. The nomination was approved, and the district went on the National Register in February 1970. The designation prompted the Friends to suggest that the DCD reconsider its HUD funding application. Instead, the department's Urban Renewal Division successfully lobbied the state historic preservation office to change the district boundaries rather than potentially lose HUD funding. The state historic preservation officer convinced the National Park Service to reduce the district from 7 acres to 1.7 acres, incorporating just the Main Market and the Corner Market.[31]

Although initially devastating to the Friends, the reduction of the proposed national historic district had a positive, if unintended, consequence. The fact that the DCD was willing to work with a 1.7-acre historic district symbolized an acceptance of preservation's role in the urban renewal plan. The Urban Renewal office and DCD agreed to work within the guidelines of a historic district. Mayor Wes Uhlman, who replaced Braman in 1970 partially because of his moderate stance toward the Pike Place Market, even suggested a city ordinance, similar to the one just enacted in Pioneer Square, protecting the 1.7-acre district.[32]

The city's willingness to incorporate historic preservation did not appease Steinbrueck and the Friends, however. If anything, it made them more determined to imprint their utopian vision on the market's landscape. When HUD approved $10.6 million for Scheme 23 in May 1971, the Friends took their crusade directly to the public, launching an initiative campaign to reestablish the 7-acre district. To get Initiative 1 on the ballot in November, the Friends easily acquired a petition with more than twenty-five thousand signatures.[33]

The Friends designed Initiative 1 to do two things. First, it would establish a 7-acre Pike Place Market historic district within the larger 22-acre urban renewal area. Second, it would create a Market Historical Commission (MHC) to oversee structural and design changes. Ironically, it did not differ significantly from the plan already proposed by the city council and Mayor Uhlman. The city had already established a Design Review Board for development projects in the central business district. Initiative 1 simply enlarged the district to 7 acres and created a historical design commission specific to the market rather than a citywide review board.[34]

The similarities in the positions of those supporting and those opposing Initiative 1 set up a confusing campaign. On the one side, the Friends, which represented Seattle's cultural elite, architects, artists, students, and activists, opposed the mayor, city council, the Desimone family, the Central Association, and the business interests, on the other side. Newspapers, broadcast media, and election propaganda tried to frame the debate in the familiar class terms. Steinbrueck argued that Scheme 23 was a land grab for private investors who did not care about the "little man" who inhabited the market. City planners countered that the urban renewal plan rewarded investors willing to risk their money to get rid of downtown blight. When Steinbrueck questioned the "humanness" of dislocating the market population, a city councilman countered that the derelicts neither voted nor paid taxes.[35]

Despite the seeming polarity in views, the opposing groups agreed that the market should be preserved; they merely disagreed on how best to preserve it. The opponents of Initiative 1 supported private development of the market supplemented by government funds. Indeed, James Braman, the son of the former mayor and the head of the DCD, claimed that the formation of the 7-acre historic district would endanger HUD funding for the entire 22-acre Pike Plaza Urban Renewal Development, which in turn would prompt investors to withdraw $150 million in private funds. Steinbrueck and the Friends, however, countered that the Pike Plaza plan would kill the market and oust the people using it by making them victims of "poisonous affluence," despite provisions in the plan to provide low-income housing and mixed-use retail outlets.[36]

In September 1971 the Alliance for a Living Market (the Alliance) joined the fight to pass Initiative 1. The Alliance was founded by a former member of the Friends who felt they were too artsy and academic to appeal to a broad range of voters. The Alliance consisted mostly of activists, young attorneys, and representatives of market businesses and targeted more politically astute, younger supporters of the market. The group opposed the Pike Plaza Urban Renewal Plan on economic grounds, showing that the recession of 1970–71 left the city's optimistic assumptions about urban renewal outdated. The Alliance volunteers focused on community outreach, working with television stations and newspapers, making presentations to city council, and talking to citizens' groups to garner support for Initiative 1.[37]

In August 1971 an organization confusingly called the Committee to Save the Market formed in opposition to the Friends. The CSM purported to represent market merchants and property owners. Richard Desimone, representative of the Desimone family interests, supported the CSM. The CSM backed Scheme 23, with the addition of a 1.7-acre historic district in the market's core.[38]

Before the election the struggle over the fate of the Pike Place Market filled the Seattle media. The Friends took out large advertisements reiterating their established arguments for preservation based on the market's role in Seattle's working-class identity. The CSM fought back by accusing the Friends and the Alliance with strangling the market by blocking funding for rehabilitation, arguing that without HUD money, the market would continue to decay. The CSM claimed *it* had the true solution to the market's problems.[39]

Since both sides claimed to be doing the same thing, a reform group called Choose an Effective City Council tried to sort out the confusion. In September 1971 CHECC asked the Friends, the Alliance, and the CSM to reveal their funding sources. The Friends and the Alliance immediately complied, showing that most of their funding came in small chunks from members and other individuals. The CSM suspiciously declined at first, but after the third request it complied. With the exception of the Desimone family's corporation, the CSM's funders read like a roll call of the downtown business establishment. The CSM's largest supporters included Sea First Bank, Washington International Hotels, Safeco, the Central Park Plaza Corporation, and the Frederick and Nelson department stores. The CSM claimed to represent thirty-seven market merchants, but none had contributed money.[40]

On November 2, 1971, Initiative 1 passed with almost 57 percent of the vote, validating the Friends' vision for the market by creating a 7-acre historic district and twelve-member historic district commission. The night of the election, DCD director James Braman appeared at the Friends' celebration with his wrists wrapped in make-believe bandages stained red. In his concession speech, Braman said, "The people have spoken." He vowed to work with the Friends to preserve Pike Place.[41]

Within a month the city council passed an ordinance reflecting the voters' mandate and emphasizing that the use of the market was the most important aspect of preservation. The "meet the producer" philosophy had been a hallmark of the Friends' determination to save the market. Now this economic function was protected by city ordinance, making the market unique among historic districts around the country.[42] The ordinance also established the Market Historical Commission to oversee design and restoration. The twelve MHC members represented a cross-section of interested groups, albeit with an emphasis on the cultural elite, and included two members each from the Friends of the Market, the Seattle chapter of the American Institute of Architects, and Allied Arts of Seattle, along with two market property owners, two market merchants, and two market residents.

The success of Initiative 1 stemmed partially from Seattle's economic and social climate in 1971. The initiative happened against a backdrop of social protest, especially against establishment interests in inner cities. Between 1963, when the Monson Plan appeared, and 1971, urban renewal promoters faced a heightened level of public awareness and involvement in civic decisions. The success of the initiative also marked the end of the cozy, paternalistic teaming of downtown businesses, major editorialists, and city hall that had seemed to be the natural order of things in 1958, when the Central Association formed to help plan the city. The social unrest of the 1960s, the Vietnam War, and the economic recession in Seattle in 1970–71 intervened to foster a new activism and a new set of players on the city's planning stage.[43]

The victory of historic preservation in the Pike Place Market did not represent a populist victory as much as a transfer of planning power from a business elite, namely, the Central Association, to a cultural elite comprising the Friends' membership of architects, artists, students, and urban design professionals. Seattle's business elite recognized that the economic function of the market was important to the reinvigoration of the central business district but had not valued the market's structure or design. The cultural elite had emphasized the importance of design, livability, historical associations, and identity over its economic potential.[44]

In addition to these competing visions of the city's physical form, the business elite and the cultural elite also held competing visions of its symbolic form. The mayor, city council, and the Central Association envisioned Pike Plaza creating an identity for Seattle as a modern, world-class city, able to compete with any city in California or the East. The Friends alternatively believed that Seattle's future resided in the past. According to the Friends, Seattle's identity was the *historic* market, as it was during its Depression-era heyday. Tobey's artwork and Steinbrueck's sketches served as the primary texts for this identity. For Steinbrueck, the run-down, haphazard buildings and the seedy, colorful characters who patronized them *were* the market. They embodied the historic, social, and aesthetic identity of Seattle, which, if destroyed, could never be re-created. Tobey's description of the market as "the heart and soul of Seattle" was widely quoted in the press. Architect Fred Bassetti's statement that the market was an "honest place in a phony time" became a slogan for the initiative struggle.[45]

The Friends based their arguments on the fact that the market was unique to Seattle. It distinguished for Seattle an identity different from that of Portland, San Francisco, or any other West Coast city. In press releases, the Friends described the identity encapsulated in the market as an "intangible benefit," something "to which a monetary value cannot be assigned." In a *Seattle Times* article shortly before the Initiative 1 election, *Washington Post* writer Wolf Von Eckardt argued, "November 2 Seattle will vote along with some mundane political matters on whether to keep its soul and an irreplaceable piece of Americana—the Pike Place Market." Six years later the *Seattle Post-Intelligencer* claimed, "The Pike Place Market is the very essence of life [in Seattle].... The people of the market are the people of Seattle." Finally, in 1976, historian Roger Sale wrote, "For many people the Public Market *is* Seattle, its one great city achievement, the place they love most, the place they take visitors first."[46]

Why was the market a utopian symbol for Seattle's cultural elite? It encapsulated an egalitarianism inherent in the city's history. The market's ethnic diversity and working-class demographics reinforced Seattle's working-class, populist roots. At the turn of the century, Seattle's middle-class reformers became radicalized, ironically, because living conditions for the middle and working classes were not that bad, leaving them time and resources to devote to improvements. During the Progressive Era, the populace voted to make Seattle one of the first publicly owned ports in America. The city also formed the nation's first municipally owned power-generating system. The formation of Pike Place Market itself represented Seattle's populist spirit. The high-water mark of Seattle's radical reform came after World War I, with the Great Strike of 1919. Labor unions throughout the city went on strike in support of unfair government treatment of the shipyard workers, bringing the city to a halt and representing a high point of the labor movement nationally. Between 1920 and 1970 conservative, business-oriented groups reasserted themselves in the city council, diluting Seattle's populist strain, but the idealism and reform of the Progressive Era resonated with the cultural elite of the 1960s and early 1970s, who saw themselves as kindred spirits with earlier labor advocates. For many Seattle residents, the market was the last physical remnant of the Progressive spirit.[47]

Fittingly, the business practices in the market represented a paradise of preindustrial capitalism. In a world of globalization, corporate consolidation, and impersonal marketing, the "meet the producer" individualism of the market harked back to a seemingly simpler era. The function and the place were intertwined in the market, so that changing the buildings would irreparably change the use. In a press release from 1970, the Friends claimed that the uniqueness of the market lay in its symbol of "the American tradition of small independent businessmen operating with enterprise and with service and personal involvement." The National Register of Historic Places designation form claimed that the market was significant because it was a "living example of free enterprise and free marketing oriented to the small businessman.... [T]he market provides a living heritage of food marketing in its simplest form where the producer meets the consumer directly.... The Pike Place marketing district is a living organism continually viable in the tradition of its simple beginnings."[48]

The purpose of Initiative 1 was to keep the market exactly as it had always been. The market was to be a place where consumption was an event rather than a cultural phenomenon. Building renovations were supposed to preserve the economic model of the market and have minimal impact on farmers, merchants, consumers, and residents. At its first meeting the newly created MHC outlined four points to inform subsequent decisions:

1. The market is a place for the farmer to sell his produce.
2. The market is a place for the sale of every kind of food product.
3. The market is a place where citizens in the low and moderate income groups can find food, goods and services, and residences.
4. The market is and will always be a place with the flavor of a widely varied shopping area.

The MHC members faced a daunting task. The MHC stood "with one foot in the past and one foot in the future, charged with preserving the special quality of the market, and with planning for the future, preserving and upgrading structures, and dealing with all of the aspirations, desires, and proposals of the many owners and tenants within the District." To be true to the "historic" functions, the MHC agreed to promote the sale of fruit, produce, flowers, meat, fish, poultry, and groceries, as well as support food sales at restaurants and cafés. They also agreed to promote uses that catered to pedestrians.[49]

Because the historic district was entirely within the twenty-two-acre urban renewal area, the MHC needed to follow the guidelines set by the Urban Renewal Division of the DCD. The market was one of the first historic preservation projects carried out with urban renewal funds and guidelines. Traditionally, urban renewal had been the enemy of historic preservation. No model existed for the marriage of the two, and thus the MHC and DCD struggled over jurisdiction. To add to the confusion, the market was also subject to the requirements of the Federal Urban Renewal Program, which sometimes did not correspond with local preservation goals. The fact that the MHC preserved a use—marketing—created opposition from HUD on funding. Seattle benefited from the fact that the Pike Place Urban Renewal Project was one of the last projects funded in the country. Because urban renewal was being phased out as national policy by the 1970s, Seattle officials negotiated with HUD to waive limits on the amount of federal funds they spent.[50]

And federal funds proved vital. From 1972 until the completion of the project in the 1980s, federal expenditures on the project, including urban renewal and HUD funds, constituted $50–$60 million, the majority of the total expenditure.[51] Washington's senator Warren Magnuson was instrumental in securing funding. As a supporter of the Friends, Magnuson promised that if Initiative 1 passed, he would use his position on the Senate Appropriations Committee to ensure that the Pike Plaza urban renewal funds transferred to preservation. Magnuson not only delivered the original $28 million but also secured an additional $10.6 million in block grants, $2 million in federal rehabilitation loans, and $2.5 million for public works and street repairs. The dependence on urban renewal funds dictated that the market comply with urban renewal's goals.

State restrictions also influenced the market's rehabilitation because they required that the city act as the urban renewal agency but limited how the city used funds. Thus, the DCD employed urban renewal funds to buy land, combine land into parcels, and sell land to private developers, but it could not develop land itself. To ensure that private developers did not fill the void, the Friends, the Alliance, and Allied Arts of Seattle suggested forming a public corporation to develop the market. Chartered in June 1973, the Pike Place Preservation and Development Authority followed the guidelines of the urban renewal project, but as a private body it was able to take out mortgages on buildings and engage in property development. The PDA became the landlord for city-owned properties. By 1981 it had an operating budget of more than $2 million, and its duties included acting as leasing agent, collecting rents, overseeing parking, and providing janitorial services, building maintenance, and security.[52]

The multiple agencies and jurisdictions involved in the market's rehabilitation forced compromises that created a district unlike either Pike Plaza or the historic market. Steinbrueck and the Friends felt compelled to ensure that any final plan was consistent with the public mandate codified by Initiative 1. Absolute compliance with the intent of the citizens' initiative was not always practical, however, and Steinbrueck soon became disillusioned with his victory. He claimed that "we won the battle, and then we put the enemy in charge of administering the peace."[53] Out of frustration, he resigned from the MHC in 1975. By 1978 Steinbrueck was openly critical of the market's rehabilitation. He lamented the number of people in the market who "looked and sounded like they were from California and New York and Montana and Cleveland." Steinbrueck observed that they were not buying but merely spectating. "It is not the Market of 1971, nor of Mark Tobey, nor of mine. It is the Market of the developer, the tourist bureau, and of 1978. Oh, well!"[54]

Steinbrueck's assessment of the market was accurate. Despite a commitment to keep the market exactly as it was, the very act of preservation transformed it. The initial goals outlined appropriate uses and ways to maintain the original market's uniqueness; revised plans added an emphasis on attracting tourists and appealing to shoppers. In the revised plan the first two goals sounded consistent with the Friends' vision to "attract farmers/sellers and support their continued roles in the Market" and "induce diversity among Market-related businesses while maintaining the predominance of the food supply function of the Market." The third and fourth goals, however, sounded more like something Scheme 23 would have advocated: to "enhance the Market as a regional attraction" and to "maintain and expand features of the Market which appeal to a broad cross-section of all people living in Seattle and the region."[55]

The rehabilitation process changed the businesses in the area. Once rehabilitation began, businesses had to be relocated within the market while buildings were renovated. Many smaller businesses, operating on thin profit margins, did not survive the upheaval. Of the original 250 businesses in the market when preservation began, only 119, fewer than half, reestablished in the market after restoration. The others either relocated outside of the market or went out of business. Additionally, rents rose in the newly preserved buildings. Despite a mandate to preserve the market's structures, the city and the PDA demolished twenty-eight buildings. By 1977 refurbishments, space shortages, and nearby private development pushed rent in renovated areas 60 percent higher than prerenovation rates, forcing other merchants to leave.[56]

When urban renewal and historic preservation ended in 1983, the market was completely different than it had been in 1971. Despite good intentions, the PDA had created a district with a design driven by elites, not the "little people." The PDA's first director, George Rolfe, recognized this phenomenon. According to Rolfe, "It is a curious reversal that the idea of a traditional Market—1930s style, meat and vegetables for low-income people—does not come from low-income people today. It comes from the upper and middle income who want to sample what life was like then."[57]

The PDA did provide services to the "working man," however. The programs to help low-income residents in the community were much more extensive than those planned by the city council. The PDA used HUD grants and loans to convert old hotels and flop houses into subsidized apartments and urged the city to build forty-three market-rate rentals, which prompted private developers to build apartments. The PDA also focused on community services, establishing a free clinic, a senior center, a food bank, a child care center, and a café providing subsidized, low-cost meals. The district even got its own newspaper—the *Pike Place Market News*—and a charitable foundation to subsidize the public programs offered in the district.[58]

Because the Pike Place Market was no longer a traditional farmers market, the PDA and the MHC had to invent a tradition to stay true to the intent of Initiative 1. The PDA acknowledged that the market's most important function was as a reminder of the way a traditional marketplace operated. According to John Turnbull, a PDA director, the PDA acted as a "local police power" to ensure that the market catered to "working people." In order to keep the forces of capitalism from driving out small producers, Turnbull observed that the PDA created a "socialist controlled economy." Turnbull claimed that the PDA promoted "internal inconsistencies and acts of randomness" to provide the proper environment for the market. The market they created was premodern, the "essence of penny capitalism . . . that is extremely important in this time of corporate giants. . . . It is a beautiful way to get business and keep business that is individual."[59]

The PDA and MHC created elaborate usage guidelines, dictating what percentage of a store's business could come from manufactured goods, what percentage could come from tourist-oriented goods, and what percentage must come from home-grown or homemade goods. The agencies prohibited national chains.[60] In general, the guidelines emphasized the sale of fresh produce, fish, and other grocery items. The PDA made a few exceptions for merchants who were not farmers but had been regularly selling their wares in the market prior to preservation.[61]

The physical structures of the market were less important than the use. Indeed, the structures remained primarily because they provided the most authentic and compatible homes for the preserved uses. All design guidelines corresponded with usage guidelines. For example, to keep the mixed-use character of the market, the Pike Place Urban Renewal Plan dictated different uses on different floors, so that retail, wholesale, storage, residential, and restaurants would all be in the same building. The plan also broke the historic district into zones, and each zone determined not only the design elements of the various buildings but also the acceptable methods of merchandising, the types of display cases allowed, the available paint colors for the interior of the shop, and preferred lighting methods.[62]

By re-creating a farmers market, the PDA and MHC harked back to a time when a "market" was a physical location and not an abstract concept. Indeed, from the Friends to the PDA, all organizations and agencies involved in the so-called preservation denied the greater capitalistic forces at work in Seattle to preserve Pike Place as a locale. Rather than defer to the economic conditions of development espoused by the Central Association, the Friends and the PDA stubbornly created a place apart and tried to regulate the use of the market to keep it from succumbing to the most potent market force, tourism. The identity preserved in the Pike Place Market was reminiscent of an early form of capitalism, where all merchandise was sold by the producer directly to the consumer.

Maintaining the market as a community-based farmers market was not always easy, however. Getting the merchants to adhere to the guidelines was one of the biggest challenges. According to one MHC chairman, "It was necessary to exert some muscle to insure that the merchants didn't allow themselves to be seduced into the whole Madison Avenue supermarket hype." One hardware store in the market repeatedly violated the historic district guidelines because it sold more Seattle key chains and coffee mugs than nuts and bolts. In 1982 City Councilman Michael Hildt challenged the usage guidelines. Hildt pushed through an amendment to the historic district ordinance, favoring artists and craftspeople and allowing for a mix of businesses that "will provide a variety of goods and services particularly to Seattle residents but also to visitors." By 1996 there were 175 craftspeople but only 125 farmers registered with the PDA.[63]

Despite efforts to maintain a farmers market, measures such as the Hildt amendment, plus larger market forces, changed the usage of space in the district. In 1974, for example, wholesale enterprise occupied 23 percent of the available space. By 1982 it was less than 8 percent. Conversely, over that same period, retail space grew from 16 percent to 56 percent. The types of businesses differed from those the Friends sought to save. Until 1970 nearly all of the businesses in the market were community based—produce vendors, thrift shops, optometrists, shoe repair shops, hardware stores, print shops, and dressmakers. By 1980 gift shops, toy stores, antiques, boutiques, gem stores, and import outlets greatly outnumbered produce vendors.[64]

Another dilemma caused by the use guidelines stemmed from the fact that there were not enough farmers to sell produce in the market. King County simply no longer supported family farms. To combat this problem, the PDA started programs to keep current farmers economically viable and to promote the establishment of new farms. The program also encouraged corporate farmers to direct-market excess produce in the Pike Place Market. The PDA-sponsored Farmer Liaison Program attracted new farmers to the market, provided marketing assistance, and worked with farmer advocacy groups. The Revolving Loan Program provided loans for new farmers who could not get commercial loans to buy equipment, seeds, and fertilizer. To ensure that the farmers were local growers and not part of a corporate farming structure, a PDA representative visited every farm yearly.[65] The PDA also organized a co-op known as the Bulk Commodities Exchange. The co-op sponsored the purchase of fresh produce from small, local farms and its resale in bulk to restaurants and buying clubs. These initiatives did help bring farmers into the market. The number of farmers selling produce in the market increased from sixty in 1976 to eighty in 1983. Still, despite the PDA's best efforts, the bulk of the produce sold in the Pike Place Market came from central Washington, east of the Cascade Mountains.

The other dilemma the governing bodies of the market faced was tourism. The successful completion of the urban renewal plan meant that there were more produce stands, more stalls for craftspeople, and more restaurant and deli space. The expanded goods and services combined with the nostalgic feel of the market drew more visitors. Market merchants catered to tourists by changing their hours. The market had originally been open until six or seven o'clock, six days a week. To attract more visitors, market merchants started opening on Sundays, but to avoid hiring more employees, they started closing at five on weekdays. The new schedule favored visitors who could come during the weekday, while penalizing people who had to come after work. The tourists helped businesses, however. In 1973 only 7 percent of market merchants reported four hundred customers in an average business day, but by 1982 some 26 percent saw that many, and 13 percent anticipated more than eight hundred daily customers.[66]

By the early 1990s the Pike Place Market was Seattle's leading tourist attraction.[67] It was also one of the most prominent symbols of the city. Visitors came in droves to sample the experience that they believed was unique to Seattle. In this regard, the supporters of the market succeeded in using it to create Seattle's civic identity. Pictures of the market graced the covers of visitor guides, tourist maps, and booster brochures. After the Space Needle, the Pike Place Market is the most recognizable man-made symbol of Seattle.

The rise of tourism and the struggle to control it illustrated the difficulty of regulating market forces. By denying the capitalistic forces at work in post–World War II American life, the PDA, the DCD's Urban Renewal Division, and the MHC created the Pike Place Market as a place where consumption was limited to a single point-of-purchase event rather than a persistent way of life. Yet by choosing what goods merchants sold, the PDA helped determine who patronized the market and established an artificial model of capitalism that could not exist without regulation. The PDA had to control the whole process, from the point of production to the point of consumption, in order to keep the market independent of the forces of standardization, consolidation, and globalization.

In the end, the market succeeded in romanticizing a preindustrial utopia. The farmers market, and the nostalgia it invoked, created the image of an agrarian paradise in the middle of the city—a time when life was simpler, people did business on a handshake, and producers and consumers met on a daily basis. In the tradition of Mark Tobey and Victor Steinbrueck, artists sit among the vegetable stands and paint scenes of the market to sell to visitors. Pictures of the neon "Public Market" sign portray the city as a small, pastoral village. To those who do not know the behind-the-scenes economics, the Pike Place Market is Seattle's working-class nirvana.

Notes

1. On urban renewal policy, see Jane Jacobs, *The Death and Life of Great American Cities* (New York: Random House, 1961); Robert M. Fogelson, *Downtown: Its Rise and Fall, 1880–1950* (New Haven: Yale University Press, 2001); and Neil Smith, *The New Urban Frontier: Gentrification and the Revanchist City* (New York: Routledge, 1996).

2. Sohyun Park Lee, "Conflicting Elites and Changing Values: Designing Two Historic Districts in Downtown Seattle, 1958–1973," *Planning Perspectives* 16 (July 2001): 243–68.

3. Alice Shorett and Murray Morgan, *The Pike Place Market: People, Politics, and Produce* (Seattle: Pacific Search Press, 1982), 13–29; *A Decade of Change: A Final Report on the Preservation and Redevelopment of the Pike Place Market* ([Seattle]: City of Seattle, 1983), 47.

4. Shorett and Morgan, *Pike Place Market*, 49, 54–65; ibid. See also *Decade of Change*.

5. Community Development Services, "A Social Ecology of the Pike Place Market," 1973, Michael Hildt Papers, City of Seattle Municipal Archives; *Minutes of the City Council Hearing on Pike Plaza Redevelopment*, 1969, Victor Steinbrueck Papers, University of Washington Manuscripts, Special Collections, and University Archives, Seattle.

6. Shorett and Morgan, *Pike Place Market*, 99–111, 121–23.

7. *Pike Place Market Design Report* (Seattle: City of Seattle, 1974); *Decade of Change*, 47. Demographic information comes from a survey conducted by Greenleigh and Associates, 1968, commissioned by the city council and presented in March 1969, transcript in Steinbrueck Papers. See also Sohyun Park Lee, "From Redevelopment to Preservation: Downtown Planning in Post-war Seattle" (Ph.D. diss., University of Washington, 2001).

8. Testimony from John W. McMahon of Research Associates at the city council hearing on Pike Plaza Redevelopment, March 19, 1969, transcript in Steinbrueck Papers.

9. *Pike Place Market Design Report*.

10. Ben Ehrlichman quoted in Shorett and Morgan, *Pike Place Market*, 125; Lee, "From Redevelopment to Preservation," 135–38.

11. Shorett and Morgan, *Pike Place Market*, 125–26; Lee, "From Redevelopment to Preservation," 133–34; transcripts of city council hearings on Pike Plaza redevelopment, Steinbrueck Papers.

12. Development Research Associates, "Land Utilization and Marketability Study," 1967, Pike Place Market Collection, Seattle Municipal Archives; McMahon testimony.

13. *Seattle Weekly,* September 23, 1981, 22.

14. J. D. Braman to the city council during hearings on Pike Plaza Redevelopment, March 19, 1969, Steinbrueck Papers.

15. Maps of area found in Steinbrueck Papers. See also report from Municipal League of Seattle to the city council, April 9, 1969, text in Steinbrueck Papers.

16. Abstract history of Friends of the Market, Friends of the Market Papers, University of Washington Manuscripts, Special Collections, and University Archives, Seattle.

17. *Seattle Times,* November 26, 1984, D1–2; Peter Steinbrueck, interview with the author, November 13, 2000, Seattle.

18. Steinbrueck to the city council, Pike Plaza Redevelopment hearings, March 21, 1969, transcript in Steinbrueck Papers.

19. Lee, "From Redevelopment to Preservation," 142–46.

20. John Morse testimony to the city council, Pike Plaza Redevelopment hearings, March 21, 1969, transcript in Steinbrueck Papers.

21. Draft of the Morse-Kirk plan, 1968, Steinbrueck Papers.

22. Steinbrueck to Mayor J. D. Braman, March 28, 1968, Steinbrueck Papers; *Seattle Times,* March 16, 1969, C9.

23. *Seattle Times,* April 4, 1968, 33.

24. Minutes of the city council hearing, Pike Plaza Redevelopment, March 19, 21, 1969, transcript in Steinbrueck Papers.

25. Ibid., March 21, 1969. See, for example, Roger Sale, *Seattle, Past to Present: An Interpretation of the History of the Foremost City in the Pacific Northwest* (Seattle: University of Washington Press, 1976), 225–27.

26. Merle Haug, testimony to the city council hearing, Pike Place Redevelopment, March 28, 1969, transcript in Steinbrueck Papers.

27. *Seattle Post-Intelligencer,* March 26, 1969, 6; April 28, 1969, 8.

28. Seattle City Ordinance 98016, August 28, 1969.

29. Pike Plaza Urban Renewal Plan, ND 401, approved 1969, copy in Steinbrueck Papers.

30. Press releases in Steinbrueck Papers.

31. Lee, "From Preservation to Redevelopment," 149–51.

32. Lee, "Conflicting Elites and Changing Values," 260–61.

33. *Seattle Times,* June 15, 1971.

34. Lee, "Conflicting Elites and Changing Values," 261.

35. *Seattle Post-Intelligencer Northwest Today Magazine,* September 26, 1971, 8.

36. Ibid., 8–9.

37. *Seattle Weekly*, September 23, 1981, 28–29. See also Shorett and Morgan, *Pike Place Market*, 36–137; and *Decade of Change*, 21.

38. *Seattle Post-Intelligencer*, August 21, 1971.

39. Friends of the Market broadside quoted in *Seattle Weekly*, September 23, 1981, 24; series of proofs for ads in both Seattle papers in Steinbrueck Papers; *Seattle Weekly*, September 23, 1981; Pike Place Market pamphlet files, University of Washington Manuscripts, Special Collections, and University Archives, Seattle.

40. *Seattle Weekly*, September 23, 1981, 30; Patrick Douglas, "Up Against the System in Seattle," *Harpers*, April 1972, 92–93.

41. Shorett and Morgan, *Pike Place Market*, 136–39, 141.

42. Ibid. See also Friends of Market press release, November 18, 1971, in Steinbrueck Papers; *Seattle Weekly*, September 23, 1981, 25; Seattle City Ordinance 100475, December 1, 1971.

43. Lee, "From Redevelopment to Preservation," 157; *Seattle Weekly*, September 23, 1981, 30.

44. Lee, "From Redevelopment to Preservation," 132–62.

45. *Seattle Weekly*, September 23, 1981, 22; Victor Steinbrueck, *Market Sketchbook* (Seattle: University of Washington Press, 1968); *Seattle Weekly*, September 23, 1981, 22. See also press releases in Steinbrueck Papers.

46. Friends of Market press release, November 25, 1968, in Steinbrueck Papers; Wolf Von Eckardt, *Seattle Times*, October 3, 1971, C1; *Seattle Post-Intelligencer*, May 19, 1977; Sale, *Seattle, Past to Present*, 169–70.

47. Sale, *Seattle, Past to Present*, 113–16; Bruce K. Chapman, remarks to the National Trust for Historic Preservation, October 5, 1974, Hildt Papers; Lee, "From Preservation to Redevelopment," 13.

48. Press release, November 25, 1970, in Steinbrueck Papers; National Register for Historic Places Nomination and Inventory Form, Pike Place Market, September 28, 1972.

49. *Pike Place Urban Renewal Plan* (Seattle: City of Seattle, 1974), 47–49.

50. *Decade of Change*, 10–11; *Pike Place Urban Renewal Plan*, 38–39. See also Richard Moe and Carter Wilkie, *Changing Places: Rebuilding Community in the Age of Sprawl* (New York: Henry Holt, 1997); and Max Page and Randall Mason, eds., *Giving Preservation a History: Histories of Historic Preservation in the United States* (New York: Routledge, 2004).

51. Shorett and Morgan, *Pike Place Market*, 146–49; *Seattle Times*, April 16, 1972, A10.

52. Charter of Pike Place Market Preservation and Development Authority, June 28, 1973, Preservation and Development Authority Records, Seattle Municipal Archives.

53. Memo to DCD, Steinbrueck Papers. See also *Decade of Change*, 7.

54. *Seattle Post-Intelligencer*, August 3, 1978, B3.

55. *Program for Rehabilitation of the Market Core* (Seattle: Pike Place Market Preservation and Development Authority), 1975.

56. *Decade of Change,* 12–15, 31, 43–44; Shorett and Morgan, *Pike Place Market,* 148–50; Pike Project Chronology, Pike Place Market Collection, Seattle Municipal Archives.

57. *Decade of Change,* 24.

58. Ibid., 51–61. See also Marlys Ericsson, interview by author, November 15, 2000, Seattle.

59. Eric Hobsbawm and Terence Ranger, eds., *The Invention of Tradition* (Cambridge: Cambridge University Press, 1983); John Turnbull, interview by author, November 14, 2000, Seattle; James Mason, director of the Pike Place Urban Renewal Project, quoted in *Decade of Change,* 6.

60. Tom Quackenbush, Seattle Department of Community Development, interview by author, October 4, 1999, Seattle. This is still true today with one exception—Starbucks. When the guidelines were written, Starbucks had only one store, in the Pike Place Market. Because it is the original store, Starbucks remains but can sell only coffee and coffee-related merchandise, like mugs. They cannot sell pastries, games, or compact discs.

61. Preservation and Development Authority, "Program for Rehabilitation of the Market Core," 1975, in Steinbrueck Papers.

62. *Pike Place Urban Renewal Plan,* 50–57.

63. David Wright quoted in *Decade of Change,* 29; Quackenbush interview; Hildt Amendment, Hildt Papers; John Pastier, "Uncommon Market," *Historic Preservation* 48 (January–February 1996): 103.

64. *Decade of Change,* 68; *Seattle City Directory* (Seattle: R. L. Polk, 1938–80).

65. Steinbrueck interview.

66. Turnbull interview; *Decade of Change,* 47–48, 73, 65–66.

67. Pastier, "Uncommon Market," 52; Steinbrueck interview.

Part III

FROM CULTURAL AND GEOGRAPHIC MARGINS TO URBAN CENTERS

By erecting legal, economic, and cultural barriers to the region's expanding suburbs and exurbs, privileged westerners created homogenous communities based on class, race, gender, and lifestyle. These homogenous communities offered their carefully selected residents lifestyle amenities, social status, and a sense of security.[1] However, in the abandoned city centers that the primarily white and affluent regional emigrants left behind, other westerners found alternative lifestyles, social acceptance, and a safe haven. Racial and ethnic groups escaped persecution and found new expressions of political power. Men and women seeking sexual freedom created a welcoming counterpublic and fought, often successfully, to change laws that prohibited sexual expression, especially those focused on persecuting homosexuals. Politically and culturally marginalized Americans created new, sometimes insurgent, communities within the same city spaces that suburban emigrants disparaged, proving that, in fact, urban living was central to community formation and empowerment for many Americans.

Of course, some people were drawn to these new, freer, urban cultural zones. Tourists to San Francisco in the mid-twentieth century sought a kind of "exotic" paradise where voyeurism was not simply tolerated but encouraged. As Nan Alamilla Boyd illustrates, early gay and lesbian nightclubs provided their customers, many of whom were not local residents, a kind of safe haven where they were sometimes protected from police harassment. The police looked away because these clubs served as tourist spending zones.

Throughout the twentieth century, gay men pursued freedom and political equality in larger western cities such as San Francisco, Seattle, or Denver, seeking refuge from persecution and creating neighborhoods based on shared sexual identity. Nonetheless, Peter Boag argues, by the 1990s many gay men—traumatized by the effect of the AIDS epidemic on gay communities and in search of homeownership opportunities, community, and access to nature—increasingly returned to their rural origins, reconfirming the central lesson of *The Wizard of Oz*, "There's no place like home." Finally, we learn from Kent Blansett that World War II propelled Indian migrations to western cities. Although initially, Indians' settlement in western cities was perceived by many Native Americans as a failure, relocation to neighborhoods, such as San Francisco's Mission District, allowed for new Indian community organizations that found political and cultural expression in the intertribalism of the 1960s.

The chapters in this part demonstrate that after many white middle-class heterosexuals left western cities in the mid-twentieth century, racial and ethnic minorities, immigrants, and gays and lesbians created new political movements and diverse neighborhoods in western cities, making them places of greater cultural heterogeneity and cultural vitality. As Blansett and Boyd demonstrate, the twentieth-century urban West was a place where minorities formed communities and movements for equality within the metropolis before expanding their political reach or, as Peter Boag writes, before beginning a process of reverse migration that led some back to the hinterland.

Note

1. Lizabeth Cohen, "Is There an Urban History of Consumption?" *Journal of Urban History* 29 (December 2003): 96.

The Making of San Francisco's Queer Urban Scene

NAN ALAMILLA BOYD

Utopian visions spark urban migrations, and San Francisco has long inspired fantasies of economic prosperity, racial harmony, and sexual liberation. Newcomers and travelers seeking pleasure or fulfillment have come to San Francisco to carve out new lives, and although some returned home frustrated that their fantasies had not materialized, others stayed and settled, transforming the landscape of San Francisco's neighborhood communities. In the post-Prohibition era, city elites clashed with entertainment-district and tourist-industry entrepreneurs who sought to capitalize on the reorganization of California's liquor interests.[1] Entrepreneurs quickly grasped the lucrative potential of San Francisco's long-standing resistance to temperance and moral reform, and they often played on the ethnic or sexual character of San Francisco's neighborhood communities in their entrepreneurial escapades. Nightclub owners in North Beach, entrepreneurs in Chinatown, and the developers of San Francisco's extravagant Golden Gate International Exposition, for example, refracted visions of a variety of historical actors as they worked to make sexualized and racialized entertainments a critical component of the city's increasingly global tourist economy. Over time, the combined efforts of neighborhood residents, entertainers, entrepreneurs, and elites worked to make sex and race tourism central to the city's local character but also to the way San Franciscans understood and marketed their city to visitors.

Capitalizing on the utopian visions of San Francisco's distinctly ethnic and sexually liberated neighborhood communities, entrepreneurs disrupted and altered the plans of San Francisco's cultural elites for a profitable and culturally sophisticated city—the jewel of the American West and a key player in the burgeoning

Pacific Rim economy. If the elite idyll of a successful San Francisco depended on social and racial hierarchies that tamed and subdued the assertion of new political identities and entitlements (and, through state action, controlled market forces), entrepreneurs, entertainers, and consumers created an alternative vision that foregrounded the possibilities of new racial and sexual constellations that promised social and economic fluidity and mobility. Through market forces (via local and global tourism), the performative reiteration of new identities (via public entertainments), and the formation of new identity-based communities out of a loosely configured cohort of voyeuristic consumers, new racial and sexual subjectivities came on the scene, eventually competing with elites for political entitlements and economic justice. Out of this mix sprang San Francisco's publicly visible queer communities in San Francisco's bawdy entertainment district, North Beach.

Historically, San Francisco's queer nightclubs could be found in the city's vice districts. When Prohibition ended in 1933 and San Francisco's vice districts expanded, queer nightlife experienced a boom, and entrepreneurs sought new ways to capture liquor revenue. Finocchio's, the North Beach nightclub that featured female impersonators, exemplifies this trend. Italian immigrant Joseph Finocchio opened Finocchio's on Stockton Street as a speakeasy during Prohibition.[2] One night, an impromptu performance by a female impersonator sparked Joseph Finocchio's interest. As journalist Jesse Hamlin notes, "A well-oiled customer got up and sang in dazzling style [a tune] that sounded exactly like Sophie Tucker. The crowd ate it up, and Finocchio saw his future." Female impersonators "were a sensation," Joe Finocchio recalls. "*Everyone* came to see the show. And to drink."[3] Initially, the show featured a female impersonator paired with an "exotic" dancer—a "hula dancer" or a "young Chinese dancer." In this way, Finocchio's combined sexualized and racialized entertainments, establishing a pattern that would continue through the postwar years.

This chapter examines the ways queer nightclubs capitalized on an already established and accepted aspect of San Francisco's unique urban culture: sex and race tourism. San Francisco's long history of prostitution, its investment in global markets, and its large migrant communities produced sexualized and racialized tourist venues that enabled San Francisco's fast-growing queer communities to grow and thrive. By closely examining three different nightclubs that staged queer entertainments in the 1930s and 1940s, this chapter links the development of San Francisco's tourist markets to the emergence and expansion of San Francisco's queer urban scene.

Mona's Club

Mona's was San Francisco's first lesbian nightclub. It opened on Union Street in 1934, just after the repeal of Prohibition, but it moved in 1936 to Columbus Avenue. Originally intending for the club to be a hangout for writers and artists, Mona Sargent and her then husband, Jimmie Sargent, covered the floors at 140 Columbus Avenue with sawdust to give the place a bohemian atmosphere.[4] Nightclub-style entertainment soon grew out of impromptu performances, and Sargent hired her most popular singers as waitresses. Over time, singing waitresses developed a floor show where women dressed as men and sang parodies of popular songs. The popularity of Mona's brought it to the attention of local writers, and the bar began to attract curious tourists.[5] Through 1936 *San Francisco Life,* a local tourist magazine, listed Mona's in its "Guide to Cocktailing, Dancing, and Dining" as a bohemian club, a code word for sexual unconventionality, and the magazine ran suggestive advertisements of individual performers. In 1938, as part of a routine check on Mona's tavern, San Francisco police sergeant Glen Hughes reported that he could not tell "which were the men and which were the women." He arrested Mona and charged her with keeping a disorderly house. Still, as Sargent remembers, "The girls came in!" The performances remained relatively informal until 1939, when Mona's moved to 440 Broadway. At this location Mona's became a tourist destination, and *San Francisco Life* ran quarter-page advertisements of the entertainers at Mona's. In the 1940s underground tourist guides like *Where to Sin in San Francisco* directed tourists "in the mood mauve" to Mona's, noting that "the little girl waitresses look like boys. The little-girls-who-sing-sweet-songs look like boys. And many of the little girl customers look like boys."[6] Located at the center of San Francisco's entertainment district, Mona's 440 brought lesbian entertainment into the public eye.

The incorporation of lesbian entertainments into San Francisco's tourist economy opened up a space for lesbian culture to grow. Longtime San Franciscan Reba Hudson remembers that Mona's was a big place: "It was a real long room with a stage at the end of it, typical nightclub kind of thing. You entered at the front and the bar was over at your left, hat-check room at the end of the bar. Then a big arch and you entered what they called the show room in nightclubs in those days. There was a line of booths down one wall, then tables in where you could utilize space around the stage."[7] The popularity of Mona's enabled other lesbian nightclubs to open, and through the 1940s lesbian bars populated San Francisco's North Beach district. There was the Paper Doll, the Artist's Club, the Beaded Bag, Mona's Candlelight, Blanco's, the Chi-Chi Club, the Beige Room, and Tommy's 299.

Through the 1950s even more lesbian nightspots opened, many of them women owned and operated. These included Tommy's Place, 12 Adler Place, Ann's 440, Miss Smith's Tearoom, the Tin Angel, the Copper Lantern, the Anxious Asp, the Front, and Our Club. All of these clubs opened on or near Broadway, at the nexus of San Francisco's vice and tourist district.

In 1941 one of the entertainers at Mona's, Babe Scott, took over the bar's management and began booking performers from New York and Los Angeles—stars like Tina Rubio, Kay Scott, and Beverly Shaw. Tina Rubio, who was called "the dynamic Latin star" in tourist magazines, combined sexual innuendo with overstylized ethnic or racialized performances. According to one review, Rubio sang in "Tahitian, Spanish, English, and Double Entendre." She performed at Mona's 440 from August 1941 until May 1942. Kay Scott, one of the more popular performers, started out at Mona's in 1936 and performed there until 1946. She dressed, as all of the entertainers at Mona's did, in a tuxedo and sang parodies of popular songs. Another favorite performer, Beverly Shaw, sang torch songs at Mona's from its inception through the mid-1940s. Perhaps the most important entertainer to appear at Mona's was African American performer Gladys Bentley. Advertised as "America's great sepia piano artist" and "the brown bomber of sophisticated songs," Bentley headlined at Mona's during the war years. According to historian Eric Garber, Bentley "packed her 250 pound frame into a tuxedo, flirted with women in her audience, and dedicated songs to her lesbian lover."[8] During the war years, sex tourism and the spectacle of gender transgression remained central to the popularity of Mona's, but "race tourism," a fascination with racial or ethnic signifiers and the racially liminal or abject body, became important aspects of the venue's performers' repertoire and, thus, Mona's tourist appeal.

Finocchio's

A second entertainment venue that became important to the expansion of queer entertainments in San Francisco was Finocchio's. In the 1930s nightclubs like Finocchio's were not gay bars in the sense that they sustained an overtly gay or homosexual-identified clientele. But as club owners profited from men willing to buy drinks for and sex from female impersonators, the nightclubs connected gay men to the city's tourist economy and established a public culture for homosexuals in San Francisco. Police records from San Francisco's Depression era reveal the public emergence of nightclubs featuring female impersonators. In 1937, for example, Police Chief Quinn "declared war" on female impersonators and announced, "Lewd entertainers must be stopped!" Following a raid on Finocchio's, he revoked the dance permit at the 201 Club at Jefferson and Taylor streets, noting that it, too, employed female impersonators on a percentage basis and that employees often mingled with guests, soliciting drinks. Shows featuring female impersonators were allowed to exist as an emblem of the city's sophistication—its desire to sustain a tourist culture—but periodic purges occurred that drew bar owners into negotiations with the police. For example, after a 1936 raid Finocchio's moved from Stockton Street to a much larger venue on Broadway. With more space, Finocchio hired a coterie of female impersonators, purchased spectacular costumes, and advertised "public entertainment that was so unusual and spectacular, that it would set the entire country talking." The use of female impersonators was risky, but Finocchio's legitimized its entertainment as a tourist attraction. "I had to fight a little bit of trouble," Joseph Finocchio remembers, "but then [the police] told me if you run the place straight everything would be fine. They don't want the entertainment to mingle with the customers. [So] I promised to run it like a regular theater."9 Finocchio's was not raided again. In fact, it became central to the development of San Francisco's North Beach tourist economy.

Through the mid-1930s tourism in San Francisco grew as the city witnessed the construction of three breathtaking architectural marvels: the Golden Gate Bridge, the San Francisco–Oakland Bay Bridge, and Treasure Island, a landfill space that rose from the bay to house San Francisco's 1939–40 Golden Gate International Exposition. As historian David Nasaw notes, expositions and fairs marketed cities to far-away tourists through hotel and railroad magazines, and "visitors to the city were fed a steady diet of urban adventure stories before they even reached the metropolis." In San Francisco hotel magazines like *San Francisco Life* and the *San Francisco Hotel Greeters Guide* called the city the "Paris of America" and cautioned police against restrictive ordinances. "Blue laws are foreign to the lightheartedness of San Francisco, a city that has always been able to distinguish between liberty and license. Away with them—let us be gay while the mood is on us." Calling itself the "Pageant of the Pacific," the Golden Gate International Exposition created a carnival-like atmosphere that complemented San Francisco's tourist entertainments. Nightclubs like Finocchio's that featured sexualized and racialized entertainments tapped into the fair's tourist appeal. Tourist magazines directed out-of-town visitors to Finocchio's, billing it as "America's most unusual night club," and the show's lineup always included Asian and Latino female impersonators who wove a variety of racial or ethnic references and signifiers into their drag performances. Li-Kar, for example, performed an "authentic and elaborate Geisha dance," and Billy Herrero impersonated Hedy Lamarr's appearance in the Hollywood film *Algiers*.[10] In 1940 Finocchio's developed a number called "Down Argentine Way" that featured South American rhythms and dancing. Later, as journalist John Stanley remembers, the show featured a wider range of racialized entertainments: "Juan Jose is a flamenco expert, clacking with castanets. Rene de Carlo is a lithe hula dancer in green skirt and bra. Bobby de Castro, billed as the 'Cuban King Kong,' performs a strip comedy complete with gorilla costume."[11]

In the postwar era Finocchio's ran four different shows, six nights a week, attracting locals, tourists, and such celebrities as Bob Hope, Frank Sinatra, Bette Davis, and Tallulah Bankhead. Finocchio's lured audiences with the titillating appeal of racialized sexual deviancy and display.[12] A 1948 edition of the San Francisco underground guidebook *Where to Sin in San Francisco* plugged Finocchio's to locals with a leading question: "Is it true what they say about Finocchio's?"

> Yes, it is. Even if the girls were women, the shows would be provocative. But the artists in the costly gowns are not women. Without saying what they are, twinkling Marjorie Finocchio does declare, "They're the only stable ones in the country." Tall, beautiful, stable Freddie Renault, the $200-a-week MC, has been here fourteen years.... Cute, Oriental Li Kar [sic], double stable after ten years, is both a dancer and the club's costume designer.... Stablest of all is Walter Hart, $275-a-week specialist in murky songs.[13]

Commenting on the loyalty of her employees at a time when entertainers were hotly in demand, Marjorie Finocchio underscores both the fascinating allure and, thus, the temporality of her performers, but also the stability and, thus, the legitimacy of Finocchio's as an institution.

With impersonators safely on stage and patrons in the audience, the clientele at Finocchio's could anticipate a pleasurably voyeuristic experience. An instructive review observed, "Guys and their gals in the know sit at least three tables from ringside and let themselves be sucked in by insidious illusion."[14] Tourists might have traveled to San Francisco to see the Golden Gate Bridge or the International Exposition, but many also sought out the city's cultural attractions and thrilled to the racialized sexual entertainments featuring a panoply of North Beach nightclubs. As tourism grew in San Francisco, Finocchio's successfully capitalized on the sexualization of both gender transgression and racial difference.

The Black Cat

Yet another venue that capitalized on and influenced the transformation of San Francisco's burgeoning tourist economy was the infamous Black Cat Café. The Black Cat grew out of a Prohibition-era tradition that combined the sex trade with queer entertainment. The Black Cat opened in 1906 at Eddy and Mason, just after the great earthquake and fire leveled much of the old Barbary Coast. Charles Ridley took over management in 1911, and like Joseph Finocchio he sought to transform the bar into "the most popular place in Bohemia." In 1913 he staged a program of events "startling for originality and uniqueness," where waiters were "costumed in carnival dress" and entertainers promised "to outshine anything ever before attempted . . . in San Francisco." The bar became famous for its unconventionality, attracting union organizers, local artists, vaudeville performers, and, later, Hollywood entertainers. California writers William Saroyan and John Steinbeck frequented the Black Cat, and entertainers Tallulah Bankhead and Bette Davis stopped in while performing in town. Between 1915 and 1919, when antiprostitution forces grew strong, the Black Cat came under scrutiny for hiring "disreputable" women. In 1921, after police commissioners witnessed women who "mingled with the guests, singing to them, sometimes eating and drinking at their tables, and usually dancing with them," the Black Cat lost its dance permit and temporarily closed.[15] It reopened after the repeal of Prohibition at 710 Montgomery Street, and Ridley again managed the place.

In the 1940s Sol Steuman purchased the Black Cat, and its patronage shifted. Ever popular with local bohemians and waterfront workers, the Black Cat became a fashionable spot for homosexuals and, increasingly, tourists seeking a taste of San Francisco's wild side. One entertainment guide announced: "Rebels have been flaunting convention at the Black Cat for over twenty years. During the war, many a Montgomery Street Bohemian went forth to work or fight, but they're back now. Any night you can watch genuine artists, intellectuals and andsoforths boisterously protesting, or being loudly indifferent to such common social practices as sobriety and amiable conversation." With large numbers of military personnel stationed in San Francisco in the postwar years, however, the Black Cat again came under police scrutiny. In 1949 the bar was raided as part of a police crackdown against nightspots "featuring lascivious entertainment and catering to lewd persons." Police arrested ten people, held seven for vagrancy, and prosecuted three.[16]

By 1951 the Black Cat also found itself on the Armed Forces Disciplinary Control Board's list of establishments "off limits and out of bounds." This ruling required that armed forces personnel stay out of the Black Cat, whether in uniform or in civilian clothing. It also required that the café post a sign advertising its "off-limits" status.[17] Still, the Black Cat's popularity soared. In fact, the management stepped up its commitment to providing a radically bohemian environment by hiring the young José Sarria as a nightly entertainer.

Sarria's nightly drag performances at the Black Cat started spontaneously but soon became the nightclub's featured event. In drag Sarria performed a regular nightclub act, singing popular songs and telling clever stories. In the early 1950s he performed three shows a night, at 9:00, 10:30, and 11:30, accompanied by a pianist. In between shows he played host, greeted people at the door, and chatted with customers. According to Sarria, the audience was one-third local, one-third tourist, and one-third gay, but Sarria addressed everyone as if they were gay. "I told everybody that once you came in here your reputation was lost." He bantered with the crowd, lavishing attention on beautiful men and mocking the discomfort of naive out-of-towners. Because business was slow on Sundays, Sarria served brunch as he staged campy interpretations of popular operas. He dressed outrageously, played all the parts, and often interrupted arias with witty repartee, political commentary, or his own interpretations of the opera's characters. As his shows grew popular, they attracted upwards of three hundred people, and the bar became, as sociologist Sherri Cavan describes, a "home territory" for gay regulars.[18]

José Sarria's history as a performer in San Francisco parallels the evolution of racialized sexual entertainments in the city's tourist districts. Born in San Francisco, he grew up during the Depression and served in the armed forces during World War II. In the postwar era, back in San Francisco, he attended college and began to venture out in drag, often with his mother. He remembers that "once in a while I would go as a girl.... My mother would take me out and we'd go, just to be crazy, just for the hell of it." In the late 1940s Sarria was arrested for sexual solicitation in the Oak Room, the all-men's bar in the St. Francis Hotel, and his career plans were dashed. "I was arrested and, well, when you were arrested you had to then carry a card. Oh, it was a mess. I had a college education, spoke languages, but where are you going to get a job?" He decided to enter a drag contest at Pearl's in Oakland and won second place, which entitled him to a two-week gig performing in drag. Next, he performed at the Beige Room in San Francisco and tried out for a spot at Finocchio's. "At the time, the lead Mexican singer at Finocchio's had died, so they came to the Beige Room. They were looking for a Mexican person. There was another boy, can't think of his name, and myself, both Latino, and I had a better voice but was not known The other boy was known, so Finocchio's took her, that person. He stayed at Finocchio's until he retired." Soon thereafter, Sarria began entertaining at the Black Cat, where he worked from the early 1950s until 1963, when the bar closed. "The tour buses would come by the Black Cat, and the drivers would say, 'You want to see a good show, go there and see this. He does four shows a night.' Just like Finocchio's but I was the star."[19]

Marketing Difference: Chinatown and the Golden Gate International Exposition

Through the 1930s cultural voyeurism in the form of racialized sexual entertainments became an important aspect of San Francisco's evolving tourist economy. San Francisco's Chinatown is a case in point. Adjacent to San Francisco's North Beach district and Broadway's tourist entertainments, Chinatown's history of vice rivaled that of the Barbary Coast.[20] Through the mid-nineteenth century, most white tourists avoided Chinatown, but toward the end of the century sightseers became interested in Chinatown, seeking "a firsthand glimpse at Oriental depravity." White tourists and bohemians seeking "realness" and "authenticity" saw Chinatown as a "preserve of authentic, pre-modern culture," as historian Raymond Rast explains. They equated authenticity with depravity and danger, and white tour guides often staged lurid and voyeuristic experiences that underscored these expectations. Soon thereafter, Chinese merchants began to capitalize on the increasingly steady flow of tourists into their neighborhood, staging their own versions of Chinese authenticity. As art historian Anthony Lee observes, "A whole subculture of abjection was constructed in order to naturalize the increasing commodification of an ethnic neighborhood and culture."[21] In other words, a highly policed and politically disenfranchised community began to construct marketable signifiers of its own race-based disenfranchisement (its most stereotypical racialized qualities) and sell them to curious outsiders in the name of Chinese authenticity. After the 1906 earthquake and fire, for instance, Chinese entrepreneurs like Look Tin Eli convinced business elites to rebuild Chinatown with "oriental-style" architecture so as to better attract tourists to San Francisco's Chinese quarter.[22] Restaurants and bars featuring American inventions like "chop suey" became more common, and the Chinese Chamber of Commerce worked to reassure visitors of their safety. In these ways Chinese merchants and entrepreneurs struggled to control Chinatown's tourist industry, stressing authentic architecture, theater, and cuisine rather than the dangers of its purported opium and prostitution dens.

By 1939 real estate developers had transformed Chinatown's central avenue into a block-long entertainment district, lavishly decorated with pagoda-style towers that safely marked the district's entrance and exit. By the early 1940s when clubs like Mona's and Finocchio's became popular with tourists, Chinese-style entertainment drew many of the same white tourists to stylish cocktail lounges like the Jade Palace, Li Po's, and Charlie Low's Forbidden City. The Forbidden City combined standard nightclub fare with what it called *authentic* and *Oriental* culture, but the Forbidden City also lured tourists with the promise of sexualized entertainments.[23] As one travel guide exclaimed, "The all-new show is titled 'Orient 66' and features a bevy of Oriental cookies, Kaouri—exotic dancing star from Japan, and the sensational act of Karnak and the 'Girl on the Sword.'"[24] Most popular was the Forbidden City's infamous "Chinese Bubble Dancer," Noel Toy, who danced nude with her body obscured by a large opaque plastic bubble. Jokingly, during an interview for Arthur Dong's documentary, *Forbidden City, U.S.A.*, Toy remembers that the show's producers marketed her performances with the tagline, "Is it true what they say about Chinese girls?"—a salacious reference to her genitalia. She would play along, she laughs, with flip comments like, "Oh yes! It's just like eating corn on the cob," but the stakes were high. The strategy of capitalizing on a voyeuristic interest in racial otherness via sexual commodification (indeed, marketing the possibility of a glimpse at Toy's genitals) increased sales and kept the Forbidden City afloat, as a bartender testifies in Dong's documentary, but controlling racialized images and their racist effects were exceedingly difficult and often exploitative.

A similar dynamic was occurring at Mona's. There, waitresses and performers would play on the fantasies of their slumming heterosexual clientele. "That's what people would come to see," Mona Sargent remembers, noting the fascination tourists had with her gender-bending employees. "They'd say, 'That's not really a girl.' I'd say, 'Yes it is.'" Kay Scott, one of the entertainers at Mona's, was slight and boyish looking—a liminal and intriguing presence. The success of Mona's rested on this intrigue, and Mona Sargent encouraged tourists to interact with her entertainers. In fact, she exploited their liminality. "Go talk to Kay," she prodded a customer one night:

> I'd say, "No, I'll tell you what . . . take her in the back room, and if you can prove to me [that Scott's a boy] I'll give her five dollars." I'd hand her a twenty-dollar bill or something like that. They'd say, "That's alright," but I'd say, "You better know what you're talking about." So I'd say, "Kay, come here . . . He doesn't think you're a girl. We're going in the back room." We went in the back room, [and] Kay took down her pants and says, "I'm a girl." So he hands her twenty bucks and says, "I didn't mean any harm. I just had to know."[25]

Just as Charlie Low marketed the sex of his Chinese bubble dancer to crowds of curious white tourists, Mona marketed the sex of her transgendered or gender-liminal entertainers to straight tourists seeking sexual stimulation or simply something outside their ken. The sexual subjection and explicit voyeurism in these two examples illustrate the body-based economy of humiliation and desire at the root of racial and sexual abjection. The curiosity of tourists, marked as innocence or deflected as humorous, was neither innocent nor humorous. It functioned to frame a knowledge-producing machine that constructed new racial and sexual subjectivities, fixing them in place as exotic or pathological even as that same curiosity seemed to (innocently) explore the social meanings of racial and sexual difference.

Marketing Chinatown to white tourists marks the beginning of a new era of cultural exploitation in San Francisco, an era when racial or ethnic difference became an increasingly valuable resource or commodity to the city. This is best exemplified by the construction of San Francisco's extravagant Golden Gate International Exposition.[26] Architects worked for two years (1936–38) to build pavilions modeled on a "Pacific Basin" theme, an amalgam of Mayan, Incan, Malaysian, and Cambodian cultural references. Anticipating California's investment in Pacific Rim economies, the exposition featured images and attractions meant to introduce Pacific Island and Latin American cultures to California and the West. According to exposition chronicler Richard Reinhardt, the fair's architecture featured a mix of cultural styles: "Around the central fountain the designers had placed more than a dozen thick-limbed, pouty-lipped statues—Indian women hunkering over stone metates, Tehuantepec boys riding alligators, Inca girls playing flutes, Polynesians strumming ukuleles and other characteristic denizens of the Pacific Basin. Chunky, sleek and imperturbable, these statues epitomized the style of the Exposition."[27]

World's Fairs like the Golden Gate International Exposition were popular in the United States through the early twentieth century, and many large American cities hosted them—not simply to attract tourists (and revenue) but to showcase the city's natural resources and summertime entertainment value. San Francisco's 1939 fair celebrated the completion of the Golden Gate Bridge, among other things, but it followed in the tradition of earlier fairs in that alongside "serious" exhibits of the uses of electricity or agricultural industry, it staged a panoply of voyeuristic sexual and cultural experiences. Sally Rand's "Nude Ranch," for instance, featured a score of women who pitched horseshoes and swung lariats in G-strings while tourists peeked through glass panels. The fair also featured ethnic festivals, rickshaw races, Jewish days, and the Gayway, an arcade of cheap amusements that included Chinese acrobats, a troop of midget cowboys, a film of nude volleyball players, and a display of premature babies in glass cases. Although these types of amusements were not unique to San Francisco's fair, the Golden Gate International Exposition fed San Francisco's growing tourist economy not simply because it attracted tourists from afar but also because it stimulated unique tourist markets within the city. Neighborhoods with distinct racial or cultural qualities like Chinatown and North Beach became revenue-netting attractions for the city. In fact, as early as 1936 Pardee Lowe quipped that Chinatown had become "the chief jewel in San Francisco's starry diadem of tourist attractions."[28]

Sex and race tourism were also primary factors in the emergence of San Francisco's publicly visible queer communities. Sex and race tourism functioned as two sides of the same coin, and it is difficult to tease out or separate the racial aspects of some performances from the sexual. Racialized entertainers like the dancing girls at Charlie Low's Forbidden City projected a highly sexualized style, and queer entertainers at places like Finocchio's and Mona's often played on racial stereotypes as an integral part of their performances. At Mona's, for instance, the headlining performers were often either gender-transgressive or nonwhite women who performed for mostly white audiences. But whereas clever parodies or sultry melodies sustained the careers of white entertainers like Kay Scott or Beverly Shaw, "Latin star" Tina Rubio made her mark with "Hawaiian war chants" and "warbles in Tahitian and Spanish as well as in U.S.A." Rose O'Neal, "the female Fred Astaire," who performed with Gladys Bentley at Mona's through 1942, sparked interest because her liminal racial features—"a blonde 'colored' gal, if you please"—drew the attention of tourist reviews. And although there's no doubt that tourists came to see Gladys Bentley's musical talents, her dark skin, mannish attire, brazen sexuality, and large body accentuated her appeal. She provided a spectacle of racial, gender, and sexual difference. "Gladys Bentley's wrestling matches with the piano are as exciting to watch as to hear when the 440 Club's famous sepia pianist lets herself go on the keyboard. And when she sings . . . no wonder they call her 'the brown bomber of sophisticated song.'"[29]

The reception and social function of sex and race tourism are difficult to untangle. The anthropology of tourism suggests that sexual, racial, and ethnic entertainments function as hegemonic texts for white or Western tourists who seek meaning and bring authenticity to their own lives through experiencing cultural practices beyond their own life sphere.[30] At the same time, through double entendre and the coded display of queer culture, male and female impersonators modeled queer representations for the nightclubs' queer clientele.[31] Performers that mixed racial, gender, and sexual transgression depended on a complex layering of social needs and identifications to make their performances work. They stabilized some social boundaries while they destabilized others. In the process, these entertainers generated a new *queer* entertainment culture in San Francisco. Popular entertainers like Gladys Bentley of Mona's, Li-Kar of Finocchio's, and José Sarria of the Black Cat drew tourists to the city in much the same way as the Golden Gate International Exposition. By staging gender-transgressive entertainments that combined queer sexuality with the spectacle of racial or ethnic difference, these entertainers redefined San Francisco's popular culture by pushing the limits of sexual propriety while capitalizing on a voyeuristic interest in cultural difference. Through their popularity, queer entertainers like Gladys Bentley, Li-Kar, and José Sarria transformed racial and sexual abjection into a consumable product.

Sex and race tourism also generated a great deal of revenue for the city. A 1940 report by an organization called Californians, Inc., noted that in 1939 tourists spent more than fifteen million dollars in the Bay Area, an increase of 123 percent over 1938. The increase in tourism was attributed to the Golden Gate International Exposition, and Californians, Inc., lobbied business leaders to fund a campaign to draw even more tourism to the San Francisco Bay Area. "The record infusion of tourist money into this part of the state was reflected in a higher level of business here . . . than obtained elsewhere in the country," John F. Forbes, president of Californians, Inc., reported.[32] With business interests pushing for increased tourism, San Francisco's tourist economy wrapped a layer of protection around clubs like Mona's, Finocchio's, and the Black Cat—clubs that elites frowned upon for their sexual immorality. By 1950, as San Francisco mayor George Christopher ushered in an era of cultural conservativism, the struggle to control San Francisco's character had already been lost to entrepreneurs like Mona Sargent, Joe Finocchio, Sol Steuman, and Charlie Low. San Francisco's bustling and increasingly global tourist economy had become firmly attached to the kinds of entertainments that showcased, indeed exploited, a variety of new racial and sexual subjectivities (same-sex, cross-race, for hire).

Interestingly, the exploitative relationships that underwrote the development of San Francisco's sex and race tourist economy enabled some artists and performers to gain a foothold in an economy that would have otherwise shunned them. A number of the male impersonators at Mona's moved on to become bar owners themselves, and entertainers at the Forbidden City remember the opportunity that paid employment singing and dancing offered them.[33] San Francisco's tourist industry, as it developed, enabled a handful of entertainers to become entrepreneurs—or activists, in the case of José Sarria.[34] And on a larger scale, the cultural capital garnered by San Francisco's investment in off-color or tawdry entertainments laid the foundation for political revolutions to come. It spawned the formation of new identity-based communities out of a loosely configured cohort of neighborhood residents, community activists, and voyeuristic consumers. New racial and sexual subjects (that is, "lesbians and gay men" and "Chinese Americans") began to compete with elites for political entitlements and economic justice.

Notes

1. Nan Alamilla Boyd, *Wide Open Town: A History of Queer San Francisco to 1965* (Berkeley and Los Angeles: University of California Press, 2003), 44–52.

2. Eric Garber, "Finocchio's: A Gay Community Landmark," *San Francisco Bay Area Gay and Lesbian Historical Society Newsletter* 3, no. 4 (1988): 1, 4–5; Stuart Timmons, *The Trouble With Harry Hay* (Boston: Alyson, 1990), 46–47; Li-Kar, "Finocchio's," undated playbill, Ephemera Collection, Gay, Lesbian, Bisexual, Transgender Historical Society of Northern California, San Francisco (hereafter cited as GLBT Historical Society).

3. Jesse Hamlin, "What a Drag: Finocchio's to Close," *San Francisco Chronicle*, November 4, 1999; Garber, "Finocchio's."

4. Mona Hood, handwritten notes, July 1992 (in author's possession).

5. Mona Hood, interview by author with Rikki Streicher and Reba Hudson, tape recording, July 25, 1992, Santa Rosa, Calif., Wide Open Town History Project, GLBT Historical Society.

6. *San Francisco Life* 4, no. 2 (1936): 29; no. 3 (1936): 46; no. 4 (1936): 48; no. 5 (1936): 48; no. 6 (1936): 54; "Cops Moan Low Down Over Mona's," *San Francisco Chronicle*, March 30, 1938, 15; Jack Lord and Jenn Shaw, *Where to Sin in San Francisco*, 1st ed. (San Francisco: Richard F. Guggenheim, 1939), 56–57.

7. Reba Hudson, interview by author, tape recording, May 29, 1992, San Francisco, Wide Open Town History Project, GLBT Historical Society.

8. *San Francisco Life* 10, no. 3 (1942): 24; 9, no. 10 (1941): 26; 9, no. 9 (1941): 22; 10, no. 7 (July 1942): 30; Eric Garber, "Gladys Bentley: The Bulldagger Who Sang the Blues," OUT/LOOK 1, no. 1 (1988): 52–61.

9. *San Francisco Chronicle*, September 9, 1937, 1; Li-Kar, undated Finocchio's playbill, Ephemera Collection, GLBT Historical Society; "Joseph Finocchio Dies," *Los Angeles Times*, January 16, 1986, Metro section, 2.

10. David Nasaw, *Going Out: The Rise and Fall of Public Amusements* (Cambridge: Harvard University Press, 1999), 64; *San Francisco Life* 7, no. 1 (1938): 8–9; 15, no. 6 (1947); Frank Kay, "I Get Around: Nite Club Review—Finocchio's," ca. 1938, Eric Garber Collection, GLBT Historical Society. Note that the epigraph that appears with this review states, "Finocchio's: Where Korea's night life is reproduced in Aphroditic form."

11. *San Francisco Life* 8, no. 15 (1940): 25; John Stanley, "Finocchio's: A Reputable Bastion of a Bizarre Art," *San Francisco Chronicle*, January 8, 1967, Datebook section, 7–8. On closing night, November 27, 1999, Finocchio's featured a host of artists including Alejandro Cruz, a.k.a. Alejandra the Puerto Rican Bombshell (Jesse Hamlin, "Strutting Into History: Laughter Gives Way to Tears as Finocchio's Ends 63-Year Drag-Show Run," *San Francisco Chronicle*, November 29, 1999, D1).

12. Silke Tudor, "Night Crawler," *San Francisco Weekly*, December 1, 1999.

13. Lord and Lloyd Hoff, *Where to Sin*, 5th ed. (1948), 145.

14. Lord and Shaw, *Where to Sin*, 4th ed. (1945), 93.

15. "Black Cat Cafe Will Celebrate Anniversary," *San Francisco Chronicle*, November 8, 1913, 14; "12 Supervisors Threaten Rolph," *San Francisco Examiner*, January 31, 1917; Michael R. Gorman, *The Empress Is a Man: Stories From the Life of José Sarria* (New York: Harrington Park Press, 1998), 124; "Cafe Owners Bar Girls' Escape" and "Cafes Quiet, Business Fair," *San Francisco Examiner*, January 31, 1917; "Police Clamp Lid on Cafes, Oust Dancers," *San Francisco Examiner*, January 8, 1921, 1; "Black Cat, Pup Dances Banned," *San Francisco Examiner*, April 26, 1921, 1.

16. Lord and Hoff, *Where to Sin*, 5th ed., 101; "Cleanup Begun at Night Spots; Cafes Warned," *San Francisco Examiner*, June 15, 1949, 1; "3 in Café Raid Convicted," *San Francisco Examiner*, June 16, 1949, 19.

17. Senior Armed Forces Disciplinary Control Board, Western Area, February 1, 1951, "Military, Off-Limits and Out-of-Bounds," 1947–57, Alcoholic Beverage Control Subject Files, California State Archives, F3718, 341–42.

18. José Sarria, interview by author, tape recording, April 15 and May 20, 1992, San Francisco, Wide Open Town History Project, GLBT Historical Society; Sherri Cavan, "Interaction in Home Territories," *Berkeley Journal of Sociology* 4 (1963): 17–32.

19. Sarria interview, April 15, 1992.

20. Connie Young Yu, "A History of San Francisco Chinatown Housing," *Amerasia* 8, no. 1 (1981): 93–109; Chalsa M. Loo and Connie Young Yu, "Heartland of Gold: A Historical Overview," in *Chinatown: Most Time, Hard Time*, edited by Chalsa M. Loo (New York: Praeger, 1991): 31–56; Victor G. Nee and Brett de Bary Nee, eds., *Longtime Californ': A Documentary Study of an American Chinatown* (Stanford: Stanford University Press, 1972), xi–xxvii.

21. Ivan Light, "From Vice District to Tourist Attraction: The Moral Career of American Chinatowns, 1880–1940," *Pacific Historical Review* 43 (1979): 367–94; Raymond Rast, "The Cultural Politics of Tourism in San Francisco's Chinatown, 1882–1917," *Pacific Historical Review* 76, no. 1 (2007): 39; Anthony Lee, "Another View of Chinatown: Yun Lee and the Chinese Revolutionary Artists' Club," in *Reclaiming San Francisco: History, Politics, Culture*, edited by James Brook, Chris Carlsson, and Nancy J. Peters (San Francisco: City Lights Books, 1998), 163–82.

22. Rast, "Cultural Politics of Tourism," 53–54.

23. *San Francisco Life* 7, no. 2 (1939): 31; 7, no. 1 (1938): 29; 7, no. 3 (1939): 31. On Charlie

Low's Forbidden City, see Thomas W. Chinn, *Bridging the Pacific: San Francisco Chinatown and Its People* (San Francisco: Chinese Historical Society of America, 1989), 217–20. See also Arthur Dong's documentary film, *Forbidden City, U.S.A.* (DeepFocus Productions, 1989).

24. *San Francisco Hotel Greeters Guide*, undated clipping (in author's possession).

25. Hood interview.

26. The Golden Gate International Exposition ran from February 19, 1939, to September 2, 1940. For the impact of World's Fairs on tourism in American cities, see John Jakle, *The Tourist: Travel in Twentieth-Century North America* (Lincoln: University of Nebraska Press, 1985), 252–54; and Warren Susman, "The People's Fair: Cultural Contradictions of a Consumer Society," in *Dawn of a New Day: The New York World's Fair, 1939–1940*, edited by Helen A. Harrison (New York: New York University Press, 1980).

27. Richard Reinhardt, *Treasure Island: San Francisco's Exposition Years* (San Francisco: Scrimshaw Press, 1973), 81. On San Francisco's investment in tourist industry revenues, see William Issel and Robert W. Cherny, *San Francisco, 1865–1932: Politics, Power, and Urban Development* (Berkeley and Los Angeles: University of California Press), 152–54; and John B. McGloin, *San Francisco: The Story of a City* (San Rafael: Presidio Press, 1978), 376–79. On the economic impact of urban tourism more generally, see Chris Ryan, *Recreational Tourism: A Social Science Perspective* (London: Routledge, 1991), 65–94; Colin Michael Hall and John M. Jenkins, *Tourism and Public Policy* (London: Routledge, 1995); and Christopher M. Law, *Urban Tourism: Attracting Visitors to Large Cities* (London: Mansell, 1993).

28. Reinhardt, *Treasure Island*; Pardee Lowe, "Chinatown's Last Stand," *Survey Graphic* 25 (1936): 88.

29. *San Francisco Life* 9, no. 8 (1941): 30; 10, no. 10 (1942): 26; 11, no. 1 (January 1943): 21.

30. Erik Cohen, "A Phenomenology of Tourist Experiences," *Sociology* 13, no. 2 (1979): 179–202; Malcolm Crick, "Representation of International Tourism in the Social Sciences: Sun, Sex, Sights, Savings, and Servility," *Annual Review of Anthropology* 18 (1989): 307–44; David Engerman, "Research Agenda for the History of Tourism: Towards an International Social History," *American Studies International* 32, no. 2 (1994): 3–31.

31. Esther Newton, *Mother Camp: Female Impersonators in America* (Chicago: University of Chicago Press, 1972).

32. "Gold Rush: '39 Tourists Brought State $80,251,626," *San Francisco Chronicle*, March 4, 1940, 13.

33. On the entrepreneurial activities of the performers at Mona's, see Boyd, *Wide Open Town*, 82–83. On the reflections of Forbidden City singers and dancers, see Dong, *Forbidden City, U.S.A.*

34. José Sarria ran for public office in 1961 as an openly gay man and helped found a number of important social and political organizations. See Boyd, *Wide Open Town*, 20–24, 56–62.

San Francisco, Red Power, and the Emergence of an "Indian City"

KENT BLANSETT

The urban environment of San Francisco encapsulated and inspired a unique utopian Intertribal vision of Tribal sovereignty. It was a vision that forged a new awareness of Native empowerment and independence during the late twentieth century. From the early 1920s San Francisco was home to a vibrant and politically active Native community. In the decades to follow, the Bay Area Indian population doubled and eventually tripled in size by the 1970s. This twentieth-century mass exodus from reservations and rural communities to western cities represented one of the greatest per capita internal migrations of a people in the United States.

Several external factors influenced this great migration: World War II, the controversial Bureau of Indian Affairs (BIA) Relocation Program, and the destructive federal policy of Termination. Each successive generation of new Indian migrants into San Francisco faced extraordinary odds: discrimination, isolation, inadequate public housing, police brutality, unemployment, assimilation, and acculturation. Indigenous San Franciscans collectively challenged these overwhelming odds by constructing political, economic, social, and cultural coalitions. These coalitions were supported by community organizations, centers, and institutions that lent their services to political objectives.

Community leaders struggled to draw enough media and public attention to unmask the truth behind Relocation and Termination. Bay Area activists competed with a counterproductive bureaucratic utopian vision that consistently enforced a paternalistic "father knows best" policy. The most well known of these policies was the BIA's Relocation Program that systematically and geographically segregated Native people throughout San Francisco—a form of de facto gerrymandering. Through these programs the federal government disenfranchised Native peoples from their Tribal communities while systematically sponsoring relocation into distant cities and districts to prevent the advent of a solid Native population and voting bloc. Whereas Termination policy was established to destroy Tribal governments, Relocation was forged under the guise of terminating individual connections to Tribal communities.

Ultimately, Native peoples transformed what appeared to be the failed experiment of urban migration and relocation, and developed a new cultural and political vision—Intertribalism. The San Francisco Indian community formed institutions, chartered organizations, infiltrated college campuses, established business networks, and politicized an entire community. By operating through these new community institutions and organizations, Native peoples erased old identity questions and stereotypes and formed a new consensus politic.

The urban Americanization experiment was reinvented by a more populated Intertribal community, as thousands of individuals from different Tribal backgrounds created political coalitions to challenge destructive government policies. Migrants who typically found themselves at the bottom of the Red Ghetto, in the North Mission District, strove to protect and reinforce their Tribal identities by accepting an Intertribal identity as "American Indians." This process of Intertribal community building is what I define as creating an "Indian city," because it served as a localized model and pattern for other urban Indian communities. By exploring this historical phenomenon, one can better understand the roots of the Red Power movement in the late 1960s. This was a movement that fused together a powerful voice on a tiny island in the Bay Area. The 1969 occupation of Alcatraz became more than just a social experiment; it was an idea. This "utopian" idea of full independence or home rule, known collectively as sovereignty, ushered in a new era of Native politics: self-determination.

Incredibly, San Francisco's 1960s Indian community has received little attention from scholars. This chapter explores the complicated invention of what I term as an "Indian city": a city that both opened and closed doors to Native peoples but also gave birth to a movement where assimilation took a backseat to intense nationalism and Intertribalism.[1] The urban environment itself did not transform Native peoples into victims, but instead urban Indians built Intertribal institutions and a community that forever altered their political relationship with the federal government. The cultural, political, social, and economic relationships that Native peoples developed in San Francisco during the 1960s raise several important questions: How did the urban space of San Francisco facilitate the growth of Intertribal identity? How was the city transformed by newly politicized Indigenous activists? What created the "Red Ghetto," and how did American Indians adapt and survive within this new space? How did Native peoples maintain distinct nationalities while creating Intertribal spaces such as cultural and political organizations, Indian bars, and Indian Centers? Using these questions as a starting point, this chapter exposes how Indigenous activists created alternatives to a life of assimilation or Tribal disaffiliation and transformed their urban neighborhoods and public and private spaces into an Intertribal "Indian city."

The Great Native Migration

The majority of historical scholarship that discusses internal migration of ethnic groups in the United States tends to focus on African Americans. However, excluding the Depression years, Native peoples migrated to urban centers at a rate of four times that of African Americans.[2] Economic necessity constituted the primary reason that Native peoples moved to cities during the early twentieth century, particularly in the postwar period. During the 1960s the average annual income on Indian reservations totaled $1,500 per family versus $2,850 per family in cities.[3] A high unemployment rate compounded this situation, reaching well above 90 percent for some communities.[4]

The top industries within reservation communities were agriculture, timber, and mining. Sociologist Joseph G. Jorgensen analyzed BIA reports from 1968 and estimated that Americans grossed $170 million from agricultural products. Of that amount, Indian agriculture accounted for only $16 million. Similarly, of 803 million board feet of lumber harvested from Native lands, Indian communities received only $15 million (this amounts to a little more than $0.18 per board foot of lumber removed from Native lands). Mineral leases yielded $31 million to select Indian communities, yet only 10,000 jobs were created for a total Indian population of 764,000.[5] Most reservation communities lacked a stable economic infrastructure to keep these profits within their borders. Additionally, much of the profits that accrued to Native peoples via agricultural and extractive industries were derived through the leasing of lands, which stripped most Tribal governments of their right to control the production of resources on Indian land.

Depopulation led to further economic disparity for many reservation communities. In the twentieth century three major events led to an increase of migration from the reservation to the city: World War II, the Bureau of Indian Affairs Relocation Program, and federal Termination policy, which was legislated in 1953.[6]

The first migration of Native peoples to urban centers was felt during and after

World War II, as approximately 44,500 Native men enlisted in the armed forces. Many of these troops were exposed to other worlds in their platoons and travels. The military proved through desegregated regiments that Indians could actively compete on the battlefield among soldiers from different backgrounds. The regimented life of the military and service in wartime industry mobilized thousands of Native peoples to actively pursue life and opportunity in an urban setting after the war. Like thousands of their comrades, many Native veterans took advantage of the GI Bill to secure loans and an education, while others applied for Veterans Administration (VA) loans to purchase homes or start businesses in western cities, and some even relocated to the burgeoning suburbs. For some veterans the urban environment was a place that would enrich their newfound foreign and domestic wartime experiences.[7] For others the city represented the ultimate escape where one could get lost in the crowded streets, delight in window-shopping, and experience new foods. It was a different and exciting reality far from the pace of reservation life or life within the many rural nonreservation communities of Oklahoma.

Enlisted men began the flow of Native peoples to western cities during World War II, but others soon followed, looking for semiskilled factory jobs in wartime industries.[8] Both Indian men and Indian women helped to desegregate industry in western cities, and many of them achieved unprecedented economic prosperity. Native women by the thousands championed the call to factories in the aircraft industries, and scholars estimate that women workers constituted about one-quarter of the Native population that left the reservation during World War II.[9] Many men and women were recruited directly from local boarding schools to work in the factories. Overall, around forty thousand Native peoples relocated to urban environments to acquire employment in wartime industries.[10]

As soldiers returned home and the war came to a close, demand for workers decreased. Native peoples were usually the first to be laid off from their newfound employment. Historian Alison R. Bernstein notes, "By 1950 the unemployment rate for urban Indians had reached fifteen percent, nearly three times that of whites." As quickly as opportunity had come to Indian wartime laborers, tragedy was just around the corner. Despite increased financial savings from the wartime years, many Native peoples survived on dual incomes—supporting family and relations back home or on the reservation while subsisting in the city. Many lacked the flexible savings to deal with the sudden loss of employment. Those who could afford it returned to their home communities, while those who lacked such funding sought affordable housing and semiskilled jobs and continued to fight for better jobs and living conditions.

SAN FRANCISCO, RED POWER, AND THE EMERGENCE OF AN "INDIAN CITY"

During the war the first wave of Native migrants to San Francisco settled in Hunter's Point, a district formed among the shipyards of Little Tokyo. However, much of the Native community was soon dispersed throughout Greater San Francisco.[11] The majority who settled in Hunter's Point were African American families who sought employment in the shipyards, and eventually former Little Tokyo became known by outsiders as Harlem West.[12] Former resident Wilma Mankiller (Cherokee) recalled:

> Shipyard employees and hourly wage earners made their homes there. Although the shipyard did not close until 1974, jobs started to become more and more scarce in the 1960s. The workers who resided at Hunter's Point fell into financial difficulties, and the housing area became little more than a ghetto.... We found a few Native Americans living at Hunter's Point, including another Cherokee family.... My Mother also became friends with people from different backgrounds.... Outside was another story. There was a great deal of animosity between black youths and Samoan youths of Hunter's Point. Sometimes it seemed like a war zone when rival gangs clashed on the streets. ... When the officers stopped to make a call and left their car unattended, every window was shattered. That was standard procedure. All of the police, across the board, were considered to be "the enemy." Living in Hunter's Point also gave me an insight into cultures I otherwise might not have ever known.[13]

Soon, Native and African American families began to compete for skilled and semiskilled employment, housing, and economic mobility.

Housing in Hunter's Point proved a more affordable solution for the thousands of laborers who relocated to San Francisco for employment during the war. Without the advantages of the VA loan, Native laborers were forced to budget, and many latched onto affordable rentals throughout Hunter's Point. Due to the huge influx of laborers relocating into the Bay Area during the war, this sudden population boom created a severe housing shortage and pushed the value of real estate far beyond the grasp of many Native families. Despite official numbers, Native peoples faced de facto discrimination and redlining when applying for mortgages, especially when buying homes in all-white neighborhoods. Coupled with high unemployment, many found themselves at the end of a very short economic stick.[14]

While military service and the promise of jobs drew many Indigenous peoples to western cities during World War II, federal Indian policy determined the nature of the migrations during the postwar years. By 1952 the BIA had launched one of the most dramatic programs in its history: the Relocation Program. The program began in 1948 when the BIA used the Hopi and Navajo Tribes as test cases.[15] In 1956

Congress passed the Indian Vocational Training Act (Public Law 959) to provide job training to migrants. Along with job training, relocatees received a one-way bus ticket to one of six relocation centers located in Chicago, Cleveland, Dallas, Denver, Los Angeles, and San Francisco. The federal government also provided temporary housing, supplementary income for furniture and household necessities, and job counseling for one year after arrival. Within that year most migrants received a monthly check of $140; when they found work, the monthly stipend was cut off.[16] However, the BIA rarely provided migrants with the promised retention-based services. Many Natives, such as LaNada Means (Shoshone/Bannock), who was in her twenties, found that the Relocation promises made by the federal government were only lies:

> The only programs the BIA has are vocational training for menial jobs, and I didn't especially want to be a beautician. Actually, I wanted to try college again, but when I told this to a BIA counselor, he said they didn't have any money for that and told me I was being "irrational and unrealistic." All types of problems develop when you're on relocation. The Indian who has come to the city is like a man without a country. Whose jurisdiction are you under, the BIA's or the state's? You go to a county hospital when you're sick and they say, "Aren't you taken care of by the Indian Affairs people?" It's very confusing. You hang around with other Indians, but they are as bad off as you are. Anyway, I started sinking lower and lower. . . . I married . . . I got pregnant again . . . things didn't work out in the marriage . . . I ended up in the San Francisco General psychiatric ward for a few weeks. I was at the bottom. . . . Indian people get to this point all the time, especially when they're relocated into the big city and are living in the slums. At that point, you've got two choices: either kill yourself and get it over with—a lot of Indians do this—or try to go all the way up, and this is almost impossible.[17]

Native peoples who participated in the Relocation Program were promised housing, jobs, and financial assistance. Most found these few options to be dead ends; as a result, Relocation was viewed by Indigenous critics as a failure. Economist Alan Sorkin calculated that "from 1953 to 1957 . . . three out of ten who were relocated returned home during that same fiscal year in which they migrated."[18] On the other hand, some people, like Yvonne Lamore-Choate (Quechan), found their experiences to be quite rewarding in the end:

> The group I was in was made up mostly of single women who were either going to attend some kind of business school or cosmetology school. It was fun getting to know each other, but by the end of the week we would all scatter to different parts of the Bay

Area: some would remain in Oakland, others would go to San Jose or Hayward, and some of us to San Francisco. Our paths would cross again over the years at one Indian bar or another. In the 1960s, there were Indian bars everywhere, and they all seemed to be doing a very lucrative business.[19]

Both LaNada Means's and Yvonne Lamore-Choate's experiences offer a different glimpse into the complex associations that Indigenous peoples forged with the program. For some, the Relocation Program and living situations in the "Red Ghetto" were far better than conditions in their homelands. Additionally, the opportunities for Native women greatly increased outside of some paternalistic and corrupt Tribal governmental systems. For couples the economic gain was twofold: Now Indian couples could enjoy the financial rewards of a double income. For Native children it meant new horizons and public education through which they avoided boarding schools. Such benefits often brought families closer together.

The advantages for many Indian families outweighed the costs of Relocation, which was strictly voluntary, and the BIA screened all applicants and searched for those they believed would adjust to urban living. Applicants were rated on age, previous work experience, police record, marital status, and education. The program, for instance, preferred married applicants over single individuals, for Relocation officers assumed that family connections increased a migrant's chance for success. Veterans held a good chance of being selected for Relocation. In fact, almost half of the Indigenous peoples who relocated to San Francisco were World War II veterans. Although the Relocation Program convinced many Native peoples to move to San Francisco, about one-third of the total Native population relocated without government assistance. There is no doubt that Relocation was a force of transformation to Native peoples. In 1969 Richard Oakes (Akwesasne Mohawk) commented on the program:

> The San Francisco Bay Area has been, as have many urban centers, recipient of a large scale Native American migration. Because of the relocation program of the Bureau of Indian Affairs, there are representatives of most of the major tribes residing here. Many are facing urban situations for the first time and find it an unknown and disruptive experience. The variety of tribal identities, the lack of communication between these, and public images of the "Indian" which are culturally undefined and often confusing in institutional application ... have added to the stress of urban "adjustment" and the formation of self-identity.[20]

By 1972 the Relocation Program had relocated 100,000 Native peoples out of a total population of 764,000 Indigenous Americans in the United States. By 1960 local Native organizations estimated that the San Francisco Indian population was around 10,000.[21] Nationally in 1960, about 27 percent of Indian Country lived in urban enclaves; by 1977 cities claimed almost 50 percent of the total Native population throughout America.[22]

The House Concurrent Resolution 108 (passed in 1953), commonly known as the "Termination Act," also affected the Native migration experience. From 1953 to 1958 this legislation ended federal trust responsibilities with 109 Indigenous Nations throughout America. Termination policy devastated many Native communities, overturning the protection of Tribal land, negating treaty rights, and threatening a way of life for thousands. Statistics on those moving into the city because of Termination legislation are lacking, but this legislation in effect accounted for a large proportion of the one-third of the Native peoples who relocated to San Francisco at their own expense.[23]

One major criticism of the Relocation and Termination era was that the government sought to exploit a large, unskilled labor force that weakened the already meager labor force on many reservations. Some statistics indicate that as much as 25 percent of the U.S. mineral wealth is located solely on Native lands.[24] Compounding this statistic was the government's increasing dependence on uranium for atomic weapons and energy, which demanded an exploitable labor force and smaller populations to limit the extent of exposure and diminished the powers of some Tribal governments against multinational corporations.[25] Coupled with the BIA's Relocation Program, large tracts of land were taken out of trust status when individuals left their reservation communities. These large plots of land created a checkerboard effect and ripped Tribal control of these lands from their respective Tribal governments.[26] Termination and Relocation legislation accelerated suspicions of resource exploitation across Indian Country, and it promoted the systematic economic and diplomatic destruction of Tribal governments.

Mission District

Before 1906 the Mission District was primarily composed of worker tenements and the famed Mission Dolores dating back to 1776. After the devastating earthquake and fire of 1906, working-class Irish families moved into the area, looking for cheaper lands for housing. Tenements were promptly built in the district for workers helping to rebuild the city. Eventually, because of the high numbers of working-class people, unions relocated their headquarters into the district. Following the unions were other ethnic laborers consisting of Italians, Germans, Russians, and Scandinavian populations. Throughout the thirties the Mission District was at the center of organized labor, which successfully sponsored strikes around the Bay Area.

By World War II the population in the area had nearly doubled. As older emigrant groups moved out, new migrant workers including African Americans, Mexican Americans, Samoans, and Native Americans replaced them. Neighborhoods like the Mission were typically characterized by low-income housing (left over from the early 1900s), high unemployment, and crime. As the incoming Native populations grew in number, they competed with other ethnic groups for services, housing, and jobs. By the 1960s the Mission District—especially the North Mission—was home to the largest concentration of Native peoples in the city and was the site of the San Francisco Indian Center.[27] LaNada Means recalled, "Whenever Mayor Alioto went to the Mission District where many of us lived, he would meet with the Latino and Spanish groups, the Mission Rebels (Blacks) and the Indians.... We were recognized as a political unit and gradually we became politicized." These coalition politics were critical to the unification of the Mission District, as Wilma Mankiller remembered: "My spirits were buoyed in the mid-1960s whenever I heard more news from the San Joaquin Valley about the National Farm Workers Association, led by Cesar Chavez.... I attended several of their benefits and consciousness-raising events held throughout the Mission District."[28] Forming alliances with the National Farm Workers Association and creating powerful coalitions was a focus for many Native peoples in the Mission District. Despite competing for scarce urban resources, coalitions could bolster municipal reform. Al Miller (Seminole), later instrumental in the formation of Native American Studies (NAS) and the Alcatraz takeover, collected the local paper *Nuestra Misión de San Francisco*, a publication put forth by the League of United Latin American Citizens.[29] The periodical was a way to organize the diverse citizenry of the Mission District into a voting bloc. Several of the articles suggested forming a separate and unique "worldwide" municipal government independent from San Francisco City Hall. These types of coalition politics created institutional and organizational support for Native peoples throughout the Mission District.

By 1960 local Native organizations estimated San Francisco's Indian population to be around ten thousand; by 1970 San Francisco contained the third-largest urban Indian population in the United States, numbering around twenty thousand, and hosting more than one hundred different Indigenous Nations.[30] Unfortunately, the majority of this population found themselves in the Mission District at the end of broken promises from the Termination and Relocation era. The development of a new infrastructure and political awareness was crucial to turning back the tide of destructive federal policies toward Indigenous peoples. An Intertribal awareness and creation of institutions that politicized Native concerns at the local, state, and national levels culminated with the advent of a new city—an Indian city.

Indian City

Although the North Mission District most closely represented an urban American Indian ethnic neighborhood, unfortunately most of the Native population was widely dispersed throughout the Greater San Francisco area. Therefore, Native peoples were typically mobile, between jobs, and increasingly migratory between urban and reservation communities. The Indian city or Native neighborhood was created and defined by Indian institutions and businesses. In San Francisco the first institution that characterized the development of an Indian city was the bar culture, or "Indian bars," the most famous one being the Klamath-owned Warren's Slaughterhouse Bar located in the North Mission District. Indian bars served as both an entry point to the city and the first stop on the road to urban survival for many Native peoples. At neighborhood bars many learned about opportunities for housing, jobs, and Tribal politics, and this atmosphere fostered a much-needed Intertribal interaction. These bars often cut across class lines, as the necessity arose to interact with other Natives who possessed a shared history and a common background. Bars were also places that promoted social interaction through dating or "cruising" for dates. For newcomers to the city bars were places where they met or located people from their community and established networks of friends. These networks were crucial for sustaining and building an Intertribal community, in that they imparted survival skills to new migrants within the urban environment. Political organizers within the community took advantage of these networks for lobbying purposes. Warren's was the first place that future American Indian Movement leader Russell Means (Lakota) learned about the policy of Termination. Ultimately, an important function of these bars fostered atmospheres of entertainment, relaxation, and refuge from the pressures of an urban environment. In particular, Warren's was also a place of employment for Native peoples, hiring managers, bartenders, and waitresses, which accented its cultural atmosphere.[31]

On the other hand, joints like Warren's sometimes fostered a hostile social setting and encouraged the habitual dependency of some of its clients. Dean Chavers (Lumbee) described Warren's as "the grungiest bar in the history of the world. . . . I went there only about once or twice, no more than that, it was a rough bar."[32] Police typically patrolled the bars of the North Mission District. They relied on racial profiling and stereotypes, which led to higher arrest rates for Native peoples.[33] A 1977 study conducted by Jensen, Stauss, and Harris revealed that arrest rates for Indians were seven to twenty-two times greater than the arrest rate for African Americans in alcohol-related offenses. The Jensen, Stauss, and Harris study goes on to further elaborate that the arrest rate for urban Indians was four times greater than any other ethnic group in the city, the total arrest rate being 27,535 per 100,000. Despite the threat of racial profiling by police outside the bar or violence inside the bar, Native peoples continued to frequent Warren's. In 1972 activist Richard Oakes, a former bartender at Warren's, wrote, "Drinking seems to fill a void in the life of many Indians. It takes the place of the singing of a song, the sharing of a song with another tribe, the sharing of experiences that another tribe member might have had. Drinking is used as a way to create feelings of some kind where there aren't any. It fills a void, that's all."[34] Within the Mission District, as competition among different ethnic groups increased over housing, jobs, and limited resources, so did crime between groups. One explanation that contemporary researchers provided for the high arrest rates was simply discrimination because Indians represented one of the most visible populations within the city.

Indian Centers coexisted with the bar culture as important institutions that facilitated a more formalized networking system. The San Francisco Indian Center, also located in the North Mission District, was a focal point for bringing the community together socially and politically. Much like the bar culture, Indian Centers served a function of networking and supplied information about jobs, housing, and health care for the Bay Area community. The Indian Center was originally established in the early fifties by the Society of St. Vincent de Paul, a Catholic organization. By the midsixties, however, the Society turned over the management of the center to the American Indian Council of the Bay Area, an Intertribal political group that offered aid to migrants in the Indian city, sponsored the Annual Indian Day Picnic, and lobbied against Termination and Relocation.[35] Wilma Mankiller recalled what the San Francisco Indian Center meant for her: "Located upstairs in an old frame building on sixteenth street on the edge of the very rough and tough Mission District, the Indian Center became a sanctuary for me. For me, [the Indian Center] became an oasis where I could share my feelings and frustrations with kids from similar backgrounds."[36] The Indian Center established programs to aid in job counseling, social work, and health outreach programs, and served as a distribution center for food and clothing. After relocatees were cut off from the aid provided by the federal program, many took refuge in the programs administered by their local Indian center.[37] Eventually, Indian Centers throughout the country competed for grants from the federal government to cover their operating expenses and program budgets. The San Francisco Indian Center created a governing board of directors responsible for appointing a director and maintaining the annual budget for the institution. For many migrants to San Francisco the Center was an organization that located temporary housing, friends, and relatives and assisted in their overall adjustment.

In 1969 the San Francisco Indian Center was destroyed in a suspicious fire. Most Natives blamed this catastrophe on the Samoan community, illustrating the depth of interethnic rivalry present in the district. A temporary Indian Center was established in a makeshift office on Sixteenth Street that eventually served as the mainland office for Indians of All Tribes—responsible for the eighteen-month occupation of Alcatraz Island.

By 1971 the San Francisco Indian Center hosted an estimated forty or more local organizations.[38] These disparate cultural and political organizations and associations became the third component in the development of the Indian city's infrastructure. Organizations ranged in function from Tribally specific (Navajo, Eskimo, Chippewa, and Tlingit-Haida Clubs) to a wider range of Intertribal associations. The Tribally specific clubs emphasized language revitalization and contact with relatives and were usually quite small in attendance. Intertribal organizations of the Bay Area were vital to the longevity of the urban Indian community, from churches to alumni associations. A total of six or more Indian churches were located in the Bay Area that ranged from the American Indian Baptist Church to the Native American Church. The Native American Church in San Francisco operated under a confederacy of roadmen devoted to Grandfather Peyote. Church culture served as the meeting ground for families and individuals that cut across Tribal and class differences.[39]

A host of different activities were arranged by organizations, which provided a recreational purpose, ranging from baseball and basketball teams to dance clubs that hosted local powwows. Powwows were sponsored by the San Francisco Indian Center once a month and served to facilitate an Intertribal awareness. On reservations powwows were strictly Tribal in nature, but as the Intertribal community increased in numbers, new Intertribal dances and songs were created. Beyond Tribalizing public spaces and cities, powwows sponsored a new consensus politic, an institution that respected both Tribal difference and Intertribal unity. Powwows were outright demonstrations of how American Indian peoples employed tradition, public action, and commerce to bolster the Indian city.[40]

Powwows became another source of income for many in the city, as traders were able to sell traditional crafts to the general public, and Indian business owners used sponsorship of these cultural activities to advertise. In California a total of 450 Indian-owned businesses were located primarily in urban areas. These businesses eventually formed a statewide association called the United Indian Development Association, which aided other Native peoples when seeking loans for commercial development.[41] Two of the most notable businesses in the San Francisco area were Adam Nordwell's Termite Business and Warren's Bar. Nordwell served on the American Indian Council of the Bay Area and was president of the local Chippewa Club. Nordwell used profits from his business to fund organizational development in the Bay Area to support agencies of protest within the community and provide jobs for those who sought employment. Warren's Bar was owned by a member of the Klamath Nation from Oregon who also utilized Indian employment and circulated money back into the Indian community. Both business owners, however, lived outside of the Mission District and Hunter's Point, which was typical of middle-income individuals but robbed the district of a much-needed tax base for redevelopment and financial infrastructure.[42]

Every Indian city relied on the formation of neighborhoods with concentrations of Native peoples. Indian neighborhoods like the Red Ghetto in the Mission District were typically characterized by low-income housing, high unemployment, and crime. As the Native population increased in the district, Native peoples increasingly found themselves competing with other ethnic groups for municipal services, housing, and jobs. One particular immigrant group that the Native community was in a constant disagreement with were the Samoans. Much of this rivalry was between street gangs of Samoans and the Native gang, better known as the Thunderbirds in the Mission District.[43] These gangs competed for dates and women and ultimately over turf rule within the district. It is hard to pinpoint a sole cause for this interethnic rivalry, yet one source might be a piece of legislation proposed in 1965 by Daniel Inouye that sought to identify Samoans as Native Americans. This measure surely eroded the already fragile relationship between leaders of both Native and Samoan communities. Native peoples viewed this as an assault on trust responsibilities and meager funding resources through the Bureau of Indian Affairs.[44]

Neighborhoods instituted their own forces of stability as families come together for civic activities, such as powwows or picnics at the San Francisco Indian Center. Much of the housing was substandard, with high rents and landlords who discriminated against Samoans or Natives. Due to prejudice and low income, many families were highly mobile, moving on average three to four times in less than a year because of eviction or other circumstances.[45] This increased mobility within the community necessitated a growing dependence on the institutions that constituted San Francisco's Indian city. Most families that came from the reservation typically had either a poor credit rating or no rating at all and represented large families, which gave some landlords the "legal" justification to discriminate.

If the Mission District was so ghettoized, why did so many Native peoples choose to stay in these circumstances? Many Natives refused to live in these conditions and returned back to their home communities, but for otheres their communities at home were often worse off than conditions in the Red Ghetto. "In 1970, 46 percent of all rural Indian housing had inadequate plumbing facilities compared to 8 percent for urban Indians . . . 19 percent is considered crowded (more than one resident per room), compared to 44 percent for rural Indians." Eventually, as federal funding for urban Indians began to rise in the late sixties, it caused competition for reservation communities. This was one of the sparks that began a political and cultural split between urban and rural or reservation Indians.[46]

The Birth of Native American Studies

Another element of the Indian city was the development of Native American Studies programs and student organizations. San Francisco State College in 1967 was engulfed in one of the most heated campus strikes to date. The strike was organ-ized by the Black Student Union around the controversial firing of an African-American faculty member who had connections with the Black Panther Party.[47] Eventually, the strikers founded a new organization, the Third World Liberation Front, and fought to establish a new Ethnic Studies Department. After countless arrests and a shutdown of the entire campus, negotiations produced an Ethnic Studies Department that housed a Native American Studies Department along with others. The university used federal funds from the Office of Equal Opportunity to recruit more than thirty Native students from the Bay Area for its first NAS class. Richard Oakes was in this first class of students and became the first coordinator for the NAS Department. In a statement of purpose Oakes wrote, "The courses which are proposed as community oriented will offer the community and the student opportunity for interaction with a philosophy of self-help based on group identification. As noted above, the San Francisco Bay Area offers a situation wherein the student might expand his studies, possibly innovate worthwhile constructive programs, seek reform and otherwise contribute to the solution of pressing urban problems."[48] By the middle of April 1969, Oakes and several other Native American students had created SCAN, the Student Coalition of American Natives. The organization served to bring Native American students together to aid in the development of Native American Studies and to serve as a voice for the Native student population at San Francisco State. The organization quickly elected Richard Oakes as its president and a young Al Miller (Seminole) as vice president.[49] Through SCAN Oakes and others provided an established network for new Native students enrolling at the college. Soon members of SCAN created the building blocks for another organization in conjunction with the San Francisco Indian Center called MANY.

Movement of American Native Youth, or MANY, was a "non profit corporation dedicated to helping American Indians through the implementation of action programs initiated by American Natives."[50] One idea outlined was to establish a Native retail outlet in which community members could sell their artwork and traditional crafts. The outlet would train members of the community in how to run and operate their own businesses. Sales from the outlet were to return to the community, helping relocatees with supplemental income during their transition. One positive outlook for the program was to draw community members together into an economic force and in the process develop a Native arts district. Art existed as a bridge connecting outside communities and neighborhoods with an appreciation for Native culture.

A third program that Oakes established was a newsletter for Native students at San Francisco State as a forum to openly publicize their views on any issue. The newsletter was aptly titled *Native American Critic and Review*. Richard Oakes urged students to take action and responsibility for their future. Slowly, NAS gathered student support for SCAN and other organizations. Oakes had a visible presence in the community as he worked among its members and expanded the enrollment numbers for the Native American Studies Department.

One of the most important decisions that Oakes made was the establishment of an NAS community advisory board, which linked the campus to the Greater San Francisco Indian community. Those selected to the board would have an overwhelming impact on the program and the community. The first positions filled were by Jeanette Henry Costo (Eastern Cherokee) and Rupert Costo (Cahuilla). Both Jeanette and Rupert Costo were instrumental in the 1964 creation of the American Indian Historical Society located on Masonic Avenue in San Francisco. The society was responsible for the groundbreaking academic journal *Indian Historian*. This publication brought together Indian scholars and scholarship from a diversity of disciplines for an interdisciplinary journal on Native American Studies.

The third member of the advisory board would forever change the students' and community's political understanding. Belva Cottier (Lakota), aside from being affiliated with the San Francisco Indian Center, was responsible for the 1964 takeover of Alcatraz Island. She informed Oakes and the other students that under treaty stipulations from the Fort Laramie Treaty of 1868, the Lakota people could reclaim any surplus land that the government had abandoned. Cottier had worked on the historical and legal research needed for the occupation, and she explained the dramatic details of the failed attempt to secure the famed island. Soon Richard Oakes and LaNada Means in their coalition of community institutions and Native Studies programs at San Francisco State and Berkeley offered the ultimate proposal to the failed government experiment of Relocation and Termination, occupation of Alcatraz Island.

Alcatraz Occupation and the Construction of an Indian City

In the late-night hours of November 20, 1969, two boats carefully deposited the occupation force of more than eighty men, women, and children onto the desolate Alcatraz Island. Overnight the organization Indians of All Tribes (IAT) set up security posts throughout the island, discouraged the Coast Guard from invading the island, and created a media barrage of press releases from the San Francisco Indian Center. After the devastating loss of the San Francisco Indian Center to a highly suspect fire, the community and student leaders had created the ultimate proposal to transform Alcatraz into an Indian city. The island would host a center for Native American Studies with a traveling university; an American Indian Spiritual Center to practice Native religion not yet protected by the federal government; an Indian Center of Ecology to formulate conservatory plans; and a Great Indian Training School, complete with a center for traditional arts and crafts, a Native restaurant, and an economic school to study ways in which to increase employment and standards of living. Finally, their proclamation called for the creation of an American Indian Museum to expose the "true" history of Native America.

Contrary to government officials who sought to evict Indians of All Tribes from the island, the IAT was highly organized. It included a mainland office, donated by Dr. Dorothy Lonewolf Miller (Blackfeet), who along with Dean Chavers, the mainland coordinator, administered all accounts and bookkeeping and established the IAT bank account.[51] The organization eventually created the *IAT Newsletter;* a radio show, *Radio Free Alcatraz;* the Big Rock School; a health care system, complete with one doctor and a registered nurse; and a host of other programs. On the island, the IAT elected a seven-member Intertribal council: Richard Oakes, Al Miller, Ross Harden (Ho-chunk), Ed Castillo (Cahuilla), Bob Nelford (Inuit),

Dennis Turner (Luiseño), and Jim Vaughn (Cherokee). The council established the housing and security committee and began a new school. The IAT improvement committee marked dangerous areas, sorted through clothing donations, planted shrubs, chopped wood, and cleared away trash, debris, vines, and weeds accumulated through years of neglect. Everyone on the island was employed to work on sanitation, day care, cooking, laundry, supply lines, or repairs. Rules were established that advocated total sobriety and a drug-free environment for all residents. The symbol and Intertribal idea of Alcatraz and Indians of All Tribes to which Bay Area students and community members gave birth became larger and larger.

Soon occupiers were attracting the attention of politicians, from California governor Ronald Reagan to President Richard Nixon, and a media frenzy that fueled national and international support for the occupiers. Although thousands of Native peoples made pilgrimages to the island and sent in monetary and logistical support, the occupation would last only nineteen months.[52]

The Native occupation of Alcatraz, beyond securing title to the island, fueled hundreds of similar occupations throughout Indian Country and became a catalyst for the Red Power movement.[53] In Seattle Bernie Whitebear (Colville) and Indians of All Tribes from Alcatraz created the United Indians of All Tribes and transformed the abandoned Fort Lawton into the Daybreak Star Center. Pit River Tribe launched a campaign to restore lands stolen by the Pacific Gas and Electric Corporation. Taos Pueblo regained control over Taos Blue Lake. The 1972 Trail of Broken Treaties March on Washington took place. Wounded Knee was occupied in 1973. Ultimately, all have long roots in the takeover of Alcatraz Island. In turn, Red Power as a national movement relied on urban Intertribal institutions and organizations forged out of Indian cities. It was also a movement that mobilized the entire San Francisco Indian community around a central belief that the path to social justice would ultimately transform Native political relationships with local, municipal, state, Tribal, and federal governments.

This path to social justice and self-determination was rooted in an urban-centered Intertribal perspective. In many ways Alcatraz and IAT were symbolic of the utopian desires of Native migrants to San Francisco, a microcosm of the ideal Indian city most wanted to live in. Alcatraz emerges not as an abandoned prison in the Indian community but as a sacred space emblematic and redefined as Native self-determination and Red Power. The rippling effect brought together Native peoples from rural, urban, and reservation communities and forged a new Intertribal reality that forever changed federal Indian policy. Richard Nixon's administration eventually passed twenty-six pieces of legislation that ended the old policies of Termination and solidified a new self-determined commitment to Indian Country.

Emerging from the development of an Indian city was a new Intertribal perspective that altered how Native peoples define themselves and their world. This new awareness affected the local political and organizational structure of groups like Aztlan, a Chicano movement, which forged together a uniquely Intertribal perspective that protected and enhanced their claim for human and civil rights. Brown Berets in Los Angeles would stage an Alcatraz-like takeover of Catalina Island. The Black Panther Party, founded by Huey Newton and Bobby Seale, explored community building through breakfast programs like those launched by the San Francisco Indian Center. The hippie movement's capital of Haight-Ashbury co-opted the Intertribal philosophy of urban Indians that defined its cultural style and political movement. In 1970 the national environmental movement founded Earth Day in San Francisco and would eventually capitalize upon Native images to commercialize its conservationist agendas. As the federal government shifted money to states and municipal governments for Indian programs, local governments had to reinvent themselves as Indian cities. The impact of Indian cities had a profound influence and ultimately reshaped national Indian policies and cities for decades to come.

Notes

1. I use the term *Intertribal* rather than the dated term *pan-Indian* because it implies that Native people do not relinquish their Tribal identities in the process of claiming an American Indian identity. An Intertribal treatment of Indian city also relies on a transnational focus that attempts to understand the complexities of members from more than one hundred different and distinct Tribal Nations who converged in San Francisco. I use the term *Intertribal* over *Supratribal* because *Intertribal* originates from the Native community and identifies both federally and state-recognized and nonrecognized Indigenous peoples. As a process of historical study *Intertribalism* in definition and application uncovers the roots of Indian cities and their relationship to the constructs of Red Power. Native peoples do not willingly give up their Tribal (political, national, social, and cultural) connections to become American Indian. Rather, these Tribal connections are protected and reinforced in Intertribal spaces and places that can promote a uniquely diverse acceptance of an overall American Indian identity for the promotion of Tribal political gains. One can trace the scholarly debates over these terms in the following sources: Hazel W. Hertzberg, *The Search for an American Indian Identity* (Syracuse: Syracuse University Press, 1971); Vine Deloria Jr., "The Rise and Fall of the First Indian Movement," *Historian* 33, no. 4 (1971): 663; Steven Cornell,

The Return of the Native: American Indian Political Resurgence (New York: Oxford University Press, 1988); and S. Levine and N. O. Lurie, eds., *The American Indian Today* (Baltimore: Pelican Books, 1970), 314.

2. Arthur Margon, "Indians and Immigrants: A Comparison of Groups New to the City," *Journal of Ethnic Studies* 4, no. 4 (1977): 18.

3. Jack O. Waddell and O. Michael Watson, "Indians and the Metropolis," in *The American Indian in Urban Society*, edited by Joseph G. Jorgensen (Boston: Little, Brown, 1971), 83; Donald Fixico, *The Urban Indian Experience in America* (Albuquerque: University of New Mexico Press, 2000), 73. For the urban figure I used the average between ten Indian cities: Oklahoma City, Los Angeles, Chicago, Minneapolis, Buffalo, Albuquerque, Seattle, San Francisco, New York, and San Diego.

4. M. Annette Jaimes, ed., *The State of Native America* (Boston: South End Press, 1992), 245.

5. Ibid., 82–83.

6. For a detailed account of the Relocation Program, see Donald Fixico, *Termination and Relocation: Federal Indian Policy, 1945–1960* (Albuquerque: University of New Mexico Press, 1986).

7. Alison R. Bernstein, *American Indians and World War II: Toward a New Era in Indian Affairs* (Norman: University of Oklahoma Press, 1991), 60.

8. Joan Ablon, "Relocated American Indians in the San Francisco Bay Area: Social Interactions and Indian Identity," *Human Organization* (1964): 297. "In 1940 the number of Indians dwelling in cities was less than five percent of the entire Indian population. By 1950, that figure had quadrupled to nearly twenty percent" (Bernstein, *American Indians and World War II*, 86).

9. James B. LaGrand, *Indian Metropolis: Native Americans in Chicago, 1945–1975* (Urbana: University of Illinois Press, 2002), 36; Nicholas G. Rosenthal, "Repositioning Indianess: Native American Organizations in Portland, Oregon, 1959–1975," *Pacific Historical Review* 71, no. 3 (2002): 419. "The War Manpower Commission offered women free training in light defense jobs that could eventually pay as much as $120 a month" (Bernstein, *American Indians and World War II*, 73).

10. Larry Burt, "Roots of the Native American Urban Experience: Relocation Policy in the 1950s," *American Indian Quarterly* 10, no. 2 (1986): 86.

11. Japanese Americans were relocated from San Francisco during the war out of fear of the American public of spying or sabotage. During the Relocation Program administrators actively sought to spread out the Indian population into diverse areas to accelerate forces of assimilation. This is more than likely a reason the return rates will be so high for relocatees at the inception of the program.

12. In 1966 a race riot erupted in Hunter's Point out of protest for the police shooting of an African American teenager who had allegedly stolen a car. The riot exacerbated the flight of white businesses from ethnic neighborhoods throughout the city, further disrupted the tax

base, decreased employment opportunities, and subsequently led to further ghettoization. These demographic and economic transformations affected the large Native populations in the Mission District and the riot eventually influenced the formation of the Oakland-based Black Panther Party in 1966. For more information on the 1966 riot, see Arthur E. Hippler, *Hunter's Point: A Black Ghetto* (New York: Basic Books, 1974).

13. Wilma Mankiller and Michael Wallis, *Mankiller: A Chief and Her People* (New York: St. Martin's Press, 1993), 108–10. Wilma Mankiller was the first woman to be elected as the Principal Chief of the Western Cherokee Nation (1985–95).

14. William Issel, "Liberalism and Urban Policy in San Francisco From the 1930s to the 1960s," *Western Historical Quarterly* 22, no. 4 (1991): 440.

15. The Outing Program originated with Carlisle Industrial Boarding School and quickly became standard policy at all federally controlled off-reservation boarding schools. During wartime Native students were outsourced to industries for cheap labor. The BIA eventually used the Outing Program as a formula for the American Indian Voluntary Relocation Program. By depopulating and disenfranchising thousands of Native citizens, Native Nations were less effective at preventing Tribal land and resource exploitation. See William Willard, "Outing, Relocation, and Employment Assistance: The Impact of Federal Indian Population Dispersal Programs in the Bay Area," *Wicazo Sa Review* 12, no. 1 (1997): 30.

16. Alan L. Sorkin, *The Urban American Indian* (Lexington: Lexington Books, 1978), 27; Peter Collier, "The Red Man's Burden," *Ramparts* (February 1970): 30.

17. Peter Collier, "Better Red Than Dead," *Ramparts* (February 1970): 30. LaNada Means was interviewed by Peter Collier for this article. Eventually, LaNada would be the primary Native student organizer on the Berkeley campus and was to become a co-coordinator with Richard Oakes of the famed Alcatraz takeover in 1969.

18. Sorkin, *The Urban American Indian*, 33. By 1959 the BIA stopped keeping statistics on its Relocation Program to avoid criticism. Therefore, little data exist except from Native organizations and the Census Bureau. Joan Ablon suggests the return rate was as high as 75 percent in the early years ("Relocated American Indians," 297).

19. Susan Lobo, *Urban Voices: The Bay Area American Indian Community* (Tucson: University of Arizona Press, 2002), 38.

20. Richard Oakes, "Native American Studies," Hayakawa Papers, San Francisco State University Archives, Ethnic Studies–NAS, 1969, 2. For more information on Richard Oakes, see also Kent Blansett, "A Journey to Freedom: Richard Oakes, American Indian Activism, and the Occupation of Alcatraz," in *American Indians in American History, 1870–2001*, edited by Sterling Evans, (Westport, Conn.: Praeger, 2002), 138–45.

21. Ablon, "Relocated American Indians," 297.

22. Sorkin, *The Urban American Indian*, 10, 25.

23. For more on Termination, see Fixico, *Termination and Relocation*; and Kenneth R. Philip, *Termination Revisited: American Indians on the Trail to Self-Determination, 1933–1953* (Lincoln: University of Nebraska Press, 1999).

24. Al Gedicks, *The New Resource Wars: Native and Environmental Struggles Against Multinational Corporations* (Boston: South End Press, 1993), 41. See also Donald Fixico, *The Invasion of Indian Country in the Twentieth Century: American Capitalism and Tribal Natural Resources* (Niwot: University Press of Colorado, 1998), 143.

25. The federal government pushed to relocate Navajos and offered free train passage and jobs on the Santa Fe Railroad to members of Laguna Pueblo. Boxcar towns were established in cities along the railroad lines and specifically in Richmond, California, located just south of San Francisco. See Kurt M. Peters, "Continuing Identity: Laguna Pueblo Railroaders in Richmond, California," in *American Indians and the Urban Experience*, edited by Susan Lobo and Kurt Peters (Walnut Creek, Calif.: Altamira Press, 2001), 117–26.

26. Burt, "Roots of the Native American Urban Experience," 92.

27. Fredrick M. Wirt, *Power in the City: Decision Making in San Francisco* (Berkeley and Los Angeles: University of California Press, 1974), 245. On Samoan and Native interactions, see Joan Ablon, "Retention of Cultural Values and Differential Urban Adaptation: Samoans and American Indians in a West Coast City," *Social Forces* (1971): 385–93.

28. LaNada Boyer, "Reflections of Alcatraz," in *Native American Voices: A Reader*, edited by Susan Lobo and Steve Talbot (Upper Saddle River, N.J.: Prentice-Hall, 2001), 507–8; Mankiller and Wallis, *Mankiller*, 154–55. On the Mission District, see Mike Miller, *A Community Organizer's Tale: People and Power in San Francisco* (Berkeley: Hey Day Books, 2009), 43; and Marjorie Heins, *Strictly Ghetto Property: The Story of Los Siete de la Raza* (Berkeley: Ramparts Press, 1972), 18–20.

29. League of United Latin American Citizens, *Nuestra Misión de San Francisco* 1, no. 3 (1969); "Mission Coalition (San Francisco)," Box 4, File 28, Al Miller Papers, San Francisco Public Library.

30. Ablon, "Relocated American Indians," 297; Ann Metcalf, "Indians in the San Francisco Bay Area," in *Urban Indians* (Chicago: Newberry Library, 1980), 90, from "Proceedings of the Third Annual Conference on Problems and Issues Concerning American Indians Today."

31. Russell Means and Marvin J. Wolf, *Where White Men Fear to Tread* (New York: St. Martin's Press, 1995), 96.

32. Dean Chavers, interview by author, August 15, 2001, tape recording—transcribed, tape 1, side 1, 8, in author's possession.

33. Troy Johnson, Joane Nagel, and Duane Champagne, eds., *American Indian Activism: Alcatraz to the Longest Walk* (Urbana: University of Illinois Press, 1997), 25.

34. Gary F. Jensen, Joseph H. Stauss, and V. William Harris, "Crime, Delinquency, and the American Indian," *Human Organization* 36, no. 3 (1977): 252–53; Richard Oakes, "Alcatraz Is Not an Island," *Ramparts* (December 1972): 36. Oakes's personal account of the takeover was published shortly after his assassination on September 20, 1972, and is the only known autobiography of the leader.

35. Ablon, "Relocated American Indians," 299.

36. Mankiller and Wallis, *Mankiller*, 111.

37. Metcalf, "Indians in the Bay Area," 97.

38. Ibid.

39. Native American Church members, despite the passage of the American Indian Religious Freedom Act of 1978, were harassed by law enforcement officials, who stereotypically viewed peyote as a narcotic rather than a religious sacrament. "Roadmen" is the proper name for spiritual leaders within the Native American Church. Further research is needed on Native church service within the San Francisco area.

40. Theorists of urban Indian migration, Alan Sorkin, Shirley Fiske, and John Price, account for only three levels of institutional infrastructure in the creation of an Indian City: Indian bars, Indian Centers, and organizations. During the late sixties other agents, such as Indian-owned businesses, Native American Studies organizations, and urban neighborhoods, must be included. On Powwow culture, see Clyde Ellis, *A Dancing People: Powwow Culture on the Southern Plains* (Lawrence: University Press of Kansas, 2003); and for an urban perspective Joan Weibel-Orlando, *Indian Country, L.A.: Maintaining Ethnic Community in Complex Society* (Urbana: University of Illinois Press, 1999), 132–52.

41. Sorkin, *The Urban American Indian*, 115.

42. On Indians in the marketplace, see Brian C. Hosmer, *American Indians in the Marketplace: Persistence and Innovation Among the Menominees and Metlakatlans, 1870–1920* (Lawrence: University Press of Kansas, 1999); and Brian Hosmer and Colleen O'Neill, eds., *Native Pathways: American Indian Culture and Economic Development in the Twentieth Century* (Boulder: University Press of Colorado, 2004).

43. Troy Johnson, *The Occupation of Alcatraz Island: Indian Self-Determination and the Rise of Indian Activism* (Urbana: University of Illinois Press, 1996), 157. The Thunderbirds became known for their trafficking in heroin and for their violent tactics of enforcing street laws to their liking. Yet for many in the Native community, the Thunderbirds were a harmless gang of young toughs.

44. Weibel-Orlando, *Indian Country, L.A.*, 189. On Samoan history, see Craig R. Janes, *Migration, Social Change, and Health: A Samoan Community in Urban California* (Stanford: Stanford University Press, 1990); and Donald Denoon et al., eds., *The Cambridge History of the Pacific Islanders* (Melbourne: Cambridge University Press, 1997).

45. Sorkin, *The Urban American Indian*, 69. "Many restrictions discriminate intentionally or unintentionally against the Indian renter: refusing children, limiting number of occupants, refusing to rent to welfare mothers, demanding a breakage fee along with rent that puts the price out of reach, and stringent credit checks" (68).

46. Ibid., 22–23. Understanding how members of both urban and reservation communities perceived each other's role in shaping further federal Indian policy deserves additional study: "Establishing rural/urban as the defining characteristic of identity is not realistic from an Indian point of view and serves to alienate Indian people from their homelands" (Lobo and Peters, *American Indians and the Urban Experience*, 76).

47. See Dikran Karagueuzian, *Blow It Up!* (Boston: Gambit, 1971); and William H. Orrick Jr., *Shut It Down! A College in Crisis* (Washington, D.C.: Government Printing Office, 1969), a report to the U.S. National Commission on the Causes and Prevention of Violence.

48. Richard Oakes, *Native American Studies* (San Francisco: San Francisco State College, 1969), 1, San Francisco Public Library, Box 4, File 32, "San Francisco State Native American Studies."

49. Letter to Hayakawa from Richard Oakes, "Request for Funds," Hayakawa Papers, San Francisco State University Archives, Ethnic Studies–NAS folder.

50. "M.A.N.Y. Movement of American Native Youth," Al Miller Papers, San Francisco Public Library, "San Francisco State—NAS," Box 4, File 32. One of the first acts this organization did was to draw attention to police action or inaction with regards to Warren's Bar. In a notice posted in the Indian Center the following MANY flyer stated, "The frequent fist fights that take place in all of the bars, the serving of minors in some of the bars in the area, the unavailability of policemen until 1:00 [a.m.] when they swoop down in numbers to harass the wrong people, bartenders looking on with indifference while people fight & the bathrooms of the bar having stopped-up, overflowing commodes. These and many other problems exist which no one seems either willing or able to do anything about" (Al Miller Papers, San Francisco Public Library, Indian Organization—American Native Youth Corp., Box 4, File 23).

51. The mainland office was also in charge of sending out telegrams; approving supply runs with the General Services Administration; approving interviews and press; writing press releases; lobbying city, state, and federal officials; sorting mail for the occupiers; and many other duties.

52. On the Alcatraz takeover, see Johnson, *Occupation of Alcatraz Island*; and Paul Chaat Smith and Robert Allen Warrior, *Like a Hurricane: The Indian Movement From Alcatraz to Wounded Knee* (New York: New Press, 1996).

53. The Red Power movement is defined as an Intertribal movement that relied on direct action to promote Native self-determination or Indian control over Indian affairs and protection of treaty and land rights and more specifically advocated for reclamation of traditional Native lands. Alcatraz is often viewed as the start of Red Power, having incorporated a myriad of these definitional characteristics, but Red Power as a movement cannot be understood historically without a detailed exploration of place and space—the Indian city.

Gay Male Rural-Urban Migration in the American West

PETER BOAG

"We're not in Kansas anymore!" Many know this classic line from the 1939 motion picture *The Wizard of Oz*. Numbers of mid- and late-twentieth-century gay American men also readily recognized it; it resonated deeply in their lives, and for a number of reasons. For one, gay icon Judy Garland, in the guise of Dorothy, uttered it. In addition to her identification with her somewhat innocently campy Wizard of Oz alter ego, Garland's popularity among gay men came from some of her other madcap stage roles, remarkable talent, vulnerability, gay-positive personal life, and later the tragic circumstances of her death. So powerful was the association that many gay males of the twentieth century had with Garland, Dorothy, and *The Wizard of Oz* that this person, character, and Hollywood production seeped into their subculture in various ways. Garland became a standard in the repertoire of drag performers. By midcentury the coded phrase "friend of Dorothy" secretly referred to others with a gay identity, while some used the expression "Dorothy and Toto" with regard to a gay couple whose more effeminate member dominated. The moniker Emerald City, or some variation of it, would eventually adorn more than one gay bar. Although apparently in no way a part of the gay flag's origins, for some its many colors reflect the rainbow that Dorothy dreamed of crossing to a better world.[1] And gay lore, if not reality, maintains that the grief and anguish resulting from Garland's suicide on June 22, 1969, partly precipitated the Stonewall riot a week later, the event that has come to mark, at least in popular memory, the beginning of the modern gay liberation movement.

The line "We're not in Kansas anymore!" itself came to mean a great deal to many mid-twentieth-century gay males. As it did for Dorothy, it epitomized their escape from the everyday drabness, the black-and-white conformity, and even the menacing oppressiveness and brutality of life in rural and middle America. Whereas Dorothy replaced all these harsh realities with the sympathetic friendship of other misfits and an amazing sojourn in the magical, colorful, and altogether fabulous land of Oz that existed somewhere over the rainbow, untold thousands of gay men traced their own yellow-brick roads out of rural America and to the city. There they more openly and easily pursued passions, formed friendships, and cultivated communities with like-minded people. While such a scenario played out across America, this real history is particularly evident in the American West, where great expanses of sparsely populated lands surround thriving metropolises, where immigration long played a major role in urban growth, and where, particularly in the post–World War II era, western cities, especially those on the Pacific Coast, came to represent a new, hopeful promise in American culture and, not surprisingly, became leading national meccas of healthy, visible, and in time politically active gay populations. But similar to Dorothy's ultimate declaration that "there's no place like home" and her ensuing return to Kansas at the end of *The Wizard of Oz*, by the late twentieth century certain hard realities and complexities that gay urban males faced led to the appearance in their culture of antiurban and even prorural utopian strains. Some gay men then even journeyed (back) to the countryside in search of new dreams.

This chapter examines such aspects of the gay male history of the twentieth-century American West. It considers the relationship between small-town, rural America and its larger cities in the growth and development of gay populations in the latter, particularly through migration. It also explores the gay urban outmigration, whether real or imagined, that took place in the latter quarter of the twentieth century. Needless to say, gay males are diverse. They come from varied backgrounds and have different desires, interests, and experiences. This chapter is a musing on a portion of that group's history; it looks primarily at internal migrations of mostly white gay men and leaves the important topic of international migration and the story of the migration of sexual minorities of color in the West to another venue. Readers should therefore not collapse all gays, gay experiences, and culture into the scenario projected here.

Homosexuals and homosexuality have long been associated with the city. As far back as the late nineteenth century, the first scientific etiologies for homosexuality, known variously at the time as sexual inversion, perversion, and degeneration, maintained that urban living was causal. In the 1890s, for example, German philosopher and physician Max Nordau attributed the apparent rise in sexual inversion to the unhealthful circumstances of the city. Nordau argued that its pollution, adulterated and contaminated foods, alcohol and drugs, and quicker pace of life due to steam power, electricity, and modern transportation and communication caused nervous exhaustion that weakened the body and rendered it vulnerable to infectious degeneracies. On the U.S. side of the Atlantic, physician James Weir similarly asserted in 1919 that "large cities are the hotbeds and breeding places of the various neuroses." Among these he included "effemination" in the American male. Other of the nation's physicians casually associated urban areas with homosexuality. In 1888 James G. Kiernan declared that sexually perverted males "exist in all large cities to-day." Some sixteen years later G. Frank Lydston held that there "are in every large community colonies of male sexual perverts and inverts, who are generally known to each other, and who usually congregate together."[2]

Contemporary commentators on cities in the American West likewise revealed the existence thereof, and the conditions they believed gave rise to, populations and even full-blown communities of homosexual men. Charles H. Hughes described in the pages of a 1907 issue of *Alienist and Neurologist* the "reverse complexion homosexual" community in St. Louis, the Gateway to the West. "Male negroes," Hughes announced, "masquerading in woman's garb and carousing and dancing with white men is the latest St. Louis record of neurotic and psychopathic sexual perversion." Hughes concluded his pithy and shocking exposé with the certitude, "These perverted creatures appear to be features of million people cities." A few years later and farther West, a Denver homosexual and university professor penned a letter that German sexologist Magnus Hirschfeld included in his 1914 publication, *Homosexuality in Men and Women*. Hirschfeld's correspondent explained that over the years he had come to know many homosexual students in Denver, and he revealed a current acquaintanceship with a number of gay residents of the city, including "five musicians, three teachers, three art dealers, one minister, one judge, two actors, one florist, and one women's tailor." One of the young artists, the professor reported, threw parties, and some of the men attended in women's clothing.[3]

The same year that Hirschfeld publicized homosexuality in Denver, officials in Long Beach, California, rounded up some fifty men on charges of social vagrancy. One young male informant caught up in the events purported that there existed "more than five thousand 'queers' in Los Angeles alone" and that he personally knew two hundred. A journalist covering the story for the *Sacramento Bee* dished out various morsels about the social networks of these so-called queers, including their "orgy" clubs, their public meeting places, and their private parties where some attended dressed in drag. Alluding to accepted knowledge of the time linking homosexuality and urbanization, the reporter distressingly affirmed, "Not a city in the United States is free from its damming[,] mind-dwarfing, soul-blasting blight and it is growing."[4]

In addition to these period anecdotes, present-day historians have revealed, some in stunning detail, the contours of gay communities that formed in western cities such as Los Angeles, San Francisco, Portland, Seattle, Denver, and even Salt Lake City by the early years of the twentieth century.[5] And like the sexologists and other observers of old, these historians generally concur that America's first gay communities formed in cities. But they agree neither with the sexologists nor with each other on exactly what conditions specifically gave rise to them. Some have emphasized that the modern city provided an atmosphere, nonextant in small towns, that allowed people to maintain multiple lives, each potentially separate from the other, thus permitting those with same-sex sexual interests to pursue them with little concern that disapproving families, coworkers, and others might find out. Other historians underscore the effects of modern capitalism and industrialization and the rise of corporations in the city; these allowed individuals to find jobs and homes on their own without having to rely on others or having to marry, permitting freedom to develop personally independent lifestyles, something notably new for larger portions of the population than in the past. Yet other scholars have proposed that the morally relaxed nature of late-nineteenth-century urban vice districts with their transient populations and specific forms of cross-gender and sexualized entertainments enabled a wide-open atmosphere in which alternative lifestyles and identities took root and blossomed.

Such theories on the rise of modern gay identity and community within the city, however, should not elide the fact that people with same-sex sexual inclinations also resided in and created forms of community in rural America from an early time.[6] In the late nineteenth century, just as often as commentaries associated homosexuality with the city, they denied that rural conditions could harbor it, save in unusual situations where foreign immigrants to the American hinterland supposedly brought their Old World debaucheries with them. Rather, they argued for the ameliorative effects of rural life.[7] Such myths have long shrouded the pervasiveness of homosexuality in the rural and small-town West, this despite the fact that as far back as 1948, Alfred Kinsey's scientific research concluded that the highest frequencies of homosexual activities he uncovered occurred in rural America and particularly in the West. "This type of rural homosexuality," Kinsey clearly asserted, "contradicts the theory that homosexuality in itself is an urban product."[8]

Kinsey, nevertheless, differentiated rural western homosexuality from its urban counterpart. In the latter it developed as "a more or less organized group activity" with "taverns, nightclubs, restaurants, and baths," while such is unknown in the former. Moreover, Kinsey argued that the virile westerners among whom he discovered homosexual activity, such as ranchmen, cattlemen, prospectors, lumbermen, and farmers, "lived on realities and a minimum of theory. Such a background breeds the attitude that sex is sex, irrespective of the nature of the partner with whom the relation is had." Kinsey instructively added, "Such a group of hard-riding, hard-hitting, assertive males would not tolerate the affectations of some city groups that are involved in the homosexual." A telling anecdote from an early-twentieth-century Wyoming traveler lends credibility to this judgment. Sometime before 1918 New York journalist Earl Lind, also known as Ralph Werther and by the alter ego Jennie June, journeyed to Wyoming on assignment. Lind described himself as an "androgyne," a young man with a "woman-soul." Wearing women's clothing and having sex with men came naturally to him. He discovered in the Rocky Mountains that western cowboys and miners were "the most prejudiced against effeminate males" he had encountered. Even though he wore male attire in Wyoming, Lind could not disguise his true nature. Soon those with whom he traveled began heaping insult upon him, using the most obscene terms they could summon "for a girl-boy." Lind also felt his life imperiled, worrying that his fellow wanderers might "push me over a precipice after tempting me to a stroll, and no one ever learn my fate. The tradition is wide-spread that bisexuals must be murdered."[9]

Not surprisingly, many young men with same-sex desires fled this rural West for the big city, where more opportunity awaited and a more fully integrated life could be had. For both the pre– and post–World War II eras, historians have only begun to assess this migration. What we know is therefore sketchy, particularly for the earlier era.[10] Logic tells us that most men with same-sex desires who could be found in western American cities at the turn of the twentieth century migrated to them from elsewhere. After all, many of these cities, such as Denver, Seattle, and Portland, only appeared in the mid- and latter nineteenth century, and all major western cities grew at remarkable rates during that era primarily through immigration. Between 1880 and 1920 San Francisco increased from a population of 233,959 to an astonishing 506,676. But other major western cities experienced even more spectacular growth during this same period: Denver from 35,629 to 256,491; Portland from 17,577 to 258,288; Seattle from only 3,533 to 315,312; and amazingly Los

Angeles from 11,183 to 576,673, give or take a few, no doubt![11] And thus a critic of Los Angeles's remarkable gay scene in 1914 tersely put it this way: Homosexual vice "attracts the indolent, the men who have money and lots of idle time and in this respect, California, the mecca of the tourists, may possibly have a larger per cent of 'queers' than some of the other large cities."[12] My study of a major homosexual scandal that broke in Portland in 1912 offers telling evidence on migration to western cities. Of more than fifty men arrested in that scandal, records reveal birthplaces for forty-five of them. Only two had been born in Portland. While some had migrated from overseas and Canada, and a few came from cities such as New York and Buffalo, most originated in small-town and rural America, in places such as Jacksonville, Estacada, and Sherman County, Oregon; Rock Falls, Illinois; Laurel, Delaware; Milan, Michigan; Lyon, Nebraska; and Baxter Springs, Kansas.[13]

But did this turn-of-the-century small-town and rural exodus of males with same-sex sexual interests result from a groundswell of feelings of isolation and misery there and a strong desire to pursue more open and fulfilling emotional and sexual lives in the city? Or, to address the knotty chicken-and-egg tautology still left tangled by current theories on the rise of urban homosexual communities, did the city introduce these men to the possibilities only after they arrived? With regard to the former question, consider Earl Lind. Even though he did not come from the West and ended up in New York City, Lind did grow up in a rural area. There he claimed he experienced "excruciating anguish in the forest" as a result of his sexual feelings. With regard to the latter question, for some the answer is undoubtedly yes, but evidence also shows, as in the case with Lind, that others, new to the city from the countryside, brought formative sexualities with them. Early Los Angeles provides an example. There a graduate student in social work at the University of Southern California encountered a homosexual man in the 1930s who had grown up on a farm, had many same-sex experiences there as a youth, and when he came to Los Angeles at age eighteen immediately began attending motion picture shows in the city's vice district where he met another man like himself and began an affair.[14]

Clearly, sexuality and sexual practices migrated with men who came to western cities at the turn of the twentieth century. Nowhere is this more evident than among members of the multinational, ethnic, and racial transient working class who frequented urban vice districts when not laboring in the region's natural resource–based industries and railroads or sailing on oceangoing vessels that periodically docked at Pacific Coast ports. San Francisco's Barbary Coast, Seattle's Skid Road, Portland's North End, Denver's Market Street, and Los Angeles's Main Street vice districts all served as temporary homes and pleasuring grounds for such men, many who, while there, readily engaged in same-sex liaisons, usually seeking out young male prostitutes for such relationships. An officer for Seattle's Juvenile Court reported in 1913 that he "frequently observed groups of twelve to fifteen-year-old boys along the streets below Yesler Way at midnight being solicited by drunks.... They were after 'easy money.'" That same year police in Portland observed a North End pool hall that served as "a clearing house for immoral boys who pander to the passions of vicious Greeks who hang around the place." An informant for the Commission on Training Camp Activities in San Francisco reported in 1918 that any number of teenage boys worked the Barbary Coast as prostitutes, and at least one, a seventeen year old who caught the attentions of a "Greek" immigrant, "was powdered and rouged and perfumed" at the time observed. A few years later a student of social work noted in Los Angeles that "several young male prostitutes" there made contacts among the vice district's "old men" at Pershing Square. "They were slender," this informant described, "smooth skinned, pink cheeked young men whose actions were effeminate. They wore men's clothing which was neatly pressed and tailored, bright ties and flowers pinned to the shirt or coat on the left lapel."[15]

Historians of western cities have offered two views on exactly what urban space provided the original fertile ground in which modern homosexual communities took root and gay identities formed. Not surprisingly, in light of the evidence just presented, one view maintains that turn-of-the-century vice districts, such as San Francisco's Barbary Coast and Seattle's Skid Road, provided this very space. Denizens of such places, this argument goes, included cross-gender dressing or acting male prostitutes who had direct and indirect links to vice-district amusements, often finding employment on the stage, in theaters, or at saloons. These individuals may very well have been the first who identified themselves as "gay," using terms such as *fruit, queer, fairy,* and *queen* when referring to themselves.[16] In my work on Portland, however, I found that class and racial prejudices provided strong barriers in West Coast cities, preventing pervasive mixing of middle-class gay males with the inhabitants of vice districts. Rather, in middle-class areas of the city, particularly the central business district, self-identified homosexual men carved out their own spaces—busy thoroughfares, parks, restrooms in posh hotels, and private apartments—for meeting, partying, and carrying on their sexual affairs.[17] In either case, both working-class and middle-class spaces of early-twentieth-century western cities drew to them from rural areas and from other cities men and youths who harbored a variety of same-sex sexual passions. In these urban areas they likewise created multiple communities replete with friends, sexual activities, and varied gay cultural forms.

Formative, even prototypical, gay communities and identities existed in large western American cities in the first half of the twentieth century. But the socially tumultuous years of World War II, to quote one historian of the gay experience, "created something of a nationwide coming out experience."[18] War mobilized for military service more than sixteen million American men and women, many who came to the West, particularly its major cities. The large coastal ports of San Diego, Los Angeles, San Francisco, Portland, and Seattle housed war installations or served as primary embarkation and debarkation points for soldiers and sailors going to and coming from the Pacific theater. Such cities, and even inland locales like Denver, also hosted colossal defense industries, particularly shipbuilding and airplane manufacturing, and thus attracted another group of migrants, people from all parts of the country hungry for lucrative employment after the lean years of the Depression. During the war years, Seattle grew 30.5 percent, Portland 33.6 percent, Los Angeles 17.8 percent, San Francisco Bay 39.9, and San Diego a remarkable 110.5 percent.[19] For any number of civilians and army and navy personnel, the World War II migrations loosened their ties to small-town and rural moorings as well as from the surveillance of family and neighbors, allowing them the freedom more easily to fathom and explore what feelings of same-sex sexuality they may have harbored. The incredible crush of people, whether permanent or transient, in the large cities of the West added to and in ways transformed gay life already existing there. All western cities witnessed their gay bars and other hangouts expand in number and size.[20] To mention only one example, instructive in its modesty, consider Denver. Historian Thomas Jacobs Noel discovered that World War II created the conditions there for the establishment of Denver's very first wholly gay bar that had any staying power. Up through the early years of the war, Mary's Tavern on Broadway continued to serve a traditionally heterosexual clientele, but soon a group of gay airmen from Lowry Air Force Base made it their favored retreat. Reportedly, their "blatantly gay behavior" soon drove off the straight patrons, and the bar became gay space.[21]

Further adding to the gay populations of western cities were the numbers of migrant war workers and service personnel, having grown to love those places during their wartime sojourns in them, who decided permanently to settle there once the worldwide conflict concluded. Take, for example, Skippy LaRue. A Texan who dressed in drag already as a nine-year-old boy, LaRue headed to Seattle during the war specifically to find employment in Boeing's aircraft plant and then remained in the city afterward, soon becoming a female impersonator in a local gay cabaret and later working at a gay bathhouse. For discharged gay and lesbian service personnel, after briefly visiting home, as historian Allan Bérubé has demonstrated in his remarkable studies of gay and lesbian experiences in the war years, many quickly abandoned family and small towns, opting instead for the larger and more tolerant conditions of American cities. Among these could be counted Elwood Burton Gerrits. He grew up in rural South Dakota and joined the navy in 1943. While stationed in the San Francisco Bay Area at Treasure Island, he had his first sexual encounter with a man, a merchant marine, at a San Francisco hotel. "Suddenly things made sense," Gerrits acknowledged. It "opened my awareness to pleasures I had dreamed but thought impossible." In 1947, subsequent to traveling elsewhere in the country and even back to South Dakota, Gerrits returned to San Francisco, claiming, "I wanted to come back. This is where my heart was." A considerably darker side to the story of postwar settlement in large western cities, however, concerns those undesirably discharged for homosexuality. Unable to go home due to the stigma they suffered, many had little choice but to remain in West Coast cities, particularly San Francisco, where any number of gays who had served in the Pacific theater were actually exposed and drummed out of the service.[22]

World War II's transformative influence on gay life reached beyond the expansion and quickening of it in the city. "By uprooting an entire generation," asserts Allan Bérubé, "the war helped to channel urban gay life into a particular path of growth—away from stable private networks and toward public commercial establishments serving the needs of a displaced, transient, and younger clientele." Although certainly not popularly accepted, gays and gay life in America's cities did indeed become more public in the postwar era. Possibly the most striking example of this is *Life*'s 1964 article and pictorial "Homosexuality in America." While this piece highlighted places such as New York City, Chicago, New Orleans, and Miami, it principally focused on San Francisco and Los Angeles, noting California's "special appeal" due to its growing postwar "reputation for easy hospitality."[23] In this article author Paul Welch boldly escorted a scandalized middle America on a tour of San Francisco's gay bars, cruising spots, drag venues, S&M clubs, and the Tenderloin vice district. He also outlined the contours and the work of California's homophile political organizations, the Mattachine Society and ONE, Inc., and he followed Los Angeles's beat police on an evening of harassing gays.

As historian Martin Meeker has shown, this *Life* exposé, plus the era's myriad newspaper and magazine reports, press coverage of municipal crackdowns, published psychological studies, communicative networks of newly founded gay and lesbian civil rights organizations, and even word of mouth spread more privately by the burgeoning gay populations, advertised, whether in a positive or negative light, the growth and evolution of thriving gay communities and cultures in America's cities during the postwar period. This advertising encouraged yet more of the country's disaffected, isolated, and dejected rural and small-town gay youth to flee to the city. In this regard, consider the case of one Klamath Falls, Oregon, youth who discovered his sexuality during his senior year in high school. At that moment he "felt very out of place, alienated, not able to meet the masculine expectations forced upon" him. At the end of the 1965–66 school year, though, he packed his bags (and his parents' credit card) and headed out. "My ticket," he explained, "was a *Life* magazine exposé of 'The Gay World.' The article explored the hidden world of the homosexual, and it also provided me with the information I needed to begin my search for others like myself. This search for community and love led me to L.A. and San Francisco." In this overall migration San Francisco likely became the single most popular destination, which is partly why *Life* could confidently declare it the "gay capital" in 1964 and many gays came to understand it as their own Oz.[24]

Also both directly and indirectly encouraging post–World War II migration to San Francisco and Los Angeles were the nation's first homosexual rights organizations, which formed in those cities in the 1950s. The Mattachine Society was the earliest of these, founded in 1950–51 in Los Angeles; it moved its headquarters to San Francisco by 1953. ONE, Inc., formed in Los Angeles in 1952. The lesbian Daughters of Bilitis organized in San Francisco in 1955. Each published journals and had distributors, in the form of sympathetic local newsstands, around the country. Information disseminated in these journals included national and some local news items from various parts of the country, short stories, positive information on sexuality, and details of the sponsoring organization's activities.

Mattachine and ONE both opened service desks to which struggling gays around the country wrote for advice and help or simply to express their heartfelt appreciation. Many rural and small-town struggling gays also requested information that might aid them in identifying other gay people and hangouts in their local areas or might assist them in migrating to California or to other large cities where they believed life would be better. Buried within these often painful letters lay a trove of information about the difficulties and isolation experienced in midcentury rural America, including the American West, but also about the migration process to larger western cities. In 1955, for example, a married man with two children in small-town Utah wrote to ONE that "should anyone in this town or in this part of the state find out I will be a social outcast for ever. They are extremely strict in this little [M]ormon community." He continued, "I am writing you this letter in hopes that you can help me fulfill a desire that is praying [sic] on me constantly." He went on to explain that he could easily get to the larger cities of Ogden and Salt Lake and hoped ONE could provide him the name of anyone in either place "with like desires." A few years later a desperate man in Salida, Colorado, begged ONE for the "name of another subscriber in my vicinity." If ONE could not oblige, he at least hoped that the organization would forward his letter to "someone in Pueblo or Denver whom you think might be interested it receiving" it. In 1966 a nineteen-year-old man in Grand Junction, Colorado, detailed to ONE his plans for moving to Denver, hoping the organization could provide information about a ONE or Mattachine chapter that might exist there. "Every job I ever had before I have been asked to leave because of being a homosexual. So I think if I can find a job where they don't care what 'sex' you are I will be better off, don't you?" On the other hand, and about the same time, a twenty-three-year-old resident of Boulder, Colorado, wrote that he could not wait to abandon the state. Apparently, the bright lights of Denver could not entice him the same way it did his Grand Junction counterpart. "I feel desperate to escape Colorado," he instead pleaded, "and get to California where I can find a measure of acceptance and where I can find productive employment."[25]

If not seeking information on or contacts in their local areas or nearby large cities to which they considered relocating, a number of these rural or small-town letter writers, like the Boulder man, expressed the desire to migrate to California. "I am wondering if you can help me in any way," an eighteen-year-old small-town Floridian wrote. "You see, I plan on coming to Los Angeles as soon as I sell my car, and can save a little money to make the trip. I intend to stay at your local 'Y,' until I could find more suitable accommodations." Another correspondent, this one from Gering, Nebraska, asserted, "Eventually I hope to come 'out west' and explore the possibility of locating in California—either Los Angeles or San Francisco—on a permanent basis."[26]

The 1960s saw the numbers of gays in large western cities grow, partly due to the continued influx of individuals like those above. But the number of out, more politically conscious gays in western cities also increased and for a number of reasons. For one, homophile organizations in these places proliferated. For example, a chapter of Mattachine formed in Denver in 1957 and helped popularize gay issues and the developing gay community there when it hosted the locally well-advertised sixth annual convention of the national organization in 1959. Although stirrings of homophile organization began in the Seattle-Tacoma area as early as 1959, the first full-fledged such group, the Dorians, finally formed in 1967. Homophiles also made themselves present in Kansas City by 1966.[27] But then, in 1969, New York's Stonewall rebellion inspired the more radical Gay Liberation Front. With an ideology more attractive to younger gays on university campuses, the GLF quickly eclipsed the older homophiles, as students founded chapters immediately in larger cities such as Los Angeles, Seattle, and Portland, but also soon enough in smaller university towns like Boulder, Colorado; Lincoln, Nebraska; Norman, Oklahoma; and Lawrence and Manhattan, Kansas. From the 1950s to the 1970s homophile and gay liberation organizations helped nudge more gays out of the closet. But the politicization of gays during this era cannot be attributed to them alone. In Los Angeles, Seattle, Denver, Portland, and especially San Francisco, fierce municipal crackdowns from the 1950s through the 1970s on gay space, particularly bars, further incited gays. They began to fight back publicly, sometimes resorting to the courtroom, sometimes simply to the streets.[28]

The growing public presence and political strength of gays by the early 1970s, combined with other factors such as inner-city decline and urban renewal projects, all led to the founding of distinctly gay neighborhoods in larger western cities. Certain segments of the gay population concentrated in them, opened their own businesses, located their political organizations and community centers there, hosted their own celebrations, purchased homes, and recreated there in various ways. Such neighborhoods helped raise the consciousness of gays and attracted yet more from the rural, small-town West. The better known of these neighborhoods include San Francisco's Castro, Seattle's Capitol Hill, Denver's Capitol Hill, San Diego's Hillcrest, and Los Angeles's West Hollywood. These highly visible gay spaces only drew to them more and more people. West Hollywood's roots as a gay neighborhood actually began in the early twentieth century when the nearby Hollywood studios started attracting workers, among them many gays, in the motion picture industry. Because West Hollywood remained unincorporated for years, it provided somewhat less expensive living, fewer regulations that facilitated the establishment of gay businesses, and considerably less surveillance by legal authorities. The Los Angeles Police Department, known for harassing gays elsewhere, had no jurisdiction there. West Hollywood's attraction to gays is evidenced by the fact that when it did incorporate as its own city in 1984, not only did it reportedly have the highest population density of any area in the western states, but an estimated one-third of this population was gay.[29]

San Francisco's Castro, on the other hand, was truly a creature of 1960s and 1970s gay social and urban developments. Situated in what is known as Eureka Valley, by the mid-1960s urban flight had left the Castro in somewhat of a deserted condition. A number of gay migrants to the city by this time had been drawn to the youthful counterculture of Haight-Ashbury just across the hill from the Castro. They soon discovered the increasingly affordable Eureka Valley and began moving in and establishing their own businesses and institutions. The Castro became more publicly visible in 1973 when gay resident and local business owner Harvey Milk, himself a migrant to the city, ran for city supervisor for the first time. By 1977 an estimated twenty thousand gays lived in the Castro.[30] If San Francisco had become by 1964, in the words of *Life,* America's "gay capital," then by a decade later, Castro had become the gay capital's main artery, through it flowing thousands of gay men from around the country during that decade. So central to American gay culture as a whole had Castro become in the '70s that it offered up the archetypal gay figure of the period: "the Castro clone," a hypermasculine character who wore, in the words of San Francisco historian Les Wright, "a body-hugging ensemble—plaid shirt or tight-fitting tee shirt, tight fitting 501 . . . blue jeans, sneakers or construction boots, a hat or cap, an earring, and facial hair, usually a mustache."[31]

The growing visibility of gays by the 1970s spilled over into other western cities where it had hardly existed before. By 1979, for example, the *Rocky Mountain Magazine* could report the existence of fifteen gay bars in Phoenix; eleven in Tucson; five in Salt Lake City; three each in Colorado Springs, Billings, and Albuquerque; two in Cheyenne; and one each in Boise and Ogden, to name only a few. Some of these and other interior western cities by 1979 counted gay political organizations, bookstores, community centers, churches, and even motorcycle clubs. That same year New York resident Lester Strong returned to his hometown of Albuquerque, from which he had fled in 1968. He admitted his "surprise" to find the Gay Co-Op located only a few blocks from his family's home. "On the one hand," Strong revealed of his conflicted feelings when visiting there, "there were my memories of homophobia and the sense of isolation I had felt as a gay youth growing up there. . . . On the other was the reality of gays living and working there, with some of the centers of that gay life even being interlaced among the scenes and places of my childhood."[32]

The spread of the gay rights and liberation movements, the number of out gays, and the visibility of gay culture and political organizations in the United States by the 1970s certainly encouraged those who remained in these then smaller western cities to begin coming out and organizing; university students in places like Manhattan, Kansas, and Lincoln, Nebraska, are examples of this. But also contributing to the growth of visible gay culture in smaller western cities by the end of the '70s was the migration to them of out gays and lesbians from larger cities. Lester Strong firmly believed that the changes that Albuquerque witnessed during his decade-long absence resulted from outsiders moving in. "It is not surprising... that gay liberation seems to have come to the area from the outside," Lester commented, "and that the most uncloseted activists I found were from among those newer arrivals." While news articles of the 1970s and early 1980s admitted that Denver's growth as a gay mecca could be attributed to its traditionally regional attractiveness to "young gays growing up in the surrounding states, from Utah clear to the eastern edges of Kansas, Nebraska, and the Dakotas," they also accredited its increasing gay atmosphere to "a lot of people who have moved here from California.... Denver offers them something different, something more laid-back and easygoing, more personal."[33]

No longer wanting to be "just another number," many self-assured gay men left the urban meccas of California for places like Denver in the late 1970s.[34] At the same time, just as San Francisco, Los Angeles, and even other West Coast cities reached new stature as gay meccas (by the '70s all of these cities had distinctly gay neighborhoods and had passed gay civil rights ordinances), a number of gay men began to turn their backs on them, heading instead, oddly enough, to small towns and the countryside. Certainly, the exodus from rural America to the city continued unabated, but by the early 1970s, and continuing through the 1990s, various hard realities of urban living led some to retrace their steps, and a retrograde migration ensued. Among these motivating factors can be counted political activist burnout, pursuit of spirituality, and the HIV/AIDS epidemic.

A number of gay male activists began to flee western urban centers in the early 1970s. In 1983, reflecting back on the early years of this urban-to-rural migration, the magazine *RFD*, the most significant mouthpiece of this gay-male back-to-the-land movement, explained simply that "gay people began to see rural life as a real option to the urban ghettos. It seems... no accident that not a small amount of energy in the early days of *RFD* came from Gay Lib 'heavies' who had either fled the urban madness or had returned to the country setting of their boyhoods." In 1976 Tom Kennedy outlined for *RFD* the political difficulties that still abided in places like his own San Francisco, despite its reputation as the gay capital: "There are those of us here in the city who are trapped... in a vicious circle of attempting to survive in a racist, classist and sexist society while at the same time attempting to maintain some integrity in our lives by being principled and political in fighting back against straight, white capitalist pigs.... We are busy in this so-called 'gay mecca' trying to get it together to just survive a bus ride without getting hassled on the way to the park. No, city life is not glamorous."[35]

In describing the difficulties confronting gays in the city, Kennedy was actually criticizing the back-to-the-land movement, accusing its adherents of abandoning the gay cause and deserting those like himself who continued to live by the liberationist slogan "The personal is political." But his assessment rang only partly true; while many gave up urban activism for refuge in "cute little dome houses nestled under a stary [sic] sky," "organic gardens," and "macrame plant hangers," a number of gay urban expatriates truly believed that rural America provided a place where their political and personal dreams could be realized. And again, in a number of cases, among these activists could be counted those who had actually originated in small towns. Jai Elliott is an example. In 1978, after having spent time in the city, he declared that he wanted to live in small-town Oregon again. Although he had painful experiences there growing up as a "sissy," he nonetheless came to realize that he identified with its people, its sense of strong community tradition, and especially its political climate of antifederalism, which he interpreted as being akin to his growing anarchism. "I see hope here," Elliott explained, "and I feel at home here. It has to do with heritage (the past), politics (the present), and struggle (the future). One builds into the other, and I feel that here is where it has/is/will be centered. This is the struggle I am committed to."[36]

Similarly, Richard Pastega, who was born in Klamath Falls, Oregon, in 1936, traveled widely before returning to his place of birth in 1969. He quickly became dissatisfied and fled to San Francisco, but soon found that city wanting as well. Although he admitted that San Francisco remained "a great place for me to visit," "exciting," and "my favorite city," he found himself unable to be "self-sufficient or productive there." But back in Klamath Falls with a new outlook, Pastega began working to end local gay oppression. "The excitement of playing a part in these developments," he revealed in 1978, "along with the deep roots I have in the community are reasons I remain in Klamath Falls and like it."[37]

For others, rural life might at the very least provide a temporary refuge where tired and worn-out urban activists could recharge. As one of the founders of the gay commune of Elwha on Washington's Olympic Peninsula explained in 1974, it would "allow city people a place to relax from the rigors of city Movement activities (as a burnt out early Gay activist I can sympathize with this trend)."[38]

Whereas a number of Seattle's and San Francisco's gay activists turned to the rural West in the 1970s due to political reasons, other gay males did so out of disaffection from the impersonal aspects of urban gay male culture, like the Castro clone, or because they simply came to the realization that urban living was not for them and they missed life in the countryside. Not surprisingly again, among them could be counted men who had originated in rural America. Jay Jackson provides an example. He left Texas for Portland sometime in the early 1970s. But he soon found the "big-city loneliness sharpened by inaccessible heights of the skyscrapers that are its heart. So there I was, contemplating how dependant gays are on the city bar games (sexual and social) to meet other gays. And wondering where my priorities were, anyway." He then retreated from Portland for a "country home" in the rural Willamette Valley of Oregon. Dean Mandel from Flushing, New York, simply asserted in 1976, "I am living in the city. I am not happy in the city for many reasons. I am 20 years old, and strong. I would like to move to the country, preferably around the southwest somewhere." Also in '76, San Francisco's Emilio Gonzalez revealed his dreams of finding a gay commune in Northern California: "It is my hope that in this way I can free myself from the city and begin to enjoy living on the land."[39]

By the end of the 1970s an organized spiritual movement, led particularly by urban gays desiring, among other things, greater connection to nature, emerged and united with elements of that decade's earlier back-to-the-land refugees. Likewise, this spiritual quest facilitated the move of more urban gays to the countryside. Dispirited by the overtly masculine and, in their view, dispassionate, superficial, and commercial gay culture they witnessed in urban bars and neighborhoods, gays in this quasi-religious movement dubbed themselves the Radical Faeries and held their first gathering atop a mountain above Benson, Arizona, in 1979.[40] A combination of 1960s counterculture, New Ageism, and paganism, the Radical Faeries also defy definition. Although mostly urban dwellers, their reverence for Mother Earth and extra-Judeo-Christian spiritual traditions has intimately connected them with the outdoors and the environment, which accounts for their early annual gatherings being hosted in rural places such as the mountaintop in Arizona; Pecos, New Mexico; Estes Park, Colorado; and a gay-owned ranch in Napa County, California. Because of their fears about the instability of the city and their concern over the growing ecological crisis, the Radical Faeries early sought a communally owned rural refuge, though something within easy access to the bulk of their numbers who, for practical reasons, had to remain in urban areas. A consortium of San Francisco faeries calling themselves Nomenus ultimately purchased land on Wolf Creek in southern Oregon (site of a gay commune associated with *RFD* since the early 1970s) where they established their sanctuary in 1987. Somewhat farther afield than originally hoped, nonetheless Wolf Creek's relative isolation from urban centers proved somewhat of a blessing as the Radical Faeries evolved. As a Nomenus member noted, isolation allowed "more intensive gatherings without the weekend vacation resort, everything is done for you, commuter atmosphere that has oft been criticized as not serving our long-range faerie vision."[41]

The back-to-the-land movement and the Radical Faeries' migration out of western cities (whether permanent or just on weekends) in search of some rural utopia were followed by another out-migration by the late 1980s, one precipitated by the darker HIV/AIDS crisis. In the United States, HIV/AIDS first showed up in the gay male population in the large coastal cities of San Francisco, Los Angeles, and New York in the very early 1980s. It hit, in the words of one historian, like a tsunami.[42] Between 1981 and June 1987, of the 3,297 reported AIDS cases in San Francisco, 3,185 were homosexual or bisexual males. Of these, 2,000 had already died. By 1990 the number of known AIDS cases in the Los Angeles area had reached 11,097; homosexual or bisexual men accounted for 9,652 of these.[43] The devastating effects became quickly apparent in gay neighborhoods such as the Castro, which historian Les Wright described as "virtually a ghost town" by 1984. Although in time Castro recovered, the nearby South of Market Street leather community was all but wiped off the San Francisco map.[44]

By the late 1980s gay men left such places for a number of reasons: fear, an overwhelming sense of loss, or to return home to die. The destination for many was small-town, rural America whence they had come. Paul Clark, who grew up in Montana, provides an example. After college he found a job as an accountant in the Los Angeles area and began participating in the city's gay scene. By 1986 he had contracted AIDS. Physically and emotionally rent, he returned to his family in Billings in the spring of 1987. "I couldn't afford to go anywhere else," Clark later explained. "My family is here. . . . And I love Montana. There are some wonderful things being here. The solitude of waking up in the morning and seeing six inches of snow hanging from the trees, and it's cold, and its really beautiful. This lifts my spirits and makes me want to live."[45]

Other gay men left large cities for rural America hoping to escape the AIDS epidemic altogether. This migration had become so noticeable just a year after Clark found his way back to Billings that the popular news magazine *Newsweek* featured an article on the phenomenon and entitled it "The Gay Refugees: Seeking an AIDS Oasis on the Great Plains." This piece highlighted the story of Mark Dilly, who had departed small-town Minnesota "for more alluring gay enclaves in Portland, Los Angeles and Denver." But when his friends there began dying of AIDS , he chose to head to Fargo in North Dakota, a state that, at that time, had very few reported cases of the disease. The article summarized the collective migration of those trying to escape the AIDS scourge in Portland, Seattle, San Francisco, Denver, and even Salt Lake City by seeking out Montana and Wyoming. Soon after this *Newsweek* item appeared, the Moorehead, Minnesota, gay publication *Communique* offered a somewhat different view, quoting Lenny Tweeden, a leader in the local gay community, who took issue with the impression *Newsweek* gave, that gays were heading to North Dakota "by the busload." But even Tweeden had to admit that fear of AIDS "might be part of the reason" some young men who had previously headed to the big city were now returning. "What we see," Tweeden explained, "is the rural farm boy who is gay move to Fargo. Then to Minneapolis or other cities, some later return." Writer Neil Miller found evidence of this very phenomenon in Minnesota in 1989. Some gays he interviewed there had moved back from the city because of the epidemic, while others he came across decided not to leave for the big city at all precisely because of HIV/AIDS.[46]

From the 1970s through the 1990s a number of gay men who had previously deserted the rural, small-town American West for greener pastures in large cities like San Francisco, Denver, and Seattle returned to their places of origin. In some essential ways their return paralleled that of the gay heroine Dorothy in *The Wizard of Oz* who in time learned that "there's no place like home." Long have historians been aware that the principal migration of gays in American history, just as it has been for all Americans more generally, has been from rural spaces to urban places. Despite this awareness, little scholarly attention has actually been devoted to this very phenomenon; not surprisingly, less has been paid to its reverse. The importance and validity of this subject should not be ignored. For one, it gives an added depth to our understanding of gays in urban spaces as well as to our understanding about rural-to-urban migration generally.

Additionally, the gay population of rural America, and particularly of the rural West, may only be growing, as evidenced in the 1990 and 2000 U.S. Censuses. For the first time, those censuses identified and enumerated same-sex couples, which, while only accounting for a portion of the overall gay and lesbian population, gives some indication of certain trends among them. For the eighteen states, including Alaska, west of the Missouri River, not surprisingly the highest percentages of same-sex couples identified in the year 2000 were to be found in the West Coast states, but also in Nevada, Arizona, New Mexico, and Colorado. The census found the lowest numbers in Oklahoma, Kansas, Nebraska, South Dakota, North Dakota, Montana, Wyoming, Idaho, and Utah.[47] But between 1990 and 2000 all western states save three (Wyoming, Alaska, and Idaho) saw the percentage of same-sex couples in their rural areas compared to their urban areas increase. Most strikingly, the Great Plains states saw the greatest growth of rural same-sex couples compared to urban: The number of same-sex couples in rural compared to urban Kansas grew by 17 percentage points, in North Dakota by 18, in Oklahoma by 22, in Nebraska by 27, and in South Dakota by 28.[48] This overall trend for the rural West and specifically for the Great Plains, on top of what we know about certain segments of the gay male population from the 1970s through the 1990s, suggests that for many, the universality of the old adage "We're not in Kansas anymore" is not quite what it used to be.

Notes

1. Les Wright, "San Francisco," in *Queer Sites: Gay Urban Histories Since 1600*, edited by David Higgs (London: Routledge, 1999), 165. Wright claims, however, that *The Wizard of Oz* was "no doubt . . . in mind when the rainbow flag was designed in 1978 by San Francisco resident Gilbert Baker" (165).

2. Max Simon Nordau, *Degeneration* (New York: Appleton, 1895), 34–37; James Weir, "Viraginity and Effemination," *Journal of Urology and Sexology* 15, no. 4 (1919): 187–88; James G. Kiernan, "Sexual Perversion and the Whitechapel Murders," *Medical Standard* 4, no. 5 (1888): 129; G. Frank Lydston, *The Diseases of Society: The Vice and Crime Problem* (Philadelphia: J. B. Lippincott, 1904), 375.

3. Charles H. Hughes, "Homo Sexual Complexion Perverts in St. Louis: Note on a Feature of Sexual Psychopathy," *Alienist and Neurologist* 28, no. 4 (1907): 487, 488; Jonathan Ned Katz, *Gay American History: Lesbians and Gay Men in the U.S.A., a Documentary History*, rev. ed. (New York: Meridian, 1992), 49–51, quote on 50.

4. Information comes from Gene I. Fisher's various article drafts and letters contained in "Homosexual Issue" file, Sacramento Archives and Museum Collection Center. See also Sharon R. Ullman, *Sex Seen: The Emergence of Modern Sexuality in America* (Berkeley and Los Angeles: University of California Press, 1997), 63–69.

5. See Ullman, *Sex Seen*; Nan Alamilla Boyd, *Wide Open Town: A History of Queer San Francisco to 1965* (Berkeley and Los Angeles: University of California Press, 2003); Wright, "San Francisco," 164–89; Peter Boag, *Same-Sex Affairs: Constructing and Controlling Homosexuality in the Pacific Northwest* (Berkeley and Los Angeles: University of California Press, 2003); Gary Atkins, *Gay Seattle: Stories of Exile and Belonging* (Seattle: University of Washington Press, 2003); Thomas Jacob Noel, "Gay Bars and the Emergence of the Denver Homosexual Community," *Social Science Journal* 15, no. 2 (1978): 59–74; and D. Michael Quinn, *Same-Sex Dynamics Among Nineteenth-Century Americans: A Mormon Example* (Urbana: University of Illinois Press, 1996).

6. John Howard, *Men Like That: A Southern Queer History* (Chicago: University of Chicago Press, 1999).

7. James G. Kiernan, "Increase of American Inversion," *Urologic and Cutaneous Review* 20, no. 1 (1916): 44.

8. Alfred C. Kinsey, Wardell B. Pomeroy, and Clyde E. Martin, *Sexual Behavior in the Human Male* (Philadelphia: W. B. Saunders, 1948), 457–58.

9. Ibid., 457, 459; Ralph Werther, *The Female Impersonators* (New York: Medico-Legal Journal, 1922), 253–54n1.

10. See John Howard, "Place and Movement in Gay American History: A Case From the Post–World War II South," in *Creating a Place for Ourselves: Lesbian, Gay, and Bisexual Community Histories*, edited by Brett Beemyn (New York: Routledge, 1997), 211–25; Nan Alamilla Boyd, "'Homos Invade S.F.!': San Francisco's History as a Wide-Open Town," in *Creating a Place for Ourselves*, edited by Beemyn, 73–95; and Boag, *Same-Sex Affairs*. For the post–World War II era, see Martin Meeker, *Contacts Desired: Gay and Lesbian Communications and Community, 1940s–1970s* (Chicago: University of Chicago Press, 2006).

11. U.S. Department of Commerce, Bureau of the Census, *Fourteenth Census of the United States: 1920* (Washington, D.C.: Government Printing Office, 1921), 1:78.

12. See Fisher's article draft, "Homosexual Issue" file.

13. See Boag, *Same-Sex Affairs*.

14. Merrill Leonard Harrod, "A Study of Deviate Personalities as Found in Main Street of Los Angeles" (master's thesis, University of Southern California, 1939), 67–68.

15. Archibald W. Frater, "Court Methods, Mothers' Pensions, and Community Dangers," in *Why Children Go Wrong*, Annual Report of the Seattle Juvenile Court for 1913 (Seattle: Seattle Juvenile Court, January 1, 1914), 9–10; Portland Police Detective Day Books, Box 9, Volume: Graddock et al., April 1, 1911, to June 13, 1914, p. 79 (April 8, 1913), Stanley Parr Archives and Records Center, Portland; Boag, *Same-Sex Affairs*, 81; Harrod, "Study of Deviate Personalities," 25–26.

16. On vice districts, working-class entertainments, and effeminate males and the origins of modern gay identity, culture, and community, see George Chauncey, *Gay New York: Gender, Urban Culture, and the Making of the Gay Male World, 1890–1940* (New York: Basic Books, 1994), 33–63; and Wright, "San Francisco," 164–72. The terms noted here can be found in period sources, including Harrod, "Study of Deviate Personalities," 26; and an oral history with "Vilma" partially reproduced in Don Paulson with Roger Simpson, *An Evening at the Garden of Allah: A Gay Cabaret in Seattle* (New York: Columbia University Press, 1996), 20–28.

17. Boag, *Same-Sex Affairs*, 84–129.

18. John D'Emilio, *Sexual Politics, Sexual Communities: The Making of a Homosexual Minority in the United States, 1940–1970* (Chicago: University of Chicago Press, 1983), 24.

19. Marilynn S. Johnson, *The Second Gold Rush: Oakland and the East Bay in World War II* (Berkeley and Los Angeles: University of California Press, 1993), 6, 8.

20. On World War II and gays and American urban spaces generally, see Allan Bérubé, *Coming Out Under Fire: The History of Gay Men and Women in World War Two* (New York: Plume, 1991), 98–127. On San Francisco, see Boyd, *Wide Open Town*, 111–23. On Seattle, see Atkins, *Gay Seattle*, 57–64. On Portland and Seattle, see Peter Boag, "'Does Portland Need a

Homophile Society?': Gay Culture and Activism in the Rose City Between World War II and Stonewall," *Oregon Historical Quarterly* 105, no. 1 (2004): 9–14.

21. Noel, "Gay Bars," 61.

22. Atkins, *Gay Seattle*, 62, 63; Allan Bérubé, "Marching to a Different Drummer: Lesbian and Gay GIs in World War II," in *Hidden From History: Reclaiming the Gay and Lesbian Past*, edited by Martin Duberman, Martha Vicinus, and George Chauncey Jr. (New York: Meridian, 1990), 383–94; Bérubé, *Coming Out Under Fire*; Elwood Burton Gerrits, "A South Dakotan at Cal, 1948: Oral History Transcript," interview by William Benemann, 1997, Gay Bears! Oral History Project, no. 1, University Archives, Bancroft Library, University of California, Berkeley, iii (quote), iv, 2, 3 (quote), 5 (quote); Bérubé, "Marching to a Different Drummer," 388–89; John D'Emilio, "Gay Politics and Community in San Francisco Since World War II," in *Hidden From History*, edited by Duberman, Vicinus, and Chauncey, 459.

23. Bérubé, *Coming Out Under Fire*, 126; Paul Welch, photographs by Bill Eppridge, "Homosexuality in America," *Life*, June 26, 1964, 66–74, quote on 68, and also the complementary piece in the same issue, Ernest Havemann's "Scientists Search for the Answers to a Touchy and Puzzling Question: Why?" 76–80.

24. On many aspects of this history, see Meeker, *Contacts Desired*; Candor Smoothstone, "Klamath Falls No. 1: Why I Left," *RFD*, Spring 1978, 22; Welch, "Homosexuality in America," 68; and Wright, "San Francisco," 173.

25. Letter to William Lambert, Business Manager, ONE Publications, April 22, 1955, ONE Social Service File: 1955–56; letter to ONE, Inc., April 8, 1958, ONE Social Service File: 1958; letter received by ONE, October 5, 1966, ONE Social Service File: 1964; letter to Social Service Department, ONE, Inc., March 11, 1965, ONE Social Service File: 1965, ONE Institute, University of Southern California, Los Angeles. In all letters I quote from ONE's collections, I have chosen to keep the authors anonymous.

26. Letter to James V. Schneider, ONE, Inc., September 23, 1965, ONE Social Service File: 1965; letter to ONE Inc., January 10, 1963, ONE Personal Correspondence File, ONE Institute.

27. Boag, "'Does Portland Need a Homophile Society?'" 23–26; Atkins, *Gay Seattle*, 107–28; D'Emilio, *Sexual Politics, Sexual Communities*, 197–200.

28. Boyd, *Wide Open Town*, 133–236.

29. *Frontiers* (Los Angeles), May 11–25, 1983, 27; November 7–14, 1984, 9.

30. *The Castro: A Documentary*, written and directed by Peter L. Stein (San Francisco: KQED Books and Tapes, 1997); Wright, "San Francisco," 180–86.

31. Wright, "San Francisco," 183.

32. Mike Burke, "The Rocky Mountain Rush," *Rocky Mountain Magazine*, July–August 1979, 73–79; Lester Strong, "Hometown Revisited: Gay Liberation Reaches Provinces," news article contained in New Mexico Subject File, ONE Institute.

33. Strong, "Hometown Revisited"; Lance Clem, "The Queen City Gives 'Em the Business," *Advocate*, November 12, 1981, 19; Scott P. Anderson, "Denver," *Advocate*, January 11, 1979, 22.

34. Anderson, "Denver," 22.
35. *RFD*, Winter 1983, 13; Summer 1976, 3.
36. *RFD*, Spring 1978, 19.
37. Richard Pastega, "Klamath Falls No. 2: Why I Stay," *RFD* Spring 1978, 24–25.
38. *RFD*, Winter Solstice 1974, 6.
39. *RFD*, Spring Equinox, 1975, 2; Spring Equinox, 1976, 1 (note that whereas the cover of this issue states "Spring Equinox," the contents page states "Vernal Equinox"); Summer 1976, 2.
40. On the early history of the Radical Faeries, see Stuart Timmons, *The Trouble With Harry Hay: Founder of the Modern Gay Movement* (Boston: Alyson, 1990), 248–90. On the connection between the back-to-the-land movement and the Radical Faeries, see "Recalling Former Decades, an *RFD* Retrospective: Part 3, Winter 1982 to Summer 1986," *RFD*, Spring 1994, 30–32.
41. Timmons, *Trouble With Harry Hay*, 275; *RFD*, Fall 1984, 49; Jason "Chirper" Serinus, "The NOMENUS Wolf Creek Radical Faerie Sanctuary," *RFD*, Summer 1995, 62.
42. Gayle S. Rubin, "Elegy for the Valley of Kings: AIDS and the Leather Community in San Francisco, 1981–1996," in *In Changing Times: Gay Men and Lesbians Encounter HIV/AIDS*, edited by Martin P. Levine, Peter M. Nardi, and John H. Gagnon (Chicago: University of Chicago Press, 1997), 108.
43. David Werdegar, Jeffrey Amory, and George Rutherford, *AIDS in San Francisco: Status Report and Plan for Fiscal Year, 1987–88*, rev. ed. (San Francisco: San Francisco Department of Health, 1987), table 8, p. 17; David E. Kanouse et al., *Response to the AIDS Epidemic: A Survey of Homosexual and Bisexual Men in Los Angeles County* (Santa Monica: Rand, 1991), v.
44. Wright, "San Francisco," 186, 188.
45. See William Poole, "Bringing It Back Home: Snapshots of Rural AIDS," *OUT/LOOK*, Spring 1992, 36–44, quote on 43.
46. *Newsweek*, May 9, 1988, 20, 25; Tom Parker, "*Newsweek* Says Region Gay Haven," *Communique* 10, no. 4 (1988): 1; Neil Miller, *In Search of Gay America: Women and Men in a Time of Change* (New York: Harper and Row, 1989).
47. See Human Rights Campaign Foundation, http://www.hrc.org, for analysis of the 2000 census. See also David M. Smith and Gary J. Gates, "Gay and Lesbian Families in the United States: Same-Sex Unmarried Partner Households" (Washington, D.C.: Human Rights Campaign, 2001), fig. 1, "Statewide Prevalence of Gay and Lesbian Couples," http://www.hrc.org/Template.cfm?Section=Census_20001&Template=/ContentManagement/ContentDisplay.cfm&ContentID=18787. On pages 1 and 2 of this report, Smith and Gates explain the problems of comparing the 1990 census to that of 2000. However, the problems are the same for rural and urban, so then logically they should cancel each other out and we can trust that the two censuses do provide suggestive information.
48. http://www.hrc.org/Template.cfm?Section=Census_20001&Template=/ContentManagement/ContentDisplay.cfm&ContentID=13401.

CONTRIBUTORS

KENT BLANSETT (Cherokee, Creek, Choctaw, Shawnee, and Potawatomi) is a Visiting Assistant Professor in History and American Indian Studies at the University of Minnesota–Morris.

PETER BOAG is a Professor and holds the Columbia Chair in the History of the American West at Washington State University. He is the author of several books and articles, including *Same-Sex Affairs: Constructing and Controlling Sexuality in the Pacific Northwest* (2003).

NAN ALAMILLA BOYD is Professor and Chair of the Women and Gender Studies Department at San Francisco State University. Her book *Wide Open Town: A History of Queer San Francisco to 1965* (2003) charts the rise of gay and lesbian politics in San Francisco.

LINCOLN BRAMWELL is Chief Historian of the U.S. Forest Service. His most recent work includes *The Yosemite Way: An Administrative History of Yosemite National Park* (with Andy Kirk).

KATHLEEN A. BROSNAN is an Associate Professor of History, the Associate Director of the Center for Public History at the University of Houston, the author of *Uniting Mountain and Plain: Cities, Law, and Environmental Change Along the Front Range* (2002), and editor of *The Encyclopedia of American Environmental History* (2010).

CONNIE Y. CHIANG is an Assistant Professor of History and Environmental Studies at Bowdoin College. She is the author of *Shaping the Shoreline: Fisheries and Tourism on the Monterey Coast* (2008) and has published articles in the *Journal of American History, Pacific Historical Review,* and *Western Historical Quarterly.*

CONTRIBUTORS

JOHN M. FINDLAY is a Professor in the Department of History at the University of Washington–Seattle. He is the coauthor, along with Bruce Hevly, of *Atomic Frontier Days: Hanford and the American West* (2011).

RINA GHOSE is an Associate Professor of Geography at the University of Wisconsin–Milwaukee. She specializes in Urban Geography and GIS. She is the author of several articles in *Environment and Planning A, Urban Geography, Progress in Human Geography, Transactions in GIS, Cartographica, Cartography and Geographic Information Science,* and the *Journal of Urban Technology.*

STEPHANIE KOLBERG is a Ph.D. student in the Department of American Studies at the University of Texas, Austin.

JUDY MATTIVI MORLEY is the author of *Historic Preservation and the Imagined West: Albuquerque, Denver, and Seattle* (2006). She founded a heritage tourism business in Denver's historic downtown and owned Grasshopper Communications, a specialty marketing firm that works with city governments to promote historic preservation, heritage tourism, and downtown revitalization.

SUSAN S. RUGH is a Professor of History at Brigham Young University and the author of *Are We There Yet? The Golden Age of American Family Vacations* (2008) and *Our Common Country: Family Farming, Culture, and Community in the Nineteenth-Century Midwest* (2001).

JEFFREY C. SANDERS is an Assistant Professor in the History Department at Washington State University, where he teaches Pacific Northwest, U.S. West, and environmental history. He is the author of *Seattle and the Roots of Urban Sustainability: Inventing Ecotopia* (2010).

AMY L. SCOTT is an Assistant Professor of History at Bradley University. She is the author of several essays on western urban and political history.

INDEX

Page numbers with the letter *t* refer to the tables.

Abbott, Carl, 69
Ablon, Joan, 280n18
Abruzzini, Fred, 138
Adams, Ansel, 188
Adamson, Michael, 207
aesthetics: aesthetically based environmentalism, 74–76; Boulder, Colo., and, 74–76, 82–83; Irvine, Calif., and, 54–57
African Americans: boosters in Los Angeles, 17–18; in San Francisco, 265
agricultural preserves, 143–44
agricultural workers, 147
Akeman, Thom, 206
Alaska, 14
Albert, Dan, 203–4
Albuquerque Chamber of Commerce, 184
Albuquerque Journal, 192
Albuquerque (N.Mex.): debates over public art and collective memory, 187; development trends in the 1920s, 191–92; First American Celebration, 192–93; gay men in, 296, 297; McClellan Park, 179, 192, 193; the *Pioneer Mother* statue and, 179, 184–85, 192–93; tourism and, 191; Truman's visit to, 184–85
Albuquerque Tribune, 192
Alcatraz Island occupation, 262, 276–78, 283n53
Alienist and Neurologist, 286
Alliance for a Living Market, 228, 229, 233
Allied Arts of Seattle, 222, 229, 233
Alpine Meadows of Tahoe, Inc., 92, 93
Alstrom, Sven, 136
American Indian Council of the Bay Area, 271
American Indian Historical Society, 275
American Indian Religious Freedom Act of 1978, 281n39
American Indian Voluntary Relocation Program, 280n15. *See also* Relocation Program

American Institute of Architects, 229
American Road Builders Association, 180
American Skiing Company, 93, 106n17
American utopianism: boosterism and, 17–18; colonization systems and, 13–15; distinction between utopian practice and utopian rhetoric, 11; Indian reservations and, 16–17; "inverse utopias," 34n31; "postmodern," 34n38; regional optimism and, 15–16; roots of, 10; western community building and, 1–2, 3, 10–11. *See also* western utopianism
American West: colonization systems in, 14–15; definitions of, 31n2; impact of wartime mobilization and migration on, 68; postwar suburbanization in, 68–69; summer vacationing by westerners, 174n4. *See also* western cities; western community building
Anderson, Karen Lee, 168–69
Anderson, Winslow, 136
Applegate, Frank, 185, 187, 188–90
architecture: historic preservation in Cannery Row, 199–201; of Napa Valley wineries, 142–43; romanticized restructuring of Santa Fe in the 1920s, 185–86; in 1920s Albuquerque, 191
Arizona, 25, 156, 299
Armstrong, Jody, 200, 207
arsenic, 104
Aspen (Colo.), 91
"Atomic Age" utopias, 24, 25
Austin, Alice Constance, 22
Austin, Mary, 178, 185, 187–90
automobiles: highway development in the 1920s and, 179, 180; overcrowding at national parks and, 164–65
Aztlan, 278

backpacking, 166, 173
Bacon, Francis, 1
Badami, Nick and Craig, 93
Bangerter, Norman, 101

[309]

Bantam Books, 29
Banyan Tree Books, 29
bar culture: gay and lesbian nightclubs, 243, 246, 247–53, 254–55, 256, 257; gay bars, 291, 296; in the San Francisco Indian community, 270–71
Barringer, Mark Daniel, 163
Barth, Gunther, 20
Bartlett, Albert, 70, 71, 72, 78
Baxter, Chuck, 198
Bean, Trafton, 69–70
bears, 158, 169–72
Beaulieu winery, 137
Bedford (N.Y.), 55
Bellamy, Edward, 1, 2
Bender, Thomas, 2–3
Bensalem, 1
Benson (Ariz.), 299
Bentley, Gladys, 248, 256, 257
Bergara, Esther, 200
Bergara, Frank, 200, 201
Beringer Brothers winery, 137, 138, 142
Bernstein, Alison R., 264
Berry, Brian J. L., 19
Bérubé, Allan, 292
Bird, Isabella, 65–66
Black Cat Café, 251–53
Black Panther Party, 278, 280n12
Blue Line campaign, 70–74
Blue Line Charter Amendment, 71–73
boarding schools, 280n15
boosterism: by African Americans in Los Angeles, 17–18; for Boulder, Colo., 65–68; for highway projects in the 1920s, 179; for highways in the 1920s, 180–82; for "new communities," 25–26; for the West, 18
Bottles and Bins (newsletter), 139
Boulder City (Nev.), 24
Boulder (Colo.): aesthetically based environmentalism, 74–76; Blue Line campaign, 70–74; boosterism and the promotion of, 65–68; competing visions for, 63; conservationist ethic in the Progressive Era, 67–68; Danish plan, 80; development of urban aesthetic and culture in, 82–83; ecosystem-management approach to urban planning, 65; Enchanted Mesa and, 76; environmental coalitions in, 65, 83; growth during the 1950s, 70–71; "multiple resource usage" policies in the nineteenth-century, 63; open-space management in, 81–82; open-space policy, 65, 76, 78–83; PLAN-Boulder, 74–76, 78, 79; planning history of, 37–38, 69–70, 74–83; plans to protect the Boulder Valley, 76–83; political identity of, 83–84; population growth in, 70; Progressive Era civic organizations, 67; utopianism and, 28
Boulder County (Colo.), 79–80, 82
Boulder Improvement Association, 67
Boulder Planning Department, 77
Boulder Valley (Colo.): Boulder Valley Comprehensive Plan, 79–83; greenbelt program, 78–79; methods for preserving green infrastructure in, 80; satellite communities proposal, 76–78
Bourgeois Utopias (Fishman), 4
boxcar towns, 281n25
Boyle, T. C., 30
Bradbury, Ray, 6
Bragdon, Joe, 213
Braman, J. D. "Dorn," 222, 225, 227
Braman, James, 228, 229
Brannan, Sam, 136
Brave New World (Huxley), 6
Bren, Donald, 60n21
British Columbia, 30
Brittendall, Gale Lee, 171
Brown, Keith, 161
Brown Berets, 278
Brury, Newton B., 168
Bryan, Toynette, 206
Bulk Commodities Exchange (co-op), 237
Bulldozer in the Countryside, The (Rome), 47
Bureau of Indian Affairs, 261–62, 263, 265–68, 279n11, 280n15, 280n18
Burnett, Nancy, 198
Burnett, Robin, 198
Burris, Aubrey and Tom, 200

cadmium, 104
California: African American boosters, 17–18; counterculture communes, 26, 27; experimental communities in, 13, 31n7; gay migration out of, 297; history of tourism in, 135; Indian-owned businesses, 273; Land Conservation Act, 143; *Life's* exposé of homosexuals in, 292; mythic history

of, 46; "new communities," 25–26; period anecdotes of homosexuals in, 286–87; as a postwar tourist destination, 156; Water Quality Control Board, 149; wine tourism in (*see* Napa Valley; wine tourism)
California Historical Society, 201
Californians, Inc., 257
Calistoga Hot Springs, 136
Callenbach, Ernest, 28–29, 30
Calthorpe, Peter, 84n8
Camino Real, 179, 189, 190
Camino Real Highway, 179–80, 189–90
campers, 161–62. *See also* travel trailers
campgrounds. *See* private campgrounds; public campgrounds
Campoy, Al, 200, 204
campus strikes, 274
Cannery Row: chronicling the labor history of, 197–98, 199–206, 208–13; the "Great Cannery Row Reunions," 202–6, 213; historic preservation of the sardine industry, 197–213; importance to Monterey's identity, 211; oral history project, 209–10; the photography of Robert Lewis, 208–9, 210; postwar collapse in, 197; prosperity during World War II, 196–97; "rebirth" at the Monterey Bay Aquarium, 198–201; redevelopment plans in the 1950s and 1960s, 197; saving the tarpaper shacks, 206–8; Steinbeck nostalgia and, 197, 199; Steinbeck's novel of, 196
Cannery Row: The History of Old Ocean View Avenue (Hemp), 203
Cannery Row Conservation District, 211
Cannery Row Foundation, 202, 203, 204, 205
Cannery Row (Steinbeck), 196, 203
"The Canyons" ski resort, 93
Carlisle Industrial Boarding School, 280n15
Carlo, Rene de, 250
Cartibiano, Jeannie, 209
Cascadia, 30
Castillo, Ed, 276
Castro, Bobby de, 250
Castro district (San Francisco), 295–96, 300
Catalina Island takeover, 278
Cavan, Sherri, 252
Central Association of Seattle, 218, 220, 221, 224, 230
Central Park (New York City), 64

Central Park Plaza Corporation, 222
Charles Krug Winery, 139, 141–42, 150
Chautaqua campgrounds, 67
Chavers, Dean, 270, 276
Chicano movement, 278
Chinatown (San Francisco), 253–54, 255
Chong, Wing, 203
Choose an Effective City Council (Seattle), 229
Christian Brothers winery, 137, 141
Christian Science Monitor, 53
Christiansen, John, 200
Christopher, George, 257
Chudy, Kevin, 54
Church of Jesus Christ of Latter Days Saints. *See* Mormons
"Citizens for the Blue Line," 72, 73
Clark, Paul, 300
"class colonization," 116
Clos Pegase winery, 153n28
Cohen, Lizabeth, 5, 68
Collapse (Diamond), 114
colonization systems, 13–15
Colorado: impact of wartime mobilization and migration on, 68; population growth in, 69, 85n21; postwar suburbanization in, 68–69; as a postwar tourist destination, 156
Colorado Mountain Club, 66, 71, 72
Colorado Springs (Colo.), 19
Columbia River, 82
Committee to Save the Market (Seattle), 228–29
commodities: "positional good," 112
communalism, 3
communes: gay, 299–300; of the 1960s and 1970s, 26–27, 28; in the West, 12–13
Communique, 301
communitarianism: the Mormons and, 20–21; of the 1960s and 1970s, 26–27, 28; separation from society and, 3; Union Colony, 16; U.S. economic cycles and, 19; in the West, 12–13
Communities Directory: A Guide to Cooperative Living, 12
community planners, 63–64
company towns, 21–22
Comprehensive Plan for Downtown Seattle. See Monson Plan
Conaway, James, 147
Cone, Pat, 103
Considérant, Victor, 13

INDEX

consumption: effect on western community building, 5; wine consumption by the middle class, 140. *See also* culture of consumption
Cooper, Maury, 200
cooperative colonies, 12–13
corporate model towns, 25–26. *See also* Irvine
Costo, Jeanette Henry, 275
Costo, Rupert, 275
Cottier, Belva, 276
Coulee Dam, 24
counterculture communes, 26–27, 28
Crane, George, 137
Cronon, William, 7n5
cultural elite: Seattle's Pike Place Market and, 218–20, 223–27, 230–32
culture of consumption: in Missoula, Mont., 112–14; rural gentrifiers and, 121–22

Daughters of Bilitis, 293
Daughters of the American Revolution (DAR): belief in Manifest Destiny, 181, 186; highway development in the 1920s and, 180–83; the *Pioneer Mother* statue and, 183–85, 186, 188–91, 192–93; selective historical memory and, 181–82, 184, 186, 190–91
Davis, Charles, 199, 200
Daybreak Star Center, 277
Deer Valley ski resort, 93–94
defense industry, 68
deforestation, 148, 149, 154n41
De Huff, J. D., 188, 189
Delta Airlines, 95
Denver (Colo.): gay men in, 286, 291; homophile organizations in, 294; impact of wartime mobilization and migration on, 68; population growth in, 69, 85n22, 288; postwar suburbanization in, 68–69
Department of Community Development (Seattle), 222, 224, 225, 227, 232
Department of Housing and Urban Development (HUD), 221, 227, 233
Desimone, Joe, 220, 222
Desimone, Richard, 228
Desimone family, 222, 228
De Vargas Hotel, 185
Diamond, Jared, 114
Dilly, Mark, 300

Dong, Arthur, 254
Dorians, 294–95
Douglas, James, 14
drag performers, 252–53, 257
Dreyfus, Philip, 131
Drop City (Boyle), 30
Duncan, James, 55
Duncan, Nancy, 55

Earth Day, 173, 278
Ecker Hill (Utah), 106n7
ecological utopias, 28–30
ecosystems management: in Boulder, Colo., 81–82
Ecotopia, 28–30
Ecotopia (Callenbach), 28–29
Ehrlichman, Ben, 221
Eli, Look Tin, 253
Elliott, Jai, 298
Empty Quarter, 30
Enchanted Mesa, 76
Ensign, Robert, 93
environmental movement: aesthetically based environmentalism, 74–76; Boulder's Blue Line campaign, 70–74; counterculture communes and, 26; effect of suburban development on, 64; impact of Native peoples on, 278; influence on urban planning, 64–65; PLAN-Boulder, 74–76, 78, 79; suburban development and, 47
Eriksen, Stein, 94
Esherick, Homsey, Dodge, and Davis architectural firm, 198
exclusion: in western suburbs and exurbs, 5
"exotic" dancers, 246, 254, 256
"exotic dancers." *See also* performers
experimental communities: of the 1960s and 1970s, 26–27, 28
exurbs, 5, 38

Fahrenheit 451 (Bradbury), 6
family camping: postwar boom in, 159–61, 172; raising of environmental consciousness and, 173; utopian visions of, 157–62; wheeled camping vehicles and, 161–62; in Yellowstone National Park, 162–69
Farmer Liaison Program, 236
farmers: Pike Place Market and, 236–37
federal communities, 23–25

[312]

Federal Urban Renewal Program, 232
female impersonators, 246, 248–50
Fiege, Mark, 104
Fiesta de Santa Fe pageant, 189
Figeria, Bob, 53
Findlay, John, 2, 4
Fine, Eben, 66
Finocchio, Joseph, 246, 249
Finocchio, Marjorie, 250
Finocchio's nightclub, 246, 248–50
First American Celebration (Albuquerque), 192–93
Fishman, Robert, 4
Fiske, Shirley, 281n40
Fitzgerald, Donald, 199
Flagstaff Mountain, 67
Fogarty, Robert S., 12
Forbes, John F., 257
Forbidden City, U.S.A. (documentary film), 254
Forbidden City nightclub, 254, 257
Forrest, Suzanne, 188
Fort Laramie Treaty, 276
Fort Lawton, 277
Foster, Richard, 206
Foundry, 30
Fourier, Charles, 16
Franciscan Hotel (Albuquerque), 184, 191, 192
Fred Harvey Company, 191
Friedland, William H., 149
Friends of the Market (Seattle): debate over designs for the Pike Plaza project and, 223–27; Initiative 1 and historic preservation of Pike Place Market, 227–30, 232; Warren Magnuson and, 233; managing the identity of Pike Place Market, 236; Pike Place Preservation and Development Authority and, 233; vision for the meaning of the Pike Place Market, 230–32
frontier, 31n2
Fryer, Heather, 34n31

Galbraith, John Kenneth, 74
gangs, 273, 281n43
Garber, Eric, 248
garden cities, 3, 37, 41–42, 63–64
Garden Cities of To-Morrow (Howard), 2
Garland, Judy, 284
Garmero, Annie, 210
Garreau, Joel, 29–30

Gaskill, David, 168
Gay, John, 139
gay and lesbian nightclubs, 243, 246, 247–53, 254–55, 256, 257
gay bars, 291, 296
gay communes, 299–300
gay communities: homophile organizations and, 293–95; neighborhoods in western cities, 295–96; news reports, exposés, and the advertising of, 292–93; rise of, in western cities, 287, 290–97; World War II and, 291–92
Gay Liberation Front, 295
gay men: gay identity, 284; HIV/AIDS crisis and, 300–301; homophile organizations and, 293–95; migration of (*see* gay migration); notions relating homosexuality to urbanization, 285–87; organized spiritual movement in the 1970s and, 299–300; in rural America, 287–88; José Sarria, 252–53, 257, 260n34; Stonewall riot, 284; in western cities, 243–44, 289–90, 295–96; *The Wizard of Oz* and, 284–85, 301
gay migration: HIV/AIDS crisis and, 300–301; to larger western cities, 288–90; organized spiritual movement in the 1970s and, 299–300; to smaller western cities, 296–97; from urban to rural areas, 244, 297–302
gay rights organizations, 293–94, 295. *See also* homophile organizations
Gayway exhibit, 255–56
Gee, Marti, 99–100, 101, 102–3
General Electric, 133
Georgetown (Wash.), 223
Gerrits, Elwood Burton, 292
Glidden, Jim and Sarah, 124
Golden Gate International Exposition, 249, 255–56, 260n26
Golden State, Golden Youth (May), 43–44
Gonzalez, Emilio, 299
Good Roads movement, 179. *See also* highway development
Goodwin, Arthur, 219, 220
Goodwin, Frank, 219
Gorgoza Water Company, 102
Gradis, Hope, 210
Grand Canyon, 156
Grand Coulee Dam (Wash.), 24
Great Cannery Row Reunions, 202–6, 213

Great Strike of 1919 (Seattle), 231
Greeley, Horace, 16
Greeley (Colo.), 16
greenbelt programs, 78–79
"Greenbelts: Why and How?" conference, 78
groundwater: wilderburbs and, 98–99. *See also* water
Guastella, Nicholas, 210

Haight-Ashbury (San Francisco), 278, 296
Hamer, David, 17
Hamlin, Jesse, 246
Harden, Ross, 276
Harlem West, 265
Hart, Walter, 250
Haug, Merle, 226
Hayden, Dolores, 12–13, 64, 87n42
Hayes, Jeff W., 18
heavy metal contamination, 104
Helena (Mont.), 18
Hemp, Michael, 201–2, 203, 204, 205, 206
Hendrickson, Nancy, 171
Herrero, Billy, 250
Hewitt, Edgar Lee, 186
Hickman, James, 71–72
highway development: the DAR and, 180–83; in New Mexico, 179–80; Truman and, 179, 180, 182. *See also* national highway
Hildt, Michael, 236
Hine, Robert V., 7n3, 12, 31n2
hippie movement, 278
Hirschfeld, Magnus, 286
historic preservation: in Cannery Row, 197–213; Pike Place Market and, 227–30
HIV/AIDS crisis, 300–301
Holiday (magazine), 140
Holochek, Mark, 61n38
homophile organizations, 293–95
homosexuality: associations with urbanization, 285–87; demographics of same-sex couples, 301–2; in rural America, 287–88, 297–302. *See also* gay communities; gay men
Homosexuality in Men and Women (Hirschfeld), 286
Hoover Dam, 24
Hopi Tribe, 265
Hopkins Marine Station (Stanford University), 198

hotel and restaurant workers, 147
Hot Springs Hotel, 136
housing: in Hunter's Point, San Francisco, 265; in Irvine, Calif., 45; trends in Missoula, Mont., 111–12, 114; trends in Napa Valley, 146–47
Hovden sardine cannery, 198–201
Howard, Ebenezer, 2, 4, 37, 41, 63–64
Hudson, Reba, 247
Hudson's Bay Company, 14–15
Hughes, Charles H., 286
Hunter's Point (San Francisco), 265, 279–80n12
Huxley, Aldous, 6

Icaria Esperanza, 31n7
"Indian bars," 270–71
Indian Centers, 271–72
Indian City: Alcatraz Island occupation, 276–78, 283n53; bar culture in, 270–71; Indian Centers, 271–72; Indian neighborhoods, 273–74; institutional infrastructure, 281n40; Intertribal community building and, 262; Native American studies, 274–75; powwows, 273
Indian Historian (journal), 275
Indian Peaks Wilderness, 71
Indian reservations, 16–17, 263, 268
Indians of All Tribes (IAT), 276–77
Indian Vocational Training Act, 266
Indigenous Nations, 268. *See also* Native peoples
individualism: counterculture communes and, 26
industrial history: historic preservation in Cannery Row, 197–213
Initiative 1 (Seattle), 227–30, 232
Inouye, Daniel, 273
intentional communities, 12–13
Intertribalism, 262, 277–78, 278n1
"inverse utopias," 34n31
Irvine, James, 40–41, 46
Irvine, James, II, 41
Irvine, Myford, 41
Irvine (Calif.): aesthetics of comfort and, 54–57; affordable housing issue, 45; building the master-planned identity, 46–53, 57–58; downtown of, 51; early history of, 40–41; growth and urbanization of, 42–43;

INDEX

as a master-planned community, 25, 37–38, 39–40, 41–42, 44, 45; open space and, 46–47, 49–51; pastoral urbanism and, 49–51; perceived low density of, 52–53; William Pereira's plan for, 41–42; population growth in Orange County and, 48–49; Trocadero bar, 61n38; utopian hopes and aspirations of, 43–44; "villages" of, 44, 52–57

Irvine Company: advertising and promotion by, 46–47, 48–52; Donald Bren and, 60n21; development of the City of Irvine and, 39, 42, 44, 45; formation of, 41

Irvine Industrial Complex, 51

Irvine Ranch, 40–41, 42, 46–47, 48–49

Jackson, Jay, 299
Jaffe, Linda, 209
James Irvine Foundation, 41
Japanese Americans, 220, 279n11
Jefferson, Thomas, 10, 31n1
Johnson, Lyndon B., 74
Jorgensen, Joseph G., 263
Jose, Juan, 250

Kansas, 26, 27
Kansas City (Mo.), 295
Kasik, Robert and Phil, 168
Kennedy, John F., 74
Kennedy, Tom, 297
Kiernan, James G., 286
King County (Wash.), 219, 236
Kinsey, Alfred, 287–88
Kirk, Paul, 224, 225
Klamath Falls (Ore.), 298
Klamath Indian Reservation, 34n31
Klingle, Matthew, 38
Kodani, Gennousuke, 207
Krug, Charles, 137

labor history: chronicling in Cannery Row, 197–98, 199–206, 208–13
Ladies' Home Journal, 156–57
Laguna Pueblo, 281n25
Laird, Betty Jane, 165
Lakota people, 276
Lamore-Choate, Yvonne, 266–67
Land of Little Rain (Austin), 188

landscape: aestheticized, 54–57
landscape architects, 2, 63–64
Landscapes of Privilege (Duncan & Duncan), 55
LaRue, Skippy, 291–92
LaSalle Hotel (Seattle), 224
Lawrence (Kan.), 26
lead, 104
League of United Latin American Citizens, 269
Lee, Anthony, 253
Lefferdink, Allen, 70
Leimbach, August, 183
Leland Hotel (Seattle), 224
lesbian nightclubs, 243, 247–48, 254–55, 256, 257
lesbians: Daughters of Bilitis, 293; land collectives, 26
Lewis, Robert, 208–9, 210
Lewis and Clark Exposition of 1905, 183
Life and Adventures of Capt. Jacob D. Armstrong, The (Meeker), 16
Life magazine, 292, 293, 296
Li-Kar, 249–50, 257
Limerick, Patricia Nelson, 99
Lind, Earl, 288, 289
Little Tokyo (San Francisco), 265
Llano del Rio experimental community, 13, 22
Locke, John, 10
Logan, Menifee and Margaret, 209, 210
Logan, Thomas, 210
Lonewolf Miller, Dorothy, 276
Long Beach (Calif.), 286
Long-Bell Lumber Company, 21
Longview community, 21–22
Looking Backward (Bellamy), 1
Los Alamos (N.Mex.), 24, 25, 34n31
Los Angeles (Calif.): African American boosters, 17–18; counterculture communes and, 26; gay community in, 289; gay neighborhood in, 295; HIV/AIDS crisis in, 300; homophile organizations in, 293; *Life*'s exposé of homosexuals in, 292; male prostitutes, 290; population growth in, 61n28, 288–89, 29
Los Angeles Times Home Magazine, 50
Louter, David, 165
Lovel, Allis, 168
Lowe, J. M., 182
Lowe, Pardee, 256
Lydston, G. Frank, 286

[315]

INDEX

Maclean, Norman, 111
Madonna of the Trail statue. *See* Pioneer Mother statue
Magic Lands (Findlay), 4
Magnuson, Warren, 233
Major, Robert, 93
"Making of a City, The" (Roberts), 43
male prostitutes, 290
Mandel, Dean, 299
Manhattan (Kan.), 26
Manhattan Project, 24, 25
Manifest Destiny, 181, 186
Mankiller, Wilma, 265, 269, 271, 280n13
Maritime Museum of Monterey, 208
Market Historical Commission (Seattle), 227, 232, 233, 235
Market Sketchbook (Steinbrueck), 223
Marling, Karal Ann, 57
Marshall Plan, 220
Mary's Tavern, 291
Mason, Herbert, 76
master-planned communities: attitudes of exclusion and, 5; Irvine, Calif., as, 25, 37–38, 39–40, 41–42, 44, 45 (*see also* Irvine)
Mattachine Society, 293, 294
May, Kirse Granat, 43–44
McClellan Park (Albuquerque), 179, 192, 193
McCoy, Abram, 72
McGirr, Lisa, 48
McGuire, Kathleen, 201
McKelvey, Robert, 70, 71, 72, 74
Means, LaNada, 266, 269, 280n17
Means, Russel, 270
Meeker, Martin, 292
Meeker, Nathan, 16–17
mercury, 104
Mexamerica, 30
Michaux, André, 10
middle-class migration: in the Rocky Mountain region, 109–10, 123–24; rural restructuring and, 123–24; trends and motivations among newcomers to Missoula, Mont., 116–23
migration: of gay men (*see* gay migration); impact on the Rocky Mountain region, 38; internal, 116; notions of social reform and, 15; patterns and motivations among newcomers to Missoula, Mont., 115–23;

urban migration of Native peoples, 261, 263–68; during World War II, 68. *See also* middle-class migration
Milk, Harvey, 296
Miller, Al, 269, 275, 276
Miller, Neil, 301
Miller, Timothy, 12, 26, 28
mill tailings, 104
mining towns, 88–89
mining waste, 104
Minnesota, 301
minorities: exclusion from western suburbs, 5
Mirise, Kenneth, 76
Mission District (San Francisco): Native peoples in, 269–70; organized labor in, 268–69. *See also* North Mission District
Mission Dolores, 268
Missoula County (Mont.), 110, 111, 112, 124
Missoula (Mont.): community tensions in, 114, 124; consumption and privatization of open space, 124; cultural institutions and events, 113; culture of consumption in, 112–14; economy and incomes in, 111; growth-management policies in, 114–15; housing trends, 111–12, 114; migration motivation among middle-class newcomers, 118–23; migration patterns, 115–18; population growth and rural gentrification in, 38, 110–15; real estate prices in, 122–23; socioeconomic characteristics of immigrants, 126t; transitions in the downtown, 113
Missouri: highway development in the 1920s and, 180–82
model towns, 25–26. *See also* Irvine
Mona's nightclub, 247–48, 254–55, 256, 257
Mondavi, Cesare, 141
Mondavi, Peter, 141, 142
Mondavi, Robert, 140, 141–42
Monson Plan, 220–21, 224
Montana: consumption and privatization of open space in, 124; gay migration to rural areas, 300; migration motivations among middle-class newcomers, 118; population growth in, 110; rural gentrification in, 38, 110–27 (*see also* Missoula); socioeconomic characteristics of immigrants, 125t
Monterey Bay Aquarium: historic preservation

at, 199–201; planning and construction of, 198–99; promulgating the labor history of Cannery Row, 210–13; tarpaper shacks and, 207
Monterey Bay Aquarium Foundation, 198
Monterey Boiler Company, 200
Monterey (Calif.): Cannery Row Conservation District, 211; historic preservation of the sardine industry in, 197–213; history of the sardine industry in, 196–97; impact of tourism on, 132; "rebirth" at the Monterey Bay Aquarium, 198–201. *See also* Cannery Row
Monterey City Council, 207
Monterey Herald, 206
Monterey Historic Preservation Commission, 206, 207
Monterey History and Art Association, 209, 216n40
Montez, Lola, 136
More, Sir Thomas, 1
Morgan, Jefferson, 144
Mormons: Joseph Smith's conception of, 26; success of utopian communities, 24–25, 28; utopian community building and, 7–8n7, 20–21
Morse, John, 224, 225
Moss, Arlene B. Nichols, 182, 183, 184–85, 186, 188, 189, 190, 192
motor homes, 161–62
Motorland (magazine), 140
Mountain Regional Water Special Service District (Summit County, Utah), 103
Mount St. Helena, 135, 138
Movement of American Native Youth (MANY), 275, 283n50
"multiple resource usage" policies, 63
Mumford, Lewis, 41

Nader, Ralph, 29
Napa County (Calif.), 135–36, 143–44
Napa River, 149
Napa Soda Springs, 136
NapaStyle store, 150
Napa Valley (Calif.): controversy over defining a "winery," 149–50; demographic character of wine tourists, 145; designated an agricultural preserve, 143–44; gross value of grapes in, 154n39; housing trends in, 146–47; impact of wine tourism on, 131, 144–50, 154n35; loss of biodiversity in, 149; Mediterranean-style architecture in the wineries, 142–43; phylloxera infestations, 137, 149, 152n15; problems facing visitor-related employees, 146–47; problems from the development of hillside vineyards, 148–49, 154n21, 154n42; public relations campaigns, 139–40; real estate value of vineyards, 153n31; threats from development, 143; tourism in the early twentieth century, 138; tourism in the nineteenth century, 135–36; tourist numbers, 141, 144, 150; traffic congestion in, 146; wine-culture landscape of, 134–35; wine industry in, 137–38, 140–41, 147–50, 153n25; wine tourism in, 133–35, 138–40, 141–44, 145
Napa Valley Conference and Visitors Bureau, 154n33
Napa Valley Foundation, 144
Napa Valley Vintners Association, 133–34, 140, 141
Napa Valley Wine Auction, 133–34
Nasaw, David, 249
NAS community advisory board, 275–76
National Farm Workers Association, 269
national highway: the DAR and the development of, 181–83; the *Pioneer Mother* statue and, 183–85 (*see also* Pioneer Mother statue)
National Old Trails Road Association, 179, 180, 182
national park concessionaires, 163
national parks: impact of camping vehicles on, 164–66; impact of tourism on, 131–32; improvements to, in the 1960s, 166–67; park concessionaires and, 163; postwar growth in tourism at, 156–57; problems of overcrowding at, 157, 162, 163, 164–66, 173; programs to increase and improve facilities at, 157, 162, 173; public access to wilderness and, 172; utopian visions of family camping at, 157–62; visitation numbers, 162, 172. *See also* Yellowstone National Park
National Park Service: hazards of wilderness to campers and, 167; Mission 66 program, 157, 162, 173; Pike Place Market and, 227
National Register of Historic Places, 227

[317]

Native American Church, 281n39
Native American Critic and Review (newsletter), 275
Native American studies, 274–75
Native peoples: Alcatraz Island occupation, 262, 276–78, 283n53; boarding schools and, 280n15; debates over public art and collective memory in New Mexico, 187; Indian City (*see* Indian City); Intertribalism and, 262, 277–78, 278n1; migration to western cities, 244; Native American studies, 274–75; Red Power movement, 262, 277, 283n53; religious freedom and, 281n39; Relocation Program and, 261–62, 263, 265–68, 279n11, 280n15, 280n18; reservations, 16–17, 263, 268; resource exploitation and loss of lands, 268; Termination policy and, 261, 262, 263, 268, 277–78; urban arrest rates, 271; urban demographics, 268, 279n8; urban migration, 261, 263–68; urban postwar unemployment rate, 264; urban/rural split among, 274, 282n46; veterans, 264, 267. *See also* Indian reservations; San Francisco Indian community
Native women: opportunities in urban centers, 267; during World War II, 264
Nature Conservancy, 76, 81
nature tourism: impact on national parks, 131–32; postwar growth in, 156–57. *See also* family camping
Navajo Tribe, 265, 281n25
Nelford, Bob, 276
Nervo, Lawrence, 203
New Atlantis, The (More), 1
"new communities," 25–26
New Deal, 23–25
New Mexico: counterculture communes, 26, 27; the DAR's national highway and, 181, 183; debates over public history and art in, 186–87; highway development in the early twentieth century, 179–80; the *Pioneer Mother* statue and, 184–85; as a postwar tourist destination, 156; Red Power movement in, 277; 1920s debate over public art in, 178–79; tourism in the 1920s, 191
"new middle class," 116. *See also* rural gentrification

Newport Center (Irvine, Calif.), 51
New Scientist magazine, 29
Newsweek, 300
Newton, Huey, 278
"New Towns," 42
New York City, 64
nightclubs: gay and lesbian, 243, 246, 247–53, 254–55, 256, 257
Nine Nations of North America, The (Garreau), 29–30
Nixon, Richard, 277
Noel, Thomas Jacobs, 291
Nomenus, 299–300
Nonella, Charlie, 202–3, 205–6
Nordau, Max, 286
Nordwell, Adam, 273
North Beach (Calif.): gay and lesbian nightclubs, 246, 247–53, 254–55, 256, 257
North Mission District (San Francisco): "Indian bars," 270–71; Indian migrants in, 262, 269; Indian neighborhoods, 273–74; San Francisco Indian Center, 269, 271–72, 276, 278
"Nude Ranch" exhibit, 255
Nuestra Misión de San Francisco, 269
Nusbaum, Jesse, 178

Oakes, Richard, 267, 271, 274–75, 276, 281n34
Old Spanish Trail, 183
O'Leary, Cecilia, 209, 216n40
Olmsted, Frederick Law, 2, 63–64, 67
Olympic Games (2002), 94
Oñate, Don Juan de, 187
ONE, Inc., 293–94
O'Neal, Rose, 256
Ontario Mine, 89
open space: in Boulder, Colo., 65, 76, 78–83; consumption and privatization in Montana, 124; Irvine, Calif., and, 46–47
Open Space Board of Trustees (Boulder, Colo.), 80–81, 82
Open Space Department (Boulder, Colo.), 82
Open Spaces Sales Tax Amendment, 79
oral history projects, 209–10
Orange County (Calif.), 41, 48, 61n28. *See also* Irvine
Oregon: counterculture communes, 26, 27; gay communes in, 299–300; gay migration to rural areas in, 298, 299

Organic Machine, The (White), 81–82
organized labor: in San Francisco's Mission District, 268–69
Otero, Miguel, 179
Outing Program, 280n15

Pacific Gas and Electric Company, 277
Packard, Julie, 198, 200
Packard, Lucile and David, 198
Papanikolas, Zeese, 27
Park City Mountain Resort, 94
Park City Resort, 92, 93
Park City (Utah): companies headquartered in, 95; geography and climate, 91–92; impact of landscape upon development, 88, 105; major transitions in the development of, 88–89; as a mining boomtown, 88, 89–90; non-Mormon population, 90; population growth in, 88, 95; postwar decline in, 90; residential development in Snyderville Basin, 95; toxic mining waste and, 104; transformation into a ski town, 90–95; transition to a bedroom community, 38, 95–96; U.S. ski-jumping competition at Ecker Hill, 106n7; the water problems of Summit Valley, 96–105
park systems: nineteenth-century urban planning and, 63–64
Park Utah Consolidated Mining Company, 90, 92
Park West ski resort, 93
Pastega, Richard, 298
pastoral urbanism, 49–51
perceived low density, 52–53
Pereira, William, 37, 41–42
performers: racially sexualized, 254, 256; transgendered or gender liminal, 246, 247, 248–50, 251, 252–53, 254–55, 256–57
peyote, 281n39
photography: of Robert Lewis, 208–9, 210
phylloxera, 137, 149, 152n15
Pierson, George W., 15
Pike Place Market Company, 219, 220
Pike Place Market (Seattle): atmosphere of, 218; changes in the usage of space, 236; competing visions for, 218–19, 230–32; effect of rehabilitation on, 233–38; listed with National Register of Historic Places, 227; managing the identity of, 235–38;

Monson Plan, 220–21, 224; origins and early history of, 219–20; PDA-sponsored support to local farmers, 236–37; Pike Place Preservation and Development Authority, 233, 234–35, 236–38; populism in the Progressive Era and, 231; public value of, 222; Starbucks and, 241n60; tourism and, 237; urban renewal and, 218–19, 220–33 (*see also* Pike Plaza Urban Renewal Project); usage guidelines, 235
Pike Place Preservation and Development Authority, 233, 234–35, 236–38
Pike Plaza Urban Renewal Project: competing designs for, 222–27; competing visions for, 218–19; funding of, 232–33; Initiative 1 and historic preservation, 227–30, 232; origins of, 220–22; usage guidelines, 235
Pinchot, Gifford, 63
Pinebrook subdivision (Utah), 102, 103
"Pioneer Memorial Highway," 183. *See also* national highway
Pioneer Mother statue, 183–85, 186, 188–91, 192–93
Pitcaithley, Dwight, 166
Pit River Tribe, 277
PLAN-Boulder, 74–76, 78, 79
populism, 231
Portland (Ore.): boosterism and, 18; homosexual scandal of 1912, 289; 1905 Lewis and Clark Exposition, 183; male prostitutes, 290; population growth in, 288, 291
"positional good," 112
"postmodern Utopia," 34n38
Postrel, Virginia, 54
powwows, 273
Price, John, 281n40
private campgrounds, 162
Progressive Era: in Seattle, Wash., 231; urban planning and western utopianism, 22–23
Prohibition, 137, 138
Prospector Park Condominiums and Business Park (Utah), 104
prostitutes: male, 290
public art: debates over in New Mexico, 186–87; *Pioneer Mother* statue, 183–85, 186, 188–91, 192–93; 1920s debate over, in Santa Fe, 178–79, 186, 188–91, 193
public campgrounds: overcrowding of, 157,

162, 163, 164–66, 173; visitation to state campgrounds in the 1950s, 160. *See also* national parks
public works projects, 24
Puget Sound, 22
Puritans, 10–11

Quebec, 30
queer communities: rise of in San Francisco, 245–58

race riots, 279–80n12
race tourism. *See* sex and race tourism
Radical Faeries, 299–300
Ramberg, Jenny Sayre, 211
ranching towns, 89
Rancho Lomas de Santiago, 40
Rancho San Joaquin, 40
Rancho Santiago de Santa Ana, 40
Rand, Sally, 255
Rand McNally, 162
Rapoport, Amos, 52
Rast, Raymond, 253
Ravalli County (Mont.), 111, 112
real estate developers, 89, 98
Red Ghetto, 262, 267, 273, 274. *See also* North Mission District
Red Power movement, 262, 277, 283n53
Reflections (newsletter), 55
Reinhardt, Richard, 255
Relocation Program, 261–62, 263, 265–68, 279n11, 280n15, 280n18
Resettlement Administration, 42
Revolving Loan Program, 236–37
RFD magazine, 297
Rhodes, Linda, 198, 199, 200
Richland (Wash.), 24, 25
Richmond (Calif.), 281n25
Ricketts, Ed, 196, 203
Ridley, Charles, 251
riots: race, 279–80n12; Stonewall, 284
Ripley, George, 13
River Runs Through It, A (Maclean), 111
road-lobbying organizations, 180
"roadmen," 281n39
Robert Mondavi Winery, 142, 150
Roberts, Myron, 43
Robinson, Marilynne, 15, 16

Rocky Mountain Magazine, 296
Rocky Mountain region: impact of in-migration upon, 38; middle-class migration in, 109–10, 123–24; population growth in, 109; rural gentrification in, 110; rural restructuring in, 89, 123–24
Rolfe, George, 234
Rome, Adam, 47, 69
Roosevelt National Forest, 71
Rothman, Hal, 139, 150
Rotunda Hotel, 136
Rubio, Tina, 248, 256
Rudd, Sam, 78
rural communes, 26–27
rural gentrification: "class colonization" and, 116; culture of consumption and, 121–22; in Missoula, Mont., 116–23 (*see also* Missoula); origin of term, 110; rural restructuring in the Rocky Mountain region and, 110, 123–24
rural homosexuality: demographics of same-sex couples, 301–2; gay migration from urban to rural areas, 297–302; Alfred Kinsey on, 287–88
rural subdivisions: cultural connection to suburban norms, 107n25; in Park City, Utah, 88–89; rural gentrifiers in the Rocky Mountain region and, 124; stakeholders in, 89. *See also* wilderburbs
Russia, 14
Russian-American Company, 14
RVs, 161–62, 164–66

Sacramento Bee, 286
Sale, Roger, 231
sales tax, 78–79
salmon, 87n56
Salt Lake City (Utah), 7–8n7, 20–21
Salt Lake Olympic Committee, 94
same-sex couples: demographics in rural America, 301–2
Samoans, 273
San Diego (Calif.), 291
San Francisco (Calif.): Castro district, 295–96, 300; Chinatown, 253–54, 255; counterculture communes and, 26; early gay and lesbian nightclubs in, 243, 246, 247–53, 254–55, 256, 257; gay men in, 290,

292; Golden Gate International Exposition, 249, 255–56, 260n26; Haight-Ashbury, 278, 296; HIV/AIDS crisis in, 300; homophile organizations in, 293; Hunter's Point, 279–80n12; Indians in (*see* San Francisco Indian community); *Life's* exposé of homosexuals in, 292; population growth in, 288, 291; race riots, 279–80n12; sex and race tourism in the rise of the queer urban scene, 245–58. *See also* Mission District; North Mission District
San Francisco Hotel Greeters Guide, 249
San Francisco Indian Center, 269, 271–72, 276, 278
San Francisco Indian community: Alcatraz Island occupation, 262, 276–78, 283n53; arrest rates for Indians, 271; bar culture, 270–71; demographics, 268, 269; gangs, 273, 281n43; Hunter's Point, 265; Indian City, 262, 270–74; Indian migration to San Francisco, 261, 265, 267, 268; Indian neighborhoods, 273–74; Intertribalism and, 262; key questions regarding, 262–63; Mission District, 268–70; Native American studies, 274–75; North Mission District, 262, 269, 270–72, 273–74; powwows, 273; San Francisco Indian Center, 269, 271–72, 276, 278
San Francisco Life, 247, 249
San Francisco State College, 274–76
Santa Clara Valley (Calif.), 143
Santa Fe Chamber of Commerce, 185
Santa Fe New Mexican, 184, 185, 189, 190, 191
Santa Fe (N.Mex.): highway development in New Mexico and, 180; impact of tourism on, 132; the *Pioneer Mother* statue and, 178–89, 183, 184, 185, 186, 188–91; romanticized restructuring in the 1920s, 185–86, 187–88; 1920s debate over public history and art, 178–79, 186, 188–91, 193; Truman's visit to, 178, 185
Santa Fe Railroad, 281n25
Santa Fe Trail, 180, 190
Santuario de Chimayó, 188
sardine cannery workers, 200, 201
sardine industry and canneries: chronicling the labor history of, 201–6, 208–13; historic preservation in Cannery Row, 197–213;

Hovden boiler restoration, 200–201; the Monterey Bay Aquarium project and, 198–201; postwar collapse in, 197; prosperity during World War II, 196–97; redevelopment plans in the 1950s and 1960s, 197; Steinbeck's novel of, 196
Sargent, Jimmie, 247
Sargent, Mona, 247, 254–55
Sarria, José, 252–53, 257, 260n34
satellite communities, 76–78
Sattui, Dominic, 143
Saturday Evening Post, 140
Schlesinger, Arthur, Jr., 74
Scott, Babe, 248
Scott, Kay, 248, 254, 256
Seale, Bobby, 278
Seattle Cityscape (Steinbrueck), 223
Seattle Post-Intelligencer, 226, 231
Seattle Times, 224–25, 230–31
Seattle (Wash.): counterculture communes, 27; gay men in, 291–92; homophile organizations in, 294–95; impact of tourism on, 132; Initiative 1, 227–30, 232; population growth in, 288, 291; in the Progressive Era, 231; urban renewal and the Pike Place Market, 218–19, 220–33 (*see also* Pike Place Market)
Seavey, Kent, 207
Second Treatise of Government (Locke), 10
service class, 116–18
Seventh-Day Adventist Sanitarium (Boulder, Colo.), 66
sex and race tourism: in San Francisco, 245–58
Shaw, Beverly, 248, 256
Sierra Club, 154n42
Silicon Valley, 143
Silver Creek (Utah), 104
Silver King Coalition, 90
ski-jumping, 106n7
ski resorts: in Park City, Utah, 92, 93–94
Smith, Joseph, 7–8n7, 26
Smith, Stuart, 148
snowmaking, 93
Snyderville Basin (Utah), 95, 96–105
socialist colonies, 21, 22
social movements: western community building and, 3; western migration and, 15
Society of St. Vincent de Paul, 271

[321]

soil erosion: in Napa Valley, 148–49, 154n42
Solis, Lucido, 204
Sonoma County (Calif.), 137, 141
Sorkin, Alan, 266, 281n40
Soter, Greg, 100
Soter, Sam, 97, 99, 100, 101
Souza, Anthony, 200
Souza, Sara, 202
Spanish Colonial Arts Society, 188
Spanish colonization strategy, 14
Spokes of the Wheel Plan, 77–78
Springfield (Ohio), 183
St. Helena (Calif.), 144, 145, 146, 148–49
St. Louis (Mo.), 286
Stanford Research Institute, 198
Stanford University, 198
Stanley, John, 250
Starbucks, 241n60
Starr, Kevin, 46, 142
state parks: visitation in the 1950s, 160
Steinbeck, John, 196, 203
Steinbrueck, Victor, 223, 224, 225–27, 228, 230, 233
Sterling Vineyards, 142–43
Stern, Edgar, 93–94
Steuman, Sol, 251
Stonewall riot, 284
strikes, 231, 274
Strong, Lester, 296–97
Student Coalition of American Natives, 275
suburbs: attitudes of exclusion and, 5; corporate model towns, 25–26; growth of the environmental movement and, 47, 64; plans to control in Boulder Valley, Colo., 76–79; postwar development of, 68–69, 96; rise of, 4. *See also* rural subdivisions; wilderburbs
Summit County Commission, 100, 103
Summit County (Utah): growth of rural subdivisions in, 88; population growth in, 95; the water problems of Summit Valley, 96–105
Summit Park subdivision (Utah), 95
Summit Park Water Company, 101
Summit Valley subdivision (Utah), 96–105
Sun City (Ariz.), 25
Sun Valley (Idaho), 91
Superfund sites, 104

surface-water rights, 98
Sweet, Forest, 170

Tanaka, Frank, 202
Taos Blue Lake, 277
Taos Pueblo, 277
tarpaper shacks, 206–8
Tedesco, Ted, 78
Termination policy, 261, 262, 263, 268, 277–78
thermal water: hazards of, 167, 168–69
Third World Liberation Front, 274
Thomas, Charles E., 43
Thunderbirds gang, 273, 281n43
Tiguex Park (Albuquerque), 187
Timberline subdivision (Utah), 102, 103
Tingley, Clyde, 192
Tobey, Mark, 223, 230
To-Morrow: A Peaceful Path to Real Reform (Howard), 2, 41
Topaz Relocation Center, 34n31
tourism: impact on western cities, 132; in nineteenth century Napa Valley, 135–36 (*see also* wine tourism); Pike Place Market and, 237; sex and race in the rise of San Francisco's queer urban scene, 245–58; in 1920s New Mexico, 191. *See also* nature tourism
tourist guides and magazines: to San Francisco, 247, 249, 250
Toy, Noel, 254
Trail of Broken Treaties March, 277
travel trailers: impact on family camping, 161–62; overcrowding at national parks and, 164–66
Trocadero bar, 61n38
Truman, Harry: highway development and, 179, 180, 182; the *Pioneer Mother* statue and, 178, 184–85, 186; visit to Albuquerque, 184–85; visit to Santa Fe, 178, 185
Turnbull, John, 235
Turner, Dennis, 277
Turner, E. Robert, 75, 77
Turtle Rock village (Irvine, Calif.), 43, 50
Tweeden, Lenny, 301
201 Club, 249

Udall, Stewart, 172–73
Uhlman, Wes, 227

[322]

INDEX

Uinta Mountains, 91–92, 97
undeveloped land: Irvine, Calif., and, 46–47
unemployment, 264
Union Colony, 16
unions, 268–69
United Indian Development Association, 273
United Indians of All Tribes, 277
United Order movement, 20
United Park City Mines Company, 90, 91
U.S. Army Corps of Engineers, 101, 199
U.S. Bureau of Reclamation, 102
U.S. Environmental Protection Agency, 104
U.S. Forest Service, 67, 157
"University City." See Irvine
University of California, Irvine, 25, 41, 42–43, 51
University of Colorado, Boulder, 66, 70, 71
University of Montana, Missoula, 121
University of New Mexico, 191
University Park Center (Irvine, Calif.), 43
University Park Village (Irvine, Calif.), 43, 44
University Village (Irvine, Calif.), 50
uranium, 268
urban boosterism, 17–18
urban cultural zones: groups occupying, 243–44; the rise of San Francisco's queer urban scene, 245–58. *See also* western cities
urban environmentalism: Boulder's Blue Line campaign, 70–74; issues of economic growth and environmental preservation, 73–74
urbanization: theories relating homosexuality to, 285–87
of Native peoples, 261, 263–68
urban migration: of gay men, 288–90, 296–97; of gay men, 244
urban planners, 3
urban planning: in Boulder, Colo., 37–38; ecosystem-management approach, 65; federal communities, 23–25; influence of environmental activists on, 64–65; in Irvine, Calif., 37–38; park systems and garden cities models, 63–64; western utopianism and, 22–23
urban-to-rural migration: of gay men, 244, 297–302; patterns and motivations among newcomers to Missoula, Mont., 115–23
Utah Geological and Mineral Survey, 104
Utah Olympic Park, 94
Utah Public Service Commission, 101

Vaca Mountains, 135
Valencia (Calif.), 25–26
Vancouver Island, 14
Vanport (Ore.), 34n31
Vaughn, Jim, 277
veterans: Native, 264, 267
vice districts, 289–90
Vicente, Romualdo, 207–8
Village of Valley View (Irvine, Calif.), 45
Village of Woodbridge (Irvine, Calif.), 53–57
villages, 44, 52–57
Villines, Antonette, 202
Visible Knowledge Project, 216n40
Voice of the Turtle (newsletter), 50
Volstead Act, 137
Von Eckardt, Wolf, 230–31
Von Reichert, Christiane, 118
V. Sattui Winery, 143, 149, 150
Wade, Richard, 7n5
Wanship (Utah), 104
Warren's Slaughterhouse Bar, 270–71, 273, 283n50
Wasatch-Cache National Forest, 97
Wasatch Front, 92, 97
Wasatch mountain range, 91–92
Washington: company towns, 21–22; counterculture communes, 27; as a postwar tourist destination, 156; socialist colonies, 22; urban renewal law of 1957, 221
water: geology and, 102–3, 104–5; historical works on water in the West, 107n26; mountain developments in Utah and, 96–105; "paper" rights and wet-water rights, 98
Watson, Ray, 45, 53
Webster, Steve, 198
Weir, James, 286

[323]

INDEX

Welch, Paul, 292
Werther, Ralph. *See* Lind, Earl
Wester, Patricia Ramsey, 210
western cities: early notions on homosexuality in, 286–87; gay men in, 243–44, 289–90, 295–96; gay migration out of, 297–302; gay migration to, 288–90, 296–97; groups occupying cultural zones in, 243–44; HIV/AIDS crisis in, 300; migration of Native peoples to, 244, 261, 263–68; population growth in, 288–89, 291; postwar unemployment rate of Native peoples, 264; rise of gay communities in, 287, 290–97; vice districts, 289–90
western community building; blurring of physical space in, 4–5; eastern urbanism as a point of reference for, 15–16; effect of consumer behavior on, 18–19; establishment of social and cultural boundaries, 5; historical trends in, 1–6; rejection of eastern models in, 5–6; rise of the suburbs, 4; shift to acceptance of modern life in, 3–4; social movements and, 3; utopian vision in, 1–2, 3, 10–11
western utopianism: of the antebellum period, 19–21; assessing the significance of, 27–30; counterculture communes, 26–27, 28; distinction between utopian practice and utopian rhetoric, 11; ecological utopias, 28–30; federal communities period, 23–25; impact on community building, 1–2, 3; industrial and progressive period, 10–11; Mormon communitarianism, 20–21; phases in, 21–23; model towns, 25–26; Mormon communitarianism, 20–21; phases in, 19, 25–26; regional optimism and, 15–16; socialist colonies, 21, 22; urban planning and, 22–23. *See also* American utopianism
West Hollywood (Los Angeles), 295
wheeled camping vehicles, 161–62, 164–66
Wheeler, Dorothy, 200, 201, 204
Where to Sin in San Francisco, 250
White, Gordon, 204
White, Richard, 82, 87n56
White, Roger, 161
White River Agency, 16–17
White Sulphur Springs resort, 136
Whitebear, Bernie, 277
Whyte, William, 51, 70–71

Wilde, Dick, 95
wildersburbs: attitudes of exclusion and, 5; cultural connection to suburban norms, 107n23; emergence after World War II, 38; overview, 95–96; the water problems of Summit Valley, 96–105; water rights and, 98–99. *See also* rural subdivisions
Williams, Dick and Geegee, 157–59
Williams, Raymond, 136, 139
Wilson, Chris, 186
Wilson, T. V., 66
Wilson, Woodrow, 180
Wine Bibber's Bible, The, 141
wine industry (in Napa Valley): controversy over defining a "winery," 149–50; gross value of, 154n39; major wineries in the 1960s, 153n25; Mediterranean-style architecture and, 142–43; Robert Mondavi and, 141–42; origins and growth of, 137–38, 140–41, 147–50; phylloxera infestations, 137, 149, 152n12; problems from the development of hillside vineyards, 148–49; real estate value of vineyards, 153n31. *See also* wine tourism
wine tourism (in Napa Valley): demographic character of wine tourists, 145; impact of, 131, 144–50, 154n35; origins and growth of, 133–35, 138–40, 141–44, 145; public relations campaigns, 139–40
Winter Olympic Games (2002), 94
Wizard of Oz, The (film), 284–85, 301, 302n1
Wolf Creek commune, 299–300
Wolf Mountain ski resort, 93
women: highway boosterism in the 1920s and, 180–82. *See also* Daughters of the American Revolution; Native women
Woodbridge Village Association, 55. *See also* Village of Woodbridge
Woodbridge Village Association Membership Manual, 54
Woods, Flora, 203
World Cup ski tour, 93
World's Fairs. *See* Golden Gate International Exposition
World War II: impact on the American West, 68; rise of urban gay communities and, 291–92; urban migration of Native peoples and, 264

[324]

INDEX

Wounded Knee occupation, 277
Wright, Les, 296, 300
Wright, Ruth, 78
Wrobel, David, 147
Wyoming, 288

Yellowstone National Park: backcountry camping at, 166; dangers of bears to tourists, 169–72; educational programs, 167; family camping in, 162–69; hazards to campers and children, 167–69; overcrowding and visitor complaints, 163–67; as a postwar tourist destination, 156; public access to wilderness and, 172
Yellowstone River, 168
Yosemite National Park, 157–59
Young, Brigham, 7–8n7, 20, 89–90

Zimmerman, J. F., 184